CALIFORNIA REAL ESTATE FINANCE

All content, suggestions, ideas, concepts and conclusions presented in this book are subject to local, state and federal law; court cases revisions or any revisions of the same. Great care has been taken to provide the most accurate, up-to-date material, however all topics may be subject to revisions both legal and otherwise. The reader is urged to consult legal counsel regarding points of law. This publication is not intended to be used as a substitute for competent legal or accounting advice.

ISBN-13: 978-0-324-65148-5
ISBN-10: 0-324-65148-1

Reproduction of sample forms and contracts printed in this book are done so with written consent of the California Association of REALTORS.®

TABLE OF CONTENTS

CHAPTER

1

CALIFORNIA REAL ESTATE FINANCE

What you will learn in this Chapter

- History of Finance

- Property

- Mortgage Lending

- Real Estate Cycles

- Real Estate Finance—Recent Changes

Test Your Knowledge

1. What concept carried over from Spanish law into modern-day property ownership?
   a. Civil law
   b. Common law
   c. Community property
   d. None of the above

2. Which of the following conditions are characteristics of a Fee Simple Absolute Estate?
   a. Provides the owner with the most rights
   b. Holds no limitations or conditions
   c. Can be conveyed by a will
   d. All of the above

3. All of the following are characteristics of a lease EXCEPT
   a. every lease is considered a contract whether it is written or oral.
   b. tenants are required to sign all written contracts.
   c. all contracts are backed by some form of consideration.
   d. written contracts may not be altered orally.

4. Which one of the following examples is not considered a fixture?
   a. Ceiling fan
   b. Space heater
   c. Custom-made window coverings
   d. Dishwasher

5. The use of a proportionately small amount of money to secure a large loan for the purchase of a property is called
   a. leverage.
   b. interest.
   c. financing.
   d. collateral.

6. Which of the following is not considered one of the four key groups responsible for providing market information for real estate?
   a. Internet
   b. Real Estate Investment Trusts
   c. Bank and insurance analysis
   d. Interest

7. Which of the following is not a characteristic of real estate?
   a. Social
   b. Physical
   c. Tangible
   d. Economic

INTRODUCTION

When most people think of finance, specifically real estate finance, they may think of nothing but math or computing mortgages and interest. You will find throughout this book that the topics covered in real estate finance deal with much more than just math or complicated computations. You will learn about all topics or concepts related to real estate finance, and get a good review of other topics covered in your real estate principles course which also relate to real estate finance.

This chapter will introduce you to real estate finance in California. We will look at the history of finance, review real property and estates in real property, as well as look at the different characteristics of property. After this quick review, we will begin looking at real estate finance in California, lending activities and cycles in real estate. This chapter will end with an examination of the changes in real estate finance.

HISTORY OF FINANCE

We all know that the first people to live in California were Native Americans. They were here before the Spanish explorers and before Mexico began colonizing and governing California. In 1513, Spanish explorers (representing the King of Spain) advanced into California and claimed all the land that touched the Pacific Ocean. The King would make land grants to individuals for farming and ranching or make similar land grants to cities for their use. Cities did not actually need a formal grant from the King for the use of the land, however, as each city would automatically receive four leagues. Each league was roughly 4,440 acres; so each city was given a little more than 2/3 of what we now refer to as a township. The governing body of the city then decided who would be given property rights and ownership for land contained within the four leagues of the city. Local authorities were given this power to grant ownership and transfer of land directly from the King, although there were very strict rules to follow when making these grants.

Moving on to the year 1822 when Mexico won its independence from Spain, Mexico had been colonizing California while a territory of Spain. Upon gaining their independence the Mexicans were able to take possession of California as well. Under their rule, Mexican governors controlled all land grants, and then recorded the grants. The recording of the grants was known as Expedients. Expedients were a rough form of recording and did not provide a very accurate land description. This ultimately caused confusion and problems amongst landowners once California became a state.

California became a possession of the United States when the Treaty of Guadalupe Hidalgo ended the Mexican American War in 1848. Individuals who had land granted to them by the ruling Mexican governors (provided they could prove ownership of such lands) were able to retain their ownership and were given land patents by the United States government. While California was a territory of Spain and Mexico, civil law ruled land ownership. When California became a territory of the United States, civil law ended and common law was adopted (one effect of which was that squatters claimed ownership rights to the newly-acquired territory). Common laws were created by the legislature, and had to be followed along with common law customs adopted from judicial decisions. One of the concepts that carried over from Spanish and Mexican rule was the concept of **community property**. Community property outlined how property acquired by a married couple during their marriage provided for dual ownership. According to community property laws, property could not be disposed of without the consent of both spouses.

> **Remember**
> - California, under Spanish and Mexican rule, utilized Civil law regarding land ownership.
> - As part of the United States, California utilizes Common Law governing land ownership.
> - Community Property is used in California. Although it is not part of Common law, it is part of civil Law.

To resolve confusion caused by upholding the Mexican land grants as well as by the squatters' claims to land, the Board of Land Commissioners was formed. Appeals between disputing parties could be heard by the United States District Court, and sometimes appealed to the Supreme Court, to decide who the lawful owner was. In most cases, the Mexican land grants were upheld.

In many places in ancient, and perhaps, not so ancient times, ownership rights to territory came along with the military might to take and hold the property, to protect it against invasion from others who came later with bigger armies and more powerful weapons. In ancient Egypt, formal land laws were established before the first century A. D. Generally, in the U. S., property laws can be traced to the English feudal system, starting with the Norman Conquest in 1066.

As a result, William the Conqueror became the owner of all English property and source of all property rights. To reward his nobles for their service, he gave away some of these rights to them, turning over to the nobles who fought with him property previously owned by the defeated English king. Then, these nobles could delegate parcels of their land to whom they wished. As a result, an army was transformed into an economic system that controlled the ownership and use of the land. The people who now owned the land were both tenants to the noblemen from whom they received the land and lords to tenants under them. King William, and his successors, remained above this system, however, because they kept the power of assignment. The English feudal system was essentially one huge life estate, with the heirs of landholders keeping possession of the property only if the monarch allowed them to.

When King John of England signed the **Magna Carta** at Runnymede in 1215, some individual property ownership rights were recognized. This historic document secures the personal liberty of British subjects and their rights in property. Private property rights were protected and specified further by the Quia Emptores statute of 1290, which allowed feudal tenants to convey—or sell—their property interests. Quia Emptores is the foundation of land ownership in fee simple absolute, which is the form of ownership used today under the private real property **allodial** system. Fee simple absolute ownership gives the owner more rights than any other type of ownership; does not place limitations or conditions on ownership; and can be inherited.

In the U.S., property owners hold rights subject only to taxation, eminent domain, escheat, and police powers. Two of those rights are the right to finance real estate by pledging the property and using the property as loan collateral.

P R O P E R T Y

The impact of real estate permeates every aspect of modern life. Land and its non-renewable natural resources (such as petroleum, natural gas, coal, and minerals) or its ability to produce renewable resources (such as lumber and agricultural products) is the bottom line necessity for much of our industrial and commercial strength, and thus, our nation's economic success.

The work of many people—although far fewer than even as recently as 60 years ago—is directly connected to land-based resources. Farmers and miners, sanitary engineers, surveyors, land planners, home builders, furniture and paper manufacturers among others, all depend directly on real estate to make a living. Suppliers to these industries add millions more people dependent on the land for their livelihoods. Eventually, all of us have some relationship to land-related industry or commerce because, frankly, we all have to eat.

The construction industry and building trades are a major part of the U.S. economy. Housing starts is a regularly determined economic indicator. When demand for construction is down, not only do construction workers and suppliers suffer, but also financial services as well—which has impacts throughout the economy. Furthermore, this is a two-way street. When money is tight, one of the first industries affected is construction because most real estate activities rely heavily on the availability and cost of borrowed funds, as indicated by interest rates.

Property Ownership

The history of private property ownership in California follows the changes in the countries whose governments controlled the area. When California was part of the Spanish Empire, Roman Civil Law was the basis for property ownership. Royal grants of land were given to political or military agencies of the crown. These grants, called ranchos, were basically of agricultural property. However, absolute title remained in the same hands.

In 1821, after Mexico declared and won its independence from Spain, "expedientes," as formal land grants were called, were recorded by the new government.

In 1848, after the Mexican-American War, California became a U.S. possession by treaty. During this time, the expedientes were reviewed and the owners' rights affirmed according to the laws of the U.S. Just a few years later in 1850, California became the 31st state, and as in the rest of the U. S., property ownership then followed English Common Law.

Property

Property is defined as anything that can be controlled and owned. Real property refers to land and buildings that are fixed in place and are controlled and owned by individuals. However, different people can control and own the same property. For example, an apartment building owner retains all property rights, but turns over control of an apartment to a tenant who pays rent in return. By contrast, personal property can be moved relatively easily; examples of personal property are clothing, furniture, vehicles, appliances, and computer equipment.

The air around us is not property. Air above land is not property until it is enclosed by a structure. Air in an oxygen tank is property.

Water falling from the sky as rain is not property; water in the ocean is not property. However, water in a well or cistern is the property of the well or cistern's owner; water in a container is property. The water in navigable lakes and rivers in the U.S., along with the land and water up to 200 miles off U.S. coasts, are the property of the U.S. government, and as such is "owned" by all citizens of this country.

An idea, work of art, music, and literature are not property until the idea is converted into a patented invention, and the art, music or literature is trademarked or copyrighted.

Real Property

Property is anything that can be owned. Real Property refers to: land; any permanent fixtures attached to the land such as a house or building; anything appurtenant to the land such as an easement; or anything attached to the land such as trees. A broader way to think about real property is in spatial terms, such as land, airspace, mineral rights, water rights and fixtures. Ownership in real property can be defined as the bundle of rights. Generally speaking, real property is immovable.

Immovable by Law

Anything deemed immovable by law is also real property. A seller of real property cannot exclude an orchard growing on the property in the sale, as the orchard is real property. Any produce growing may be negotiated in the sale of the property, yet the trees are immovable by law and are therefore considered real property.

Personal Property

Personal property is considered movable. Any property that is not considered real property is personal property. As briefly stated earlier in this chapter, items such as mature, harvested crops, furniture in a house, a cut tree used for lumber, automobiles, stocks or money are all considered personal property. Personal property is also known as **chattel**, as it is movable and transferred or sold using a bill of sale. When real property is sold, all personal property goes with the seller unless he or she has agreed to leave such personal property on the property or include it in the contract.

Real and personal property can change form from one to the other. An example of this is a tree. While it is growing and attached to the ground it is considered real property. When it is cut down or harvested for lumber it becomes personal property. When the lumber is used to build a house, it again becomes real property. If the house is torn down, and the lumber is recycled for different use, it again becomes personal property.

As discussed earlier, **emblements** (such as crops that are sold, mortgaged or harvested) are considered personal property. The actual plant itself is not personal property; it is real property. The crop it yields is personal property.

> **Remember**
> - Personal property is also called **chattel**
> - Property may change form from real to personal and back to real.

Fixtures

A fixture is real property that began as personal property. It has become real property because it is now permanently attached to another real property. Examples of this include: a refrigerator, a ceiling fan, or custom-built shelves for a closet. One important note to make is that cost is NOT a test for fixtures.

Trade Fixtures

Trade fixtures are personal property affixed to real property for use in a trade, business or craft. These fixtures can be removed, provided that their removal causes no damage to the real property. This is especially important when a tenant attaches his or her trade fixtures to a rented space.

> **Examples of Trade Fixtures**
> - Built-in work benches
> - Dividing screens or temporary walls
> - Cash registers

Types of Estates in Real Property

An estate is ownership or interest in real property. Thus, real estate or real property means ownership. There are two types of estates in real property: freehold estate and less-than-freehold estate (or leasehold estate). The type of estate a person has in property determines the degree of ownership, or claim, the property owner has in his or her estate.

Freehold Estates

A **freehold estate** is the highest form of ownership. The term freehold stems from medieval England, where the landowner was free from the demands of his overlord and could use the land in any way he desired. A freehold estate may continue for an indefinite period, or be limited to a specific number of years. Additionally, although the freehold estate allows the owner the most freedom of use, this use may still be limited.

There are two types of freehold estates: **fee simple estate** and **life estate**.

> ### Remainderman
> The person a life estate reverts to upon the death of the current owner, not the original owner of the estate.

If a person should die before the individual whose life measures the life estate, then the estate will transfer to the holder's heirs for the duration of the measuring life.

California is a **community property** state. The concept of community property goes back to the Spanish law that governed California before 1848. Under community property laws, husbands and wives own equal interest in all property acquired after their marriage that is bought with funds they share. When either the husband or wife dies, the deceased's half interest is inherited by the person named in the will. In states without community property, property owned by a married couple automatically reverts to the surviving spouse under a "joint-and-survivor" system. On July 1, 2001, however, new regulations stipulated that community property may also carry the right of survivorship. So, now in California, when a spouse dies, the surviving spouse automatically becomes the sole owner of the property.

To avoid probate, joint tenancy allows property to automatically revert to the surviving owners when any one of the owners dies. Joint tenancy is usually arranged within families because this system eliminates the right of an owner to distribute the property in a will. With this form of automatic survivorship, shares in the property are equally distributed to the surviving tenants. So, in a two-party joint tenancy arrangement between a married couple, if the wife dies, her half interest immediately becomes the property of her husband. In a three-party joint tenancy arrangement among a father, mother, and child, the death of one owner means that the survivors' interests increase from one-third of the property to half for each.

Leasehold Estates

A **leasehold estate** (or less-than-freehold estate) contains fewer bundles of rights than a freehold estate. People who own this type of estate are called **renters** and **tenants**. The owner of a leasehold estate has exclusive right of possession of the land and everything attached to it during the duration of the lease. The lease will outline the conditions for use, duration of rental and occupancy of the property. The bundle of rights a tenant or renter holds with a leasehold includes the right of possession, use and enjoyment.

- The tenant, or lessee, is someone who acquires the use of property for a specific time period as outlined by the lease and holds the right of exclusive possession

- The landlord or lessor is the person who owns the title to the property or reversion during the lease

- The tenant will pay the landlord rent at predetermined time periods for use of the property

Remember

A leasehold estate is a lease between a tenant, or lessee and a landlord, or lessor.

Leaseholds are considered personal property or **chattel real**. Tenants hold the right of possession and use of the property, yet it is not considered real property, as they cannot encumber or convey the property and only hold possession of the property for the duration of the lease.

There are four different types of leasehold estates. They are
- Estate for years

- Estate from period to period

- Estate at will

- Estate at sufferance

These will be explained further a little later in this book, but for now, be aware there is more than one type of lease a person can enter into.

Characteristics of Every Lease

- All leases are contracts whether they are in written or oral form. The landlord must sign all written contracts. Tenants, on the other hand, are not required to sign a written contract as occupancy is considered his or her acknowledgement of the lease and its terms

- Contracts must have clear terms understood by both parties backed by consideration or a form of rent

- Once written, a contract cannot be altered by oral means

Characteristics of a Lease

- Landlords must sign all written contracts

- Possession by a tenant is considered his or her acknowledgement of a lease contract

- Contracts must be backed by some form of consideration (or a form of rent)

- Once written a contract cannot be altered by oral means

Physical, Economic, and Social Characteristics of Real Estate

As collateral for financing, real estate has physical, economic, and social properties that qualify it for this purpose, Physically, real estate is considered to be fixed in place. Even with the changes that can occur with avulsion caused by flooding, twisting from earthquakes, and human-initiated removal of hills, land stays fairly identifiable. This fixity of land provides lenders with some degree of security: they know that the land a borrower puts up today as collateral will still be there tomorrow in case he or she should default on the loan.

Land is also viewed as indestructible. Although the quality of land may change, its durability has made it an attractive investment over the years. Also, a parcel of land is considered unique. You cannot buy perfectly equal pieces of land the way you can buy perfectly alike articles of clothing, for example. Legally, each parcel of land can be specifically identified by its individual boundaries, description, and ownership. As a result, all contracts related to specific properties are relatively easy to enforce—which also adds to the security so prized by lenders.

Economically, land is scarce because land on which people want to live and work is in short supply—which, of course, makes it valuable. Overall however, the supply of land is almost unlimited, especially if its use could be made more intensive; however, when you eliminate land that is not hospitable or attractive to humans and land that would be too expensive or difficult to make hospitable, the supply of land decreases to relative scarcity. For the most part, a very large proportion of the earth's population lives on only a small part of the land, mostly in cities, where employment and cultural opportunities are greater. As a result, there is high demand for a relatively small, fixed supply of land, which means that this land carries a high economic value that seems to go up every year. As real estate agents repeat, everything is location, location, location.

Besides permanence of the land itself, the fixity of improvements built or put on the land furthers its security and value as collateral for financing. Most construction is done to last a long time. When such improvements with significant life expectancies are combined with the scarcity of usable land, lenders find financing loans backed by such collateral relatively easy decisions to make.

Another economic value of land is its location in relation to other parcels of land. This attribute makes it relatively simple for lenders to determine the value of the land accurately, which is important information when a borrower is asking for a specific loan amount.

In terms of factors related to the overall society however, real estate is one interface where the rights of individual owners to do whatever they wish to and on their property meets—and sometimes collides—with the rights of the public at large.

The rights of the owner of private property are set down in statutes and common law. An owner's highest bundle of rights is limited by government police power, which regulates the uses of property for the public welfare and by eminent domain. In short, government has sovereign powers of condemnation of private property for the community's benefit. When police power is invoked, compensation to the property owner does not usually occur. However, when eminent domain is invoked, private property is essentially "taken" for public use. It is usually required that the owner be compensated for the fair market value of the property.

In 1987, two significant cases related to private property rights were handed down by the U.S. Supreme Court. In the first case, *First English Evangelical Lutheran Church of Glendale v. County of Los Angeles*, the church argued that Los Angeles County's denial of its right to rebuild church camp buildings washed away by flooding in the Angeles National Forest in 1978 was an "illegal taking" of the church's property. The Supreme Court agreed with the church.

The second case, *Nollan v. California Coastal Commission*, concerned two Ventura County homeowners who wanted to replace a small beachfront cottage with a significantly larger two-story home. The Coastal Commission required that the public be allowed to walk across the beach in front of the home in exchange for the right to build the larger house on the land. The Nollans objected. The Supreme Court agreed with the Nollans, saying that the right to build on one's property is subject only to reasonable regulation.

Currently, private property rights are being reduced to control uses that can negatively affect the environment. Pollution and improper land use can damage the health and safety of the public now and for generations to come. Such social controls can have significant impact on property values and community development. Because such controls can often reduce the number of homes that can be build on a certain-sized parcel of land, for example, the result can be most clearly seen in rising real estate prices, as the scarcity attribute discussed earlier increases in impact.

MORTGAGE LENDING

Most real estate loans are made by commercial banks, savings banks (thrifts), and life insurance companies, although other sources exist; these are discussed later in this book. The foundation of real estate financing is individual savings and investments in the real estate secondary market. This money is loaned to borrowers, who pay for the right to use the money in the form of interest on the loan amounts for the life of the loans. This interest paid by borrowers is used, in part, to pay interest to savers on their deposits in banks and dividends to investors in the secondary real estate market (more on this subject later in this book).

Currently, interest rates paid on deposits to savings and commercial banks are the lowest in decades, and stay fixed over long periods, although future rates are unpredictable. On the other hand, the interest rates that borrowers agree to pay on loans fluctuate with market rates. Furthermore, lenders can, in some cases, call loans, so borrowers may have to pay back their loans or arrange for new financing with little advance notice.

Rarely do home buyers pay cash for their houses; even those selling one house and buying another usually need to borrow to purchase the new house. If sources for home loans were limited or interest rates too high, few homes would be built and fewer would be sold. When real estate financing is tight, the entire construction industry is affected, and ramifications are felt throughout this economic sector.

Mortgage lending is affected by a number of U.S. federal and California state agencies and programs—as well as the basic economic laws of supply and demand. The cost of money—interest rates—is controlled by the Federal Reserve Board. The loan insurance and guarantee programs of the Federal Housing Administration (FHA) and the Department of Veterans Affairs (DVA) can reduce or expand the breadth of homes for which certain buyers are qualified. Furthermore, California home loan bond programs for moderate income buyers, local regulations inhibiting growth, and financing for real estate all are affected by national and local economic conditions, which fluctuate over time.

In the past, when rising interest rates have made conventional real estate lending difficult, alternative loan arrangements were developed to maintain the flow of buying and selling homes, apartments, and commercial buildings. Participation finance, adjustable interest rates, and variable payment patterns were all designed to enable financing to go forward under any economic conditions and allow lenders to stay in business. These alternative financing arrangements are discussed in depth later in this book. In short, however, these alternative financing methods transferred the risk and other factors arising from changes in the economy to the consumer.

Credit in Our Economy

Our society is oriented toward the use of credit—buying today and paying for it later by charging the item to a credit card or charge account. Using credit allows us to own more goods that, supposedly, make our lives better.

Buying on credit, and therefore, enjoying the use of something while paying for it, is the basis of real estate finance. A real estate purchase involves large sums of money and usually a long time to repay the loan. Real estate loans are usually for many thousands of dollars and have periods of 15 or 30 years, or even longer.

The systematic repayment of real estate loans over these long periods, usually in specified monthly amounts, sustains the ability of lenders to collect savings, pay interest to depositors, and redistribute funds to borrowers, and thus, maintain the pace of economic growth in the community. However, this rhythm is lost when prolonged **disintermediation** occurs; when people who used to deposit their savings in banks seek higher returns and move their funds to financial instruments that provide those yields. This competition for available money is continuous among individual borrowers, financial institutions, the commercial stock and bond markets, and governments (for example, U.S. Treasury securities, municipal bonds). Depending on the balance that arises and other economic factors, interest rates go up and down.

Financing Relationships

Real estate financing usually means pledging real property as collateral to back up a promise to repay a loan. A borrower uses a building and/or land that he owns to guarantee to a lender that the terms of a loan contract will be met. If the borrower defaults on the repayment, the lender can legally foreclose on the property and sell it to recoup the loan balance.

Real estate financing can also be described as **hypothecation**. The borrower keeps possession and control of the property while the lender holds an underlying, equitable right—or a **lien**—in the property. If the borrower repays the loan according to the terms of the contract, the lender releases the underlying lien. If the borrower defaults, then the lender "perfects the lien" into full ownership, that is, a fee simple absolute.

Hypothecation also occurs when a tenant pledges leasehold rights as collateral for a loan. Lenders can pledge rights in receivable mortgages, deeds of trust, or land contracts as collateral for other loans. Life tenants and remaindermen can mortgage their rights, and farmers can pledge unharvested crops as collateral for a loan. In these cases, borrowers keep possession, control, and use of the collateralized property while taking out a loan against its value.

A third way to explain real estate financing is through the concept of leverage. When leverage is used, a relatively small amount of money secures a large loan for a purchase of property. Basically, people who borrow money to buy property use other people's savings to secure the purchase. These buyers invest a comparatively small amount of their own money as a down payment and then leverage that investment by borrowing the much larger balance needed to make up the difference between the down payment and the purchase price.

Leverage is an important concept. An eligible military veteran may leverage 100% of a home's purchase price under certain circumstances and not have to risk any personal funds at all. Other buyers may have to make down payments of 5, 10, 20 or 25% of the total price of the home before they are considered qualified to borrow the balance. The degree of leverage depends on the specific situation and the type of loan. As is obvious, the cash required for the down payment and other charges at closing has a considerable impact on a buyer's ability to purchase property.

Local Real Estate Markets

Local real estate lenders are tightly interconnected with whatever is going on in the local real estate market. Anything that affects local property values is vitally important to the bankers, mortgage lenders, and others who provide financing for property.

Government zoning decisions, for example, can dramatically raise or lower property values. Road building, location of intersections and exits, and other political decisions related to community growth or no-growth policies, pollution control, building standards, and the preservation of coastlines and wildlife habitats can significantly affect a community's property values and its attractiveness to potential home buyers. The quality of schools is a major factor in people's decisions about where to buy their homes.

When economic conditions are not good, when unemployment is higher or money tight, local financial institutions approve fewer mortgages—which actually contributes to the downward cycle of reduced confidence and economic stagnation. In good times, mortgage lending goes back up to serve the growing demand.

National Real Estate Markets

When the demand for mortgage money is high, local lenders may deplete locally available funds. In the same vein, when the economy is sluggish, these same lenders may have enough low-risk outlets for excess funds. To balance and smooth out geographic peaks and valleys in the availability of mortgage money, a national mortgage market was established.

The bank deregulation of the 1980s along with the rise of regional commercial banks and bank holding companies, investment trusts, and a sophisticated secondary mortgage market have made it possible for local lenders to participate in a national market. Now, local institutions can buy and sell mortgages and deeds of trust that originate across the country while at the same time, continue to serve their local markets.

Fannie Mae, or the Federal National Mortgage Association (FNMA); Freddie Mac, or the Federal Home Loan Mortgage Corporation (FHLMC); and Ginnie Mae, or the Government National Mortgage Association (GNMA), form the secondary market for real estate mortgages nationwide. These agencies stabilize and smooth out the fluctuations in the mortgage market by making funds available in capital-deficient areas and by providing low-risk investments for the funds of financial institutions where mortgage lending is less active. Lenders in slow-growth areas can invest their surplus funds by purchasing mortgages from these agencies. Lenders in areas with faster growth, where home and commercial real estate mortgages are in demand, can sell their mortgages on the secondary market to obtain additional funds for more loans.

REAL ESTATE CYCLES

Impact of Supply and Demand

The overriding economic impact of the laws of supply and demand is the primary factor affecting real estate cycles. In the short term, general business conditions that support employment and investment growth create the demand that determines the current amount of real estate activity. When and where business is good and demand is greater than the available supply of real estate, purchase prices go up. This demand also encourages more construction, which increases the supply of real estate until there is a surplus. Now the supply exceeds the demand, the situation switches to a buyer's market, and price increases slow, and prices may decrease. Continuing to build new homes and commercial buildings under these conditions is economically unsound. However, after a time, the surplus is exhausted, and the cycle repeats.

The available supply of mortgage money is a second variable affecting real estate cycles. Tight money (high interest rates) occurs when competition heats up for the more or less fixed supply of money invested or deposited. Along with bank savings accounts, the federal government needs to borrow to meet its budgetary commitments, and private industry goes to the money markets to finance inventories, plant expansions, and operating expenses when cash flow is not optimal. When money is tight and these different entities are competing for dollars, interest rates—the cost of capital—go up, further depressing the housing market. Such a situation occurred in the early 1980s when interest rates on new home loans reached 20%.

To help smooth out the peaks and valleys of the traditional real estate cycles, better market information and increased openness about real estate dealings, financing, and new construction are necessary. Today, movement on these fronts is occurring because

1. Bond analysts and rating agencies now submit detailed information to investors in the mortgage-backed securities markets, which represent 14% of the real estate debt market

2. Real Estate Investment Trust (REIT) analysts provide full disclosure of data in this field, which now controls about 40% of commercial real estate

3. Bank and insurance analysts publish underwriting market data

4. The Internet makes large amounts of data available to anyone with access

Impact of Population Attributes

Changes in population size as well as age and income proportions also affect long-term real estate cycles. Historically, large, steady shifts of people from rural areas to cities could be expected. Today, the trend had reversed in certain parts of the country. Some large cities are losing population. Some rural communities are experiencing unexpected growth—and the need to provide services they never needed to consider before. Meanwhile, in some center cities, condominiums in buildings that used to house department stores and offices are selling rapidly for very high prices.

The 2000 Census reported growth of the overall U.S. population with existing trends continuing in certain regions, Western states grew the most; southern states grew significantly; the Northeast and Midwest retained about the same population as they had in the previous census. Not surprisingly, weather appears to be a major factor determining where people want to live and work; generally Americans left cold, wet areas for warm, dry ones.

California's population grew about 13.5% between 1990 and 2000, to more than 33.8 million, some of which resulted from immigration of people from other countries, along with the migration of people from other states in the U.S. California's continued economic success has been partially based on its supply of affordable housing for its growing population. But now, the demand for housing has far outstripped the supply and as a result, purchase prices have risen dramatically. Cable television shows compare what a home buyer gets in California to what the same money will buy in other parts of the country. Needless to say, the latter is much more house.

Birth rates and changing family structures affect the demand for housing of different sizes. More than 10% of California's population are senior citizens who currently live in or may need congregate care facilities and nursing homes in the near future. Baby-boomers comprise about one-third of the state's population currently. While some are interested and have the wherewithal to trade up to larger, more expensive homes, others are looking to downsize because they no longer have children living at home and want to reduce the amount of effort involved in caring for their residences.

Only about 25% of California households are "traditional," in that the family unit is composed of two parents and two children. Another 25% of the state's households are made up of singles; of these, 60% are women; about half of these single women are widows.

Political Attitudes

Real estate cycles are also influenced by predominant political attitudes. Historically, California communities wanted fast growth. Local governments offered concessions to industries to locate plants and other operations in their communities. Today, however, planned growth is preferred, and local leaders are running on platforms of limiting new construction to satisfy citizen demands for less growth, less noise, less traffic, and lower taxes. The effects of growth limitation policies are dramatic for example; prices of existing ocean-side properties have skyrocketed since a moratorium on building along the entire California coastline was instituted.

Impact of Income Taxes

The Tax Reform Act of 1986 (TRA '86) eliminated many benefits enjoyed by real estate investors in the past and affected real estate cycles. With few exceptions, under TRA '86, excess losses from property investments no longer could shelter other income. The Act's elimination of special treatment for capital gains income and the extension of depreciation time periods reduced real estate investment profits considerably. Although lower tax rates may have offset some of these negative results, many economists agree that TRA '86 profoundly affected the commercial and investment real estate markets. While some property values appear to behave in a contrarian way, most values will follow real estate cycles. In addition, over the long run, the value of most real estate rises.

The secondary mortgage markets have stabilized some of the volatility in real estate that caused localized booms and busts. Furthermore, the policies of the Federal Reserve Board (Fed) and the U.S. Treasury have largely reduced long-term overreactions to these cycles. Both the Fed and the Treasury largely control how much money is in circulation. They try to anticipate cyclical economic variations and adjust the cost of capital— the interest rate on available money. As a result, the peaks and valleys of the cycles are smoothed out and flattened to a degree so their impact is less extreme. However, there have been a few occasions when the Fed, in trying to reduce inflation, restricted the money supply too much, which resulted in high interest rates and a downturn in the real estate cycle.

Tax Relief Act of 1997 (TRA '97)

The U.S. Congress passed the Tax Relief Act of 1997 to give homeowners broad exemptions from capital gains taxes on profits on the sale of their residences. Replacing the one-time exemption of $125,000 in profit available to sellers older than 55, TRA '97 exempts up to $500,000 of profit from taxes for a married couple filing jointly or up to $250,000 for a single if the property has been their primary residence for at least two years within the five years prior to the sale.

Sellers can take advantage of these benefits every two years. Furthermore, new IRS regulations say that if the property meets the entire exclusion, the transaction does not need to be reported. TRA '97 effectively eliminates taxes on capital gains from the sale of most taxpayers' principle residences. It also eliminates the need to keep extensive records of improvements that result in changes to the property's tax basis—unless the gain from the sale is greater than the exemption.

R E A L   E S T A T E   F I N A N C E — RECENT CHANGES

Over the past 25 years, interest on real estate loans fell from a high of 20%+ in the early 1980s to 8% in the 1990s and to between 5 and 7% more recently. Double digit inflation rates of earlier years now hover around 3%. A highly regulated banking system with very stringent loan requirements switched gears when deregulated in the 80s and became free and easy by comparison in financing construction. Some appraisals were highly overstated, but financing was still readily available. The pendulum eventually swung back however; in response to such irresponsibility that led to a number of bank failures, the U.S. Congress past the Financial Institutions Reform, Recovery and Enforcement Act of 1989 (FIRREA), which reestablished strict banking controls.

Although today's real estate market is very strong (in fact, some say it is overheated), some degree of slowdown is expected to occur soon. However, in California, returns on real estate investment are likely to remain high because the supply of desirable housing has not yet satisfied demand here. If real estate returns on investment (ROI) continue to be good, real estate can become a separate and seriously considered asset class for institutional portfolios.

The following factors make real estate a good investment as a hedge against recession

1. Supply and demand are in equilibrium.

2. Real estate yields are about 3% higher that the yield on 10-year U.S. Treasury bonds, which provides investors with a safe risk cushion.

3. The supply of housing is likely to grow only slowly; developers have shown surprising restraint, perhaps as a result of having lived through several valleys in the real estate cycle.

4. Lease structures are now set up so only a small number expire each year.

5. The low real estate interest rates appear to be relatively permanent, enabling homeowners to refinance mortgages and thus, increase cash flows toward home improvements and increasing the value of the housing stock.

S U M M A R Y

Real estate is a major factor in the economic well-being of the nation, both directly and indirectly

A large proportion of the population is involved in industries directly connected to real estate, such as construction, mining, lumber, and agriculture. The addition of suppliers and service providers to these industries raises the number of employees dependent on real estate much higher.

Most real estate purchases are financed through loans. Savings collected by banks, savings associations (thrifts), life insurance companies, pension funds, and other formal financial intermediaries are borrowed by builders and developers to finance their projects. Other loans are made to buyers of existing and new homes and commercial buildings, thus providing financial institutions with ongoing, low risk, outlets for investment of the funds they receive. These investments, that is, the loans, are repaid with interest, making more funds available for new loans to further stimulate growth. For example, by the end of the third quarter of 2001, mortgage loans in the U.S. amounted to more than $7 trillion.

Real estate financing is relatively simple. The real estate is pledged as collateral to guarantee the repayment of a loan. The borrower continues to possess, control, and use the collateralized real estate during the term of the loan. The financial institution granting the loan can, if the borrower defaults, sell the property to recoup the loan balance.

An arrangement in which the borrower keeps control of the property while borrowing against it is called hypothecation. It is also related to leverage; in other words, the borrower puts down a relatively small amount of his or her own personal funds to secure a much larger loan for the purchase of property. If the borrower breaks the promise to repay the loan, the lender can take possession the collateral property and sell it to recover the investment.

Real estate is fixed in place, as are any buildings placed on it. The value of real estate is affected by local economic, political, and social conditions. Local conditions usually have the greatest impact on property values. Most real estate loans are made locally in the primary market, funded by savings deposited by people in the same community.

National markets for real estate financial instruments have developed under the auspices of Fannie Mae, Freddie Mac, and Ginnie Mae. These federal agencies form secondary markets for the buying and selling of mortgages nationally. As a result, money from an area with a relatively slow real estate market can be invested in real estate debt instruments in a region with a hotter market, thus increasing the mortgage money supply there. This national level secondary market reduces the impact of extreme changes in local real estate conditions.

Real estate cycles are very dependent on the economic forces of supply and demand. Excess demand usually drives new construction until excess supply reverses the cycle. Following the forces of supply and demand is the availability of financing at reasonable interest rates. Other variables that affect real estate cycles are population changes, social issues, and political attitudes that can affect policies on growth and development.

Broad controls of the money supply, inflation, and taxes are in the hands of the Federal Reserve and the U.S. Treasury. By controlling the amount of money in circulation and interest rates (cost of capital), these agencies try to keep the economy in balance.

TERMS AND PHRASES

Appurtenances   Rights, privileges and improvements that belong to and pass with the transfer of real property but are not necessarily a part of the actual property

Chattel   Personal property

Chattel Real   Item of personal property which is connected to real estate (e.g., a lease or an easement)

Consideration   Exchange, usually rent, given to a lessor by a lessee in a leasehold estate

Doctrine of Correlative User   Doctrine which states that a property owner may use only a reasonable amount of the total underground water supply for his or her benefit

Emblements   Annual crops produced for sale. Emblements are considered personal property and belong to the grower whether he or she is the tenant or landlord

Estate   Legal interest in land; defines the nature, degree, extent and duration of a person's ownership in land or property

Estate in Fee   Most complete form of ownership in real property; a freehold estate that can be passed by descent or by will after the owner's death (also known as estate of inheritance or fee simple estate)

Estate of Inheritance   See estate in fee

Fee Simple Absolute   Estate in fee with no restrictions on the land's use

Fee Simple Estate   See estate in fee

Fee Simple Defeasible /Qualified   Estate in which the holder has a fee simple title, subject to return to the grantor if a specified condition occurs

Fixture   Personal property that has become part of, or affixed to, real property

Freehold Estate   Estate in real property that continues for an indefinite period of time

Less-Than-Freehold Estate   Leasehold estate, or rental agreement, that exists for a definite period of time or successive periods of time until the end of the contract or lease

Life Estate   Estate that is measured by the life of the grantee or the life of another person dictating the length of the estate

Measuring Life   Person's lifespan on which the life estate duration is based. The measuring life may be based on the lifespan of the grantee of the life estate or the lifespan of a neutral third party

Personal Property   Anything moveable that is not real property

Property   Rights or interests an individual has in something owned

Trade Fixture   Fixture used for business that has been affixed onto rented or leased property. Trade fixtures are considered personal property as they may be removed from the real property as long as there is no damage to the real property at the end of a lease

Real Property   Land, fixtures on the land, appurtenances to the land, or anything immovable by law

C H A P T E R   Q U I Z

1. What concept carried over from Spanish law into modern-day property ownership?
    a. Civil law
    b. Common law
    c. Community property
    d. None of the above

2. What are the two types of freehold estates?
    a. Fee Simple and Life Estate
    b. Absolute and Qualified
    c. Defeasible and Life Estate
    d. Fee Simple and Leasehold Estate

3. Which of the following conditions are characteristics of a Fee Simple Absolute Estate?
    a. Provides the owner with the most rights
    b. Holds no limitations or conditions
    c. Can be conveyed by a will
    d. All of the above

4. In reference to a life estate, a measuring life is
    a. the life duration of the grantor of the life estate.
    b. the life duration of the person on whose life the estate is based.
    c. a life estate in reversion.
    d. none of the above.

5. All of the following characteristics are correct regarding a leasehold estate EXCEPT
   a. the owner of a leasehold estate possesses more bundles of rights than a freehold estate.
   b. the owner of the leasehold has exclusive right of possession.
   c. the landlord holds title to the property.
   d. people holding a leasehold estate are referred to as tenants or renters.

6. Which of the following are considered the lowest form of estate?
   a. Fee Simple Defeasible
   b. Estate at Will
   c. Estate at Sufferance
   d. Estate in Reversion

7. All of the following are characteristics of a lease EXCEPT
   a. every lease is considered a contract whether it is written or oral.
   b. tenants are required to sign all written contracts.
   c. all contracts are backed by some form of consideration.
   d. written contracts may not be altered orally.

8. Property is considered
   a. anything that can be owned.
   b. real.
   c. personal.
   d. All of the above

9. An example of real property is
   a. grain harvested from plants.
   b. a car.
   c. the airspace immediately above the property.
   d. money.

10. Another term for personal property is
    a. chattel.
    b. appurtenance.
    c. fixture.
    d. MARIA.

11. Property can change from real to personal and back to real property.
    a. True
    b. False

12. Which one of the following examples is not considered a fixture?
    a. Ceiling fan
    b. Space heater
    c. Custom-made window coverings
    d. Dishwasher

13. Which one of the following is NOT considered a test of a fixture?
    a. Method of attachment
    b. Emblement
    c. Relationship between parties
    d. Adaptability

14. Trade fixtures are considered
    a. personal property.
    b. real property.
    c. both A and B.
    d. neither A nor B.

15. Which of the following is not a characteristic of real estate?
    a. Social
    b. Physical
    c. Tangible
    d. Economic

16. A person must live in his or her home a minimum of how many years to be eligible for the tax relief act?
    a. 1
    b. 2
    c. 5
    d. 7

17. A single person may qualify for property exemption of
    a. $125,000.
    b. $250,000.
    c. $500,000.
    d. $700,000.

18. What economic principle directly or indirectly affects real estate?
    a. Interest
    b. Soft Money
    c. Hard Money
    d. Supply and Demand

19. Which of the following is not considered one of the four key groups responsible for providing market information for real estate?
    a. Internet
    b. Real Estate Investment Trusts
    c. Bank and insurance analysis
    d. Interest

20. The use of a proportionately small amount of money to secure a large loan for the purchase of a property is called
    a. leverage.
    b. interest.
    c. financing.
    d. collateral.

CHAPTER

2

MONETARY SYSTEM

What you will learn in this Chapter

- Money
- The Fed—History and Purpose
- United States Treasury
- Federal Home Loan Bank System
- California Agencies for Real Estate Financing

Test Your Knowledge

1. Disposable income is
   a. any earned income such as wages, commissions or returns on investments.
   b. earned income less savings and short term reserves.
   c. earned income less bills, taxes and mortgage or rent.
   d. all of the above.

2. The Federal Reserve System is made up of how many districts?
   a. 10
   b. 12
   c. 14
   d. 16

3. Which of the following is NOT a tactic used by the Fed to regulate the money supply?
   a. Open market operations
   b. Reserve requirements
   c. Supply of gold
   d. Discount rate

4. The interest rate member banks must pay to the Fed to borrow money is referred to as
   a. interest.
   b. discount rate.
   c. open market operation.
   d. unusable funds.

5. Which creditors are required to abide by Regulation Z?
   a. Those who make 20 non-secured loans a year
   b. Those who make 3 collateral-secured loans a year
   c. Those who make 27 non-secured loans a year
   d. All of the above

6. Treasury bonds have terms of
   a. 2–5 years.
   b. less than 2 years.
   c. 5–30 years.
   d. one of the above.

7. The state agency providing real estate loans for low-income families through approved lenders is the
   a. California Housing Finance Agency.
   b. Department of Savings and Loans.
   c. Department of Insurance.
   d. Department of Banking.

INTRODUCTION

The mortgage market is a significant part of the U.S. monetary system. Money is printed and minted by the federal government. Certain agencies of the federal government, notably the Federal Reserve and the U.S. Treasury Department, control the money supply by monitoring and sometimes manipulating the prime interest rate (the rate that banks are charged to borrow money from one another). These agencies and others—for example, the Securities and Exchange Commission—monitor various fiduciary entities to protect the principal funds of bank depositors, to ensure the fair and accurate disclosure of corporate earnings, and so on.

Besides the Federal Reserve (Fed), the U.S. Treasury, and the Federal Home Loan Bank (FHLB) system, other agencies with links to real estate transactions include the Federal Deposit Insurance Corporation (FDIC); the Bank Insurance Fund (BIF); and the Savings Association Insurance Fund (SAIF).

MONEY

Money is a convenient means of exchange. It enables a value to be placed on the results of physical and mental efforts that can then be used to obtain the results of other people's physical and mental efforts. Money can be defined in the following ways

- A means of payment

- Purchasing power

- Agreed-upon value standard

In primitive societies, money may have been in the form of beads, salt, shells, and so on—whatever is accepted by the society as representing a specific value. Usually, whatever means was used was relatively scarce, and therefore had an intrinsic value. Today, convenience is a major factor in the form our money takes; paper money and coins are used throughout the world as the means of exchange.

Today, money is only a representation of the goods and services that we can buy with it. We work and invest to obtain money so we can buy food, clothing, and shelter—the basic necessities. Beyond these needs, people usually want additional funds so they can enjoy their lives, feel more secure and safe, and otherwise fulfill their desires.

Individual personal income comes from wages, salaries, and commissions received from employment plus interest, dividends, and profits from self-employment, businesses, or investments. Disposable personal income is total income minus taxes, mortgage or rent, and other non-tax payments. After some portion of these funds are spent to meet other expenses, whatever is left can be saved or invested for future

needs. These savings dollars are separated into two categories: short-term reserves and long-term investment, also known as discretionary income.
Here is an example of how your income might be distributed:

1. *Personal income from all sources*   *$105,000*
2. *Taxes, mortgage, other payments*   *$ 59,000*
3. *Disposable income*   *$ 46,000*
4. *Other expenses (personal consumption)*   *$ 39,000*
5. *Funds available for savings*   *$ 7,000*
6. *Short-term reserves*   *$ 3,000*
7. *Discretionary income*   *$ 4,000*

Paper Money

Paper money was used originally by goldsmiths who issued receipts for deposits of gold and other valuables left with them for safekeeping. It soon was obvious that it was more convenient for depositors to exchange these paper receipts for specific amounts than to withdraw, exchange, and redeposit the precious metals. Essentially, this developed into banking and checking accounts. Holders of receipts for gold could expect that they could withdraw the value stated on the receipt in gold at any time. The goldsmiths' paper receipts—or money—were as good as the gold they held in their vaults. Gold was one of the first precious metals used to evaluate the worth of goods or services.

The U.S. maintained a gold standard for its paper money until 1933. Until that time, each paper dollar represented 23.22 grams of pure gold that was held by the U.S. government. However, besides jewelers and artists, few citizens wanted to hold gold itself and use it as a means of exchange. It was much more convenient to write checks or use bills and coins.

The Great Depression of the early 1930s resulted in international currency devaluations, and the gold standard was replaced by the gold exchange standard, which is still used today.

In 1934, the U.S. Congress passed the Gold Reserve Act, which stipulated that 13.71 grams of pure gold now backed up each dollar. This gold was held in federal depositories. More significantly, the Act also eliminated citizens' rights to exchange coins or paper money for gold. The federal government said that only licensed dealers could purchase gold from the U.S. Treasury—and then only for domestic, industrial, medical, or artistic use. The government also asked citizens to turn in all gold coins then in circulation. Other forms of money in use in 1934—paper bills, silver coins, and bank notes—were declared legal tender for paying all public and private debts. This money could be exchanged for silver. Paper money issued at this time was called "silver certificates."

Since 1960, dollars have not been redeemable in silver, either. Silver certificates have been replaced by Federal Reserve notes. Bottom line, today's monetary system is largely based on the confidence people have in the stability of their government and their country's economic viability. As long as we can exchange symbolic paper money for commodities that have been deemed to be of the value represented by a specific amount of money, the system works. When that confidence is shaken, as in does in countries where political turmoil leads to economic unrest, the ability of money to buy goods and services goes down fast, leading to more instability.

Money, Supply and Demand

The supply of money and how great the demand is for it, as indicated by how much people are willing to pay in terms of interest, are the foundation of a country's economic stability. Usually, the greater the supply of money in circulation, the more economic activity can go forward. When people have more money to spend, they usually do so, and production of goods also rises because inventories need to be replenished to meet the increased demand for goods. Increased production usually means more people at work. More employment means people have more money to spend. And so the cycle goes.

If this description of economic cycles were entirely true, then the opposite—tightening the money supply—should slow the economy down. However, this is a simplistic view of a much more complicated process. Economic activity is affected by a number of factors beside the quantity of money available, including how quickly this "permanent" asset circulates or turns over. In other words, the money supply has two components: its actual physical amount and how fast its velocity of circulation is.

Economists use specifically defined monetary aggregates when they measure the money supply

- **MI "Narrow Money"**   includes cash in public hands, private checking accounts at commercial banks, credit union share accounts, and demand deposits at thrift institutions

- **M2 "Broad Money"**   includes all of MI plus money market mutual fund shares, savings deposits, and time deposits of less than $100,000 at all depository institutions

- **M3**   includes all of M2 plus large time deposits at all depository institutions

In today's economy, national monetary policy has gone beyond its earlier emphasis on fine-tuning the economy by controlling interest rates to attempts to vary the money supply. Today, interest rates are correlated with marketplace changes rather than by governmental edict. When interest rates are higher, borrowing is reduced and so is economic activity. To spur the economy, the Fed may tweak the supply and cost (interest rates) of money to raise borrowing and increase economic activity.

Other factors can affect economic activity as well. When the U.S. Congress passed the **Depository Institutions Deregulation and Monetary Control Act of 1980 (DIDMA)**, all depository institutions came under Fed control and were given the ability to "create" money through credit. Functions that used to be performed only by savings institutions could now be offered by brokerage houses, mutual fund managers, insurance companies, and credit card services and vice versa. As a result, checking accounts are now available from brokerages like Merrill Lynch; banks like Bank of America offer mutual funds and money market accounts; and electronic fund transfers are available from credit card companies like Visa.

THE FED — HISTORY AND PURPOSE

Shortly after the Revolutionary War, the legislature of the new state of Pennsylvania chartered the Bank of North America. It was successful but limited to serving only customers in the immediate area. In 1791, the First Bank of the United States was established as the earliest attempt at forming a national banking system. The First Bank failed in 1811. Five years would pass until the Second Bank of the United States was formed in 1816, and it operated until 1836, when it also failed.

Until 1913 and the formation of the Federal Reserve System (the Fed) and the organization of the Federal Reserve Bank, no federal bank existed in this country. Each state in the union issued its own currency and controlled the supply of its money and interest rates.

President Woodrow Wilson signed the Federal Reserve Act in 1913. The original purposes of the Federal Reserve were to set up facilities for selling and/or discounting commercial paper and to supervise banking. However, since that time, the Federal Reserve has extended its influence and impact to be a major factor in the operations of the U.S. monetary system, especially in the areas of money supply and the cost of capital and credit, that is, interest rates.

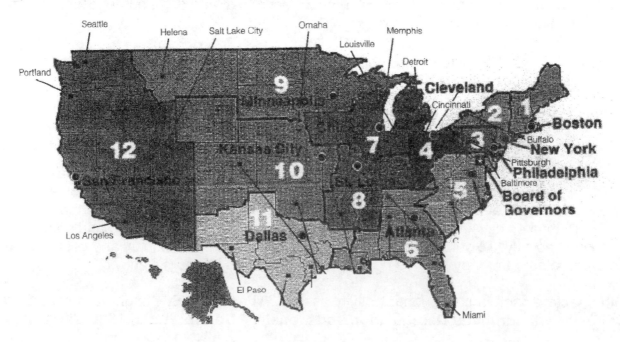

The Fed is the central bank of the U.S. Its overall goal is to ensure that long-term money and credit growth can maintain rising standards of living for all citizens. In the short term, the Fed varies its policies to prevent deflationary or inflationary pressures from affecting the economy adversely. The Fed is also the lender of last resort, so it also uses its policy instruments to prevent national liquidity crises and financial panics.

Organization of the Federal Reserve

The Fed is composed of 12 Federal Reserve districts, each served by a district Federal Reserve bank. Each district is coordinated by the seven-member Federal Reserve board in Washington, D.C. Board members are appointed by the President of the U.S. with the consent of the Senate. These districts and their branch territories are shown on the map on the previous page. Each Federal Reserve bank is not controlled by a government agency, but is responsible to a board of nine directors in each Federal Reserve district.

All nationally chartered commercial banks must be part of the Federal Reserve System; some state-chartered banks also are members. Each member bank must buy capital stock in its district Federal Reserve Bank that amounts to no more than 6% of the member bank's paid-in capital and surplus. Currently, most member banks own an amount of stock equal to about 3% of their paid-in capital and surplus. The Fed can, however, have member banks buy more, if necessary.

Member banks are also required to maintain sufficient reserves to meet Fed standards and to clear checks through the Federal Reserve system. In addition, member banks, and now, nonmember banks as well, must comply with Fed-imposed regulations governing loans and maintaining monetary stability.

Member banks may borrow money from their district Federal Reserve Bank when they need funds, take advantage of the information services provided by the Fed, and receive the protection of the Federal Reserve System.

Functions of the Federal Reserve
- Issuing currency in the form of Federal Reserve Notes
- Supervising and regulating member banks
- Clearing and collecting checks issued on member banks

Fed functions most closely associated with real estate financing

- Regulation of the size of member banks' reserves
- Determination of discount (interest) rates
- Open market operations
- Ensuring that Truth-in-Lending Act (Regulation Z) requirements are met

Reserve Requirements of Member Banks

Fed member banks must maintain reserve funds equal to a specific proportion of that bank's total funds on deposit with its federal district bank. This **reserve requirement** protects a bank's depositors by guaranteeing they can withdraw their funds from the bank whenever they want. However, protecting deposits is only the tip of the iceberg. Setting bank reserve requirements also enables the Fed to effectively "manage" the national money market by adjusting the size of reserves. The Fed can "cool off" a money market considered too "hot" by raising the reserve requirements. Banks now have less money available for lending. To spur a sluggish economy, the Fed can ease reserve requirements, thus releasing more funds for borrowing. Also, the member banks themselves can reduce the amount of money they keep on deposit at their district Federal Reserve Bank, giving the member bank more cash to lend. As a result of controlling reserve requirements, the Federal Reserve System fulfills its purpose of keeping the national economy in balance.

Member banks reserves vary from 3% to 22% of their deposits. Larger reserves are necessary to meet the liquidity requirements of checking accounts than savings accounts, for example. A member bank in a city must keep larger reserves just because more activity is likely to take place there in comparison to a bank located in a smaller community.

The Depository **Institutions Deregulation and Monetary Control Act of 1980 (DIDMA)** expanded the Fed's control to nonmember banks by requiring them to meet reserve requirements, as well.

Discount Rates and the Prime Rate

Commercial banks finance personal property and short-term business needs. The loans these bank issues are called **commercial paper**. One of the first tasks of the new Federal Reserve System in 1913 was to enable member banks to sell or discount their commercial paper. The Fed still operates a market for selling bank commercial paper at a discount, which gives member banks more funds to lend.

When banks borrow funds from their district Federal Reserve Bank, they pledge their commercial paper as collateral. The Fed charges the borrowing bank interest on these loans. This interest rate is the **discount rate**. This rate is the basic or prime interest rate the bank uses to determine the interest rate it must charge its borrowers. So, if you borrow funds from a Fed member bank, you will pay a higher rate of interest than the bank itself is paying for its funds. The higher the interest rate that the Fed charges to banks that borrow from it, the higher will be the interest rates that those banks will charge their real estate borrowers.

In real estate finance, the discount or prime rates charged by the Fed to borrowing banks are the base interest charges for short-term mortgage loans. Borrowers pay the prime rate or higher rates, depending on their credit standings. Borrowers whose credit standings are less than perfect will pay higher interest rates because they are considered greater risks.

When the Fed raises its discount rate, member banks reduce sales of their commercial paper and as a result, have less money available to borrowers. Less credit is now available locally, and theoretically, the economy slows. The reverse occurs when the discount rate goes down. The current Fed discount rate is reported in most newspapers, in financial news broadcasts, and on financial Web sites.

Federal Funds Rate
The Fed also lends money to its member banks without requiring collateral. These usually short-term loans carry an interest called the federal funds rate. This rate is published daily and is another benchmark banks use to determine the interest rates they charge borrowers.

Open-Market Operations
Fed **open-market operations** also help fulfill the purpose of balancing the economy. Open-market operations include the Fed purchasing or selling government securities in lots. Most of these are U. S. Treasury securities, but may also involve paper issued by federally sponsored housing and farm credit agencies, including the Federal Home Loan Bank System (FHLB), the Federal Housing Administration (FHA), and the Government National Mortgage Association (Ginnie Mae), to name just a few.

Open-market bulk trading of these securities generally averages several billion dollars per day. Special dealers are authorized to buy and sell these securities "over the counter." These dealers and their customers communicate by a national electronic system that enables these huge volumes of securities to transfer almost instantaneously.

These operations are directed by the system's Federal Open-Market Committee (FOMC), which meets monthly to decide on current policies. The FOMC has 12 members, seven of whom are also the members of the Federal Reserve's board of governors. The other five members are the president of the Federal Reserve Bank of New York and four other district reserve bank presidents elected to serve one-year terms.

A decision by FOMC to buy or sell securities immediately affects the money supply. When FOMC sells securities, the economy slows down because money available for credit is withdrawn from the market. When FOMC buys securities, it effectively pumps money into the economy, leading to economic expansion. As is obvious, FOMC is one of the most powerful committees in the U.S. government. The impact of its buying and selling on the availability of funds for real estate purchases is as significant as the effect of the Fed's raising or lowering the discount rate.

Truth-in-Lending Act (Regulation Z)
The Truth in Lending Act (also called Regulation Z) of the Federal Reserve Board requires creditors to fully disclose the meaning of various credit terms to the borrower. As a result, borrowers can better make informed decisions when choosing among sources of credit.

Creditors are those who extend credit or make loans to borrowers (more than 25 times each year for non-secured loans; 5 times each year for those loans requiring real property as security for the loan). A written arrangement, outlining payment amount, timing and other terms of the loan, is required. A creditor is allowed to charge interest on the loan, provided that the interest on the loan is payable in at least four installments and that there is written agreement to these terms. It is important to note that the person arranging credit is not the creditor. Rather, the institution, or actual person making the loan, is the creditor. For example, a loan officer at Wells Fargo Bank is not a creditor; Wells Fargo Bank is the creditor.

There are certain transactions that are exempt from the Truth in Lending Act. These transactions are commercial, agricultural or business loans. Loans made for more than $25,000 are exempt from Regulation Z, unless it is a purchase money loan (where the loan must be secured by real or personal property) and the borrower plans to use the property as his or her primary place of residence. Any loans made to purchase, maintain or improve a rental property fall under different regulations and rules. If this rental property will be owner-occupied within one year, the following rules apply

- Loans made to acquire rental property consisting of one or more units are considered business loans, and are regulated as such.

- Loans made to improve or maintain a property consisting of four or more units are also considered business loans and are regulated as such.

Any loans acquired for the purpose of purchasing, maintaining or improving a rental property that will not be owner occupied will always be considered a business loan.

Customers who have decided not to go ahead with the purchase of a property may cancel the loan. This is known as the **right to rescind**. A borrower has three days to cancel any loan involving a security interest in the borrower's principal residence. The three-day period will end at midnight on the third business day.

The following events must occur for the borrower to rescind

- Use of the transaction

- Borrower has received the truth in lending disclosure statement

- Borrower has received notice of the right to rescind

The right to rescind does not apply to the following situations

- Refinancing a loan secured by property that is not occupied by the owner

- Residential purchase money, first mortgage, or trust deed loans

- Borrower refinances a loan, and no new funds are advanced to the borrower

In emergency situations, the right to rescind may be waived so that the lender can fund the borrower's loan as fast as possible. Such situations may occur when closing needs to happen at a specific time for the purchase contract to be accepted.

There are certain disclosures required by Regulation Z. All disclosures must be grouped together, with the information set off by a box apart from the rest of the information on the loan. A different type style, bold type, or a different color background is also required, so that the disclosures will clearly stand out. These disclosures must be made before the transaction is completed (which is generally before closing). Usually, this disclosure statement will be delivered to the borrower at the same time as the loan commitment information is sent. This is normally after the loan has been approved, but before the loan has been funded.

The required disclosures pertain to financial information. It is necessary to state the name of the creditor, the description of the security interest, the amount of money to be financed, the finance charge associated with the loan, the annual percentage rate, the total amount of the payments, and the total sales price. The borrower must be informed of any prepayment penalties, rebates or late payment charges, so that there are no surprise charges associated with an early payoff or a late payment. When insurance is not a requirement of the loan, and the borrower wishes to obtain insurance on the item to be purchased, the borrower must sign a request for insurance. When a signature is not required, the borrower's initials must be placed on the document.

Five Most Important Disclosures
• Amount to be financed
• Finance charge
• Annual percentage rate
• Total amount of the payments
• Total sales prices (for any credit sales)

Loans may be assumable when the borrower wishes to sell the property to another buyer. A borrower in a residential mortgage transaction must be informed of whether or not this is possible with their loan. This should be included in the disclosure statement. Regulation Z also governs the types of advertisements that may be made for loans.

In any advertisement, the ad must state the annual percentage rate of the loan, along with its payment terms. Specific information regarding the different forms of adjustable rate loans must also be included in the advertisement.

Along with the Federal Reserve, the U.S. Treasury is also tasked with operating to maintain economic balance in the country. The Treasury is the fiscal manager of the U.S. and controls the daily operations of the federal government in terms of money collected in the form of taxes and borrowing and money spent. The Treasury manages the enormous debt of the federal government and supervises banking systems through the **Federal Deposit Insurance Corporation (FDIC)**. The overall credit conditions and climate of the U.S. are very dependent on the ability of the Treasury to balance government income against its long and short-term debt obligations.

The Office of the Comptroller of the Currency (OCC)

Established during the Civil War (1863) to institute a national currency, the OCC charters, regulates, and supervises all banks in the U.S. Assessments on national banks and income from U.S. Treasury securities are sources of the OCC's budget (see www.occ.treas.gov).

The Functions of the U.S. Treasury

The Treasury collects funds to cover government expenses from federal income taxes, Social Security payments, and other sources. Employers regularly send payroll deductions for Social Security (usually noted as FICA on pay stubs) and income tax withholding to the nearest federal bank. All these payments are deposited in Federal Reserve banks and other insured domestic and foreign banks.

When money thus received by the federal government is not enough to cover federal spending, either in terms of amount or when it arrives, a **deficit** occurs. When the government funds on deposit in the nation's banks are not enough to cover the payments needed, for example, to keep federal agencies operating, to meet balance of payments obligations with foreign countries, to pay out funds to various entitlement programs, the Treasury must borrow money.

To generate these funds, the Treasury sells short and long-term debt **securities**. The "collateral" for these securities are the full faith and credit of the U.S. government, with its financial stability backed by its taxing power. Essentially, the real evidence of the U.S. economic health is the confidence that citizens have in the country as shown by their readiness to buy government security issues, or in other words, to take on the risk that the government will repay its debts.

Today's national debt of more than $8 trillion is composed of various securities of different denominations, with different interest rates and with short and long terms, coming due at different times in the future. **Treasury bonds** are long-term debt instruments and have terms of 5 to 30 years. **Treasury notes** have intermediate terms of 2 to 5 years. **Treasury bills** are short-term securities that have terms of up to one year. As existing debt instruments come due, they are either repaid, thus reducing government debt, or refinanced by a new issue of bonds, notes, and/or bills.

How the Treasury decides on the mix of short and long-term debt securities to issue and whether to pay down or refinance securities coming due has a significant impact on the money supply and thus, an indirect influence on the availability of real estate financing, Theoretically, if the Treasury issues more securities, more money should be withdrawn from a "hot" economy to buy those relatively risk-free instruments. So, as a result, the economy should slow down and interest rates increase to reflect the reduced availability of funds, similarly to the effect of the FOMC selling bank commercial paper. In the same way, paying down the federal debt should pump money into a sagging economy.

However, because of fiscal pressure, the Treasury's efforts can sometimes have results opposite to the goals of the Federal Reserve. For example, to spur a slow economy, the Fed might reduce its reserve requirements and discount rates. However, if the Treasury floats a huge securities issue to meet unusually large deficits at the same time, it is essentially working counterproductive to the Fed.

The Treasury is also involved in real estate financing as it is a major contributor to the financial foundations of the Federal National Mortgage Association (Fannie Mae), the Federal Home Loan Mortgage Corporation (Freddie Mac), and the Government National Mortgage Association (Ginnie Mae)—the national secondary mortgage markets. Furthermore, the Treasury funds the Farm Credit System, which has assisted farmers for many years. For more information about the Treasury Department, see www.treasury.gov.

The Financial Institutions Reform, Recovery and Enforcement Act of 1989 (FIRREA)

In 1989, the U.S. Congress passed FIRREA to reform, recapitalize, and consolidate the Federal Deposit Insurance Corporation (FDIC) and to clarify and extend the supervisory and enforcement activities of federal agencies in regulating financial institutions. FIRREA was passed largely in reaction to a number of savings and banking failures after deregulation in the early 1980s led to some fraudulent activities and mismanagement.

The purposes of FIRREA are listed in Title I, Section 101 of the Act as follows

1. To promote, through regulatory reform, a safe and stable system of afford able housing finance.

2. To improve the supervision of savings associations by strengthening capital, accounting, and other supervisory standards.

3. To curtail investments and other activities of savings associations that pose unacceptable risks to the federal deposit insurance funds.

4. To promote the independence of the Federal Deposit Insurance Corporation from the institutions holding the deposits it insures by providing an independent board of directors, adequate funding, and appropriate powers.

5. To put the federal deposit insurance funds on a sound financial footing.

6. To establish, under the Department of the Treasury, the Office of Thrift Supervision (OTS) to manage this nation's savings and loan institutions.

7. To establish a new corporation to be known as the Resolution Trust Corporation (RTC), to contain, manage, and resolve failed savings associations. (RTC has since been dissolved.)

8. To provide funds from public and private sources to deal expeditiously with failed depository institutions.

9. To strengthen the enforcement powers of the federal regulators of depository institutions.

10. To strengthen the civil sanctions and criminal penalties for defrauding or otherwise damaging depository institutions and their depositors.

Federal Deposit Insurance Corporation (FDIC)

During the Great Depression, the Banking Act of 1933 created the Federal Deposit Insurance Corporation (FDIC) to help reinstate the public's confidence in the commercial banking system by insuring the safety of deposits. Initially, FDIC covered up to $5,000 in each account. This coverage has increased over the years to its current $100,000 per account. The FDIC now insures accounts to this amount in all member institutions, both banks and savings associations.

The FDIC is directed by a board of governors, consisting of two permanent members— the Comptroller of the Currency and the Director of the Office of Thrift Supervision, plus three U.S. citizens appointed by the President, with the consent of the Senate. These appointees serve for a maximum of six years. No more than three members of the board may be from the same political party. The chair and vice-chair of the FDIC board are chosen by the President, with approval by the Senate, from the three appointed members. The chair and vice-chair can serve no more than five years in these capacities.

The FDIC supervises its member banks and savings associations and regularly examines their operations. Before FIRREA, many warnings issued by FDIC examiners were ignored because of political pressure and, in some cases, fraud. Under FIRREA however, supervision has become much stricter.

The FDIC is appointed receiver or conservator in the event of the reorganization or liquidation of failed banks and savings associations. When serving as receiver or conservator, the FDIC acts autonomously and is not under the supervision of any other federal agency or state agency.

If a savings institution fails, the FDIC can do anything that is appropriate to reinstate the solvency of the insured institution. The FDIC can appropriate funds to fulfill the business of the institution, conserve its assets and property, and, if necessary

- Place the insured depository institution in liquidation and dispose of its assets, with consideration for the credit conditions in the local area

- Organize a new federal savings association to take over the failed institution's assets or liabilities

- Merge the insured deposits of the failed institution with those of another insured depository organization

In the event of a liquidation, the payment of insured deposits is made by the FDIC as soon as possible, either in cash or by transferring deposits to another insured depository institution (see www.fdic.gov).

Deposit Insurance Fund (DIF)
Established by FIRREA, the **Deposit Insurance Fund (DIF)** changed the federal deposit insurance system by eliminating the Federal Savings and Loan Insurance Corporation (FSLIC), which had not been able to meets all its obligations when so many savings institutions failed after deregulation. The DIF is administered by the FDIC.

Under the DIF, the **Bank Insurance Fund (BIF)** and the **Savings Association Insurance Fund (SAIF)** were formed and maintained as separate funds to preserve the integrity of the commercial bank insurance fund. The SAIF receives extra insurance premiums from the savings associations that are its current members to reimburse the FSLIC that was depleted to such an extent during the 1980s.

The insurance premiums required by the BIF from member commercial banks comprise 0.2% of their total annual average insured accounts. The BIF reported income of $1.6 billion for the year 2001 compared to a $198 million loss for 2000. The SAIF reported income of $478 million for 2001 compared with $441 million in 2000. At the end of 2001, both funds were in good financial position.

Recent legislative changes will affect how these funds operate, however. On February 8, 2006, President George W. Bush signed the Budget Reconciliation Bill (S. 1932), which contains deposit insurance reform provisions to modernize the Federal deposit insurance system. Among other provisions, this legislation

- Merges the Bank Insurance Fund (BIF) and the Savings Association Insurance Fund (SAIF) into the new Deposit Insurance Fund (DIF)

- Indexes the $100,000 deposit insurance limit to inflation beginning in 2010 and every succeeding five years while giving the Federal Deposit Insurance Corporation (FDIC) and the National Credit Union Administration (NCUA) boards authority to determine whether raising the standard maximum deposit insurance is warranted

- Increases the deposit insurance limit for certain retirement accounts to $250,000 and indexes that limit to inflation

- Allows the FDIC Board to set assessments

- Requires final regulations to be issued no later than 270 days after enactment with an effective date not later than 90 days after publication

FEDERAL HOME LOAN BANK SYSTEM

Similarly to a number of other banking regulations, the **Federal Home Loan Bank (FHLB)** system was established in 1932—during the Great Depression—to return stability to U.S. savings and loan associations, particularly in rural areas. Most of these types of institutions had operated with little public supervision or scrutiny since their inception. Many of them, like most financial institutions, faced failure during the Depression. Their failures and closings had resulted in terrible losses to their depositors, and public confidence in them was negligible.

The FHLB provides a central credit clearing facility for all member savings associations, establishes rules and regulations for its members, and supervises a deposit insurance program to cover deposits.

Organization of the FHLB

Similar to the Federal Reserve System, the FHLB is composed of 12 regional federal home loan district banks. The FHLB is directed by the Federal Housing Finance Board, an independent regulatory agency of the executive branch of government, tasked with improving home mortgage financing by making more funds available. The Finance Board is supported by assessments from the 12 FHLB district banks (see www.fhfb.gov).

Office of Thrift Supervision (OTS) of the FHLB

FIRREA created the **Office of Thrift Supervision (OTS)** under the U.S. Treasury Department to charter and regulate member associations in the FHLB. The OTS replaced the Federal Home Loan Bank Board (FHLBB). The OTS may issue charters to nonbank entities, such as insurance companies and other large financial organizations. An OTS charter preempts state laws and allows an institution to operate in all 50 states, as opposed to their needing to be licensed in each individual state (see www.ots.treas.gov).

FHLB membership is required of all federally chartered savings associations. However, state-chartered savings and loan institutions, life insurance companies, and savings banks may also join by meeting qualifications largely related to financial stability and sound management policies.

Activities of the FHLB

The FHLB provides its members with a national market for their securities. Member associations may borrow directly from their district Home Loan Banks for up to one year without collateral, but to receive the longer-term loans necessary for them to offer real estate financing, the associations must pledge collateral. Acceptable collateral includes government securities and existing real estate mortgages held in the association's investment portfolio. If savings associations capitalize on their stock-in-trade—real estate mortgages—they can receive more funds to expand, similarly to how commercial banks discount their commercial paper with their Federal Reserve district banks.

The **Individual Development and Empowerment Account Program (IDEA)**, administered by the FHLB, matches money 3 to 1 that prospective, low-income home buyers deposit in special no-fee savings accounts at local participating banks, up to a maximum match of $15,000. Participating households must save for a minimum of 10 months, successfully complete a homebuyer counseling program, and find a home and qualify for a mortgage. The subsidy must be used only toward down payment or closing costs on a home purchased as the homebuyer's primary residence. The income of the household must be 80% or less of the HUD (Housing and Urban Development) area median income.

California Department of Savings and Loans
- Regulates state savings and loan associations

California Housing Finance Agency (CHFA)
- Provides real estate loans for low-income families through approved lenders
- Obtains funds for the purchase of these loans by the sale of tax-free bonds. Approved lenders make the loans, which are then sold to the CHFA

California Department of Banking
- Supervises all state-chartered banks, foreign banking corporations in California, and institutions that exercise trust powers while doing business in the state
- Licenses business and industrial loan companies, issuers of travelers' checks, and transmitters of money to other countries
- Supervises banks by appraising bank assets, general conditions, ability to meet depositor demand, adequacy of capital, earning ability, management, and compliance with banking laws and regulations

California Department of Insurance
- Regulates insurance companies and monitors their financial stability
- Checks insurance companies' rating and underwriting procedures for compliance with the Open Competition Rating Law of California
- Issues Certificates of Authority for insurance companies to operate in California.
- Administers the agents' licensing examinations

California Department of Corporations (DOC)
- Handles securities transactions
- Franchises businesses
- Licenses thrift and loan companies, credit unions, money order issuers, escrow companies, and broker dealer investments
- Conducts periodic audits of these organizations
- Involved in licensing, regulating, and providing surveillance and control of companies lending money and/or selling securities or commodities, or advising or receiving funds from the public in a fiduciary capacity
- Regulates real estate syndications

California Department of Real Estate (DRE)
- Enforces real estate law to protect purchasers of real property and people dealing with real estate licensees

- Investigates complaints against licensees

- Regulates subdivisions, nonexempt franchises, and real property securities

- Screens and qualifies applicants for licenses

- Investigates nonlicensees allegedly doing business without a real estate license

- The Real Estate Commissioner cannot settle or litigate commission disputes or give legal advice.

Office of Real Estate Appraisers (OREA)
- Implements the requirements of FIRREA regarding appraisals of real property.

S U M M A R Y

Today, the U.S. monetary system is based primarily on the confidence citizens have in the country's economy and stability rather than on a precious metal. Money is a medium of exchange. The value of money lies in its ability to be exchanged for goods and services that have been deemed to have the same value as that represented by the money. When money is available at relatively low interest rates, the economy booms— but too much expansion can lead to inflation and instability. When interest rates are high however, the economy contracts and unemployment rates can go up.

The federal government's role in real estate finance can be seen from the very foundations of financial activity. The Federal Reserve and the U.S. Treasury determine the supply and cost (interest rates) of funds circulating in our monetary system. As a result, these agencies have profound impact on the amount of credit available and the rates of interest it carries.

The Federal Reserve System manages the money of the U.S. Created in 1913 to stabilize the commercial banking system, the Fed regulates its member banks' reserves, determines discount rates, handles the buying and selling of government securities, enforces the Truth-in-Lending Act, and regulates and controls the U.S. commercial banking system. The Fed attempts to anticipate changes in the economy, and balances the money supply to reduce inflationary or deflationary trends.

Fluctuations in the money supply affect the cost (interest rate) of borrowed funds. Because real estate finance depends heavily on how much money and credit is available for loans, the actions of the Federal Reserve have a great deal of influence on the number and dollar amounts of mortgage loans,
The U.S. Treasury also affects real estate financing. The Treasury manages the national debt and balances the federal budget. The Treasury offsets budget deficits selling government securities to raise funds. The amount of Treasury securities for sale affects the money supply and the cost of capital (interest rates).

The Treasury currently supervises U.S. depository institutions through the FDIC, OCR, and OTS. Reorganized under FIRREA, the FDIC's overall job is to maintain balance and stability in the banking industry.

The BIF insured accounts in commercial banks, and the SAIF insured savings institution accounts, both under the supervision of the FDIC. In February 2006, these two insurance funds were combined, plus insurance on bank deposits and IRAs are now to be regularly indexed against inflation.

The FHLB System, operating similarly to the Federal Reserve System, regulates U. S. savings and loan associations.

The FHLB determines member associations' reserve requirements and provides an important secondary source of funds for them.

In California, agencies involved in real estate finance include the Department of Savings and Loans, the California Housing Finance Agency, the Department of Banking, the Department of Insurance, the Department of Corporations, the Department of Real Estate, and the Office of Real Estate Appraisers.

T E R M S   A N D   P H R A S E S

Annual Percentage Rate (APR)   Effective interest rate of a loan

Discount Rate   Rate that the Fed charges its member banks for funds borrowed on collateralized loans

Discretionary Income   Earned funds left over for investment after allocations for necessities and reserves

Disposable Income   Total income after allocations for necessities; available for personal consumption

FDIC   Federal Deposit Insurance Corporation; provides insurance of $100,000 per account and supervises the operations of banks that qualify for membership in the insurance program

Fed   United States Federal Reserve System

Federal Funds Rate   Rate the Fed recommends that member banks charge each other

FHLB   Federal Home Loan Bank System; serves the nation's savings associations

FIRREA   Financial Institutions Reform, Recovery and Enforcement Act of 1989

FOMC   Federal Open Market Committee; directs and regulates the Federal Reserve System's open-market operations

FSLIC   Federal Savings and Loan Insurance Corporation; provides insurance for its member savings accounts. Replaced by the DIF

M1, M2 and M3   Measurements of the money supply

Open-Market Operations   Techniques employed by the Fed in buying and selling government securities that, in turn, control the amount of money in circulation

OTS   Office of Thrift Supervision

Personal Income   Person's gross income from all sources

Primary Interest Rate   Interest rate charged by fiduciary institutions to their AAA rated borrowers

Regulation Z   Truth-in-lending provision that requires lenders to reveal the actual costs of borrowing

Reserve Requirements   Flat percentage of deposits, required by the Federal Reserve, to be set aside by member banks as a safety measure

SAIF   Savings Institutions Insurance Fund

1. Money can be viewed as a
   a. standard of value.
   b. medium of exchange.
   c. storehouse of purchasing power.
   d. All of the above

2. Disposable income is
   a. any earned income such as wages, commissions or returns on investments.
   b. earned income less savings and short term reserves.
   c. earned income less bills, taxes and mortgage or rent.
   d. All of the above

3. Our current money system is based on
   a. the value system.
   b. the gold standard.
   c. paper.
   d. raw materials such as silver and bronze.

4. M1 is described as
   a. money market mutual fund shares and savings deposits less than $100,000.
   b. cash in public hands, checking accounts and demand deposits.
   c. large deposits at all depository institutions.
   d. both B and C.

5. Current interest rates are primarily established by
   a. marketplace realities.
   b. government edicts.
   c. foreign influences.
   d. None of the above

6. The Federal Reserve System is made up of how many districts?

   a. 10
   b. 12
   c. 14
   d. 16

7. Which of the following is NOT a tactic used by the Fed to regulate the money supply?
   a. Open market operations
   b. Reserve requirements
   c. Supply of gold
   d. Discount rate

8. The amount of money each member bank of the Federal Reserve has in reserves is
   a. regulated by the Fed.
   b. accessible to make loans.
   c. based on a percentage of deposits that may not be used.
   d. both A and C

9. The interest rate member banks must pay to the Fed to borrow money is referred to as
   a. interest.
   b. the discount rate.
   c. open market operation.
   d. unusable funds.

10. The directorial board of the FED is made up of how many governors?
    a. 5
    b. 7
    c. 10
    d. 12

11. The Fed's board of governors is appointed by
    a. the President and approved by the Senate.
    b. the Senate and approved by the President.
    c. Congress.
    d. each district elects one representative.

12. Member banks in the Federal Reserve banking system are
    a. only nationally chartered banks.
    b. both nationally and state chartered banks.
    c. only state chartered banks.
    d. none of the above.

13. Which creditors are required to abide by Regulation Z?
    a. Those who make 20 non-secured loans a year
    b. Those who make 3 collateral-secured loans a year
    c. Those who make 27 non-secured loans a year
    d. All of the above

14. Which of the following loans would be exempt from Regulation Z requirements?
    a. A loan made for more $25,000 secured by real property
    b. A non-secured residential loan for under $25,000
    c. An agricultural loan
    d. None of the above

15. Disclosures required by Regulation Z are
    a. included on a separate addendum to the loan.
    b. included in regular type in the loan document.
    c. offset by a box, type style, color and bold lettering in the loan document.
    d. made verbally by the loan originator.

16. Which of the following is not a disclosure to be made by Regulation Z?
    a. Finance charge
    b. Total sales price
    c. Amount to be financed
    d. Date each installment is due

17. What agency supervises the Federal Deposit Insurance Corporation (FDIC)?
    a. Fed
    b. Federal Reserve System
    c. United States Treasury
    d. Each individual region supervises their local FDIC

18. Treasury bonds have terms of
    a. 2–5 years.
    b. less than 2 years.
    c. 5–30 years.
    d. None of the above

19. The state agency providing real estate loans for low-income families through approved lenders is
    a. California Housing Finance Agency.
    b. Department of Savings and Loans.
    c. Department of Insurance.
    d. Department of Banking.

20. The state agency handling securities transactions is called the
    a. Department of Banking.
    b. Department of Corporations (DOC).
    c. Office of Real Estate Appraisers (OREA).
    d. Department of Insurance.

CHAPTER

LAND TITLE
AND
ESTATES

What you will learn in this Chapter

- Types of Estates in Real Property

- Real Property

- Personal Property

- Fixtures and Trade Fixtures

- Descriptions of Land

- Encumbrances

- Homestead Declaration

- Marketability of Title

- Title Insurance

Test Your Knowledge

1. What are the two types of freehold estates?
   a. Fee Simple and Life Estate
   b. Absolute and Qualified
   c. Defeasible and Life Estate
   d. Fee Simple and Leasehold Estate

2. Property is considered
   a. anything that can be owned.
   b. real.
   c. personal.
   d. all of the above.

3. Trade fixtures are considered
   a. personal property.
   b. real property.
   c. both A and B.
   d. neither A nor B.

4. Which of the following is NOT considered an encumbrance on real property?
   a. Lien
   b. Encroachment
   c. Homestead
   d. Easement

5. What is the maximum homestead exemption a person 65 years of age or older can declare on his or her residence?
   a. $150
   b. $75
   c. $50
   d. $85

6. A certificate of title will tell what about a property?
   a. Vesting
   b. Encumbrances
   c. Neither A nor B
   d. Both A and B

7. A standard title insurance policy will guard against all of the following except
   a. federal tax liens.
   b. forgery.
   c. water rights.
   d. fraud.

INTRODUCTION

Owning property, or **ownership**, is the basic concept for the subject of real estate. In this chapter we will examine the different types of ownership, or **estates**, that a person can have in property. We will also look at the different ways property can be transferred from one person to another and the length of time of ownership. The concepts of owning, leasing and renting will become clear to you as they are differentiated and explained.

You will also learn the definition of **real property** and the difference between real and **personal property**. **Fixtures** and **trade fixtures** are other concepts, which will be differentiated and explained. The distinction between fixtures and trade fixtures is important, as the two are often confused with one another. Finally, we will discuss **land descriptions, divisions** and **area**.

TYPES OF ESTATES IN REAL PROPERTY

An **estate** is ownership or interest in real property. Thus, **real estate** or **real property** means ownership. There are two types of estates in real property: **freehold estate** and **less-than-freehold estate** (or **leasehold estate**). The type of estate a person has in property determines the degree of ownership, or claim, the property owner has in his or her estate.

Estates in Land		
Freehold Estates	Fee Simple	Fee Simple Absolute
		Free Simple Qualified/fee Simple Defeasible
	Life Estate	
		Estate in Reversion
		Estate in Remainder
Leasehold Estates		Estate for Years
		Estate for Period to Period
		Estate at Will
		Estate at Sufferance

Freehold Estates
A **freehold estate** is the highest form of ownership. The term "freehold" stems from medieval England, where a landowner who was free from the demands of his overlord could use the land in any way he desired. A freehold estate may continue for an indefinite period, or be limited to a specific number of years. Additionally, although the freehold estate allows the owner the most freedom of use, this use may be limited.

There are two types of freehold estates: **fee simple estate** and **life estate**.

Fee Simple Estate

Fee simple estate allows the property owner to use the property now and for an indefinite number of years. It provides the owner with the largest bundle of rights of any type of estate. A fee simple estate may also be known as an **estate of inheritance** since it can be conveyed by a will. A fee simple estate that holds no conditions or limitations is called a **fee simple absolute**. This estate is generally transferred through a normal real estate transaction.

If a fee simple estate is transferred with limitations, conditions or qualifications, it is referred to as a **fee simple qualified** or **fee simple defeasible**. Under the provisions of a fee simple qualified or defeasible estate, the interest in the property can be limited or taken away in the event of misuse of the property per any agreed-upon conditions.

> *Example*
> *Adam gives 420 acres of land to Peter, a developer, to build a new amusement park. Adam grants the gift with the condition that no trees are cut down in the development of the park. During construction, Adam learns that 100 acres have been stripped of all vegetation to allow for a parking garage. Since Peter broke the condition against Adam's wishes, Adam can take the property back and repossess it for his own use.*

Life Estate

A **life estate** is an estate that is granted for a definite period of time. The owner of the property has the right to use and possess the property for the duration of his or her lifetime, or the **measuring life** of another individual. Upon the death of the land-owner or specified individual, the estate will revert back to the original owner who made the life estate.

> ### Measuring Life
>
> A person's lifespan upon which the life estate duration is based; this may be the grantee of the life estate or a neutral third party.

A life estate is a type of freehold estate. As a result, the owner has all the rights associated with fee ownership EXCEPT conveyance of the property by will. The owner may sell the property with the condition that the property reverts back to the original owner upon the death of the individual whose life measures the length of the estate.

Taxes and maintenance of the property are the sole responsibility of the holder of the life estate. The property may be rented out, encumbered or disposed of at his or her discretion. However, any interest in the property that extends beyond the life of the person by whom the life estate is measured will become invalid upon that individual's death.

Possession returns to the original owner of the property when the life estate ends if the original owner has a reversion. Sometimes the property will revert to a third party when the life estate ends and the owner does not have a **reversion**; this person holds a life estate in remainder during the existence of the life estate. This person is referred to as the **remainderman**.

> ### Remainderman
> The person a life estate reverts to upon the death of the current owner, not the original owner of the estate.

Leasehold Estates

A leasehold estate (or **less-than-freehold estate**) contains a smaller bundle of rights than a freehold estate. People who own this type of estate are called **renters** and **tenants**. The owner of a leasehold estate has exclusive right of possession of the land and everything attached to it during the duration of the lease. The lease will outline the conditions for use, duration of rental and occupancy of the property. The bundle of rights a tenant or renter holds with a leasehold includes the right of possession, use and enjoyment.

- The **tenant**, or **lessee**, is someone who acquires the use of property for a specific time period as outlined by the lease and holds the right of exclusive possession.

- The **landlord**, or **lessor**, is the person who owns the title to the property or reversion during the lease.

- The tenant will pay the landlord **rent** at predetermined time periods for use of the property.

> ### Leasehold Estate
> A leasehold estate is a lease between a tenant, or lessee, and a landlord, or lessor.

Leaseholds are considered personal property or **chattel real**. Tenants hold the right of possession and use of the property, yet it is not considered real property as they cannot encumber or convey the property, and only hold possession of the property for the duration of the lease.

There are four different types of leasehold estates. They are

- Estate For Years
- Estate From Period To Period
- Estate At Will
- Estate At Sufferance

Estate for Years
An **estate for years** is a lease agreement that will continue for a definite period of time, which is agreed upon in advance. The term of this type of lease can extend to 99 years. This term can be broken down into years, months, weeks or days. No notice is required from either party to vacate the property or terminate the agreement.

Estate from Period to Period
An estate from period to period is one that continues for a specified period of time such as week-to-week, month-to-month or year-to-year. This type of lease is automatically renewed for the same type of time period, unless the tenant or landlord gives notice to vacate the property or terminate the lease agreement. Periodic tenancies generally have month-to-month terms and require one month's notice from either party to vacate or terminate the lease.

Estate at Will
An **estate at will** is a lease for an indeterminable amount of time with no express rent promised for the occupancy. This type of lease is uncommon.

Estate at Sufferance
An **estate at sufferance** occurs when a tenant remains on the land after the lease has run out. Additionally, an estate at sufferance may be formed when a tenant gives the landlord a notice to vacate but then does not leave the property by the specified time. In both instances the landlord has not given the tenant permission to stay on the property. This type of leasehold estate contains the smallest bundle of rights, making it the least desirable form of estate, as the landlord may start eviction proceedings at any time or the tenant may vacate the property with no notification required.

Leasehold Estates Include
- Estate for years
- Estate from period to period
- Estate at will
- Estate at sufferance

Written agreements are helpful in any leasehold situation. However, a written contract is required if the lease is going to last longer than one year. Written agreements or contracts help both parties avoid any misunderstandings regarding the property, terms of the lease or length of occupancy. A written contract is also required if a lease is going to end more than one year in the future, even if the lease term is less than one year.

Characteristics of Every Lease

- All leases are contracts whether they are in written or oral form. The landlord must sign all written contracts. Tenants, on the other hand, are not required to sign a written contract as occupancy is considered his or her acknowledgement of the lease and its terms.

- Contracts must have clear terms understood by both parties backed by **consideration** or a form of rent.

- Once written, a contract cannot be altered by oral means.

Characteristics of a lease

- Landlords must sign all written contracts
- Possession by a tenant is considered his or her acknowledgement of a lease contract.
- Contracts must be backed by some form of consideration or rent.

R E A L   P R O P E R T Y

Property is anything that can be owned. **"Real property"** refers to land, any permanent fixtures attached to the land such as a house or building, anything appurtenant to the land such as an easement, or anything attached to the land such as trees. A broader way to think about real property is in spatial terms, such as land, airspace, mineral rights, water rights and fixtures. Ownership in real property can be defined as the **bundle of rights; some of the rights in the "bundle" may be held by different persons**. Generally speaking, real property is immovable.

Airspace
The airspace above a building to a specific height is considered personal property. Homeowners, including condominium owners, may restrict the use of the airspace immediately above their property if it is being used in a disruptive way.

Minerals
Solid minerals contained in the ground are considered real property until taken out of the ground. Coal is an example. Once the coal is taken out of the ground, it becomes personal property. You will learn more about personal property later in this chapter.

Non-solid minerals such as oil and gas are not considered real property because of their fluid nature. The property owner has the right to drill for gas or oil on his or her own land, but it does not become property until it is reduced to possession after drilling.

Water Rights

Water is considered real property, but it cannot be owned. A property owner cannot dam surface water to collect it for his or her own use; nor can water be channeled for the benefit of any one person. Under the **Doctrine of Correlative Rights**, the landowner may take a reasonable share of the ground water.

The different types of water rights include
- **Littoral**   the rights of a property owner who owns a piece of land bordering a lake or ocean

- **Surface**   these rights outline rain runoff rights and regulations

- **Riparian**   rights to use rivers and streams bordering a piece of property, as defined in the doctrine of correlative rights

- **Underground**   a landowner's right to use percolating or underground water

- **Right of Appropriation**   allows the state to allocate non-riparian property owners to take surplus ground water for their own beneficial use. An example of this would be for agricultural production

Permanent Attachments

Real property not only includes water rights, mineral rights and the land itself. It also includes those items permanently attached to the ground itself. These include

- Buildings or other structures resting on the land

- Growing plants attached to the ground with roots

- Items permanently fixed (referred to as fixtures) in or on a house or building

Growing plants such as trees, shrubs and vines are considered real property. Industrial crops are considered real property only until they are harvested for sale, severed, cut or mortgaged. Once these crops are harvested they become personal property.

Emblements are growing crops that are considered personal property and are an exception to the rule of growing crops as real property. Such crops may be owned by the landowner or by a tenant leasing land from a landlord. The crops themselves are considered personal property, while the land on which the crops are growing is NOT considered personal property. An example of this is a peach tree orchard. The peaches themselves are personal property to the grower; the trees themselves are real property attached to the land. Personal property will be further discussed in the next section.

Appurtenances

An appurtenance is anything used with the land for its benefit. An example is an easement, which gives others the right to use the property for a specific purpose, such as a right-of-way to cross another person's property. Stock in a mutual water company is another type of appurtenance. These appurtenant rights are sold with the land as they are considered real property.

Immovable by Law

Anything deemed immovable by law is also real property. A seller of real property cannot exclude an orchard growing on the property from the sale, as the orchard is real property. Any produce that is growing may be negotiated in the sale of the property yet the trees are immovable by law and are therefore considered real property.

> **Real Property Includes**
> - Land—including airspace, minerals, and water rights
> - Attachments to the land such as buildings and tree
> - Appurtenances such as easements
> - Objects immovable by law

P E R S O N A L   P R O P E R T Y

Personal property is considered movable. Any property that is not considered real property is personal property. As briefly stated earlier in this chapter, items such as mature, harvested crops, furniture in a house, a cut tree used for lumber, automobiles, stocks or money are all considered personal property. Personal property is also known as **chattel**, as it is movable and transferred or sold using a bill of sale. When real property is sold, all personal property goes with the seller unless he or she has agreed to leave such personal property on the real property, or include it in the contract.

Real and personal property can change form from one to the other. An example of this is a tree. While it is growing and attached to the ground it is considered real property. When it is cut down or harvested for lumber it becomes personal property. When the lumber is used to build a house, it again becomes real property. If the house is torn down, and the lumber is recycled for a different use, it again becomes personal property.

As discussed earlier, emblements (such as crops that are sold, mortgaged or harvested) are considered personal property. The physical plant itself is not personal property; it is real property. The crop it yields is personal property.

- Personal Property is also called **chattel**
- Property may change form from real to personal and back to real

FIXTURES AND TRADE FIXTURES

A fixture is real property that began as personal property. It has become real property because it was permanently attached to real property. Examples of this include a refrigerator, a ceiling fan, or custom-built shelves for a closet.

There are five tests to determine what items are fixtures

1. Method of attachment or degree of permanence
2. Adaptability
3. Relationship of the parties
4. Intention of the person who attached it
5. Agreement between the parties

As you can see, an easy way to remember these determinations is the acronym MARIA, as is spelled by the first letter of each test. One important note to make is that cost is NOT a test for fixtures.

Method of Attachment
The greater the degree of attachment or permanence, the more likely the item is a fixture. For example, a ceiling fan wired into the electrical system of a home has a high degree of attachment and is considered real property.

Adaptability
The more an item is adapted to a specific room or place, the more likely it is a fixture. To revisit the ceiling fan example, the fan was purchased intentionally for one room in a home, with consideration of size, style and color. On the other hand, a floor fan plugged into a wall can be moved from one room to another. As the floor fan is not adapted for specific needs or purposes of a room, it is personal property – while the ceiling fan is real property.

Relationship of the Parties
Relationships between parties can be of the buyer-seller or landlord-tenant type. Courts can determine whether an item is a fixture or not, based on the relationship of the parties. If a seller of land attaches a fixture onto the land before a sale, the fixture will be considered real property and will transfer to the new owner upon sale of the property.

Intention of the Person Attaching the Item
If a person intends to remove a piece of personal property upon the sale of said property, he or she should not attach it to the property itself. **This is the most important test of a fixture**. If a tenant purchased a ceiling fan for the bedroom of an apartment and informed the landlord that she planned on removing it and taking it with her upon moving, the ceiling fan will not be considered a fixture. It will instead be considered personal property.

Agreement between Parties
Parties should put their intentions into writing to avoid disputes about fixtures and personal property. This determines the intentions of each party more clearly.

Five Fixture Tests

- Method of attachment

- Adaptability

- Relationship of the parties

- Intention of the person attaching the item

- Agreement between parties

Trade fixtures are personal property affixed to real property for use in a trade, business or craft. These fixtures can be removed, provided that their removal causes no damage to the real property. This is especially important when a tenant attaches his or her trade fixtures to a rented space.

Examples of Trade Fixtures

- Built-in work benches

- Dividing screens or temporary walls

- Cash registers

Every piece of land is unique, as no other piece of land has exactly the same characteristics. Some pieces of land may look very similar to one another, with similar topography and features. Still, the land's physical geographical positioning makes it unique in itself. Street names and addresses are used to describe areas of land or locations, but this is not an adequate distinction for all parcels of land. Rural areas cannot be adequately described by addresses, while areas currently under development are undergoing constant changes or reconstruction.

Today, legal descriptions of land are used to describe a specific property. These legal descriptions are required before a property can be sold to a new owner or a deed can be recorded. There are three methods used to describe land for legal purposes. They are

- Lot, block and tract system
- Metes and bounds
- U.S. government section and township survey

Lot, Block and Tract System
The **lot, block and tract system** is also called the **subdivision system**. The subdivision is mapped out with a **Plat Map** showing the divisions of tracts, blocks within the tracts and the lots within each block. Each deed to a property that uses a plat map description will contain the tract, the block and the lot number. This description will be unique to the parcel of property and separate from any other parcel. The tract is the largest area on a plat map, which can be broken down into blocks and then again into lots, which are the smallest portion on the map. Below is the Plat Map of 10304 S. Central Avenue in Los Angeles.

Plat Maps

Plat Maps are used to show the division within the lot, block and tract system.

Metes and Bounds

The **metes and bounds** measurement system is used when Lot, Block and Tract or U.S. government section and township survey are not practical, or would not work. Metes and bounds are used mostly to describe complicated or irregularly shaped properties. Metes and bounds describe property based on measurements between boundaries or landmarks. These measurements are based on the distance, direction or angle from a given point.

"Metes" most closely describe the distance or measurement between two given points, while **"bounds"** refers to the boundaries, or points, being referenced in the measurement between landmarks or monuments. Bounds can include both artificial and natural features. Examples of artificial bounds are roads, canals or stakes. Examples of natural bounds are rivers, streams, lakes, boulders, land formations and trees.

A metes and bounds description starts at a well-known landmark or point and follows the natural boundaries of the land to another landmark or point. The distance between the boundaries and back to the original starting point is measured to determine the metes and bounds.

Example of a Metes and Bounds Description

Commencing from a point one-half mile upstream from Smith Bridge on Jones Creek, proceed northeast 500 feet to Spring Hill, ten northwest to the large oak tree, then southwest to the large rock in the middle of Jones Creek, then along Jones Creek to the origin. (See left side of map on next page)

Be cautioned that metes-and-bounds surveys are liable to create problems. Since surveys were done as land was claimed, the result was often overlapping claims—and lengthy court battles. Even today, land titles are more difficult to verify in areas surveyed by metes and bounds. A larger problem is that the boundary markers (oak tree, big rock, etc.) are eventually obliterated. The result is often an ambiguous boundary. One measure used to avoid such ambiguity is to replace landmarks or boundary markers with exact compass directions and distances (also known as "Coordinate Geometry"). So, using coordinate geometry, the description above might be replaced with the following

Example
Commencing from a point one-half mile upstream from Smith Bridge on

Jones Creek, proceed N 45° E 500 feet, then N 50° W 324 feet, then S 35° W to Jones Creek, then along Jones Creek to the origin. (See right side of map below)

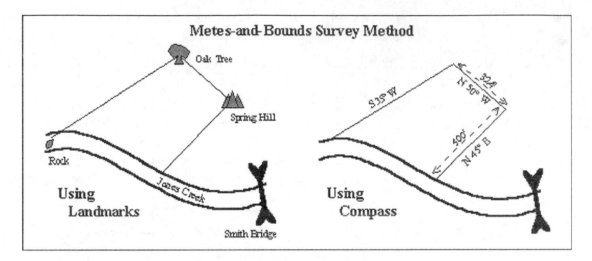

Metes-and-Bounds Survey Method

The metes and bounds survey method is used when the township survey or lot, block and tract systems would not be sufficient survey methods. This occurs primarily in cases of irregularly-shaped plots of land, or land that is difficult to survey (such as wetlands or mountainous terrain).

U.S. Government Section and Township Survey

Most of the land in the U.S. is described under the U.S. government's section and township survey. This system is used in 30 of the 50 states. A rational, rectangular survey is called the **Public Land Survey (PLS)** system, which was enacted under the Northwest Land Ordinance of 1785. The township survey system starts out with a coordinate system for a given area.

Principal meridians are lines running north and south. **Baselines** are the lines that run east and west. Each baseline is given a name, so that each land parcel may be identified by that name.

- Meridians run north and south
- Baselines run east and west

US Public Land Survey

Major Principal Meridians and Baselines

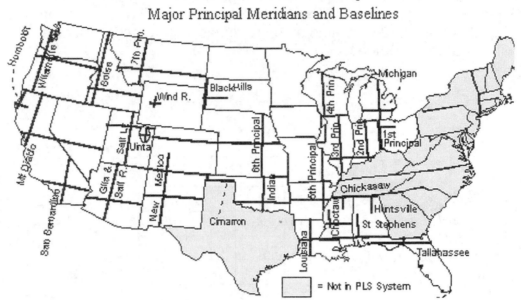

California has tree principal meridian / baseline pairs

- San Bernardino meridian (Southern California
- Mount Diablo meridian (most of Northern California)

The initial point is the intersection of the principal meridian and baseline. From this point, townships are marked off east/west and north/south. Each **township** is 6 miles on a side, or 36 square miles. Townships are designated on the east-west direction as being a certain number of **ranges** east or west of the principal meridian. The township is also a certain number of **townships** north or south of the baseline. For example, the township that is just on the southeast corner of the initial point is Township 1 South, Range 1 East (usually abbreviated T. 1 S, R. 1 E). Another example: T. 4 S, R. 5 E would be the fourth township south of the baseline and five townships to the east.

- Range lines are every 6 miles east and west of the meridian.
- Township lines are every 6 miles north and south of the base line.

Each township was divided so that individuals could afford to purchase one **section**, or a portion of each section further divided (see graphic below). The township was divided into 36 sections of one square mile each. Each of the sections is numbered consecutively from 1 to 36, starting at the northeast corner and snaking around the rows, with 36 at the southeast corner.

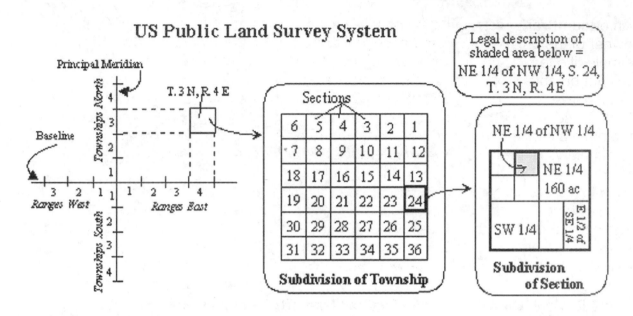

Sections can be broken down into halves, quarters or eighths, designated by a compass direction. If they are divided in half, we have either east/west halves, or north/south halves. If divided into quarters, we have the NE, NW, SW, and SE quarters. Quarters can be broken down further if necessary. For example, an eighth of a section might be designated by the NE quarter of the SE quarter. One section contains 640 acres, while a quarter section contains 160 acres. Property descriptions must include a township number, section number, and fraction of a section. So, a property description may read

SW 1/2 of SE 1/4, Sect. 4, T. 87 N, R. 34 E, 6th Principal Meridian

The township survey system is not a flawless system. There are irregularities in certain geographic areas. Section and township lines are not always exactly north/south and east/west, and sections are sometimes less than a full square mile (in the event that the sections are less than a full square mile, they are called **government lots**). The irregularities of the township survey system arise from several different sources. The following are just a few possible reasons for irregularities

Meridians converge to the north, so as surveyors moved north, townships didn't match up with those that were further south. Often east-west correction lines were set up, along which townships were re-aligned. You'll notice this effect when driving north or south along a country road when you have to take a sudden turn right or left, then turn north/south again after a short distance.

California Real Estate Finance

Surveying in difficult terrain where there are mountains or adverse weather conditions caused some lines to go astray. Once set up, however, the errors were kept, and these lines were never resurveyed or redrawn.

E N C U M B R A N C E S

An **encumbrance** is a limitation on real property imposed by someone who is not the owner of the property. Encumbrances must be identified because they will affect the fee simple title to real estate or the use of the property. A property that has an encumbrance will not be able to be sold until the encumbrance is cleared. An encumbrance is most often a legal obligation against the title of the property, though not all encumbrances are bad. Some encumbrances require property in certain developments or zoned areas to maintain a certain standard of property improvements for the good of the entire community. The end result is a more attractive community in which to live.

Encumbrances may affect the marketable title to property. A title free of any liens or encumbrances is one an informed buyer is likely to accept. When a title has a debt against it, this is referred to as a **"cloud on the title."** Property with a cloud on the title is less attractive to sell, often causing the property owner to sell below market value. In extreme cases, it may even prevent the property owner from selling the property at all.

There are two types of encumbrances: money and non-money encumbrances. **Money encumbrances** are also called **liens**, or debt against the title of the property. Liens form a legal obligation to repay a debt that was secured by real property. These liens may be voluntarily or involuntarily acquired. The different types of liens are mortgages and trust deeds, tax liens, mechanic's liens, judgments, attachments and special assessments.

Non-money encumbrances are limitations on the use of the property; building restrictions or codes, zoning requirements and encroachments are all considered non-money encumbrances (or physical restrictions) placed on property.

> **Two Types of Encumbrances**
>
> - Non-money encumbrances: easements, building restrictions, zoning requirements ad encroachments.
>
> - Money encumbrances: restrictions or liens such as mortgages and trust deeds, tax liens, mechanic's liens, judgments, attachments and special assessments.

Liens encumber property for a debt secured against the property. **General liens** apply to all property owned by the debtor, while specific liens attach only to one specific property. Some examples of general and **specific liens** are mechanic's liens, court judgments, and trust deeds or mortgages. Mechanic's liens and trust deeds are specific liens that attach only to the property being financed (trust deed) or improved (mechanic's lien), while a court judgment is a general lien that attaches to all property owned.

Liens are not always a negative thing. A loan secured against property, lines of credit, mortgages and trust deeds and other financial advances to be used to make improvements to a property or to purchase desired items such as a car, boat or additional property are all examples of positive results of a lien. Such liens are **voluntary liens**, meaning that the property owner agreed to the lien. Liens such as mechanic's liens, tax liens or judgments are **involuntary liens**, meaning that the property owner did not willingly seek these liens. Rather, they were imposed upon the owner.

Mechanic's liens will secure a payment for any services performed, materials consumed or work done to improve a property. Any party or supplier who contributes to the improvement of a property is eligible to file a mechanic's lien to ensure payment for services rendered. Professionals who are eligible to file a mechanic's lien include

- Contractors
- Subcontractors
- Architects
- Engineers
- Surveyors
- Material Suppliers
- Machinists
- Equipment Lessors
- Truckers
- Laborers or Workers

Professionals who indirectly supply materials or sub-contractors not working directly for the property owner can utilize the mechanic's lien to ensure they are paid for services they render to a contractor who is working for the property owner. If the property owner pays the contractor or builder, but does not pay the material supplier or subcontractors working through the contractor, these professionals have the option of filing a mechanic's lien to receive payment. Sometimes the property owner will pay the contractor in full for the job performed, and the contractor will in turn fail to pay the subcontractor or suppliers. In this situation, the homeowner will be held liable for the money still owed to the subcontractors and suppliers. One way a homeowner can prevent this situation is by requiring the contractor to obtain a payment bond. A **payment bond** is a form of insurance where the issuing company will compensate the property owner if a contractor does not follow through with all agreed-upon obligations. The bonding company will see to it that all parties receive payment. This relieves the property owner from liability in the event the contractor fails to pay all other subcontractors and suppliers.

The enforcement of a mechanic's lien results in foreclosure on a property. Once the property has been sold through judicial sale, all lien holders are paid from the proceeds, and any funds left over after the sale of the property are returned to the property owner. All mechanic's liens must be enforced within 90 days of filing. Lien holders may grant an extension to the property owner, but only for a period of not more than one year after the work has been completed.

Anyone filing a mechanic's lien must be sure to follow the procedures to make sure the lien is valid. All mechanic's liens must be verified and recorded.

The following is a list of steps that must be taken to initiate a valid mechanic's lien.

1. **Preliminary Notice**   Written notice that is given to a property owner within 20 days of when work first begins or when materials are delivered. This serves as notice to the property owner that if they fail to pay for any materials or labor, a lien may be filed. The Preliminary Notice may be hand-delivered or mailed (via first class registered mail or certified mail) to the property owner, general contractor or construction lender

2. **Starting Time**   Begins when construction on a project begins, and determines when the preliminary notice must given

3. **Completion Time**   When the project is completed, when the property owner begins to use the new improvement, when the work has been accepted, or when construction has been stopped for 60 days

4. **Notice of Completion**   An owner may file a Notice of Completion with the county recorder 10 days after the project has been finished. Once this notice is filed, contractors have 60 days to file a mechanic's lien; all others have 30 days to file their mechanic's liens. If the owner does not file a Notice of Completion, all parties filing a mechanic's lien have 90 days to file

5. **Foreclosure Action**   After a mechanic's lien is filed, the person filing the lien has 90 days to bring foreclosure action against the property owner. If the person who filed the lien does not bring action against the property owner within the 90-day period, the lien filer will lose the right to foreclose on the property and will not be compensated for the work performed.

Mechanic's Lien Time line

1. Materials are delivered or work begins on the project

2. Preliminary 20-day notice is given

3. Work has been completed

4. Notice of completion is recorded*

5. Lien Recorded

6. Foreclosure Action Recorded

7. Service of Process

8. Court Decision

*The property owner does not always file notice of completion. It is important to understand the difference in timeframe between when a completion is filed and when one is not.

The order in which a lien will be paid upon foreclosure is determined by the order (by date) of when a lien was filed. This order will be followed only if there is more than one lien against a property. Mechanic's liens are the exception to this rule, as a mechanic's lien takes priority over all other liens—including trust deeds. A trust deed may be recorded months ahead of any mechanic's lien; however, the mechanic's lien will be the first to be paid in full upon foreclosure.

If a property owner did not authorize any work to be done, but a contractor begins working in spite of this, the property owner may file a **notice of non-responsibility**. This notice must be recorded with the county recorder and posted on the property where the work is taking place. This will relieve the property owner from any responsibility to pay for unauthorized work. The notice of non-responsibility must be filed within 10 days of any construction or work beginning on the property and must include the following: a property description; name, address and property interest of the person giving notice (usually the owner); and a statement of non-responsibility.

Tax liens and special assessments   When a property owner fails to pay property taxes, the amount of the unpaid tax becomes a lien against the property. If there is a utility project or local improvement levied against the property owner which is not paid by the agreed-upon time, this amount also becomes a lien. Special assessments and local taxes are **specific liens** attaching only to one specific piece of property, while any government tax will become a **general lien** attaching to all property owned.

Attachments and Judgments   An **attachment** occurs when the court orders a freeze on personal or real property that has been awarded to another in a lawsuit. A **judgment**

is the decision of the judge in a court case. The losing party has the right to appeal the judgment to a higher court to reverse the decision. However, once a judgment is final, the judgment becomes a lien. A court judgment is a **general lien**. This general lien will also be applied to all property—including property acquired after the judgment has been made. A **writ of execution** may be requested from the lien holder to pay off a lien. A writ of execution is a court order directing an officer of the court to satisfy a judgment out of the debtor's property. A portion of the property will be sold to raise the funds to pay off the lien or debt. The property to be sold may include the nonexempt property or exempt property, subject to the judge's discretion.

Lis Pendens   a cloud on a title of a property pending litigation which can often prevent the sale or transfer of a property until litigation is completed and judgment rendered.

Easements or **right-of-way**   the right to use someone else's land for a specific purpose. An easement is a **nonposessory** interest, meaning that the person benefiting from the easement does not own the land. The property owner giving the easement is known as the **servient tenement** and the person receiving the right to use the easement is known as the **dominant tenement**.

Easements are useful in that they allow an individual to access property or landmarks not accessible from a main road, or from one's own property. For example, Joe owns a house on a lot that is not accessible from any main street. In order to get to his house, Joe must utilize 30 feet of his neighbor's driveway to reach his own property. The 30 feet of his neighbor's driveway is the easement. Again, it is important to note that Joe does not own any portion of his neighbor's driveway, but is allowed to use it to gain access to his own property. When Joe sells his home, the person buying the house will also have access to the easement. Easements are appurtenant and are automatically sold with the property of the dominant tenement. You will remember that appurtenances to the land, whether they are easements, fixtures or stock in a mutual water company, will be transferred with the property. The seller will not retain ownership rights.

Easements don't only benefit persons owning property. Easements can allow access to streams, lakes, camping sites or other recreational areas requiring the crossing of someone's land. For example, a canoe outfitter regularly takes his patrons to Millers Landing to launch a 36-mile canoe trip downriver. In order to access Millers Landing, the canoe outfitter must cross 40 yards of private land. An easement will allow the canoe outfitter to legally cross the land in both directions. Without this easement, Millers Landing would be inaccessible to everyone except the landowner.

Easements in Gross are easements that benefit public utilities. This type of easement is not appurtenant to one property. If or when a utility company needs to cross private land to reach a utility pole, transformer or any other structure, they will be allowed access due to easement in gross. This type of easement is similar to a license. However, unlike a license, an easement in gross cannot be terminated.

Creation of an Easement Requires

- Contract
- Express Grant from the property owner
- Express Reservation
- Implied Grant/Reservation
- Necessity
- Prescription

Contract   An easement created by a contract is one where the property owner (servient tenement) grants use to cross his or her property to another individual (dominant tenement). The person receiving the easement may not need to own property adjacent to the granting property owner, depending on the type of easement that is created.

Express Grant   An easement is created through express grant when the servient tenement grants an easement by deed to the person who will benefit from the easement (the dominant tenement).

Express Reservation   An easement is created through express reservation when the dominant tenement sells his or her property to another but reserves the easement rights in the deed for use by the new property owner.

Implied Grant/Reservation   Occurs when an easement is created through an implication of law. No formal mention of such easement need be made in the deed. However, due to the proximity of one piece of property to another, an easement may be necessary and obvious.

Necessity   An easement is created through necessity when there is no other way to reach a landlocked property. If or when an alternative way on or off the property is created, the easement will automatically be terminated. An example of this is when city blocks are drawn and interior lots with no street access are created. The person purchasing the interior lot will need to cross a neighbor's property to reach his or her own. Usually this is done by utilizing the neighbor's driveway as an easement.

Prescription   An easement is created through prescription when **open and notorious use** of someone else's land has occurred continuously for five or more years. The person using the land against the property owner's will, however, must have a valid reason for crossing the land.

Eight Ways to Terminate an Easement

1. Express agreement between both parties
2. Lawsuit
3. Abandonment
4. Estoppel
5. Merger of the easement between the dominant and servient tenements
6. Destruction of the servient tenement
7. Adverse possession
8. Excessive use

Express Agreement   Agreement that terminates an easement when the dominant tenement surrenders the use of the servient tenement's land through a **quitclaim deed**. A quitclaim deed transfers property with no warranty.

Lawsuits   Or quiet title actions, are court proceedings to establish title to property, to terminate an easement that can be brought upon the dominant tenement by the servient tenement.

Abandonment   If an easement created through prescription is not used for a continuous period of five years, the easement will be terminated.

Estoppel   Occurs when the easement is not being used, if the dominant tenement implies that the easement is no longer necessary, or if the servient tenement utilizes the land based on recommendations made by the dominant tenement.

Merger of the Easement   Occurs when the dominant tenement purchases the property containing the easement from the servient tenement.

Destruction of the Servient Tenement   When a servient tenement destroys an easement, the easement is terminated.

Adverse Possession   Occurs when the servient tenement performs all the actions necessary for adverse possession, ultimately taking the easement rights away from the dominant tenement.

Excessive Use   If the dominant tenement uses the easement more frequently than originally intended, or uses it for a different purpose than originally stated in an agreement, the easement will terminate.

Restrictions   Limitations placed on a certain property or group of properties in a certain area. Zoning laws, development or building restrictions and building requirements are all considered restrictions. Private individuals, developers or the government may place these restrictions on a property. Private restrictions are placed on a property by a previous owner, creating a restriction for a single property or development only. Alternatively, zoning laws are created by the government and designed to benefit the public in a large area consisting of multiple properties. A restriction is placed in the deed at the time of sale or may be created during the planning of a subdivision.

Restrictions are often placed on property to insure the conformity or unity of an area. For example, if a subdivision is known for its view, a restriction of house heights or number of stories in condominium buildings may be placed to ensure that every unit or property has an optimal view. Because a restriction dictates what people can do on or with their own personal property, it is a form of encumbrance, but it is usually done for the benefit of an area.

When there is more than one restriction in place for a given area, the stricter regulations, rules, zoning ordinances or restrictions will be the one(s) that must be followed.

Restrictions are also called **C.C. & R.'s or covenants, conditions and restrictions**. A **covenant** is a promise to either engage in, or abstain from, a certain action. Breach of a covenant will most often result in monetary penalties. An example of a covenant is when a property owner purchases a plot of land with the agreement that it will only be used for raising agricultural crops, rather than development of a subdivision.

Condition   Similar to a covenant, but, if a condition is not met, the penalty is to surrender the property to the original owner or grantor. There are two types of conditions. The first is **condition subsequent**, where a restriction is placed in the deed regarding a property. If this condition is violated, the property will revert back to the original grantor. The second type is **condition precedent**, wherein certain actions or events must take place before a property may pass to its new owner.

Encroachments   Improvement on real property that crosses adjacent property lines. An example is a privacy fence that crosses property lines and extends six inches into the neighbor's back yard. By law, the owner of the property encroached upon has three years to remove the improvement. Examples of encroachments are fences, walls, trees, shrubs, buildings or drives. If the encroachment fulfills the requirements for an easement by prescription or adverse possession, the owner of the improvement may earn the right to use the encroached-upon land. In the above example, if the fence crosses six inches into the neighbor's lot, and its existence was not contested for five years, the owner of the fence has full right to use the encroached-upon land.

Examples of Encroachments

- Fences
- Walls
- Buildings
- Trees / Shrubs
- Drives or Walkways

HOMESTEAD DECLARATION

We learned earlier in this chapter that a lien may be attached to a property to satisfy a debt against the property owner. If the lien is not satisfied, foreclosure may occur against the homeowner or property owner. A **homestead exemption** is a recorded document protecting a certain amount of a homeowner's investment. This protection will guard against foreclosure from certain creditors as well as judgments rendered against the property owner. It is important to note that a property that has been homesteaded is not protected against trust deeds, mechanic's liens, or other liens recorded prior to the homestead declaration.

California allows the head of household to homestead $75,000 of a home's value to be protected against creditors. Persons 65 years of age or older or persons with a mental or physical disability are entitled to $150,000 homestead exemption. All other individuals falling outside of the above mentioned parameters are entitled to a $50,000 homestead exemption.

Each homeowner may file only one homestead. If a homeowner owns more than one property, only one property may be homesteaded at a time. If the homeowner chooses to terminate the homestead on one property in favor of another, an **abandonment of homestead** must be filed on the property where the homestead will be terminated and only then may a new homestead be filed for the newly-favored property. Sale of a property will automatically terminate a homestead on that property.

MARKETABILITY OF TITLE

When a person is ready to sell property, it is important that he or she has a **marketable title** to the property. This does not mean that the title is perfect in the legal sense, but it does mean that a person likely and willing to purchase the property would be confident of no challenge to the title or purchase of property. A **chain of title** will reveal the actual owner of the property. This chain of title can be found in the county recorder's office in the county where the property is located. The chain of title is the original basis to establish marketable title.

Marketable Title

A marketable title is on that a person is likely to accept in confidence that it will be free and clear of any challenge of ownership.

In times before accurate recordkeeping, **abstractors** were used to research a property to determine the current or lawful owner. The abstractor would search all available documents to trace any conveyances or ownership changes, and put together an abstract of title listing such information. A prospective buyer would then consult this **abstract of title** to ensure that none of the previous property owners had a legal claim to the property.

These days, records are organized such that any person can go into the county recorder's office and conduct a title search for him or herself. Records are kept in a **title plant**, an organized system of filing title information, which will provide any interested party with information regarding the **certificate of title**. A certificate of title will detail how the property is currently vested to the owner, as well as outlining any encumbrances attached to the title. Title insurance is also used now to guarantee the title to real property. This is important, in that it protects any interested parties against loss in the case of an unmarketable title.

T I T L E   I N S U R A N C E

Title insurance is used to guarantee a marketable title against risk. Properties maintain value as long as they are capable of being sold. When the property cannot be sold due to a cloud on the title, the value of the property decreases.

Due to the high demand for property and the value associated with it, land or property may be bought and sold several times during the documented periods. Marriage rights associated with community property, joint tenancy, and property legally willed to an heir can all create complications for freely selling or buying property.

How are we to be sure the property being sold is being sold by its rightful owner? Records are kept regarding change of ownership for each piece of property in a given county. Any interested person can search the **chain of title**, which is a record of all owners of a specific property during the time that records have been kept.
This chain of title search reveals the **abstract of title**, a record of each time a property has changed ownership, as well as prior owners. Abstract of title is used, along with an **attorney's opinion of title**, to determine any claims of ownership on a property.

Although it is a very good way of ensuring there is a marketable title, the process can be very time-consuming.

The chain of title, abstract of title and an attorney's opinion of title are good resources for determining who is the lawful owner of a property. In some cases, however, they may be faulty methods, as in cases of fraud or forgery. In cases such as this, a marketable title may be contested. The last thing a new property owner wants to worry about is whether or not the title to his or her property will be contested. Title insurance companies can help guard against recorded and unrecorded risks that may affect the marketable title to property.

There are two different types of title insurance: the standard policy and the extended policy.

> **Two Types of Title Insurance**
> - Standard Policy
> - Extended Policy

A **standard policy** of title insurance protects against matters of record already on file with the county recorder's office. It also protects against matters that would not be on record, such as forgery, fraud, impersonation, or the failure of a competent party to create or enter into a contract. In addition, a standard policy will protect against federal tax liens and any expenses incurred in legally defending the title to a property. The standard policy will NOT protect against the following

- Title defects either known to the policyholder at the time of insurance or shown in a survey
- Rights or claims of people in physical possession of the property, even those rights or claims that would not show up in public record
- Easements and liens not shown in public record
- Changes in land use dictated by zoning laws
- Water rights
- Mining claims
- Reservations

The **California Land Title Association (CLTA)** is an association of California title companies that provides all members with a standard form for insurance. Note that this form is only used by those who choose to take out a standard policy. Those individuals who choose extended coverage will fill out a different form.

For an additional cost, most risks not covered in a standard policy can be covered in an **extended policy**. The **American Land Title Association (ALTA)** offers a policy known as the **ALTA Owner's Policy**, which covers the same items as in the standard policy. In addition, the policy protects the insured against the claims of people who may be in physical possession of the property, but have no recorded interest; marketability of title, water rights, mining claims, recorded easements and liens, rights or claims discovered from a proper survey, and reservations in patents. Lenders, as well as property owners, usually take out this type of policy to protect their investment.

S U M M A R Y

The "bundle of rights" is the set of rights or privileges associated with ownership of property. The number of rights associated with ownership, through the bundle of rights, is determined by the type of estate. Freehold estates are the highest form of property ownership and come with the largest bundle of rights.

Freehold estates are considered real property. Leasehold estates contain fewer rights for the owner, as a leasehold estate is considered personal property. Individuals holding a leasehold estate are tenants or renters. Real property consists of land and anything fixed to the land such as buildings, easements or trees. Real property is extended to airspace, mineral rights and water rights. Personal property is moveable. Examples of personal property include: harvested crops, cars, trees cut for lumber and stocks.

Another name for personal property is "chattel." A fixture is real property that began as personal property. An example of this would be kitchen cabinets. The cabinets started out as lumber constructed into cabinets and then affixed to the walls of the kitchen, thus becoming part of the house and thereby becoming real property. Trade fixtures are considered fixtures, but retain their status as personal property because they are moved out when a tenant or business owner vacates. The trade fixture is legally moveable as long as no real property is damaged in the trade fixture's removal.

Legal descriptions are used to describe a specific piece of property. There are three methods to describe land: lot, block and tract; metes and bounds; and U.S. government section and township survey system. Before real property can be sold, there must be a legal description of the land.

T E R M S / C O N C E P T S

ALTA (American Land Title Association) Owner's Policy   policy of extended title insurance, which can be purchased by either a lender or buyer

Appurtenances   rights, privileges and improvements that belong to real property, and pass with property when it is transferred, but are not necessarily a part of the actual property

Base Line   survey line running east and west, used as a reference when mapping land

Bill of Sale   written agreement used to transfer ownership of personal property

Bundle of Rights   ownership concept describing all the legal rights that attach to the ownership of real property

California Land Title Association   trade organization consisting of the state's title companies

Chattel   personal property

Chattel Real   item of personal property which is connected to real estate (e.g., a lease or an easement)

Condition Precedent   condition that requires something to occur before a transaction becomes absolute and enforceable (e.g., a sale that is contingent on the seller clearing up a mechanic's lien)

Condition Subsequent   condition which, if it occurs at some point in the future, can cause ownership of a property to revert back to the grantor (e.g., a requirement contained in a grant deed that restricts a buyer from consuming alcohol on the property)

Consideration   exchange, usually rent, given to a lessor by a lessee in a leasehold estate

Constructive Notice   recording of a deed or possession of property

Conveyance   written transfer of title to land from one person to another

Declaration of Homestead   recorded document that protects a homeowner from foreclosure by certain judgment creditors

Doctrine of Correlative Rights   doctrine which states that a property owner may use only a reasonable amount of the total underground water supply for his or her benefit

Dominant Tenement   property that benefits from an easement

Easement   or right-of-way, is the right to use another's land for a specified purpose

Easement in Gross   easement that is not appurtenant to any one parcel (e.g., public utilities)

Emblements   annual crops produced for sale. Emblements are considered personal property and belong to the grower, whether he or she is the tenant or landlord.

Encroachment placement of permanent improvements on adjacent property owned by another

Estate legal interest in land; defines the nature, degree, extent, and duration of a person's ownership in land or property

Estate in Fee **estate of inheritance** or **fee simple estate,** is a freehold estate that can be passed by descent or by will after the owner's death.

Estate of Inheritance or estate in fee, is a freehold estate that can be passed by descent or by will after the owner's death.

Extended Policy extended title insurance policy

Fee Simple Absolute **the** most complete ownership recognized by law; an estate in fee with no restrictions on the land's use

Fee Simple Estate or **estate of inheritance** is freehold estate that can be passed by descent or by will after the owner's death.

Fee Simple Defeasible / Qualified estate in which the holder has a fee simple title, subject to return to the grantor if a specified condition occurs

Fixture personal property that has become part of, or affixed to, real property

Freehold Estate estate in real property that continues for an indefinite period of time

Guarantee of Title assurance that a title to property is clear

Instrument written legal document setting forth the rights and liabilities of the parties involved

Less-Than-Freehold Estate leasehold estate, or rental agreement, that exists for a definite period of time or successive periods of time until termination of the contract or lease

Lien claim on the property of another for payment of a debt

Life Estate estate that is measured by the life of the grantee or the life of another specified person

Lis Pendens recorded notice that indicates pending litigation affecting title on a property. Lis pendens will prevent a conveyance or any other transfer of ownership until the lawsuit is settled and the *lis pendens* is removed.

Littoral bordering a lake, ocean, or sea

Marketable Title   clear, salable title that is reasonably free from risk of litigation over possible defects

Measuring Life   person's lifespan on which a life estate duration is based. The measuring life may be based on the lifespan of the grantee of the life estate or the lifespan of a neutral third party.

Meridian   survey line running north and south, used as a reference when mapping land

Metes and Bounds   survey method by which land is described by the distance and angle between landmarks or boundaries

Monument   fixed landmark used in metes and bounds land description

Personal Property   anything moveable that is not real property

Plat Map   map of a town or subdivision showing the division of property into tracts, blocks, and lots

Property   rights or interests an individual has in something owned

Range   land description used in the U.S. government survey system consisting of a strip of land located every six miles east and west of each principal meridian.

Real Property   land, fixtures on the land, appurtenances to the land, or anything immovable by law

Riparian Rights   rights of a landowner to reasonable use of the water flowing from his or her property when said property or land is located next to a natural watercourse

Section   640 acres of land, considered 1/36th of a township. Each section measures one mile by one mile.

Servient Tenement   property that is burdened by an easement

Standard Policy   policy of title insurance covering only matters of record

Title   evidence of land ownership

Title Insurance   insurance policy that protects the insured against loss or damage due to defects in the property's title

Township   surveyed area of land totaling 36 individual sections of land comprised of 36 square miles, or six miles by six miles

Trade Fixture   fixture used for business that has been affixed onto rented or leased property. Trade fixtures are considered personal property as they may be removed from the real property as long as there is no damage to the real property at the end of a lease.

C H A P T E R   Q U I Z

1. Which of the following is considered a money-restricted encumbrance?
   a. Encroachment
   b. Judgment
   c. Easement
   d. None of the above

2. The American Land Title Association (ALTA) provides an extended title insurance policy which guards against which of the following?
   a. Water rights
   b. Mining claims
   c. Unrecorded liens
   d. All of the above

3. What does "estate" refer to?
   a. Land
   b. Property
   c. Ownership
   d. Buildings

4. What are the two types of freehold estates?
   a. Fee Simple and Life Estate
   b. Absolute and Qualified
   c. Defeasible and Life Estate
   d. Fee Simple and Leasehold Estate

5. Which of the following conditions are characteristics of a Fee Simple Absolute Estate?
   a. Provides the owner with the largest bundle of rights
   b. Holds no limitations or conditions
   c. Can be conveyed by a will
   d. All of the above

6. In reference to a life estate, a measuring life is
   a. the life duration of the grantor of the life estate.
   b. the life duration of the person on whose life the estate is based.
   c. a life estate in reversion.
   d. none of the above.

7. All of the following characteristics are correct regarding a leasehold estate EXCEPT
   a. the owner of a leasehold estate possesses a larger bundle of rights than the owner of a freehold estate.
   b. the owner of the leasehold has exclusive right of possession.
   c. the landlord holds title to the property.
   d. people holding a leasehold estate are referred to as tenants or renters.

8. Which of the following are considered the lowest form of estate?
   a. Fee Simple Defeasible
   b. Estate at Will
   c. Estate at Sufferance
   d. Estate in Reversion

9. All of the following are characteristics of a lease EXCEPT
   a. every lease is considered a contract whether it is written or oral.
   b. tenants are required to sign all written contracts.
   c. all contracts are backed by some form of consideration.
   d. written contracts may not be altered orally.

10. Property is considered
    a. anything that can be owned.
    b. real.
    c. personal.
    d. All of the above

11. An example of real property is
    a. grain that has been harvested.
    b. car.
    c. the airspace immediately above the property.
    d. money.

12. Which of the following is NOT considered a water right for a property owner?
    a. Riparian
    b. Right of appropriation
    c. Littoral
    d. Emblement

13. Another term for personal property is
    a. chattel.
    b. appurtenance.
    c. fixture.
    d. MARIA.

14. Property can change from real to personal and back to real property.
    a. True
    b. False

15. Which one of the following examples is not considered a fixture?
    a. Ceiling fan
    b. Space heater
    c. Custom-made window coverings
    d. Dishwasher

16. Which one of the following is NOT considered a test of a fixture?
    a. Method of attachment
    b. Emblement
    c. Relationship between parties
    d. Adaptability

17. Trade fixtures are considered
    a. personal property.
    b. real property.
    c. Both A and B
    d. Neither A nor B

18. All of the following are descriptions of land EXCEPT
    a. lot, block and tract system.
    b. metes and bounds.
    c. U.S. government section and township survey.
    d. encroachment.

19. Metes and bounds land descriptions are most commonly used when
    a. land is irregularly shaped and would be difficult to describe with any other system.
    b. developers divide up land into lots and record a plat map.
    c. using meridians and baselines.
    d. using a grid system.

20. A plot of land containing 36 square miles most likely describes
    a. 1 township.
    b. 6 townships.
    c. 36 sections.
    d. Both A and C

CHAPTER

INSTRUMENTS
OF
FINANCE

What you will learn in this Chapter

- The Lending Process

- Promissory Note

- Transfer of Property by the Buyer

- Special Clauses in Financing Instruments

- Junior Trust Deeds

- Other Types of Loans Secured by Trust Deeds of Mortgages

- Unsecured Loads

- Alternative Financing

- Short Pay

Test Your Knowledge

1. Promissory notes are considered negotiable instruments. Which of the following is also considered to be a negotiable instrument?
   a. Personal Check
   b. Credit Card
   c. Collateral
   d. None of the above

2. Which one of the following characteristics is not found in a partially amortized note?
   a. Interest-only payments
   b. Partial payment of principal, full payment of interest
   c. Balloon payment
   d. Periodic fixed payments

3. Which of the following is NOT a special clause found in financial instruments?
   a. Acceleration
   b. Subordination
   c. "Or more"
   d. Redemption

4. In a hybrid note
   a. interest is fixed for the life of the loan.
   b. interest is variable for the life of the loan.
   c. interest is fixed for a set number of years, and then becomes variable,
   d. tied to an index.

5. An unsecured loan has which of the following characteristics?
   a. Does not utilize a trust deed
   b. Does not require any collateral
   c. Does not utilize an index to determine the variable interest rate
   d. Does not charge a prepayment penalty fee

6. Sellers who finance a buyer with a wrap-around loan often
   a. carry back a note on the property.
   b. charge the buyer a higher interest rate then he or she currently pays on the original trust deed.
   c. collect the money directly from the buyer for the AITD.
   d. require a high down payment from the buyer.

7. Which of the following is a cost associated with obtaining a home equity line?
   a. Appraisal fee
   b. Pest inspection fee
   c. Transaction fee
   d. Both A and C

INTRODUCTION

Home ownership is one of the largest (if not the largest) investments a person can make. Since very few people can afford to purchase a home with cash, the vast majority of homeowners are currently paying off a mortgage (or trust deed, as it is called in California). Thus it is important for you, the real estate agent, to understand how financing works, and provide advice to your clients accordingly. By knowing what programs are available to your client, and providing the client with advice and guidance to speak with a mortgage broker, you can help homeownership become a more realistic goal than he or she might have thought possible. By allowing a home buyer to obtain a loan for the difference between the sales price and the down payment, real estate lenders have provided the solution to the problem of how property can be bought and sold without the requirement of an all-cash sale.

In this chapter, we will learn about instruments of finance. We will look at the different programs and options people have when financing a home and how those financing options function. Real estate finance has evolved far beyond obtaining a loan at a local bank; yet, it is still often just as simple as that. Pay close attention to terms or concepts to which you are introduced, as most ideas in real estate finance are related to each other in some fashion.

What started out as a simple loan by a local bank, with an agreement that the borrower pay it all back in a timely manner, is now a complex subject. Buyers and sellers need to rely on experts to explain all the choices relating to financing the purchase or sale of property.

THE LENDING PROCESS

When a person obtains a loan, he or she uses the property that he or she wishes to purchase as collateral to secure the loan. Lenders require collateral on loans of this size to ensure the loan will be repaid in full. If the borrower defaults on the loan, the house can be sold to pay the note's remaining balance.

The loan itself is called a **note**. A person who wishes to obtain a loan signs a document called a **promissory note**. The promissory note is a statement of intention to pay back the loan in the installments agreed upon with the lender. The promissory note itself is the evidence of debt, and is held by the lender until the entire amount of the note is paid.

Most of us are familiar with the term **mortgage**. We take out a mortgage when we purchase a home. California uses **trust deeds**, which are essentially the same as a mortgage. A trust deed is the security for the note. Usually there is a neutral third party, called a **trustee**, who holds bare legal title (though he or she has no rights or interest in the property), until the note is paid in full. Once the note is paid in full, the trustee reconveys the deed from the lender to the trustor. The borrower takes possession of the home during the time the note is being paid, but must make all payments on time. Otherwise, the home may be sold in order to satisfy the debt against it.

A person is said to be **leveraging** when he or she is using an investor's money to purchase property for him or herself. By leveraging money, a homeowner can risk very little of his or her personal money in the purchase of a home. However, the buyer may take possession of the property immediately. This is a clear advantage for a person who has the means to make a monthly payment on property, but does not have a large sum to pay for the property at once. An investor will also benefit from interest earned on the loan that is given to the property owner.

Remember

A homeowner secures a note from a lending institution by promising to use the property being purchased as collateral against the note. If the homeowner fails to pay back the note, the property may be sold to satisfy any debt against the property.

There are several reasons leverage is appealing to both the home buyer and the investor. The principal advantage to the home buyer is that he or she does not have to amass the entire purchase price to become a home owner. The investor can use leverage to control several investments, rather than just one, each purchased with a small amount of personal funds, and a large amount of a lender's money. The investor can then earn a return on each property, therefore increasing the amount of yield on investment dollars.

Remember

The Promissory note is the evidence of the debt; the trust deed, or mortgage, is the security for the debt.

P R O M I S S O R Y   N O T E

As mentioned earlier, a promissory note is the written document that a borrower signs, stating to the lending institution that he or she will repay the entire amount of the loan. The promissory note is held by the lender. A lender will use the property itself as security or collateral for the note. Promissory notes are often referred to simply as 'notes'. So, when you see that term used by itself, you will know it means.
The borrower is the **maker** of the note, as he or she is 'making' a personal promise to repay the loan in full. The lender is referred to as the **holder** of the note.

California Real Estate Finance

Promissory notes are secured by trust deeds, which are held by a trustee or third party. The trustee holds bare legal title, which means that the trustee has the authority to sell the property in the event that the lender forecloses on the borrower. Outside of this authority, the trustee has no rights or interest in the property. More on trust deeds will be covered later in this chapter.

There are four different types of notes: **straight, partially amortized, fully amortized** and **adjustable rate**. The difference between these types of notes is the manner in which they are repaid.

Straight Note
The straight note requires only the payment of interest each month, followed by a large payment against the principal at the end of the note.

Fully Amortized Note
In fully amortized notes, both the principal and interest are being paid throughout the life of the loan. Payments will remain the same from the beginning to end, with the loan being paid in full at the end of the note term.

Partially Amortized Note
A partially amortized note is a combination of both straight note and fully amortized note. Partially amortized notes allow the borrower to pay on both the interest and principal, but with only a portion of the principal covered by the monthly payments. In addition, a balloon payment is required at a specific time, or at the end of a certain term, to cover the remaining balance of the principal. A **balloon payment** is a lump sum of money, larger than a regular monthly payment.

Adjustable Rate Note
An adjustable rate note fluctuates in accordance with market conditions. When interest rates drop, interest on the note will reflect this drop, in the form of a lower monthly payment. When interest rates rise, the note will also reflect this change by charging the lender a higher rate, thus increasing the monthly payment.

Promissory notes are considered negotiable instruments, as they are a promise to pay money to another party. You might compare a promissory note to a personal check. When you write a personal check, you are promising the party receiving the check that there is money in your account. You are further promising that they may deduct the amount that you are authorizing, in payment for a good or service. Additionally, if endorsed, a promissory note may be transferred to another party, much the same as if you endorse a personal check made payable to one party, and pass it on to a third party. A promissory note, accurately prepared, can even be used as cash.

All negotiable instruments must be in written form, promising to pay a specific sum of money back to the holder of the note. The note is considered a legal contract that can only be made between two legally competent parties. The note must be signed by the borrower and delivered to the lender. Promissory notes are voluntary, with both parties entering into the agreement for mutual benefit. The person making the note will be able to secure and take possession of property, while the holder of the note will make a profit on the return of the note. Promissory notes are paid either at specific intervals, or on demand. If a lender **calls** the note, the borrower must be able to repay the entire sum of the loan. Otherwise, the property may be sold to satisfy the debt.

Four Types of Promissory Notes

1. Straight note – equal monthly payments sufficient to cover the interest only, with the principal due at the end of the note

2. Fully amortized note – equal monthly payments of both interest and principal

3. Partially amortized note – equal monthly payments for a certain term, followed by a balloon payment (required to cover the difference between the percentage of principal paid and the percentage of principal owed for that term)

4. Adjustable rate – monthly payments vary because interest rates may change, depending on market conditions

The holder of the note may also sell the promissory note to another individual, or even give it away. The person buying the note, or receiving it, will now be the individual who is owed monthly payments on the property. As long as the promissory note is prepared correctly, it is very easy for it to change hands quickly. The person now holding the note is called the **assignee** or **transferee**, depending on the conditions the original holder has in place upon giving or selling the note to another individual. The new holder of the note becomes the **holder in due course**. A holder in due course is someone who takes on a note, but receives more benefits than the original holder of the note (provided the note was prepared properly and is considered a transferable instrument). When the note is transferred to another person as holder in due course, this fact must be clearly written on the note. A holder in due course takes the promissory note in good faith and without notice that anyone else may have claim on the note.

A holder in due course takes a note

- In good faith
- For Value
- Without notice of defense.

NOTE

November 15, 2002

Property Address

1. BORROWER'S PROMISE TO PAY

In return for a loan that I have received, I promise to pay **Three Hundred Forty Nine Thousand Three Hundred and 00/100 Dollars (U.S. $349,300.00)** (this amount will be called "Principal"), plus Interest, to the order of the Note Holder. The Principal may include points, origination fees and other amounts permitted by applicable law. The Note Holder is **Wonderful Bank of Anywhere, National Association**, a national banking association organized and existing under the laws of the United States of America. I understand that the Note Holder may transfer this Note. The Note Holder or anyone who takes this Note and who is entitled to receive payments under this Note will be called the "Note Holder."

2. INTEREST

I will pay Interest at an annual rate of **6.23%** ("Interest"). Interest will be charged on the unpaid Principal and will continue until the full amount of Principal has been paid. Interest shall continue to accrue at this rate after the maturity or default of this loan. Each payment I make on this Note will be applied first to scheduled Interest, next to unpaid Principal, and then other charges, if any, until the entire indebtedness, evidenced by this Note, is fully paid.

3. PAYMENTS

I will pay Principal plus Interest by making payments each month ("monthly payments"). My monthly payment will be the sum of U.S. **$2,146.16**.

[X] If checked, I will make **360** monthly payments on the **1st** day of each month beginning on **January 01, 2003**. If on, **December 01, 2032**, any sum still remains unpaid, I will pay what I owe in full on that date.

[ ] If checked, this loan contains a Balloon Payment feature. I will make _____ monthly payments on the _____ day of each month beginning on _____. These payments are based upon a _____ month amortization. I understand that these payments will not completely amortize the outstanding Principal, Interest and other charges, and that there will be an outstanding balance remaining on my loan at maturity. I agree to pay the Note Holder in full the remaining outstanding Principal balance plus Interest and any other charges which are due under the terms of this Note in a single balloon payment which shall be due and payable on _____.

I will make my monthly payments payable to GoodEq Servicing Corporation and mailed to P. O. Box 55555, Anywhere, CA 00000-0000, or at a different address if required by the Note Holder.

I agree that if, during the term of this Note, if in the Note Holder's sole discretion, the Note Holder permits me to modify or defer my obligation to the Note Holder, or request other services related to servicing or administering my loan for which the Note Holder has a scheduled charge, I will pay the Note Holder the then-current fee for such services or request if the Note Holder agrees to perform such service or request.

4. BORROWER'S FAILURE TO PAY AS REQUIRED

(A) **Late Charge for Overdue Payments:** If the Note Holder has not received the full amount of any of my monthly payments by the end of fifteen (15) calendar days after the date it is due, I will promptly pay a late charge to the Note Holder. The amount of the charge will be four (4%) of the full monthly payment. I will pay this late charge only once on any late monthly payment.

(B) **Default:** I will be in default under this Note if any of the following things happen:
   (1) if I fail to make any payment or comply with any of the terms of this Note or any other note with the Note Holder now or in the future; or
   (2) if I make any false, incorrect or misleading representation or warranty at any time during the application process; or
   (3) if I die or become involved in any bankruptcy or insolvency proceeding; or
   (4) if I fail to abide by the term(s) of any Security Instrument which secures payment of this Note; or
   (5) if I fail to furnish financial statements or other financial information reasonably requested by the Note Holder.

I understand that the loan is subject to repayment in full upon demand of the Note Holder in the event the real estate securing this debt is sold, conveyed or otherwise transferred.

(C) **Notice of Default:** If I am in default, then the entire Principal balance, accrued Interest fees, and collection costs, permitted to be collected under applicable law will be immediately due and payable. At its option or if required by law, the Note Holder may send me a written notice informing me of said default and acceleration. If I make any payment after the Note Holder has demanded payment of the entire balance due, my payment will be applied to the Unpaid Balance due under the Note. The Unpaid Balance consists of the Principal Amount remaining due, plus accrued finance charges, unpaid late charges, collection costs, and all other amounts due to the Note Holder under this Note. The Note Holder shall also have other rights and remedies provided by law. If the net proceeds of collateral sold do not pay my indebtedness in full, I will pay the Note Holder the difference, plus Interest at the Note Interest Rate until the Unpaid Balance is paid in full. Any default of this Note will also constitute an event of default of any separate Mortgage, Deed of Trust or Security Deed securing this Note ("Security Instrument"). Upon default, Note Holder may proceed to enforce the terms of the Note or enforce any rights that it may have under the Security Instrument.

(D) **No Waiver by Note Holder:** Even if, at a time when I am in default, the Note Holder does not require me to pay immediately in full as described above, the Note Holder will still have the right to do so if I am in default at a later time.

(E) **Payment of Note Holder's Costs and Expenses:** If the Note Holder has required me to pay immediately in full as described above, the Note Holder will have the right to be paid back for all of its costs and expenses to the extent not prohibited by applicable law. Those expenses include, for example, reasonable attorneys' fees for an attorney who is not the Note Holders salaried employee, foreclosure fees and court costs.

(F) **Check Collection Charges:** If I present the Note Holder with a check, negotiable order of withdrawal, share draft or other instrument in payment that is returned or dishonored for any reason, I will pay a check collection charge to the Note Holder for each time such instrument is returned. The amount of the charge will not be greater than U.S $25.00.

5. THIS NOTE SECURED BY A SECURITY INSTRUMENT

In addition to the protections given to the Note Holder under this Note, the Security Instrument, on real property (the "Property") described in the Security Instrument and dated the same date as this Note, protects the Note Holder from possible losses which might result if I do not keep the promises which I make in this Note. The Security Instrument describes how and under what conditions I may also be required to make immediate payment in full of all amounts I owe under this Note. I agree to these conditions. I acknowledge that I may obtain property insurance and/or credit life insurance from any insured.

6. BORROWER'S PAYMENTS BEFORE THEY ARE DUE

Subject to the order of application of payments described in Section 2, I have the right to make payments of Principal at any time before they are due. A prepayment of all of the unpaid Principal is known as a "full prepayment." A prepayment of only part of the unpaid Principal is known as a "partial prepayment."

If I make a partial prepayment, my next due date will not be advanced. I must still make each subsequent payment as it becomes due and in the same amount.

[ ] If checked, I may make a full or partial prepayment at any time without penalty.

[X] If checked, I may make a full or partial prepayment at any time, however, if within the first 24 months from the date of this loan I make any full prepayment of the Principal amount of this loan, I will pay a prepayment charge equal to 2% of the outstanding Principal balance.

7. BORROWER'S WAIVERS

I waive my rights to require the Note Holder to do certain things. Those things are (a) to demand payment of amounts due (known as "presentment"); (b) to give notice that amounts due have not been paid (known as "notice of dishonor"); and (c) to obtain an official certification of nonpayment (known as "protest"). Anyone else who agrees to keep the promises made in this Note, or who agrees to make payments to the Note Holder if I fail to keep my promises under this Note, or who signs this Note to transfer it to someone else, also waives these rights. These persons are known as "guarantors," "sureties" and "endorsers."

8. GIVING OF NOTICES

Unless applicable law requires a different method, any notice that must be given to me under this Note will be given by delivering it or by mailing it by first class mail addressed to me at the Property Address described herein. A notice will be delivered or mailed to me at a different address if I give the Note Holder a notice of my different address.

Any notice that must be given to the Note Holder under this Note will be given by mailing it by first class mail to the Note Holder at the address stated in Section 3. A notice will be mailed to the Note Holder at a different address if I am given a notice of that different address.

9. PAYMENT IN FULL

I AGREE THAT THE NOTE HOLDER MAY ACCEPT PAYMENTS MARKED "PAID IN FULL" WITHOUT ANY LOSS OF THE NOTE HOLDERS RIGHTS UNDER THIS NOTE UNLESS I SEND THEM FOR SPECIAL HANDLING TO GOODEQ SERVICING CORPORATION, 4837 BETTY AVENUE, SUITE 000, SOUTH YOURTOWN, CA 00000, ATTN: PAYOFF PROCESSING – M05334.

10. RESPONSIBILITY OF PERSONS UNDER THIS NOTE

If more than one person signs this Note, each of us is fully and personally obligated to pay the full amount owed and to keep all of the promises made in this Note. Any guarantor, surety, or endorser of this Note (as described in Section 7 above) is also obligated to do these things. The Note Holder may enforce its rights under this Note against each of us individually or against all of us together. This means that any one of us may be required to pay all of the amounts owed under this Note. Any person who takes over my rights or obligations under this Note will have all of my rights and must keep all of my promises made in this Note. Any person who takes over the rights or obligations of a guarantor, surety, or endorser of this Note (as described in Section 7 above) is also obligated to keep all of the promises made in this Note. This Note is intended by Note Holder and me as a complete and exclusive statement of its terms, there being no conditions to the enforceability of this Note. This Note may not be supplemented or modified except in writing signed by me and the Note Holder. This Note benefits Note Holder, its successors and assigns, and binds me and my heirs, personal representatives and assigns.

11. APPLICABLE LAW

This Note shall be governed by the laws of the State of Anywhere and applicable federal law. If a law which applies to this loan and sets maximum loan charges is finally interpreted so that the interest and other charges collected or to be collected in connection with this loan exceed the permitted limits, then: (A) any such interest or other charge shall be reduced by the amount necessary to reduce the interest or other charge to the permitted limit; and (B) any sums already collected from me which exceeded permitted limits will be refunded to me. The

Note Holder may choose to make this refund by reducing the Principal I owe under this Note or by making a direct payment to me. If a refund reduces Principal, the reduction will be treated as a partial payment.

12. EXTENSIONS AND MODIFICATIONS

All endorsers, sureties and guarantors and I further consent to any and all extensions of time, renewals, waivers or modifications which may be granted or consented to by the Note Holder as to the time of payment or any other provision of this Note. If an extension, renewal or modification is made to this Note, I agree to pay a charge, as additional Interest, of the greater of $50.00 or one-quarter (1/4) of one percent (1%) of the loan balance then outstanding. All makers, sureties, guarantors, and endorsers hereby waive presentment, notice of dishonor, and protest hereof. This Note is the joint and several obligation of each maker and shall be binding upon them and their heirs, successors and assigns.

NOTICE TO BORROWER:

1. CAUTION – IT IS IMPORTANT THAT YOU READ ALL PAGES OF THIS NOTE BEFORE YOU SIGN IT.
2. DO NOT SIGN THIS NOTE IF IT CONTAINS ANY BLANK SPACES.
3. You are entitled to a copy of this Note.
4. You acknowledge receipt of a completed copy of this Note.
5. This Note provides for the payment of a penalty if you wish to repay the loan prior to the date provided for repayment in this Note.

By signing and sealing this Note, I agree under seal to the terms set forth above.

_____ [SEAL]

_____ [SEAL]

(Sign Original Only)

The reason that a holder in due course is in a more favorable position than the original holder of the note is because the new holder is protected from defenses the maker (borrower) may bring against the note. If a court case is brought, the maker cannot use any of the following defenses against the holder in due course

1. The maker cannot claim that he or she never received the promised funds or property in exchange for the note
2. The maker cannot claim that the note has already been paid in full unless marked accordingly on the note (in this case, the note would never have been sold or transferred to the assignee)
3. Cancellation
4. Setoff (the difference of what is owed on the note and what is owed to the holder of the note)
5. Fraud

Any of the above defenses may be used by the maker of the note against the original holder of the note. However, none of these may be used against the new assignee if it is written on the note and he or she takes the note as holder in due course. This does not mean that the maker of the promissory note is now without defense, however. There are certain defenses that may be made by the maker against the original holder or the holder in due course. These defenses are

- Incapable maker (the maker is a minor or not mentally competent to enter into a contract)

- Forgery (if the maker did not actually sign the note)

- Changes to the note of which the maker was not aware

- The note is connected to an illegal act

In any of these situations, the maker has a valid defense against any holder of the note.

Adjustable Rate Mortgage (ARM) An adjustable note, or ARM (adjustable rate mortgage), is a note whose interest rate is tied to a movable economic index. The interest rate of the note varies upward or downward over the term of the loan, depending on the money market conditions and an agreed-upon index.

This type of loan was first offered as a result of the major recession and banking crisis in the early 1980s. Currently, these ARMs come in many flavors. The basic adjustable loan, however, is one whose interest rate is tied to a certain government economic index.

A lender may offer several choices of interest rate, term, payments, or adjustment periods to a borrower with an ARM. The initial interest rate is determined starting with the current rate of the chosen index. Then, a margin, which might be anywhere from one to three percentage points, is added to the initial interest rate to determine the actual beginning rate the borrower will pay. The margin is maintained for the life of the loan and does not change. The interest rate may change, however, as the chosen index changes, depending on the economic conditions that drive it.

The borrower's payment will stay the same for a specified time period, which might be six months or a year, depending on the agreement with the lender. At the agreed upon time, the lender re-evaluates the loan to determine if the index has changed, either up or down, and calculates a new payment based on the changed interest rate plus the same margin. That will then be the borrower's payment until the next 6 months or year passes and the loan will be reviewed again.

There is usually a limit on how much the interest rate can change on an annual basis, as well as a lifetime cap, or limit, on changes in interest rate. The annual maximum increase is usually 1 to 2%, while the lifetime cap is usually limited to no more than five or six points above the starting rate.

ARM Characteristics
Not all ARMs are the same, but they are similar enough to share the following characteristics.

Introductory Rate
Many adjustable rate loans (ARMs) have a low introductory rate or start rate, sometimes as much as 5.0% below the current market rate of a fixed loan. This start rate is usually good for a period of one month to as long as 10 years. As a rule, the lower the start rate, the shorter the time period before the loan makes its first adjustment.

Index
The index of an ARM is the financial instrument that the loan is tied to, or adjusted to. The most common indices, or indexes, are the 1-Year Treasury Security, LIBOR (London Interbank Offered Rate), Prime Rate, 6-Month Certificate of Deposit (CD) and the 11th District Cost of Funds (COFI). Each of these indices moves up or down based on conditions in the financial markets.

Margin
The margin is one of the most important aspects of ARMs because, it is added to the index to determine the interest rate that a borrower pays. The margin plus the index is known as the **fully indexed rate**. As an example, if the current index value is 5.50% and the loan has a margin of 2.5%, the fully indexed rate is 8.00%. Margins on loans range from 1.75% to 3.5%, depending on the index and the amount financed in relation to the property value.

Interim Caps
All adjustable rate loans carry interim caps. Many ARMs have interest rate caps of 6 months or 1 year. There are also loans that have interest rate caps of 3 years. Interest rate caps are beneficial in rising interest rate markets, but can also keep the interest rate higher than the fully indexed rate if rates are falling rapidly.

Payment Caps
Some loans have payment caps instead of interest rate caps. These loans reduce payment shock in a rising interest rate market, but can also lead to deferred interest or negative amortization. These loans generally cap the annual payment increases to 7.5% of the previous payment.

Lifetime Caps
Almost all ARMs have a maximum interest rate or life-time interest rate cap. The lifetime cap varies from company to company and loan to loan. Loans with low lifetime caps usually have higher margins, and the reverse is also true. Those loans that carry low margins often have higher lifetime caps.

ARM Index
Several index options are available to fit individual needs and risk tolerance with the various market instruments. ARMs with different indexes are available for both

purchases and refinances. Choosing an ARM with an index that reacts quickly lets a borrower take full advantage of falling interest rates. An index that lags behind the market lets a borrower take advantage of lower rates after market rates have started to adjust upward.

Standard ARM Indexes and Programs

6-Month Certificate of Deposit (CD) ARM
- Has a maximum interest rate adjustment of 1% every 6 months.

- The 6-month Certificate of Deposit (CD) index is generally considered to react quickly to changes in the market.

1-Year Treasury Spot ARM
- Has a maximum interest rate adjustment of 2% every 12 months.

- The 1-Year Treasury Spot index generally reacts more slowly than the CD index; but more quickly than the Treasury Average index.

6-Month Treasury Average ARM
- Has a maximum interest rate adjustment of 1% every 6 months.

- The Treasury Average index generally reacts more slowly in fluctuating markets, so adjustments in the ARM interest rate will lag behind some other market indicators.

Standard ARM Indexes and Programs (cont.)

LIBOR (London Interbank Offered Rate)
- LIBOR is the rate on dollar-denominated deposits, also known as Eurodollars, traded between banks in London. The index is quoted for 1 month, 3 months, 6 months, or 1 year.

- LIBOR is the base interest rate paid on deposits between banks in the Eurodollar market. A Eurodollar is a dollar deposited in a bank in a country where the currency is not the dollar. The Eurodollar market has been around for over 40 years and is a major component of the international financial market. London is the center of the Euromarket in terms of volume.

- The LIBOR rate quoted in the Wall Street Journal is an average of rate quotes from five major banks: Bank of America, Barclays, Bank of Tokyo, Deutsche Bank and Swiss Bank.

COFI (Cost of Funds Index)
- The 11th District Cost of Funds is more prevalent in the West and the 1-Year Treasury Security is more prevalent in the East. Buyers prefer the slowly moving 11th District Cost of Funds, and investors prefer the 1-Year Treasury Security.

- The monthly weighted average for the 11th District has been published by the Federal Home Loan Bank of San Francisco since August 1981. Currently more than one-half of the savings institutions loans made in California are tied to the 11th District Cost of Funds Index. (COFI)

Hybrid Note

While many consumers prefer the more familiar types of loans, a new loan called a **hybrid mortgage** may be suitable for some borrowers. The interest rate is fixed for an initial period of 3, 5, 7 or 10 years; after that the interest rate is tied to an economic index and adjusts every year. It's called a hybrid mortgage because it combines the features of a fixed-rate loan with those of the adjustable rate loan.

A hybrid note may be desirable for borrowers who plan on selling their homes or paying off their loans within a few years, because the initial interest rates on these loans are typically lower than a fixed rate loan, but allow the security, as least for the first years of fixed payments, of a fixed rate loan.

The borrower can then decide to either sell the property or refinance the loan when it turns into an adjustable loan, especially if prevailing interest rates at the time are higher, requiring a higher monthly payment. The borrower takes a gamble with a hybrid loan, hoping that interest rates will be low when the interest rate adjusts.

Holder in Due Course
As we have seen, notes are negotiable instruments, easily transferable from one person to another. However, the transferee or buyer of a note must have confidence in getting the money when the note is paid.

A holder in due course is someone who obtains (buys) an existing promissory note (negotiable instrument) for value, in good faith, and without notice that it is overdue or has been dishonored or claimed by another person.

The holder in due course takes a negotiable instrument which is

- Complete and regular in appearance and form

- Without notice that it is overdue, or has been dishonored or has any claim on it by any person

- Taken in good faith for valuable consideration

A holder in due course has a favored position with respect to the instrument because the maker (borrower) cannot raise certain "personal defenses" in refusing to pay. Personal defenses include lack of consideration, setoff and fraud.

The favored position that the holder in due course enjoys is a greater claim to the note's payment than the original holder. If a court action is necessary to bring payment on the note, the maker cannot use any of the following defenses to refuse payment to a holder in due course, even though they could be used against the original lender.

Defenses Not Allowed by the Maker of a Note

- The maker cannot claim non-receipt of what the payee promised in exchange for the note

- The maker cannot claim the debt was already paid. Even if it was, if there is no proof (as in marking the note "paid"), and the original payee transfers the note to a holder in due course, the original maker might still be required to pay

- The maker cannot use fraud (in the original making of the note) as a defense

- The maker cannot claim a setoff. For example, if the amount owed is $10,000, but the payee owes $15,000 to the holder, the difference cannot be used as a defense against paying the note

All the above defenses may be used against the original payee, or lender, but are not good against a holder in due course. Indeed, some real defenses are good against any person, a payee or holder in due course.

Defenses Allowed Against Anyone

- Forgery, if the maker didn't really sign the note

- Secret material changes in the note

- Incapacity, if the maker is a minor or an incompetent

- Illegal object, if the note is connected to an illegal act or if the interest rate is usurious

Because of this preferred treatment or "safety net" for a holder in due course, people are more willing to accept such instruments without needing to check the credit of the borrower or even knowing the borrower.

Conflict in Terms of Note and Trust Deed

As you recall, a note is the evidence of a debt. A trust deed or mortgage, even though it is the security for the debt, is still only an incident of the debt. A trust deed or mortgage must have a note to secure, but a note does not need a trust deed or mortgage to stand alone. If there is a conflict in the terms of a note and the trust deed or mortgage used to secure it, the provisions of the note will control. If a note is unenforceable, the presence of a trust deed will not make it valid. However, if a note contains a due on sale acceleration clause, the trust deed must mention it as well for the clause to be enforceable.

The term that describes the interest of a creditor (lender) in the property of a debtor (borrower) is **security interest**. The security interest allows certain assets of a borrower to be set aside so that a creditor can sell them if the borrower defaults on the loan.

Proceeds from the sale of that property can be taken to pay off the debt. The rights and duties of lenders and borrowers are described in a document called a **security instrument**. In some states, trust deeds are the principal instruments used to secure loans on real property and in other states, mortgages are used.

Mortgages accomplish the same thing as trust deeds, and are used as security for real property loans. You will hear the term "mortgage" used loosely in California and some other trust deed states, as in "mortgage company," "mortgage broker" and "mortgage payment"—but the "mortgage" referred to really is a trust deed.

About Notes, Trust Deeds and Mortgages

- A trust deed or mortgage must have a note to secure, but a note does not need a trust deed to stand alone.

- If the conditions of a note and trust deed or mortgage are in conflict, the terms of the note have the authority.

TRANSFER OF PROPERTY BY THE BUYER

Under certain circumstances, a property owner may transfer responsibility for the loan to the buyer when he or she sells the property to another party. A buyer may assume an existing loan, or may buy a property subject to an existing loan.

Loan Assumption

When a property is sold, a buyer may **assume** the existing loan. Usually with the approval of the lender, the buyer takes over primary liability for the loan, with the original borrower secondarily liable if there is a default. What that means is that even though the original borrower is secondarily responsible, according to the loan assumption agreement, no actual repayment of the loan may be required of that person. As long as a deficiency judgment is not allowed under the laws of the particular state, the original borrower's credit will be affected by the foreclosure, but he or she will not be required to pay off the loan. If the new owner defaults, the property is foreclosed by the lender, the current owner loses the property and the former owner gets a ding on his or her credit for the foreclosure.

The original borrower (seller) can avoid any responsibility for the loan, however, by asking the lender for a substitution of liability, known as a **novation**, relieving the seller of all liability for repayment of the loan.

In most cases, a buyer assumes an existing loan with the approval of the underlying lender. However, an **alienation clause**, sometimes known as a **due-on-sale** clause, in the note would prevent a buyer from assuming the loan.

"Subject To"

A buyer may also purchase a property **"subject to"** the existing loan. The original borrower remains responsible for the loan, even though the buyer takes title and makes the payments. In this case, also, the property remains the security for the loan. In the case of default, it is sold and the proceeds go to the lender, with no recourse to the original borrower. Again, the default would show up as a ding against the original borrower's credit. In some states, the lender can get a deficiency judgment against the original borrower, holding him or her personally responsible for the loan, to make up for any loss suffered by the lender in the event that the property sold for less than the loan amount.

When a buyer takes a property "subject to" the existing loan, the underlying lender may not always be informed. The buyer simply starts making the payments and the seller hopes he or she is diligent and does not default.

The occurrence of "subject to" sales is relative to economic and market conditions. In a real estate market where there are more buyers than sellers (a seller's market), a homeowner does not need to sell "subject to" his or her loan. When money is tight and interest rates high and sellers are wondering where all the buyers are, a "subject to" sale might be more attractive to a seller.

SPECIAL CLAUSES IN FINANCING INSTRUMENTS

Lenders take a risk each time they make a loan to a borrower for any purpose. This is especially true when the l o a n is made for the purchase of property, due to the amount that must be borrowed. As we have seen in this chapter, there are ways for a lender to retrieve monies that have been lent; but there are situations where the lender may not be repaid in full, due to the type of loan granted. For lenders to protect themselves, they will usually include a **special clause** or requirement in the loan.

A lender will use the **acceleration clause** if payment of the entire note is required in certain circumstances. Examples of times when a lender might call the note are: in the event of default for taxes, insurance or payment of the note; or, if the buyer decides to sell the property.

Just as the acceleration clause requires that the entire amount of the loan be paid in certain circumstances, the **due-on-sale** or **alienation clause** demands that the entire amount of the note be paid in the event that a property owner transfers ownership to another individual. A lender will typically do this to protect itself from unqualified borrowers assuming the original loan, thus protecting the lender's interest from default.

As we just discussed in the section above, the **assumption clause** allows the buyer to take over an existing loan from the seller with the knowledge and approval of the lender. The new buyer assumes primary responsibility for this loan, while the original borrower holds secondary responsibility for the loan.

Special Clauses
• Acceleration
• Alienation or due-on-sale
• Assumption
• Subordination
• "Subject to"
• Prepayment
• "Or more"

In the event that a borrower defaults on a loan, the lender or creditors are paid from the sale of the property in the order in which the liens were recorded against the property. Trust deeds are considered liens, and will be paid accordingly. There are certain circumstances in which there may be more than one trust deed on a property with subsequent deeds recorded after the first. A **subordination clause** will change the priority of these trust deeds, or any other financial instrument. If a note is recorded, and an additional note is recorded after the original but is considered higher priority than the original, a subordination clause will allow the second note to be paid first in the event of default. The most common example of when this might occur is when land is purchased for future construction, requiring separate financing at the time of building. The lender who is financing the development of the land would naturally prefer to be first in line in the event of default. The lender would use the subordination clause to position the later-recorded trust deed ahead of any previously recorded deeds.

Just as the assumption clause was discussed in the previous section, the **"subject to"** clause was also discussed. The difference between the assumption clause and the "subject to" clause is that in the assumption clause, the lender is made aware of and approves the new buyer's taking over the loan. In the "subject to" clause, the lender is not made aware of any changes in property ownership, leaving the original owner responsible for the loan. The "subject to" clause also allows for deficiency judgments for any hard money loans, meaning that the original owner may be liable for a new buyer's default on a loan.

Common sense dictates that if a loan is paid off early, there will be less total interest paid on the note. This is good for consumers, but bad for banks. In these cases, banks may lose a portion of their return on the investment. To prevent this, banks may attach a **prepayment clause**, which basically penalizes the consumer if the note is paid in full before the loan period expires. If a borrower has the means to pay off a note early, he or she may pay a penalty on the loan, to help the lender recover some of the interest lost as a result of the early payoff. The good news for consumers is that banks are limited as to the amount they can charge for this prepayment clause. On residential property, the prepayment penalty may not exceed six months' interest. A borrower may prepay up to 20% of the loan amount in any 12-month period, with no penalty charge. On any payment over 20%, a prepayment penalty may be applied. Different rules and regulations apply to non-residential properties.

The final clause in financing instruments is the **"or more"** clause, which is the opposite of the prepayment clause. The "or more" clause allows a borrower to pay off a loan early with no penalty, by making one lump payment or higher monthly payments.

J U N I O R   T R U S T   D E E D S

California is known, nationwide, for having one of the most expensive housing markets. Properties appreciate very quickly, leaving lucky homeowners with quite a bit of equity in their homes. For first-time homebuyers, this creates a challenge. The challenge is trying to save enough money for a down payment while securing a loan large enough to cover the purchase price of the home. Often, the amount of the down payment plus the loan will not cover the entire cost of the house. In such cases, the homeowner needs to take a second trust deed. These secondary loans or trust deeds are called **junior trust deeds**. A junior trust deed is recorded after the first deed, and is secured by taking out a second deed on the home. There are three ways to obtain a junior trust deed: seller financing, outside financing, and home equity loans.

Three ways to obtain a junior trust deed

1. Seller financing

2. Outside financing

3. Home equity loans

When a buyer finds that he or she is not able to afford a home by paying only the down payment plus the first trust deed, he or she must seek alternative financing. One way for a seller to obtain the necessary funds through a junior trust deed is by seller financing. Seller financing occurs when the seller of the property makes a secondary loan to the buyer, and records this loan only after the first trust deed is recorded. In these cases, the seller becomes the lender and will receive a monthly payment or other installment payment to satisfy the debt. The act of the seller making a junior trust deed is sometimes referred to as **"carrying back"**.

The loan a seller provides to a buyer is considered a **purchase money loan**, as it is intended for one purpose (that is, to cover any funds needed for the purchase of the property). It not only works in favor of the buyer, but also in favor of the seller. If the seller has sold his or her home for an amount substantially more than the original purchase price (and thus stands to make a large gain), the seller can use some of this additional money as part of the junior trust deed - to avoid a large tax liability. The seller is at an advantage because he or she can accept monthly payments and avoid paying capital gains on a large sum of money received all at once.

The idea of a seller financing a portion of the loan may be a bit confusing. After all, financial professionals are educated and are presumed to know more about interest rates, payment schedules and the technical aspects of a loan. The second trust deed that a seller may provide to a buyer must be negotiated between both the buyer and seller. There are no banks involved; it is simply an agreement between the two parties. The buyer and seller agree upon the interest rate, how the loan will be paid, whether it will be in monthly installments, quarterly, etc., with no payments at all, or with a large lump sum due after a specific amount of time. In addition, the buyer and seller decide if the loan will be a straight note, partially amortized or fully amortized. After all terms of the loan have been discussed and agreed upon, instructions will be carried through the escrow process.

CALIFORNIA
ASSOCIATION
OF REALTORS®

SELLER FINANCING ADDENDUM AND DISCLOSURE
(California Civil Code §§2956-2967)
(C.A.R. Form SFA, Revised 10/02)

This is an addendum to the ☐ Residential Purchase Agreement, ☐ Counter Offer, or ☐ Other _____
_____, ("Agreement"), dated _____,
On property known as _____ ("Property"),
between _____ ("Buyer"),
and _____ ("Seller").
Seller agrees to extend credit to Buyer as follows:

1. **PRINCIPAL; INTEREST; PAYMENT; MATURITY TERMS:** ☐ Principal amount $ _____, interest at _____ %
    per annum, payable at approximately $ _____ per ☐ month, ☐ year, or ☐ other _____,
    remaining principal balance due in _____ years.

2. **LOAN APPLICATION; CREDIT REPORT:** Within 5 (or ☐ _____) **Days** After Acceptance: **(a)** Buyer shall provide Seller a completed
    loan application on a form acceptable to Seller (such as a FNMA/FHLMC Uniform Residential Loan Application for residential one to four
    unit properties); and **(b)** Buyer authorizes Seller and/or Agent to obtain, at Buyer's expense, a copy of Buyer's credit report. Buyer shall
    provide any supporting documentation reasonably requested by Seller. Seller, after first giving Buyer a Notice to Buyer to Perform, may
    cancel this Agreement in writing and authorize return of Buyer's deposit if Buyer fails to provide such documents within that time, or if
    Seller disapproves any above item within **5 (or ☐ _____) Days** After receipt of each item.

3. **CREDIT DOCUMENTS:** This extension of credit by Seller will be evidenced by: ☐ Note and deed of trust; ☐ All-inclusive
    note and deed of trust; ☐ Installment land sale contract; ☐ Lease/option (when parties intend transfer of equitable title);
    OR ☐ Other (specify) _____

**THE FOLLOWING TERMS APPLY ONLY IF CHECKED. SELLER IS ADVISED TO READ ALL TERMS, EVEN THOSE NOT
CHECKED, TO UNDERSTAND WHAT IS OR IS NOT INCLUDED, AND, IF NOT INCLUDED, THE CONSEQUENCES THEREOF.**

4. ☐ **LATE CHARGE:** If any payment is not made within _____ **Days** After it is due, a late charge of either $ _____,
    or _____ % of the installment due, may be charged to Buyer. **NOTE:** On single family residences that Buyer intends to occupy,
    California Civil Code §2954.4(a) limits the late charge to no more than 6% of the total installment payment due and requires a
    grace period of no less than 10 days.

5. ☐ **BALLOON PAYMENT:** The extension of credit will provide for a balloon payment, in the amount of $ _____
    plus any accrued interest, which is due on _____ (date).

6. ☐ **PREPAYMENT:** If all or part of this extension of credit is paid early, Seller may charge a prepayment penalty as follows (if
    applicable): _____. Caution: California Civil Code
    §2954.9 contains limitations on prepayment penalties for residential one-to-four unit properties.

7. ☐ **DUE ON SALE:** If any interest in the Property is sold or otherwise transferred, Seller has the option to require immediate
    payment of the entire unpaid principal balance, plus any accrued interest.

8.* ☐ **REQUEST FOR COPY OF NOTICE OF DEFAULT:** A request for a copy of Notice of Default as defined in California Civil
    Code §2924b will be recorded. **If Not**, Seller is advised to consider recording a Request for Notice of Default.

9.* ☐ **REQUEST FOR NOTICE OF DELINQUENCY:** A request for Notice of Delinquency, as defined in California Civil Code §2924e,
    to be signed and paid for by Buyer, will be made to senior lienholders. **If not**, Seller is advised to consider making a Request for
    Notice of Delinquency. Seller is advised to check with senior lienholders to verify whether they will honor this request.

10.*☐ **TAX SERVICE:**
    A. If property taxes on the Property become delinquent, tax service will be arranged to report to Seller. **If not**, Seller is
    advised to consider retaining a tax service, or to otherwise determine that property taxes are paid.
    B. ☐ Buyer, ☐ Seller, shall be responsible for the initial and continued retention of, and payment for, such tax service.

11. ☐ **TITLE INSURANCE:** Title insurance coverage will be provided to **both** Seller and Buyer, insuring their respective interests
    in the Property. **If not**, Buyer and Seller are advised to consider securing such title insurance coverage.

12. ☐ **HAZARD INSURANCE:**
    A. The parties' escrow holder or insurance carrier will be directed to include a loss payee endorsement, adding Seller to
    the Property insurance policy. **If not**, Seller is advised to secure such an endorsement, or acquire a separate
    insurance policy.
    B. Property insurance **does not** include earthquake or flood insurance coverage, unless checked:
    ☐ Earthquake insurance will be obtained; ☐ Flood insurance will be obtained.

13. ☐ **PROCEEDS TO BUYER:** Buyer will receive cash proceeds at the close of the sale transaction. The amount received will be
    approximately $ _____, from _____ (indicate source of
    proceeds). Buyer represents that the purpose of such disbursement is as follows: _____.

14. ☐ **NEGATIVE AMORTIZATION; DEFERRED INTEREST:** Negative amortization results when Buyer's periodic payments are
    less than the amount of interest earned on the obligation. Deferred interest also results when the obligation does not
    require periodic payments for a period of time. In either case, interest is not payable as it accrues. This accrued interest
    will have to be paid by Buyer at a later time, and may result in Buyer owing more on the obligation than at its origination.
    The credit being extended to Buyer by Seller will provide for negative amortization or deferred interest as indicated below.
    (Check A, B, or C. CHECK ONE ONLY.)
    ☐ **A.** All negative amortization or deferred interest shall be added to the principal _____
    (e.g., annually, monthly, etc.), and thereafter shall bear interest at the rate specified in the credit documents (compound interest);
    OR ☐ **B.** All deferred interest shall be due and payable, along with principal, at maturity;
    OR ☐ **C.** Other _____.

*(For Paragraphs 8-10) In order to receive timely and continued notification, Seller is advised to record appropriate notices and/or to
notify appropriate parties of any change in Seller's address.

Buyer's Initials (_____)(_____)
Seller's Initials (_____)(_____)

EQUAL HOUSING
OPPORTUNITY

Reviewed by _____ Date _____

SELLER FINANCING ADDENDUM AND DISCLOSURE (SFA PAGE 1 OF 3)

Property Address: _____ Date: _____

15. ☐ **ALL-INCLUSIVE DEED OF TRUST; INSTALLMENT LAND SALE CONTRACT:** This transaction involves the use of an all-inclusive (or wraparound) deed of trust or an installment land sale contract. That deed of trust or contract shall provide as follows:

   A. In the event of an acceleration of any senior encumbrance, the responsibility for payment, or for legal defense is: _____ _____ ; OR ☐ **Is not** specified in the credit or security documents.

   B. In the event of the prepayment of a senior encumbrance, the responsibilities and rights of Buyer and Seller regarding refinancing, prepayment penalties, and any prepayment discounts are: _____ ; OR ☐ **Are not** specified in the documents evidencing credit.

   C. Buyer will make periodic payments to _____ (Seller, collection agent, or any neutral third party), who will be responsible for disbursing payments to the payee(s) on the senior encumbrance(s) and to Seller. **NOTE:** The Parties are advised to designate a neutral third party for these purposes.

16. ☐ **TAX IDENTIFICATION NUMBERS:** Buyer and Seller shall each provide to each other their Social Security Numbers or Taxpayer Identification Numbers.

17. ☐ **OTHER CREDIT TERMS** _____ _____

18. ☐ **RECORDING:** The documents evidencing credit (paragraph 3) will be recorded with the county recorder where the Property is located. **If not,** Buyer and Seller are advised that their respective interests in the Property may be jeopardized by intervening liens, judgments, encumbrances, or subsequent transfers.

19. ☐ **JUNIOR FINANCING:** There will be additional financing, secured by the Property, junior to this Seller financing. Explain: _____

20. **SENIOR LOANS AND ENCUMBRANCES:** The following information is provided on loans and/or encumbrances that will be **senior** to Seller financing. **NOTE:** The following are estimates, unless otherwise marked with an asterisk (*). If checked: ☐ A separate sheet with information on additional senior loans/encumbrances is attached

		1st	2nd
A.	Original Balance	$ _____	$ _____
B.	Current Balance	$ _____	$ _____
C.	Periodic Payment (e.g. $100/month):	$ _____	$ _____ /
	Including Impounds of:	$ _____	$ _____ /
D.	Interest Rate (per annum)	_____ %	_____ %
E.	Fixed or Variable Rate:	_____	_____
	If Variable Rate: Lifetime Cap (Ceiling)	_____	_____
	Indicator (Underlying Index)	_____	_____
	Margins	_____	_____
F.	Maturity Date	_____	_____
G.	Amount of Balloon Payment	$ _____	$ _____
H.	Date Balloon Payment Due	_____	_____
I.	Potential for Negative Amortization? (Yes, No, or Unknown)	_____	_____
J.	Due on Sale? (Yes, No, or Unknown)	_____	_____
K.	Pre-payment penalty? (Yes, No, or Unknown)	_____	_____
L.	Are payments current? (Yes, No, or Unknown)	_____	_____

21. **BUYER'S CREDITWORTHINESS:** (CHECK EITHER A OR B. Do not check both.) In addition to the loan application, credit report and other information requested under paragraph 2:

   A. ☐ No other disclosure concerning Buyer's creditworthiness has been made to Seller;

OR B. ☐ The following representations concerning Buyer's creditworthiness are made by Buyer(s) to Seller:

Borrower _____	Co-Borrower _____
1. Occupation _____	1. Occupation _____
2. Employer _____	2. Employer _____
3. Length of Employment _____	3. Length of Employment _____
4. Monthly Gross Income _____	4. Monthly Gross Income _____
5. Other _____	5. Other _____

22. **ADDED, DELETED OR SUBSTITUTED BUYERS:** The addition, deletion or substitution of any person or entity under this Agreement or to title prior to close of escrow shall require Seller's written consent. Seller may grant or withhold consent in Seller's sole discretion. Any additional or substituted person or entity shall, if requested by Seller, submit to Seller the same documentation as required for the original named Buyer. Seller and/or Brokers may obtain a credit report, at Buyer's expense, on any such person or entity.

Buyer's Initials (_____)(_____)
Seller's Initials (_____)(_____)

Reviewed by _____ Date _____

SELLER FINANCING ADDENDUM AND DISCLOSURE (SFA PAGE 2 OF 3)

Property Address: _____ Date: _____

23. CAUTION:

    A. If the Seller financing requires a balloon payment, Seller shall give Buyer written notice, according to the terms of Civil Code §2966, at least 90 and not more than 150 days before the balloon payment is due if the transaction is for the purchase of a dwelling for not more than four families.

    B. If **any** obligation secured by the Property calls for a balloon payment, Seller and Buyer are aware that refinancing of the balloon payment at maturity may be difficult or impossible, depending on conditions in the conventional mortgage marketplace at that time. There are no assurances that new financing or a loan extension will be available when the balloon prepayment, or any prepayment, is due.

    C. If **any** of the existing or proposed loans or extensions of credit would require refinancing as a result of a lack of full amortization, such refinancing might be difficult or impossible in the conventional mortgage marketplace.

    D. In the event of default by Buyer: (1) Seller may have to reinstate and/or make monthly payments on any and all senior encumbrances (including real property taxes) in order to protect Seller's secured interest; (2) Seller's rights are generally limited to foreclosure on the Property, pursuant to California Code of Civil Procedure §580b; and (3) the Property may lack sufficient equity to protect Seller's interests if the Property decreases in value.

If this three-page Addendum and Disclosure is used in a transaction for the purchase of a dwelling for not more than four families, it shall be prepared by an Arranger of Credit as defined in California Civil Code §2957(a). (The Arranger of Credit is usually the agent who obtained the offer.)

_____
Arranger of Credit - (Print Firm Name)   By _____   Date _____

Address _____ City _____ State _____ Zip _____

Phone _____ Fax _____

BUYER AND SELLER ACKNOWLEDGE AND AGREE THAT BROKERS: (A) WILL NOT PROVIDE LEGAL OR TAX ADVICE; (B) WILL NOT PROVIDE OTHER ADVICE OR INFORMATION THAT EXCEEDS THE KNOWLEDGE, EDUCATION AND EXPERIENCE REQUIRED TO OBTAIN A REAL ESTATE LICENSE; OR (C) HAVE NOT AND WILL NOT VERIFY ANY INFORMATION PROVIDED BY EITHER BUYER OR SELLER. BUYER AND SELLER AGREE THAT THEY WILL SEEK LEGAL, TAX AND OTHER DESIRED ASSISTANCE FROM APPROPRIATE PROFESSIONALS. BUYER AND SELLER ACKNOWLEDGE THAT THE INFORMATION EACH HAS PROVIDED TO THE ARRANGER OF CREDIT FOR INCLUSION IN THIS DISCLOSURE FORM IS ACCURATE. BUYER AND SELLER FURTHER ACKNOWLEDGE THAT EACH HAS RECEIVED A COMPLETED COPY OF THIS DISCLOSURE FORM.

Buyer _____ Date _____
               (signature)

Address _____ City _____ State _____ Zip _____

Phone _____ Fax _____ E-mail _____

Buyer _____ Date _____
               (signature)

Address _____ City _____ State _____ Zip _____

Phone _____ Fax _____ E-mail _____

Seller _____ Date _____
               (signature)

Address _____ City _____ State _____ Zip _____

Phone _____ Fax _____ E-mail _____

Seller _____ Date _____
               (signature)

Address _____ City _____ State _____ Zip _____

Phone _____ Fax _____ E-mail _____

SURE·TRAC The System for Success™   Published by the California Association of REALTORS®

Reviewed by _____ Date _____   EQUAL HOUSING OPPORTUNITY

SFA REVISED 10/02 (PAGE 3 OF 3)

SELLER FINANCING ADDENDUM AND DISCLOSURE (SFA PAGE 3 OF 3)

Once a seller makes a secondary trust deed to a buyer, the seller is not bound to the loan until it is paid off. If the seller chooses to sell the secondary trust deed, he or she may sell it to an investor or to a mortgage broker. The mortgage broker will purchase the note and junior trust deed at a discounted rate. This means that the loan will be sold for less than the buyer owes the original seller. The advantage to the seller is that he or she will be repaid immediately, even if he or she is not receiving the full amount of the loan.

> *Example*
> *Deborah wishes to sell her home and puts it on the market for $400,000. Because of the neighborhood and economic conditions, the home sells fast, for the asking price. The buyer offers a 10% down payment, or $40,000, and secures a new first loan for $320,000. Deborah agrees to make a loan to the buyer in the amount of $40,000 (so the transaction will go through, and Deborah will be able to move into her new home).*
>
> *Immediately after escrow closes and Deborah moves into her new home, she finds that her monthly payment is quite a bit harder to make than she originally thought. She chooses to sell the loan and junior trust deed to a mortgage broker, to cash out and use the money to make her own home payments. She finds an investor willing to purchase the loan at a 10% discount. This means that she immediately receives $36,000 for the loan (which is $4,000 less than made originally). However, it also means she will be able to make her monthly payment with no problem.*

There are, of course, disclosure statements that must be signed by the buyer and seller in a transaction where the seller provides a junior trust deed. These disclosures are required by law, and provide both the buyer and seller with all the appropriate information to make an educated decision regarding this type of financing. The disclosure statements will allow the seller to see if the buyer is financially able to make the payment, and his or her credit rating. This is very important information for the seller, to help determine if the loan is feasible, and if it will be paid back in a timely manner. The buyer can see which loans are currently taking precedence over the junior trust deed that would potentially be created. A real estate professional can be used to arrange credit, to ensure all laws regarding the transaction have been followed.

If the seller is not in a position to make the second trust deed to a buyer, there are a few other options available to the buyer to secure the additional funds needed to purchase the property. The buyer can attempt to obtain outside financing through more traditional sources, such as a mortgage banker, traditional bank or outside investor.

This second trust deed is considered a purchase money loan and will be sent to escrow for disbursement upon closing. The trust deeds will be recorded sequentially (first trust deed recorded first; and the second loan backed by a second or third trust deed).

The third way to obtain a junior trust deed is to secure, if possible, a **home equity loan**. A home equity loan is equal to the amount of equity, or value, a home has above the amount owed on the loan against the home. If there is positive equity in the home, a homeowner may apply for a loan to withdraw money as a cash loan for any purpose. Some reasons for this withdrawal might be to make improvements to the home, take a vacation, purchase a vehicle, etc.

A smart lender is careful not to make home equity loans to unqualified persons or against a property that may not appreciate and/or may actually lose money in the long term. A lender also does not usually loan 100% of the difference between the money owed on the loan against the home and the determined value of the home.

Typically, 80–90% of the equity in the home is loaned. This is to protect the lender from losing money in the event that the property depreciates in value.

Home equity loans are considered **hard money loans** and are naturally secured by a deed of trust. As you might remember, a hard money loan leaves the homeowner open to the possibility of a deficiency judgment in a judicial foreclosure.

> *Example*
> *Emily has a home worth $150,000, with a first loan of $75,000. She wished to take out a home equity loan of $65,000 to build a guesthouse and pool. When Emily begins looking for a lender, she finds that she cannot secure a loan of that amount because its total is more than 80% of her equity in the home. The largest loan she can secure is $60,000, as $60,000 is 80% of the $75,000 of equity she has in her home.*

Balloon Payment Loans

A balloon payment is an installment payment or final payment that is substantially more than other payments, resulting in the complete payoff of a debt. A balloon payment will be made when a loan is not fully amortized during the term of the loan, thus requiring a large payment to completely satisfy the principal amount of the loan.

A balloon payment may happen on first trust deeds of over $30,000, second trust deeds of over $20,000, or when a seller is rescinding a junior trust deed upon selling his or her home to a qualified buyer. These balloon payments are discussed at the onset of the loan, so that the consumer is aware of the obligation. Still, laws require a lender to notify the borrower of this obligation again. This must be done 90 to 150 days before the payment is actually due. Balloon payments are utilized on hard money loans, not for purchase money loans. As you might recall, a purchase money loan is specifically made to finance property, where a hard money loan is made in exchange for cash for any purpose.

Junior trust deeds may also have balloon payments for a hard money loan of under $20,000. For junior trust deeds of less than three years, a final balloon payment may be required, but the amount of the balloon payment must not exceed twice the amount of the smallest installment payment.

Facts regarding balloon payments

- Utilized on hard money loans

- First trust deed of $30,000 or more, and a junior trust deed of $20,000 or more

- Junior trust deeds under $20,000 must have a term of less than three years, with a restricted balloon payment of no more than twice the smallest installment payment

- Lender must give 90–150 days' notice before the payment is due

Remember

Hard money loans are made in exchange for cash, as opposed to a loan made to finance a certain property.

OTHER TYPES OF LOANS SECURED BY TRUST DEEDS OR MORTGAGES

Home Equity Loan

Another way a junior loan can be created is by way of a home equity loan. Assuming there is enough equity, i.e. the difference between the value of a home and the money that is owed against it, a homeowner can apply for a cash loan against that equity for any purpose.

A lender uses strict standards about the amount of equity required in a property before loaning money, and particularly for a junior loan. The reason is simple. All a lender wants is to get his or her money back in a timely manner, along with the calculated return on the investment. Care must be taken, in case of a decrease in the value of the subject property, to make sure there is enough of a margin between the total amount owed and the value of the property. If the lender has to sell the property at a foreclosure sale, he or she will be assured of getting the money back. By only loaning up to 75%-90% of the property value, the lender leaves some room for loss.

Example
Michael's home was appraised at $100,000, with a $40,000 first trust deed recorded against it. Michael wants a $40,000 home equity loan. To determine whether or not to make the loan, the lender adds the amount owed to the amount desired in the loan to determine the percentage of the value that would be encumbered by the existing first trust deed added to the desired second trust deed. If the lender will only loan up to 80% of the appraised value of the property, will Michael get his loan?

The priority of the loan will depend on what other instruments are recorded ahead of it, but it will be known as a hard money loan (subject to state laws) and will be secured by a deed of trust or mortgage against the property. (Of course Michael does get his loan, because he has enough equity in the property to qualify.)

Home Equity Line of Credit (HELOC)
More and more lenders are offering home equity lines of credit. By using the equity in their homes, borrowers may qualify for a sizable amount of credit, available for use when and how they please, at an interest rate that is relatively low. Furthermore, under the tax law, depending on each borrower's specific situation, he or she may be allowed to deduct the interest because the debt is secured by the home.

What is a home equity line of credit?
A home equity line of credit is a form of revolving credit in which a borrower's home serves as collateral. Because, in most cases, the home is likely to be a consumer's largest asset, many homeowners use their home equity credit lines only for major items such as education, home improvements, or medical bills and not for day-to-day expenses.

With a home equity line, a borrower will be approved for a specific amount of credit—the credit limit—meaning the maximum amount he or she can borrow at any one time.

Many lenders set the credit limit on a home equity line by taking a percentage (75%–90%) of the appraised value of the home and subtracting the balance owed on the existing mortgage. For example

Formula for Setting Credit Limit

Appraisal of home $100,000	$100,000
Percentage of appraised value	x 75%
	$75,000
Less balance owed on existing mortgage	- 40,000
Potential credit line	$35,000

In determining the borrower's actual credit line, the lender also will consider his or her ability to repay, by looking at income, debts, and other financial obligations, as well as a borrower's credit history.

Home equity plans often set a fixed time during which a homeowner can borrow money, such as 10 years. When this period is up, the plan may allow the borrower to renew the credit line. But in a plan that does not allow renewals, the borrower will not be able to borrow additional money once the time has expired. Some plans may call for payment in full of any outstanding balance. Others may permit a borrower to repay over a fixed time, for example 10 years.

Once approved for the home equity plan, usually a borrower will be able to borrow up to the credit limit whenever he or she wants. Typically, a borrower will be able to draw on the line by using special checks.

Under some plans, borrowers can use a credit card or other means to borrow money and make purchases using the line of credit. However, there may be limitations on how the borrower may use the line. Some plans may require the homeowner to borrow a minimum amount each time he or she draws on the line (for example, $300) and to keep a minimum amount outstanding. Some lenders also may require that the borrower take an initial advance when he or she first sets up the line.

Interest Rate Charges and Plan Features

Home equity plans typically involve variable interest rates rather than fixed rates. A variable rate must be based on a publicly available index (such as the prime rate published in some major daily newspapers or a U.S. Treasury bill rate); the interest rate will change, mirroring fluctuations in the index. To calculate the interest rate that the borrower will pay, most lenders add a margin of one or two percentage points, which represents the profit the lender will make, to the index value. Because the cost of borrowing is tied directly to the index rate, it is important to find out what index and margin each lender uses, how often the index changes, and how high it has risen in the past.

Sometimes lenders advertise a temporarily discounted rate for home equity lines—a rate that is unusually low and often lasts only for an introductory period, such as six months.

Variable rate plans secured by a dwelling must have a ceiling (or cap) on how high the interest rate can climb over the life of the plan. Some variable-rate plans limit how much the payment may increase, and also how low the interest rate may fall if interest rates drop.

Some lenders may permit a borrower to convert a variable rate to a fixed interest rate during the life of the plan, or to convert all or a portion of the line to a fixed-term installment loan.

Agreements generally will permit the lender to freeze or reduce a credit line under certain circumstances. For example, some variable-rate plans may not allow a borrower to get additional funds during any period during which the interest rate reaches the cap.

Costs to Obtain a Home Equity Line

Many of the costs in setting up a home equity line of credit are similar to those a borrower pays when he or she buys a home. For example

- A fee for a property appraisal, which estimates the value of the home

- An application fee, which may not be refundable if the borrower is turned down for credit

- Up-front charges, such as one or more points (one point equals 1 percent of the credit limit)

- Other closing costs, which include fees for attorneys, title search, mortgage preparation and filing, property and title insurance, as well as taxes

- Certain fees during the plan. For example, some plans impose yearly membership or maintenance fees.

- The borrower also may be charged a transaction fee every time he or she draws on the credit line

How Will the Borrower Repay the Home Equity Plan?

Before entering into a plan, a borrower should consider how he or she will pay back any money that is borrowed. Some plans set minimum payments that cover a portion of the principal (the amount borrowed) plus accrued interest. But, unlike the typical installment loan, the portion that goes toward principal may not be enough to repay the debt by the end of the term. Other plans may allow payments of interest alone during the life of the plan, which means that the borrower pays nothing toward the principal. If the homeowner borrows $10,000, he or she will owe that entire sum when the plan ends.

Regardless of the minimum payment required, the borrower can pay more than the minimum and many lenders may give the borrower a choice of payment options. Consumers often will choose to pay down the principal regularly, as they do with other loans.

Whatever the payment arrangements during the life of the plan—whether the borrower pays some, a little, or none of the principal amount of the loan—when the plan ends the borrower may have to pay the entire balance owed, all at once. He or she must be prepared to make this balloon payment by refinancing it with the lender, by obtaining a loan from an-other lender, or by some other means.

Comparing a Line of Credit and a Traditional Second Mortgage Loan

If a homeowner is thinking about a home equity line of credit, he or she also might want to consider a more traditional second mortgage loan. This type of loan provides a fixed amount of money repayable over a fixed period. Usually the payment schedule calls for equal payments that will pay off the entire loan within that time. A HELOC gives the borrower more flexibility, but the traditional second mortgage is likely to give the borrower more security.

Disclosures from Lenders

The Truth in Lending Act requires lenders to disclose the important terms and costs of their home equity plans, including the APR, miscellaneous charges, the payment terms, and information about any variable-rate feature. And in general, neither the lender nor anyone else may charge a fee until after the borrower has received this information. The borrower usually gets these disclosures when he or she receives an application form, and will get additional disclosures before the plan is opened. If any term has changed before the plan is opened (other than a variable-rate feature), the lender must return all fees if the borrower decided not to enter into the plan because of the changed term.

Package Loan

A loan on real property that is secured by more than the land and structure is known as a **package loan**. It includes fixtures attached to the building (appliances, carpeting, drapes, air conditioning) and other personal property.

Blanket Loan

A trust deed or mortgage that covers more than one parcel of property may be secured by a **blanket loan**. It usually contains a release clause that provides for the release of any particular parcel upon the repayment of a specified part of the loan. Commonly, it is used in connection with housing tracts, or construction loans.

Open-Ended Loan

An additional amount of money may be loaned to a borrower in the future under the same trust deed. The effect is to preserve the original loan's priority claim against the property with this open-end loan.

Swing Loan

A **swing loan** or **bridge loan** is a temporary, short term loan made on a borrower's equity in his or her present home. It is used when the borrower has purchased another property, with the present home unsold, and needs the cash to close the sale of the new home. The new loan is secured by a trust deed or mortgage against the borrower's home. Usually there are no payments, with interest accruing during the term of the loan. When the borrower's home sells, the swing loan plus interest is repaid, through escrow, from the proceeds of the sale.

Wrap-Around Loan

Wrap-around loans are another way to finance property. Sometimes these loans are called an **all-inclusive trust deed (AITD)**. A wrap-around loan usually consists of both the existing note held by the seller, and the new loan secured by the buyer. The new loan "wraps around" the existing loan, and one payment is made to cover both loans. One loan consumes all the present encumbrances of the property, plus the amount of the new loan.

Because this is not a blanket loan or open-ended loan, there is a hierarchy which makes the AITD subordinate to any previously recorded trust deed on the property. If the property should be foreclosed, any previous trust deeds must be paid first (even though the wrap-around loan is making the payments for these loans). One difference regarding the AITD loan versus other financing is that, with an AITD loan, the buyer receives the title to the property at closing. Usually an AITD is utilized when a seller and buyer are both financing a property. In a traditional loan assumption, or when the seller carries back a note on the property, the buyer takes a loan to cover the cost of the existing loan plus the difference in the sale price of the home. The seller benefits from this situation, because he or she receives the full price for the home. The buyer generally benefits through a lower down payment, and also does not have to endure the traditional qualifying process to obtain the loan.

The AITD includes the unpaid principal balance of the existing loan plus the amount of the new loan being made by the seller to the buyer. The seller continues to make payments on the loan that he or she has taken out from his or her financial institution, while the buyer makes payments to the seller for the AITD. Of course, payment from the buyer will be enough to cover the original loan, plus a higher interest rate to the seller. This acts in concert with the additional money borrowed from the seller, to cover the difference between the original trust deed and the selling price of the property.

While this type of loan seems like a great idea for a buyer, there are situations when it simply does not work out as well. If a seller needs to cash out of a loan for the purchase of another property, or for any other reason, he or she will not be able to do so with an AITD loan. The seller is obligated to repay the entire original note to the lender, which is wrapped around by the loan the seller has provided to the buyer. Some loans contain a "due on sale" clause, meaning the seller would not be able to wrap around a loan to the existing loan, as the original loan must be paid off when the home is sold. If there is no "due on sale" clause, the lender may have to approve the wrap-around loan, and there are some cases when the buyer may not qualify (for example, because of his or her credit score or debt to asset ratio). In a market with high interest rates, an AITD may not be the best choice, because the buyer ends up paying a much higher rate than the current market demands for the wrap-around loan. This higher rate is, however, financially attractive to the seller.

The buyer typically does not make payments directly to the seller, although in theory that is what is happening. Instead, the buyer will usually make payments to a collection company, which will then distribute the money to the appropriate parties.

The original lender will receive a monthly payment, while the seller will receive the amount predetermined by the contract. This is done to protect the buyer from mismanagement on the seller's behalf and to ensure that the original note is being paid according to the promissory note's terms and conditions. This protects all parties involved, and ensures that this type of financing remains feasible and functional.

Wrap-around loan / All-inclusive trust deed

- Seller finances the buyer, by providing a loan encompassing all payments to the first and any subsequent trust deeds
- Buyer's payment to the seller includes the payment on the original loan, plus the higher interest rate, as well as the difference between the principal owed on the first note and the amount of the sale price of the home
- Wrap-around loan is subordinate to the original loan
- Buyer takes the title to the home
- Buyer makes payments to a collection company, ensuring that all funds are distributed to the appropriate parties

---

Example
Arthur wanted to sell his house, and listed it for $100,000. The existing first trust deed was for $50,000 at 8%, payable at $377 monthly. He thought about carrying a second trust deed at 10%, counting on the income from the note. However, Bonnie, his listing agent, explained he could get a greater return from carrying an all-inclusive trust deed (AITD) instead of just a note and second trust deed from a buyer. She also told him any offer that included an AITD should be referred to an attorney. Arthur, with his attorney's approval, accepted the following offer soon after listing the house.

Sales Price	*$100,000*
Buyers Down Payment	*-20,000*
AITD in favor of Arthur	*$80,000*

- *Payments on new AITD of $80,000 at 10% to be $702, made monthly to Arthur*

- *Payments on existing first trust deed of $50,000 at 8%, in the amount of $377 monthly, to be paid by Arthur to original lender*

AITD payment to Arthur	*$702*
Existing First Trust Deed payment	*-377*
Monthly difference to Arthur	*$32*

Wrap-Around Loans are secured by a trust deed that "wraps" or includes all existing financing, plus the amount to be financed by the seller.

Benefits to the seller
- Usually gets full-price offer

- Increased percent on amount carried

Benefits to the buyer
- Low down payment

- No qualifying for a loan or payment of loan fees

U N S E C U R E D L O A N S

The **unsecured loan** is a promissory note that does not have any collateral to secure the payment of the note. The lender is taking a risk in making this type of loan, as the only way to receive payment for the note in the event of default is through court action.

A L T E R N A T I V E F I N A N C I N G

Alternative financing describes the different programs available to consumers. Whereas in the past, only one type of loan was available to those attempting to purchase a home, there are now many different types of programs available to match the individual needs of homebuyers. Depending on market conditions, a consumer's credit or the down payment that is feasible, one or more of these types of loans may be ideal to help a consumer achieve the goal of home ownership.

The programs available to consumers include

- Graduated Payment Adjustable Mortgage

- Contract of Sale

- Shared Appreciation Mortgage

- Variable / Adjustable Rate Mortgage (ARM)

- Rollover Mortgage

- Reverse Annuity Mortgage

The **Graduated Payment Adjustable Mortgage** (also known as a **flexible rate mortgage**) is a loan that defers part of the principal until the end of the loan. The payments for the first few years will be lower than the payments for the final few years, allowing people who anticipate making more money at their jobs in the future to purchase property now, and thus defer paying down some of the principal until a later time. Both interest and principal will be paid down with each payment, but the amount of principal being included in each payment is adjusted from the beginning of the loan to the end of the loan.

Contract of sale is a unique financing option, because the seller of the property remains the legal owner of that property until the buyer has made his or her final payment. For those who are familiar with a traditional car note (where the bank or finance company legally owns the car until the note has been paid in full), this concept is similar. This type of financing may be attractive for buyers with below average credit or those in a very tight money market.

The buyer (sometimes referred to as the vendee) will receive possession of the property and may use the property as intended at the time of purchase. Additionally, the buyer holds equitable title, while the seller (or vendor) holds legal title to the property. A contract of sale is very similar to the AITD or wrap-around loan. The vendor continues to pay the original note on the property, while the vendee pays the vendor for the property itself. The main difference between these two types of financing is that those who finance with a wrap-around loan will take the title to the property immediately, while those who finance with contract of sale will only receive equitable title, as the legal title remains with the vendor.

A **shared appreciation mortgage** allows the buyer to enjoy more attractive loan terms, by sharing the appreciation in the home with the lender. The lender will use their share of this appreciation as security for the loan. The lender and buyer must mutually agree to these terms for the life of the loan.

Variable rate mortgage / adjustable rate mortgages (ARM) fluctuate with changes in market interest rates. When interest rates rise, interest on the loan will reflect the increase, and thus increase the amount of each monthly payment. Correspondingly, a decrease in market interest rates will have the opposite effect, decreasing the monthly payment of the note. In addition to the amount of the monthly payment, the term and monthly payment of the loan may change.

Sometimes a note is renegotiated after many years, to adjust the interest rate and monthly payment in keeping with market conditions. This loan is called a **rollover mortgage**. Typically, a rollover mortgage is reviewed or renegotiated every five years.

Reverse Annuity mortgages are basically the opposite of a traditional home loan.

FORM 2

SPACE ABOVE THIS LINE FOR RECORDER'S USE

LONG FORM SECURITY (INSTALLMENT) LAND CONTRACT
WITH POWER OF SALE

THIS AGREEMENT, made and entered into this _____ day of _____ , 20 ____ , by and
between _____ (Vendor's name),
whose address is _____
(hereinafter sometimes referred to as "Vendor"), and

_____ (Vendee's name), whose address is _____
_____ (hereinafter sometimes referred to as "Vendee"); and

CONTINENTAL LAND TITLE COMPANY (hereinafter sometimes referred to as "Trustee")

W I T N E S S E T H :

WHEREAS, Vendor is now the owner of certain real property situated in the County of _____
State of California, commonly known as _____
_____ (Property street address), and described as follows:

WHEREAS, Vendor has agreed to sell, and Vendee has agreed to buy said real property on the terms and conditions hereinafter set forth;

WHEREAS, Vendor shall retain legal title as a security interest in said real property until the payment of the balance of the purchase price has been paid by Vendee to Vendor as set forth below.

NOW, THEREFORE, THE PARTIES HERETO DO HEREBY AGREE AS FOLLOWS:

PURCHASE PRICE

1. Vendor agrees to sell, and Vendee agrees to buy all of the aforedescribed real property for the sum of
_____ (Total purchase price) ($ _____).

lawful money of the United States, as hereinafter more fully set forth.

REQUEST FOR NOTICE OF DEFAULT

2. In accordance with Section 2924b, Civil Code, request is hereby made by the undersigned Vendor and
Vendee that a copy of any Notice of Default and a copy of any Notice of Sale under Deed of Trust recorded
_____ in Book _____ Page _____ , Official Records of
_____ County, California, as affecting above described property, executed by
_____ as Trustor in which _____
is named as beneficiary, and _____ as Trustee, be mailed to Vendor
and Vendee at address in paragraph 3 below.

NOTICES AND REQUEST FOR NOTICE

3. Notices required or permitted under this agreement shall be binding if delivered personally to party
sought to be served or if mailed by registered or certified mail, postage prepaid in the United States mail
to the following:

Vendor: _____
_____
_____

Vendee: _____
_____
_____

Vendor and Vendee hereby request that notice of default and notice of sale hereunder be mailed to them at the above address.

PAYMENT OF PURCHASE PRICE

4. Vendee shall pay the purchase price of $ _____ as follows:
   (a) Vendee shall pay to Vendor the sum of $ _____ (down payment) as and for a down payment.
   (b) The balance of purchase price of $ _____ shall be paid by Vendee to Vendor and shall bear interest at the rate of
_____ percent per annum of any balance unpaid. Said sum shall be paid in installments of $ _____ on the
_____ day of each and every month commencing _____ and continuing
thereafter until paid in full; each payment first to be credited to interest with balance to principal. This agreement will require
_____ years and _____ months to complete payment in accordance with its terms. Vendor shall make payment
of any installments on existing first, second and/or third deeds of trust in accordance with paragraph (c) hereinbelow.

Title Order No. _____   Escrow or Loan No. _____

TT-281

Most people seek a loan to purchase property; however, a reverse annuity mortgage takes a property that has been owned for many years (and may even be paid off), and begins drawing money against the equity in the home. This is attractive to retirees, who may have been living in their home for many years and are living on a fixed income. When they find that this fixed income does not meet their standard of living, they may begin drawing a monthly payment against their home.

Generally, this money does not have to be paid off until the person dies or chooses to sell the property. At this time, the debt to the bank is paid, and any remaining monies are paid to the seller (or the seller's estate or family in the event of death).

> **Difference Between AITD and Contract of Sale**
> - AITD: buyer gets title to property
> - Contract of sale: seller keeps title until loan is paid off

SHORT PAY

Sometimes a trustor owes more money on his or her home than the home is actually worth. It is hard to imagine this situation in California, since property values appreciate so much and so fast. Yet, it is a possibility. When this occurs, the lender may allow the buyer to sell the property at market value and walk away from the debt, even if the market value of the property is less than the loan amount.

The process described above is called **short payoff**. A short payoff may seem undesirable to a lender, as the lender does not receive the entire loan amount in return. However, in some cases a short payoff is better than the alternative. Many lenders will use either a foreclosure (to send the property to a trustee's sale) or judicial foreclosure (to sell the property through a court order) as an alternative. This will generally, though not always, bring in the amount owed on the loan.

The trustee's sale and judicial foreclosure also may not bring in enough money to pay off the loan, or the home may not sell at all. The buyer may back out of the sale due to lack of funds, or there may be no bidders on the property. In this case, the lender purchases the property for the amount owed on the note. This is not attractive to the lender; as the lender would much rather sell the property to earn their money back. By taking a short payoff versus acquiring the property, the lender may see a return of some of their money. The advantage to that is that the lender does not have to worry about paying for the trustee's sale, court proceedings, interest and fees associated with these proceedings, or perhaps be stuck with a property that they do not want.

Short Payoff

- Allows a borrower to sell his or her home at market value, less what is owed on the loan, to avoid foreclosure and further financial hardships.

- Attractive to a lender because they receive some of their initial investment back, and does not have to tie up additional monies in a judicial foreclosure, trustee's sale or ownership of property worth less than the original investment.

S U M M A R Y

This chapter covered promissory notes, trust deeds and mortgages and financing options for homebuyers. A person who has taken out a loan out on a home, and has not paid the note in full, may transfer this loan responsibility to another individual who wishes to purchase the property or assume the debt. This is done by the buyer assuming the debt, or by the seller carrying back a note for the buyer. In either case, if the buyer defaults on the loan, the original borrower may suffer. He or she may have his or her credit adversely affected. or he or she may be held liable for any hard money loans against the property in a default judgment.

There are special clauses in financing which may describe the hierarchy (or importance) of trust deeds or may require specific action on a loan in the event ownership changes. Additionally, junior trust deeds may be used to secure additional funding, in the event that the first trust deed and down payment are not sufficient to cover the selling price of the home.

Alternative financing is intended for those people who may have special situations or circumstances that make a traditional real estate loan impossible or unattractive. These loan programs allow rates, payments and terms of the loan to fluctuate with the needs of the borrower. Additionally, balloon payments may be utilized, allowing a low monthly payment and a large installment due at the end of the loan. This is attractive for those people who foresee higher incomes in the future, but are only able to make smaller payments now.

T E R M S   A N D   P H R A S E S

Acceleration Clause   condition of a loan that states that the entire payment for the loan is due in certain circumstances (such as upon sale of the property)

Adjustable Rate Mortgage (ARM)   loan with a flexible interest rate that increases or decreases with market interest rate changes

Agreement of Sale   financing option in which the seller finances the property for the buyer, without giving up legal title to the property. The buyer (vendee) receives possession of the property, but does not receive the title to the property until the loan is paid in full

Alienation Clause   condition of a loan that allows the lender to require full payment of the loan in the event the property is going to be sold

Assignment of Rents   agreement between the property owner and the holder of a trust deed or loan on the property. In this case the holder has the right to collect rents from any tenants occupying the property, as security for the loan. The holder of the loan will only receive this right if the property owner defaults on the note.

Assumption Clause   financing option where the buyer takes over the existing loan on a property and is thereby liable for the note. The seller still remains secondarily liable in the event the buyer defaults on the loan. The buyer can only take over the existing loan if approved by the lender.

Balloon Payment   note requiring a large payment at the end of its term to cover the debt in full. This is used when only a small percentage of the principal is being covered by each of the monthly payments.

Beneficiary   lender or financial institution that provides a loan to the borrower

Blanket Loan   loan covering several properties, whereby each individual property can be released by paying a specific amount on the loan.

Collateral   object of value that is pledged as security for the purchase of another object of value. In real estate, collateral is the property that is pledged as security for the note as evidenced by the trust deed.

Contract of Sale   financing option where the seller finances the property for the buyer, but does not give up legal title to the property. The buyer receives possession of the property, but does not receive the title to the property until the loan is paid in full.

Default   failure by the trustor to pay the monthly or installment payments on the promissory note for the property purchased

Equitable Title   interest in property held by a trustor or vendee before the entire loan has been paid off

Equity   appreciated value in a property over what is owed on the loan after all the debts have been paid off

Fully Amortized Note   note where the installment payments pay both the interest and principal in equal amounts until the debt is paid off in full

Graduated Payment Adjustable Mortgage financing option where the loan installment payment gradually increases during the life of the loan, until it eventually levels off

Hard Money Loan type of trust deed or loan given in exchange for cash. The borrower can utilize the money for any purpose; it need not be used to purchase property.

Holder party to whom the promissory note is made payable (usually the lender)

Holder in Due Course person who has obtained a negotiable instrument (such as a check, promissory note or any other legal tender document) in the ordinary course of business, before it is due, in good faith, for value, and without knowledge that it has been previously dishonored

Home Equity Loan loan made to a homeowner against the equity built up in his or her home, which generally will not exceed 80 to 90% of the equity in the home

Interest cost a lender will charge when lending money to a borrower

Land Contract financing option in which the seller finances the property for the buyer, but does not give up legal title to the property. The buyer receives possession of the property, but does not receive its title until the loan is paid in full.

Legal Title title to property that is complete, with no encumbrances. This title may be held by a trustee in a trust deed, to be reconveyed to the trustor when the note is paid in full.

Maker borrower who requests funds from a lender. The borrower will make a promissory note and become liable for the debt against him or her. Usually, the promissory note is accompanied by the trust deed in a real estate purchase.

Mortgage legal document pledging property as security for a debt

Mortgagee lender loaning the money for the purchase of real estate

Mortgagor borrower requesting a loan to purchase real estate

Naked Legal Title title allowing a trustee to reconvey title to property upon satisfactory payment of a debt, or foreclosure (in the event of default). This title does not grant any ownership privileges to the property.

Negotiable Instrument written document that may be transferred by endorsement or delivery from one party to another

Novation substitution of a new obligation for an old one

Open-Ended Loan   financing option whereby the borrower is allowed to request additional funds secured by one existing trust deed

"Or More" Clause   clause in a note that allows a borrower to pay off the funds early, incurring no penalties

Package Loan   financing option where a loan can be secured not only by real property, but by personal property or the fixtures attached to that property

Partially Amortized Installment Note   loan that will require a balloon payment at the end. The installment payments will cover the interest and part of the principal amount, but will not be sufficient to fully pay the principal at the end of the loan term, making a balloon payment necessary.

Pledge   transferring property to a lender as security for a loan. In this situation, the lender will take possession of the property.

Power of Sale   clause in a loan that allows the lender to sell a property in the event that a borrower defaults on the loan

Prepayment Clause   clause in a loan that penalizes a borrower from paying the loan back early. In the event the loan is paid off early, a percentage of the loan may be collected as penalty.

Principal   amount of a loan, not including the interest

Promissory Note   written promise a borrower makes to a lender pledging to pay back the loan. This promissory note is the evidence of debt.

Purchase Money Loan   loan made specifically for the purchase of real estate

Second Trust Deed   junior trust deed, or evidence of a debt that is recorded after the original trust deed

Security   collateral used to secure a loan

Straight Note   financing option where payments of only the interest on a loan are made during the term of the note with a large lump sum due at the end of the note to pay off the principal. Straight notes may also be set up so that there are no payments required until the end of the loan, at which time both the interest and principal are due.

"Subject To" Clause   buyer takes over an existing loan, and makes payments on it yet is not responsible for the loan itself

Subordination Clause   clause in a loan that allows a subsequent loan, or a loan recorded later to take precedence

Swing Loan   short-term loan allowing the seller of property to purchase another property to replace the one being sold. Upon the sale of the first property, the loan will be called.

Trust Deed   document where the title to property (bare legal title) will pass to a third party (called a trustee) as security for the debt

Trustee   holds bare legal title to property where there is a deed of trust

Trustor   borrower in a trust deed

Usury   act of lending money and charging an interest rate more than what is allowed by law

Variable Rate Mortgage   loan with a flexible interest rate that increases or decreases when market interest rates change

Wrap-Around Loan   financing option in which a new loan is placed in a secondary position. The new loan includes both the unpaid principal balance of the first loan as well as whatever sums are loaned by the lender. Wrap-around loans are sometimes called all-inclusive trust deeds (AITD).

C H A P T E R   Q U I Z

1. When a person signs a promissory note to purchase property, he or she generally uses what as security?
   a. Trust Deed
   b. Collateral
   c. Leverage
   d. Both A and B

2. Promissory notes are considered negotiable instruments. Which of the following is also considered to be a negotiable instrument?
   a. Personal Check
   b. Credit Card
   c. Collateral
   d. None of the above

3. Which of the following is not considered a promissory note?
   a. Adjustable note
   b. Full Reconveyance
   c. Straight note
   d. Amortized note

4. Which one of the following characteristics is not found in a partially amortized note?
    a. Interest-only payments
    b. Partial payment of principal, full payment of interest
    c. Balloon payment
    d. Periodic fixed payments

5. Which of the following parties in a trust holds the trust deed?
    a. Trustee
    b. Beneficiary
    c. Trustor
    d. None of the above

6. In a 6-Month Certificate of Deposit Adjustable Rate Mortgage (ARM), what is the maximum the interest may fluctuate in a 6-month period?
    a. 0.25%
    b. 0.5%
    c. 0.75%
    d. 1%

7. In a trust deed, who holds the original deed to the property before the promissory note is paid in full?
    a. The trustor
    b. The trustee
    c. The lender
    d. Both A and B

8. Which of the following is NOT a special clause found in financial instruments?
    a. Acceleration
    b. Subordination
    c. "Or more"
    d. Redemption

9. Which best describes the "subject to" clause?
    a. A buyer takes over the existing loan from the seller without the lender's knowledge. The seller, or original owner, is responsible for the loan and may be held liable for any deficiency judgments.
    b. The borrower is subject to a credit check before being approved for a loan.
    c. The borrower is subject to a loan based on the inspection and appraisal of the property of interest.
    d. The buyer takes over the existing loan with the knowledge and approval of the lender.

10. The unsecured loan has which of the following characteristics?
    a. Does not utilize a trust deed
    b. Does not require any collateral
    c. Does not utilize an index to determine the variable interest rate
    d. Does not charge a prepayment penalty fee

11. Which of the following is (are) considered a junior trust deed?
    a. Seller financing
    b. Outside financing
    c. Home equity loans
    d. All of the above

12. If a seller finances a junior trust deed to the buyer of his or her property, what options does the buyer have regarding the loan?
    a. The seller may carry the note until it is paid in full.
    b. The seller may sell the note at a discounted rate to a mortgage broker.
    c. The seller may force the buyer into paying the note back earlier than originally planned, because they need the money for a new car.
    d. Both A & B

13. Louise wishes to obtain a home equity loan to remodel her living room and have money to go back to school. Her home is worth $320,000, and she currently has a first loan balance of $150,000. She wishes to pull out $100,000 to cover both her remodeling project and tuition. Will a lender be willing to do this for Louise?
    a. Yes. Louise has plenty of equity in her home for this loan.
    b. No. Louise cannot take out money for any purpose other than the purchase of property.
    c. No. Louise does not have enough equity in her home for this size of loan.
    d. None of the above.

14. Balloon payments
    a. are used on hard money loans.
    b. require a large final payment to completely repay the debt.
    c. require a 90 to 50 day notice from the lender to the borrower that the payment is forthcoming.
    d. all of the above.

15. In a hybrid note
    a. interest is fixed for the life of the loan.
    b. interest is variable for the life of the loan.
    c. interest is fixed for a set number of years, and then becomes variable, tied to an index.
    d. none of the above.

16. Sellers who finance a buyer with a wrap-around loan typically do which of the following?
    a. Carry back a note on the property
    b. Charge the buyer a higher interest rate then he or she currently pays on the original trust deed.
    c. Collect the money directly from the buyer for the AITD.
    d. Require a high down payment from the buyer.

17. Which of the following loans allow individual properties to be released from the responsibilities of the loan, provided there is a sufficient payment?
    a. Blanket loan
    b. Wrap-around loan
    c. Open-ended loan
    d. Unsecured loan

18. Which of the following mortgage types best describes a loan similar to the wrap-around loan or all-inclusive trust deed?
    a. Graduated payment adjustable mortgage
    b. Rollover mortgage
    c. Shared appreciation mortgage
    d. Contract of Sale

19. What is the term for selling a property at market value, below what is owed on the loan?
    a. Short Pay
    b. Walk away
    c. Foreclosure
    d. Trustee's sale

20. Which of the following is a cost associated with obtaining a home equity line?
    a. Appraisal fee
    b. Pest inspection fee
    c. Transaction fee
    d. Both A and C

5

TRUST DEEDS AND MORTGAGES

What you will learn in this Chapter

- Trust Deeds

- Junior Trust Deeds

- Benefits of a Trust Deed

- Mortgage

- Foreclosure Under a Trust Deed

- Foreclosure Under a Mortgage

Test Your Knowledge

1. Assignment of rents allows
   a. the lender to take possession of a foreclosed property and collect rent from any tenants
   b. the owner in default to continue to collect rents from any tenants on property until all payments are caught up
   c. the tenants of a foreclosed property to forego paying rent, as the owner no longer has control of the building.
   d. none of the above.

2. Who is responsible for foreclosing a property in the event of default on the loan?
   a. Trustor
   b. Trustee
   c. Lender
   d. Courts

3. What is the redemption period?
   a. The time during which junior lien holders or the mortgagee's successors may repurchase a property after a foreclosure sale.
   b. The act of seeking a personal judgment against the person defaulting on the promissory note.
   c. The time by which a bidder must pay the amount in full for the property he or she is purchasing.
   d. The time between the notice of sale and the actual sale of the foreclosed property.

4. Which of the following are benefits of a trust deed to the lender?
   a. No redemption after foreclosure
   b. Trust deeds never expire
   c. Short foreclosure process
   d. All of the above

5. Which of the following is not a method of foreclosure?
   a. Nonjudicial
   b. Strict
   c. Sheriff
   d. Judicial

6. A non-judicial foreclosure is also known as
   a. reconveyance.
   b. power of sale.
   c. deficiency judgment.
   d. trustees sale.

7. Which of the following liens is not eliminated in a foreclosure?
   a. Junior lien
   b. Property tax lien
   c. First trust deed
   d. None of the above

California Real Estate Finance

INTRODUCTION

When a consumer enters into an agreement to buy real property, he or she normally pays a small portion of the price as a down payment and borrows the rest of the money, usually from a mortgage lender. The borrower then executes a **promissory note** and either a **trust deed** or **mortgage** to secure the loan.

The interest of a **creditor** (lender) in the property of a **debtor** (borrower) is called the security interest, with the trust deed or mortgage as evidence of that security interest. The security interest allows the creditor to sell the identified property if the borrower defaults on the loan. Proceeds from the sale of that property can be taken to pay off the debt. The rights and duties of lenders and borrowers are described in a document called a **security instrument**. In California, and other states mentioned below, trust deeds are the principal instruments used to secure loans on real property.

Mortgages accomplish the same thing as trust deeds, and are used in some states as security for real property loans. You will hear the term mortgage used loosely in California and other trust deed states, as in "mortgage company", "mortgage broker" and "mortgage payment"—but the "mortgage" referred to really is a trust deed.

TRUST DEEDS

California is one of only 14 states that use trust deeds as security for a promissory note. As we have learned, if a borrower defaults on a loan, the lender may instruct the trustee to foreclose the property in an effort to raise the necessary funds to pay off the promissory note. Foreclosing on a trust deed generally takes less than four months. We will examine this in detail later in this chapter.

In a previous chapter, we learned about liens, and how they attach to property. There are liens that are voluntary and liens that are involuntary. A trust deed is a voluntary lien assumed by the homeowner. Once the trust deed is recorded, a lien is placed on the property, securing the note.

Under the **power of sale clause**, the lender gives the trustee the right to sell the property in the event the homeowner defaults on the note. The power of sale clause allows the trustee to foreclose, sell and then convey the property to a new buyer, using the proceeds of the sale to repay the promissory note. Additionally, if the person who purchased the property intended it for rental, the lender may take possession of the property and collect any rents the property may bring in.

Trust deeds may be difficult to understand if you are unfamiliar with the terminology used to describe a trust deed. So, let's make sure you are clear on the different parties involved in a trust deed and the names by which those parties are commonly called.

Financial institutions or private investors lending money are referred to as either the **lender** or **beneficiary**. This person or institution will receive monthly payments on the promissory note. The lender holds both the trust deed to the property and the promissory note.

The person wishing to purchase a home and who makes the promissory note is called the **borrower** or **trustor**. The trustor approaches the lender and requests a trust deed in the amount of the difference between the down payment and the purchase price of a property. The trustor is allowed to take possession of the property, but does not take possession of the title until the note is paid in full. The trustor does, however, hold equitable title in the property immediately.

The neutral third party who holds **bare legal** title is known as the **trustee**. The trustee is responsible for reconveyance of the property's deed upon paying off the promissory note, or foreclosing on the property (if the homeowner defaults on his or her loan). Bare legal title refers to either the reconveyance or foreclosure. The trustee does not have any rights to the property and can only reconvey the deed or foreclose on the property when instructed to do so by the lender.

Remember
- Beneficiary = the lender
- Trustor = the borrower
- Trustee = the neutral third party holding bare legal title to the property

The biggest difference between a mortgage and a trust deed is the conveyance of title to a trustee. As mentioned above, the trustee holds bare legal title to the property. The trustor basically owns the property, but he or she does not hold the deed to the property until the promissory note is paid in full.

Remember

- An "assignment of rents" clause allows the lender to take possession of the property and collect any rents being paid if the borrower should default on the loan

- A "power of sale" clause gives the trustee, or lender, the right to foreclose on the property and sell the property to another purchaser if the borrower should default on the loan.

Trust

The trust will allow the trustee to either foreclose on the property or reconvey the deed back to the trustor at the time the promissory note is paid in full. The trustee acts on the directions given him or her by the beneficiary. If the property is to be foreclosed, the beneficiary will direct the trustee to do so. If the note has been paid in full, the beneficiary signs the note and instructs the trustee to deliver it to the trustor. To illustrate the extent of the power that a trustee has, the trustee usually does not know that reconveyance or foreclosure is happening - until it is requested by the lender.

When a note is paid in full, the trustee will receive the original note and trust deed from the lender. The trustee is instructed to record the conveyance (along with any fees associated with the recording of the deed) within 21 days of receiving the original note and deed. The reconveyance deed given to the trustor is recorded, to give public notice that the note against the property has been paid in full.

The original trust deed must be signed by the borrower, so that it may be recorded in the county where the property is located. The purpose of recording the trust deed is to publicly announce that there is a lien on the property (in the event the property might be sold or transferred to another individual before the promissory note is paid in full). After the trust deed is recorded, it goes back to the lender, who will hold the trust deed for the life of the loan.

In the event that a trustor defaults on his or her loan obligation, the beneficiary has the option to request a trustee's sale or a judicial foreclosure. Either action may be chosen to dispose of the property and receive the necessary funds to repay the note and all fees. However, there is a 4-year statute of limitations on judicial foreclosure. The power of sale in a trust deed never expires, and the property can be sold at any time to satisfy the debt. The trustee's sale is made possible via the trust instrument (the deed itself). To initiate the trustee's sale, the beneficiary must notify the trustee of the reason for default by filing a declaration of default. The beneficiary must attach the original note and trust deed in the declaration of default.

There are a few guidelines that must be followed for a notice of default to be valid. For instance, the first statement of the notice must be printed in bold type. The notice must also clearly state that the entire amount of the note is due upon the sale as the result of default. Otherwise, the amount cannot be collected upon sale of the property. The statement must also be in Spanish if either the trustor requests it, or if the original note and trust deed were negotiated in Spanish.

The notice of default must be sent via certified or registered mail. Recipients of the notice are: the trustor; junior lien holders; State Controller, if necessary; all parties who have filed a request for notice with the county recorder's office; and any successor in interest to the trustor. In the event that there are other parties involved (other than the original trustor), the notice must be published in a newspaper of general circulation once each week for four weeks.

If there has been a notice of default filed against a trustor, the trustor can reinstate the note. The trustor may only do so if all overdue payments have been made prior to five business days before the date of sale. A notice of trustee sale will be given, no later than three months after the notice of default, and the trustor has until five days before this sale to clear the overdue payments on the note. If the trustor cannot, or has not, made the necessary payments, the sale will happen as scheduled.

Requirements for a trustee's sale

- Written notice of default including the amount delinquent must be issued via certified mail
- A Notice of Trustee's Sale must be issued within three months of the notice of default
- Trustor may reinstate the note if all payments are made within five days of the trustee's sale
- Notice of the trustee's sale must run in a general circulation paper once each week for four weeks
- All sales are final, and there is no right of redemption
- There is no deficiency judgment allowed in a trustee's sale
- An unlawful detainer must be used to evict any previous property owner who refuses to vacate the property

Upon sale of the property, the beneficiary will accept payments in the form of cash or cashier's check. Any other forms of payment must be mentioned as optional payment methods in the notice of trustee sale. When selling the property at a trustee sale, the purchaser takes possession immediately. The trustor who was in default has no right of redemption after the sale is final. This is distinctly different from a judicial foreclosure.

If, after a trustee's sale, the former owner refuses to give up possession of the property, the new owner must obtain an unlawful detainer. An unlawful detainer is a court order, directing the sheriff to evict the present occupant. It is a risk that the bidder must factor into the process if purchasing property at a trustee sale.

With no right of redemption, the lender's risk in the promissory note is minimized. If the borrower defaults, the lender is usually paid in full with the proceeds from the trustee's sale. This is true despite the fact that a power of sale prohibits a deficiency judgment. In a deficiency judgment, the lender may seek a personal judgment against the trustor for any amount or fees not covered by the sale of the property.

Once a trustor pays off his or her promissory note in full, the lender delivers the original trust deed and note to the trustee. The trustee is directed to issue a deed of reconveyance to the trustor and to record this reconveyance with the county recorder's office. The original deed and trust may be delivered to the trustor with a written request from the trustor for the original deed. It is important that the lender remembers to clear the title to the trustor's property. If the lender does not clear the title, he or she may be subject to civil and criminal penalties. A trustee is obligated to carry out all reconveyances and recordings, or the trustee may be penalized.

JUNIOR TRUST DEEDS

California is known, nationwide, for having one of the most expensive housing markets. Properties appreciate very quickly, leaving lucky homeowners with quite a bit of equity in their homes. For first-time homebuyers, this creates a challenge. The challenge is trying to save enough money for a down payment while securing a loan large enough to cover the purchase price of the home. Often, the amount of the down payment plus the loan will not cover the entire cost of the house. In such cases, the homeowner needs to take a second trust deed. These secondary loans or trust deeds are called **junior trust deeds**. A junior trust deed is recorded after the first deed, and is secured by taking out a second deed on the home. There are three ways to obtain a junior trust deed: seller financing; outside financing; and home equity loans.

Three ways to obtain a junior trust deed

1. Seller financing
2. Outside financing
3. Home equity loans

When a buyer finds that he or she is not able to afford a home by paying only the down payment plus the first trust deed, he or she must seek alternative financing. One way for a seller to obtain the necessary funds through a junior trust deed is by seller financing. **Seller financing** occurs when the seller of the property makes a secondary loan to the buyer, and records this loan only after the first trust deed is recorded. In these cases, the seller becomes the lender and will receive either a monthly or another installment payment to satisfy the debt. The act of the seller making a junior trust deed is sometimes referred to as "**carrying back**."

The loan a seller provides to a buyer is considered a purchase money loan, as it is intended for one purpose (that is, to cover any funds needed for the purchase of the property). It not only works in favor of the buyer, but also in favor of the seller. If the seller has sold his or her home for an amount substantially more than the original purchase price, and thus stands to make a large gain, the seller can use some of this additional money as part of the junior trust deed, to avoid a large tax liability. The seller is at an advantage because he or she can accept monthly payments and avoid paying capital gains on a large sum of money received all at once.

The idea of a seller financing a portion of the loan may be a bit confusing. After all, financial professionals are educated and are presumed to know more about interest rates, payment schedules and the technical aspects of a loan. The second trust deed that a seller may provide to a buyer must be negotiated between both the buyer and seller. There are no banks involved; it is simply an agreement between the two parties. The buyer and seller agree upon the interest rate, how the loan will be paid, whether it will be in monthly installments, quarterly, etc., with no payments at all, or with a large lump sum due after a specific amount of time. In addition, the buyer and seller decide if the loan will be a straight note, partially amortized or fully amortized. After all terms of the loan have been discussed and agreed upon, instructions will be carried through the escrow process.

Once a seller makes a secondary trust deed to a buyer, the seller is not bound to the loan until it is paid off. If the seller chooses to sell the secondary trust deed, he or she may sell it to an investor or to a mortgage broker. The mortgage broker will purchase the note and junior trust deed at a discounted rate. This means that the loan will be sold for less than the buyer owes the original seller. The advantage to the seller is that he or she will be repaid immediately, even if he or she is not receiving the full amount of the loan.

> *Example*
> *Deborah wishes to sell her home and puts it on the market for $400,000. Because of the neighborhood and economic conditions, the home sell fast, for the asking price. The buyer offers a 10% down payment, or $40,000, and secures a new first loan for $320,000. Deborah agrees to make a loan to the buyer in the amount of $40,000 (so the transaction will go through, and Deborah will be able to move into her new home). Immediately after escrow closes and Deborah moves into her new home, she finds that her monthly payment is quite a bit harder to make than she originally thought. She chooses to sell the loan and junior trust deed to a mortgage broker, to cash out and use the money to make her own home payments. She finds an investor willing to purchase the loan at a 10% discount. This means that she immediately receives $36,000 for the loan (which is $4,000 less than made originally). However, it also means she will be able to make her monthly payment with no problem.*

There are, of course, disclosure statements that must be signed by the buyer and seller in a transaction where the seller provides a junior trust deed. These disclosures are required by law, and provide both the buyer and seller with all the appropriate information to make an educated decision regarding this type of financing. The disclosure statements will allow the seller to see if the buyer is financially able to make the payment, and find out his or her credit rating. This is very important information for the seller, to help determine if the loan is feasible, and if it will be paid back in a timely manner. The buyer can see which loans are currently taking precedence over the junior trust deed that would potentially be created. A real estate professional can be used to arrange credit, to ensure all laws regarding the transaction have been followed.

A trust deed turns out to be an attractive alternative to a mortgage in some states. In locales where trust deeds are used, the benefits to both lender and borrower are numerous.

Benefits of a Trust Deed to a Lender

- No redemption after foreclosure
- Short foreclosure process
- In the event of default, the lender takes possession of the property and has the right to collect rents
- Trust deeds never expire
- The trustee, or lender, holds title and can easily grant title to a buyer at a foreclosure sale

Whether a trust deed or mortgage is used to secure a promissory note, both lender and borrower have the full power of the law, depending on which state the property is in, to enforce their rights regarding repayment of a debt.

Benefits of a Trust Deed to a Borrower

- The only security the borrower is required to give for the loan is the property itself, and there are no deficiency judgments allowed. In the event of foreclosure, the borrower will only lose the property in question, and no other assets.

Upon the trustor paying off the note in full, the trustee will

- Receive the original trust deed and note from the lender, and sign these documents
- Issue a deed of reconveyance to the trustor
- Clear the title to the property of all encumbrances related to the trust deed
- Record the reconveyance at the county recorder's office

Not all states use the trust deed as a security instrument. Other states use mortgages. Surely most of us are more familiar with the term "mortgage" and understand its concept. The trust deed essentially serves the same function, with some differences. The following states primarily use trust deeds as the basic security instrument

- Alaska
- Arizona
- California
- Colorado
- District of Columbia
- Idaho
- Maryland

- Mississippi
- North Carolina
- Oregon
- Tennessee
- Texas
- Virginia
- West Virginia

Other states use partial trust deeds. Those states include

- Alabama
- Delaware
- Hawaii
- Illinois
- Montana

- Nevada
- New Mexico
- Utah
- Washington
- Nevada

The terms "mortgage" and "trust deed" are often used synonymously, though this is a mistake. Mortgages and trust deeds basically function in the same way. They secure a note so that the buyer or borrower may obtain property and use it (per the mortgage or trust deed) as security for the note. However, there are distinct differences between mortgages and trust deeds, as you will see in this section.

REQUEST FOR FULL RECONVEYANCE

A Full Reconveyance will be issued only when original note or notes, together with the Deed of Trust securing payment thereof, are surrendered to the Trustee for cancellation, accompanied by this Request signed by all owners of the note or notes, together with the reconveyance fee.

Date _____ , 19 ____

The undersigned Beneficiary is the legal owner and holder of the _____ promissory

note _____ for the total sum of $ _____ and all other indebtedness secured by

Deed of Trust dated _____ , 19 ____ executed by _____

_____ , Trustor, to _____

_____ , Trustee, and recorded _____ , 19 ____

as Instrument No. _____ , in Book _____ Page _____

of Official Records in the office of the Recorder of _____ County, State of California. You are notified hereby that said note or notes and all other indebtedness secured by said Deed of Trust have been fully paid, and said note or notes and the said Deed of Trust the herewith surrendered to you for cancellation. You are therefore requested, upon payment to you of all sums owing to you under the terms of said Deed of Trust, to reconvey, without warranty to the "person or persons legally entitled thereto," the estate now held by you and acquired through said Deed of Trust.

Mail recorded reconveyance to:

_____   _____

_____   _____

_____   _____

0-57

A mortgage is similar to a trust, in that it is an instrument that secures payment of a debt. In our situation, the property itself is the security for the promissory note (evidenced by the presence of a mortgage). The mortgage will create a lien on the property. If the property owner (or mortgager) defaults on the note, the mortgagee (or lender), may utilize a **judicial foreclosure**, which is court-ordered. There is another method of foreclosure called a **power-of-sale provision**, which functions much like the trustee's sale in a trust.

In a judicial foreclosure, the court will order the property to be sold to satisfy the debt against it. The sale must occur in the county where the property or the majority of the property is located. The property is sold in a manner similar to public auction; that is, the property will go to the highest bidder. A sheriff or court-appointed commissioner will oversee the sale to ensure the sale is carried out properly. Just as in a trustee's sale, proper notice is required before conducting a judicial foreclosure.

The person who places the highest bid is required to place a deposit on the property, with full payment due within 10 days of the sale. The deposit for a property selling for more than $5,000.00 is the greater of either $5,000.00 or 10% of the selling bid. Any bidder who chooses to make a deposit, with the full amount due later, is also responsible for any interest that may accrue on the property during that time. In the event that the person who won the bid defaults on payment, the property sale will be held again. Those people who successfully win the bid, but are not able to pay for the property, may be held liable for any costs of the original sale, plus attorney fees, interest and the difference, if any, between the original bid and the new bid. Sale may also be postponed if there are no satisfactory bids.

If the sale was a success, and the bidder paid the full amount he or she bid for the property, the commissioner or sheriff will issue the purchaser a certificate of sale. The new property owner should record this document immediately to both protect his or her interest in the property, and prevent claims made as such.

Once the property is sold, proceeds from the sale will be used to pay off the note on the house. Once the note is paid, any remaining proceeds will be distributed to any lienholders in order of priority (i.e., the order in which the lien was recorded). If there is any money remaining from the sale of the property once all debts against it have been paid, the remaining proceeds will be given to the mortgagor. The best case scenario is when all debts have been paid and the mortgagor receives the remaining amount, though this is not always the case. In some situations, the proceeds of the sale will not be sufficient to pay off the mortgagee. At that time, the mortgagee may seek a deficiency judgment against the mortgagor for the remaining debt. A mortgagee may NOT seek a deficiency judgment against a mortgagor if the mortgagee was the original seller of the property to the mortgagor. A mortgager may also seek a deficiency judgment if the loan was used to pay all or part of the purchase price of an owner-occupied residential dwelling consisting of no more than four units.

The mortgagee can reinstate the mortgage if he or she makes all delinquent payments plus any costs incurred during the foreclosure proceedings.

Judicial foreclosures are very time-consuming. First, it takes many months before the sale is held. At that time, the person who purchases the property receives only a certificate of sale. The purchaser does not take possession of the property at this time, as that occurs only after the statutory **redemption period**. The statutory redemption period is the amount of time following the sale of a property when the former owner's heirs or successors may buy back the property. This redemption period must be taken into account by the purchaser of the property when making a bid. In fact, there is a chance the purchaser will never take possession of the property.

Steps in a Judicial Foreclosure

- Court orders the sheriff or commissioner to sell the property

- Judicial sale is held, and creditors may seek a deficiency judgment in the event the sale does not raise enough money to cover the debt against the property

- Certificate of sale is issued to the purchaser of the property

- Redemption period must be satisfied before purchaser takes possession of the property

The old rule regarding the redemption period (for mortgages that were assumed before July 1, 1983) allowed junior lienholders to also buy back the property. The stipulation was that junior lienholders had to act within 3 months of the sale of the property if the proceeds of the sale were enough to cover all costs and interest. The redemption period for all others with an interest in the property is one year, unless the mortgagee waives his or her right to this time period, or is prohibited from obtaining a deficiency judgment. Since this is the old rule for mortgages made prior to July 1, 1983, it is advisable to consult an attorney for all foreclosures made after this time.

A mortgage is held by the lender for the life of a loan, or until the borrower pays it off. There are some similarities to a trust deed, and some differences, as we shall see in the following examination of mortgages.

A mortgage may create a lien on real property or give actual **title** to the lender, depending on the laws of the state where the property is located. Title may be vested in the borrower, or—like a trust deed where a deed of trust gives title (bare legal title) to a trustee—to the lender. In both cases, possession of the property remains with the borrower.

The **Statute of Limitations** runs out on a note secured by a mortgage in four years. This means a lender must sue within four years of nonpayment to get his or her money back.

Under a mortgage, a borrower in default may reinstate the loan by paying all delinquencies, plus all costs of the foreclosure action, at any time before the court approves the foreclosure.

Upon the payment in full of a mortgage, the lender will deliver the original note and mortgage to the party making the request. When the mortgage is released and delivered, it should be recorded so that there is public record of the encumbrance being paid in full.

Trust Deed vs. Mortgage

The major differences between a trust deed and mortgage are

- Number of parties involved in the process
- Statute of Limitations
- Available upon default
- Conveyance of the title
- Reinstatement period
- Deficiency judgment
- Redemption period
- Procedure following satisfaction of the debt

The trust deed offers lenders a bit more security in their investment. The trust deed allows the lender a faster and cheaper way to get its money back, in the event the trustor defaults on the note. There is also no guarantee that there will be bidders at a foreclosure sale. In such cases, the lender will be forced to purchase the property back from the owner. This is an undesirable scenario for any lender.

FORECLOSURE UNDER A TRUST DEED

Foreclosure is the unfortunate event that happens when a borrower is unable to repay his or her loan to a lender, and falls behind on payments. If the payments have been delinquent for an extended period, the lender is able to foreclose on the property. Remember, the property itself is used as security or collateral for the promissory note as evidenced by the trust deed. So, the lender is able to sell the property to repay the debt against it. This not only pays back the lender for the promissory note against the property, but may also pay other liens encumbering the property.

Trust deeds can be foreclosed by a trustee's sale or through judicial action as determined by the courts. Mortgages, however, require judicial foreclosures. Since California primarily uses trust deeds, we will focus our attention on the trustee's sale in this section, while discussing judicial foreclosure, or foreclosure under a mortgage, in the next section.

In a deed of trust, you will remember, there are three parties involved. These parties are the lender, the borrower (or trustor) and the trustee (or third party holding bare legal title to the property). The trustee is the one called upon in the event of foreclosure. The trustee will conduct a **trustee's sale**, which is the most common way to foreclose on property utilizing a trust deed. The trustee is given the power of sale by the buyer when the buyer signs the trust deed at closing. A trustee's sale is the fastest way for property to be foreclosed, as there is no right of redemption after the sale, and deficiency judgments are not allowed against the trustor.

Application Number:

DEED OF TRUST

THIS DEED OF TRUST is made this day of **November 15, 2002**, among the Trustor,
and   HUSBAND AND WIFE, TRUSTEES OF THE   FAMILY TRUST
DATED MAY 10, 2001, whose mailing address is the property address (herein "Borrower"), and FIRST
BANKER TITLE INSURANCE COMPANY whose mailing address is 1 FIRST BANKER   WAY, ,
YOURTOWN, CA 00000, (herein "Trustee"), and the Beneficiary,   **Good Bank of Anywhere, National
Association**, a national banking association organized and existing under the laws of the United States
of America, whose address is One George Circle, 000 Banker Street, Yourtown, CA 00000   (herein
"Lender").

WHEREAS, Borrower is indebted to Lender in the principal sum of U.S. **$349,300.00**, which indebtedness
is evidenced by Borrower's note dated **November 15, 2002** and extensions, modifications and renewals
thereof (herein "Note"), providing for monthly installments of principal and interest, with the balance of
indebtedness, if not sooner paid, due and payable on **December 01, 2032**;

TO SECURE to Lender the repayment of the indebtedness evidenced by the Note, with interest thereon;
the payment of all other sums, with interest thereon, advanced in accordance herewith to protect the
security of this Deed of Trust; and the performance of the covenants and agreements of Borrower herein
contained, Borrower does hereby grant and convey to Trustee in trust with power of sale the following
described property located in the County of **COUNTY**, State of **CALIFORNIA**:

SEE ATTACHED SCHEDULE A.

Parcel No. 000-00-000 which has the address of   (herein
"Property Address");

CA Deed of Trust   Page 1

TOGETHER with all the improvements now or hereafter erected on the property, and all easements, rights, appurtenances and rents all of which shall be deemed to be and remain a part of the property covered by this Deed of Trust; and all of the foregoing, together with said property (or the leasehold estate if this Deed of Trust is on a leasehold) are hereinafter referred to as the "Property."

Any Rider ("Rider") attached hereto and executed of even date is incorporated herein and the covenant and agreements of the Rider shall amend and supplement the covenants and agreements of this Deed of Trust, as if the Rider were a part hereof.

Borrower covenants that Borrower is lawfully seized of the estate hereby conveyed and has the right to grant and convey the Property, and that the Property is unencumbered, except for encumbrances of record. Borrower covenants that Borrower warrants and will defend generally the title to the Property against all claims and demands, subject to encumbrances of record.

UNIFORM COVENANTS. Borrower and Lender covenant and agree as follows:

1. Payment of Principal and Interest. Borrower shall promptly pay when due the principal and interest indebtedness evidenced by the Note and late charges as provided in the Note. This Deed of Trust secures payment of said Note according to its terms, which are incorporated herein by reference.

2. Prior Mortgages and Deeds of Trust; Charges; Liens. Borrower shall perform all of Borrower's obligations, under any mortgage, deed of trust or other security agreement with a lien which has priority over this Deed of Trust, including Borrower's covenants to make payments when due. Borrower shall pay or cause to be paid all taxes, assessments and other charges, fines and impositions attributable to the Property which may attain a priority over this Deed of Trust, and leasehold payments or ground rents, if any.

3. Hazard Insurance. a) Borrower shall keep the improvements now existing or hereafter erected on the Property insured against loss by fire, hazards included within the term "extended coverage", and any other hazards, including floods or flood, for which Lender requires insurance. This insurance shall be maintained in the amounts and for the periods that Lender requires. The insurance carrier providing the insurance shall be chosen by Borrower subject to Lender's approval which shall not be unreasonably withheld. If Borrower fails to maintain coverage described above, Lender may, at Lender's option, obtain coverage to protect Lender's rights in the Property in accordance with paragraph 5.

b) All insurance policies and renewals shall be acceptable to Lender and shall include a standard mortgagee clause. Lender shall have the right to hold the policies and renewals. If Lender requires, Borrower shall promptly give to Lender all receipts of paid premiums and renewal notices. In the event of loss, Borrower shall give prompt notice to the insurance carrier and Lender. Lender may make proof of loss if not made promptly to Borrower.

c) Unless Lender and Borrower otherwise agree in writing, insurance proceeds shall be applied to restoration or repair of the Property damaged, if the restoration or repair is economically feasible and Lender's security is not lessened. If the restoration or repair is not economically feasible or Lender's security would be lessened, the insurance proceeds shall be applied to the sums secured by this Security Instrument, whether or not then due, with any excess paid to Borrower. If Borrower abandons the Property or does not answer within 30 days a notice from Lender that the insurance carrier has offered to settle a claim, then Lender may collect the insurance proceeds. Lender may use the proceeds to repair or restore the Property or to pay sums secured by this Security Instrument, whether or not then due. The 30-day period will begin when the notice is given.

d) Except as provided in subparagraph 3(e) below, should partial or complete destruction or damage occur to the Property, Borrower hereby agrees that any and all instruments evidencing insurance proceeds received by Lender as a result of said damage or destruction, shall be placed in a non-interest bearing escrow account with Lender. At Lender's discretion, Lender may release some or all of the proceeds from escrow after Borrower presents Lender with a receipt(s), invoice(s), written estimates(s) or other document(s) acceptable to Lender which relates to the repair and/or improvements of the Property necessary as a result of said damage and/or destruction. Absent an agreement to the contrary, Lender shall not be required to pay Borrower any interest on the proceeds held in the escrow account. Any amounts remaining in the account after all repairs and/or improvements have been made to the Lender's satisfaction, shall be applied to the sums secured by this Deed of Trust, Deed to Secure Debt, or Mortgage. Borrower further agrees to cooperate with Lender by endorsing all, checks, drafts and/or other instruments evidencing insurance proceeds; and any necessary documents. Should Borrower fail to provide any required endorsement and/or execution within thirty (30) days after Lender sends borrower notice that Lender has received an instrument evidencing insurance proceeds, or document(s) requiring Borrower's signature, Borrower hereby authorizes Lender to endorse said instrument and/or document(s) on Borrowers behalf, and collect and apply said proceeds at Lender's option, either to restoration or repair of the Property or to sums secured by this Deed of Trust, Deed to Secure Debt, or Mortgage. It is not the intention of either party that this escrow provision, and/or Lender's endorsement or execution of an instrument(s) and/or document(s) on behalf of Borrower create a fiduciary or agency relationship between Lender and Borrower.

e) Unless Lender and Borrower otherwise agree in writing, any application of proceeds to principal shall not extend or postpone the due date of the monthly payments referred to in paragraph 1 or change the amount of the payments. If under paragraph 15 the Property is acquired by Lender, Borrower's right to any insurance policies and proceeds resulting from damage to the property prior to the acquisition shall pass to Lender to the extent of the sums secured by this Security Instrument.

4. Preservation and Maintenance of Property; Leaseholds; Condominiums; Planned Unit Developments. Borrower shall keep the Property in good repair and shall not commit waste or permit impairment or deterioration of the Property and shall comply with the provisions of any lease if this Deed of Trust is on a leasehold. If this Deed of Trust is on a unit in a condominium or a planned unit development, Borrower shall perform all of Borrower's obligations under the declaration or covenants creating or governing the condominium or planned unit development, the by-laws and regulations of the condominium or planned unit development, and constituent documents.

5. Protection of Lender's Security. If Borrower fails to perform the covenants and agreements contained in this Deed of Trust, or if any action or proceeding is commenced which materially affects Lender's interest in the Property, then Lender, at Lender's option, upon notice to Borrower, may make such appearances, disburse such sums, including reasonable attorneys' fees, and take such actions as is necessary to protect Lender's interest.

Any amounts disbursed by Lender pursuant to this paragraph 5, with interest thereon from the date of disbursal, at the Note rate, shall become additional indebtedness of Borrower secured by this Deed of Trust. Unless Borrower and Lender agree to other terms of payment, such amounts shall be payable upon notice from Lender to Borrower requesting payment thereof. Nothing contained in this paragraph 5 shall require Lender to incur any expense or take any action hereunder.

6. Inspection. Lender may make or cause to be made reasonable entries upon and inspections of the Property, provided that Lender shall give Borrower notice prior to any such inspection specifying reasonable cause therefore related to Lender's interest in the Property.

7. Condemnation. The proceeds of any award or claim for damages, direct or consequential, in connection with any condemnation or other taking of the Property, or part thereof, or for conveyance in lieu of condemnation, are hereby assigned and shall be paid to Lender subject to the terms of any mortgage, deed of trust or other security agreement with a lien which has priority over this Deed of Trust.

8. Borrower Not Released; ForbearanceBy Lender Not a Waiver. The Borrower shall remain liable for full payment of the principal and interest on the Note (or any advancement or obligation) secured hereby, notwithstanding any of the following: (a) the sale of all or a part of the premises, (b) the assumption by another party of the Borrower's obligations hereunder, (c) the forbearance or extension of time for payment or performance of any obligation hereunder, whether granted to Borrower or a subsequent owner of the property, and (d) the release of all or any part of the premises securing said obligations or the release of any party who assumes payment of the same. None of the foregoing shall in any way affect the full force and effect of the lien of this Deed of Trust or impair Lender's right to a deficiency judgment (in the event of foreclosure) against Borrower or any party assuming the obligations hereunder, to the extent permitted by applicable law.

Any forbearance by Lender in exercising any right or remedy hereunder, or otherwise afforded by applicable law, shall not be a waiver of or preclude the exercise of any such right or remedy.

9. Successors and Assigns Bound; Joint and Several Liability; Co-signers. Borrower covenants and agrees that Borrower's obligations and liability shall be joint and several. However, any Borrower who co-signs this Security Instrument but does not execute the Note (a "co-signer"): (a) is co-signing this Security Instrument only to mortgage, grant and convey the co-signer's interest in the Property under the terms of this Security Instrument; (b) is not personally obligated to pay the sums secured by this Security Instrument; and (c) agrees that Lender and any other Borrower can agree to extend, modify, forbear or make any accommodations with regard to the terms of this Security Instrument or the Note without the co-signer's consent.

Subject to the provisions of Section 14, any Successor in Interest of Borrower who assumes Borrower's obligations under this Security Instrument in writing, and is approved by Lender, shall obtain all of Borrower's rights and benefits under this Security Instrument. Borrower shall not be released from Borrower's obligations and liability under this Security Instrument unless Lender agrees to such release in writing. The covenants and agreements of this Security Instrument shall bind and benefit the successors and assigns of Lender.

10. Notice. Except for any notice required under applicable law to be given in another manner, (a) any notice to Borrower provided for in this Deed of Trust shall be given by delivering it or by mailing such notice by first class mail addressed to Borrower or the current owner at the Property Address or at such other address as Borrower may designate in writing by notice to Lender as provided herein, and any other person personally liable on this Note as these person's names and addresses appear in the Lender's records at the time of giving notice and (b) any notice to Lender shall be given by first class mail to Lender's address stated herein or to such other address as Lender may designate by notice to Borrower as provided herein. Any notice provided for in this Deed of Trustshall be deemed to have been given to Borrower or Lender when given in the manner designated herein.

11. Governing Law; Severability. The state and local laws applicable to this Deed of Trust shall be the laws of the jurisdiction in which the Property is located. The foregoing sentence shall not limit the applicability of Federal law to this Deed of Trust. In the event that any provision or clause of this Deed of Trust or the Note conflicts with applicable law, such conflicts shall not affect other provisions of this Deed of Trust or the Note which can be given effect without the conflicting provision, and to this end the provisions of this Deed of Trust and the Note are declared to be severable. As used herein "costs", "expenses" and "attorneys' fees" include all sums to the extent not prohibited by applicable law or limited herein.

12. Borrower's Copy. Borrower shall be furnished a conformed copy of the Note, this Deed of Trust and Rider(s) at the time of execution or after recordation hereof.

13. Rehabilitation Loan Agreement. Borrower shall fulfill all of Borrower's obligations under any home rehabilitation, improvement, repair or other loan agreement which Borrower enters into with Lender.

CA Deed of Trust
Page 4

Lender, at Lender's option, may require Borrower to execute and deliver to Lender, in a form acceptable to Lender, an assignment of any rights, claims or defenses which Borrower may have against parties who supply labor, materials or services in connection with improvements made to the Property.

14. Transfer of the Property or a Beneficial Interest in Borrower, Assumption. As used in this Section 14, "Interest in the Property" means any legal or beneficial interest in the Property, including, but not limited to, those beneficial interests transferred in a bond for deed, contract for deed, installment sales contract or escrow agreement, the intent of which is the transfer of title by Borrower at a future date to a purchaser.

If all or any part of the Property or any Interest in the Property is sold or transferred (or if Borrower is not a natural person and a beneficial interest in Borrower is sold or transferred) without Lender's prior written consent, Lender may require immediate payment in full of all sums secured by this Security Instrument. However, this option shall not be exercised by Lender if such exercise is prohibited by federal law.

If Lender exercises this option, Lender shall give Borrower notice of acceleration. The notice shall provide a period of not less than 30 days from the date the notice is given in accordance with Section 10 within which Borrower must pay all sums secured by this Security Instrument. If Borrower fails to pay these sums prior to the expiration of this period, Lender may invoke any remedies by this Security Instrument without further notice or demand on Borrower.

15. Default Acceleration; Remedies. If any, monthly installment under the Note is not paid when due, of if Borrower should be in default under any provision of this Deed of Trust, or if Borrower is in default under any other Deed of Trust or other instrument secured by the Property, the entire principal amount outstanding under the Note and this Deed of Trust and accrued interest thereon shall at once become due and payable at the option of Lender without prior notice and regardless of any prior forbearance. In such event, Lender, at its option, may then or thereafter deliver to the Trustee a written declaration of default and demand for sale and shall cause to be filed of record a written notice of default and of election to cause to be sold the Property. Lender shall also deposit with the Trustee this Deed of Trust and any Notes and all documents evidencing expenditure secured thereby. After the lapse of such time as then may be required by law following recordation of such notice of default, and notice of sale having been given as then required by law following recordation of such notice of default, that notice of sale having been given as then required by law, the Trustee, without demand on Borrower, shall sell the Property at the time and place specified by such Trustee in such notice of sale, or at the time to which such noticed sale has been duly postponed, at public auction to the highest bidder for cash in lawful money of the United States, payable at time of sale, except that Lender may offset his bid to the extent of the total amount owing to him under the Note and this Deed of Trust, including the Trustee's fees and expenses. The Trustee may sell the Property as a whole or in separate parcels if there is more than one parcel, subject to such rights as Borrower may have by law to direct the manner or order of sale, or by such other manner of sale which is authorized by law. The Trustee may postpone the time of sale of all or any portion of the Property by public declaration made by the Trustee at the time and place last appointed for sale.

The Trustee shall deliver to such purchaser its deed conveying the Property so sold, but without any covenant or warranty, express or implied. The recital in such deed of any matters of fact shall be conclusive proof of the truthfulness thereof. Any person, including Borrower, the Trustee or Lender may purchase the Property at such sale. After deducting all costs, fees and expenses of the Trustee, and of this Deed of Trust, including costs of evidence of title in connection with such sale, the Trustee first shall apply the proceeds of sale to payment of all sums expended under the terms of this Deed of Trust, not then repaid, with accrued interest at the rate then payable under the Note or Notes secured thereby, and then to payment of all other sums secured thereby and, if thereafter there be any proceeds remaining, shall distribute then to the person or persons legally entitled thereto.

(continued)

16. Borrower's Right to Reinstate. Notwithstanding Lender's acceleration of the sums secured by this Deed of Trust, Borrower shall have the right to have any proceedings begun by Lender to enforce this Deed of Trust discontinued if: (a) Borrower pays Lender all sums which would be then due under this Deed of Trust, this Note and Notes securing Future Advances, if any, had no acceleration occurred; (b) Borrower cures all breaches of any other covenants or agreements of Borrower contained in this Deed of Trust; (c) Borrower pays all reasonable expenses incurred by Lender and Trustee in enforcing the covenants and agreements of Borrower contained in this Deed of Trust, and in enforcing Lender's and Trustee's remedies as provided in Paragraph 15 hereof, including, but not limited to, reasonable attorneys' fees; and (d) Borrower takes such action, as Lender may reasonably require to assure that the lien of this Deed of Trust, Lender's interest in the Property and Borrower's obligation to pay the sums secured by this Deed of Trust shall continue unimpaired. Upon such payment and cure by Borrower, this Deed of Trust and the obligations secured hereby shall remain in full force and effect as if no acceleration had occurred.

17. Assignment of Rents; Appointment of Receiver. As additional security hereunder, Borrower hereby assigns to Lender the rents of the Property, provided that so long as Borrower is not in default hereunder, Borrower shall have the right to collect and retain such rents as they become due and payable.

Upon Borrower's default or abandonment of the Property, Lender, in person or by agent, shall be entitled to collect all rents directly from the payors thereof, or have a receiver appointed by a court to enter upon, take possession of and manage the Property and to collect the rents of the Property including those past due. All rents collected by the receiver shall be applied first to payment of the costs of management of the Property and collection of rents, including, but not limited to receiver's fees, premiums on receiver's bonds and reasonable attorneys' fees, and then to the sums secured by this Deed of Trust. The receiver shall be liable to account only for those rents actually received.

18. Loan Charges. If the loan secured by this Deed of Trust is subject to a law which sets maximum loan charges, and that law is finally interpreted so that the interest or other loan charges collected or to be collected in connection with the loan exceed permitted limits, then: (1) any such loan charge shall be reduced by the amount necessary to reduce the charge to the permitted limit; and (2) any sums already collected from Borrower which exceeded permitted limits will be refunded to Borrower. Lender may choose to make this refund by reducing the principal owed under the Note or by making a direct payment to Borrower. If a refund reduces principal, the reduction will be treated as a partial prepayment under the Note.

19. Legislation. If, after the date hereof, enactment or expiration of applicable laws have the effect either of rendering the provisions of the Note, the Deed of Trust or any Rider, unenforceable according to their terms, or all or any part of the sums secured hereby uncollectible, as otherwise provided in this Deed of Trust or the Note, or of diminishing the value of Lender's security, then Lender, at Lender's option, may declare all sums secured by the Deed of Trust to be immediately due and payable.

20. Satisfaction. Upon payment of all sums secured by this Deed of Trust, this Deed of Trust shall become null and void and Lender or Trustee shall release this Deed of Trust. If Trustee is requested to release this Deed of Trust, all instruments evidencing satisfaction of the indebtedness secured by this Deed of Trust shall be surrendered to Trustee. Borrower shall pay all costs of recordation, if any. Lender, at Lender's option, may allow a partial release of the Property on terms acceptable to Lender and Lender may charge a release fee.

21. Substitute Trustee. Lender may from time to time at Lender's discretion and without cause or notice, remove Trustee and appoint a Successor Trustee to any Trustee appointed hereunder. Without conveyance of the Property, the Successor Trustee shall succeed to all the title, power and duties conferred upon the Trustee herein and by applicable law.

CA Deed of Trust   Page 6

(continued)

22. Waiver of Homestead. Borrower hereby waives all rights of homestead exemption in the Property and relinquishes all marital property rights in the Property.

23. Hazardous Substances. Borrower shall not cause or permit the presence, use, disposal, storage, or release of any Hazardous Substances on or in the Property. Borrower shall not do, nor allow anyone else to do, anything affecting the Property that is in violation of any Environmental Law. The preceding two sentences shall not apply to the presence, use, or storage on the Property of small quantities of Hazardous Substances that are generally recognized to be appropriate to normal residential uses and to maintenance of the Property.

Borrower shall promptly give Lender written notice of any investigation, claim, demand, lawsuit, or other action by any governmental or regulatory agency or private party involving the Property and any Hazardous Substance or Environmental Law of which Borrower has actual knowledge. If Borrower learns, or is notified by any governmental or regulatory authority, that any removal, or other remediation of any Hazardous Substance affecting the Property is necessary, Borrower shall promptly take all necessary remedial actions in accordance with Environmental Law.

As used in this paragraph 23, "Hazardous Substances" are those substances defined as toxic or hazardous substances by Environmental Law and the following substances: gasoline, kerosene, other flammable or toxic petroleum products, toxic pesticides and herbicides, volatile solvents, materials containing asbestos or formaldehyde, and radioactive materials. As used in this paragraph 23, "Environmental law" means federal laws and laws of the jurisdiction where the Property is located that relate to health, safety, or environmental protection.

(continued)

IN WITNESS WHEREOF, Borrower has executed this Deed of Trust.

_____[SEAL]
      TRUSTEE OF THE   FAMILY TRUST DATED MAY 10, 2001

_____[SEAL]

_____[SEAL]
      TRUSTEE OF THE   FAMILY TRUST DATED MAY 10, 2001

_____[SEAL]

[Space Below This Line For Acknowledging]

STATE OF **CALIFORNIA**   )
) ss
COUNTY OF _____   )

On   (date) _____, _____ before   me
_____, (name & title of the officer), personally appeared
                             , TRUSTEE OF THE   FAMILY TRUST DATED MAY 10,
2001 personally known to me (or proved to me on the basis of satisfactory evidence) to be the person(s) whose name(s) is/are subscribed to the within instrument and acknowledged to me that he/she/they executed the same in his/her/their authorized capacity(ies), and that by his/her/their signature(s) on the instrument the person(s), or the entity upon behalf of which the person(s) acted, executed the instrument.

WITNESS my hand and official seal

Signature: _____ (SEAL)

My Commission Expires: _____

REQUEST FOR RECONVEYANCE

TO TRUSTEE:

The undersigned is the holder of the note or notes secured by this Deed of Trust. Said note or notes, together with all other indebtedness secured by this Deed of Trust, have been paid in full. You are hereby directed to cancel said note or notes and this Deed of Trust, which are delivered hereby, and to reconvey, without warranty, all the estate now held by you under this Deed of Trust to the person or persons legally entitled thereto.

Dated: _____   _____
                                                     Vice President

MORTGAGE

THIS INDENTURE, made as of the _____ day of _____, 20__, by and between _____, (Mortgagor), and _____, (Mortgagee).

AMOUNT OF LIEN:

WHEREAS, Mortgagor is justly indebted to Mortgagee in the sum of _____ dollars ($ _____) and has agreed to pay the same, with interest thereon, according to the terms of a certain note (Note) given by Mortgagor to Mortgagee, which is attached hereto as Exhibit A.

DESCRIPTION OF PROPERTY SUBJECT TO LIEN:

NOW, THEREFORE, in consideration of the premises and the sum set forth above, and to secure the payment of the Secured Indebtedness as defined herein, Mortgagor by these presents does grant, bargain, sell and convey unto Mortgagee the property located at _____, more particularly described as:

Together with all buildings, structures and other improvements now or hereafter located on, above or below the surface of the property; and,

Together with all the common elements appurtenant to any parcel, unit or lot which is all or part of the Premises; and,

ALL the foregoing ecumbered by this Mortgage being collectively referred to herein as the Premises;

TO HAVE AND TO HOLD the Premises hereby granted to the use, benefit and behalf of the Mortgagee, forever. Conditioned, however, that if Mortgagor shall promptly pay or cause to be paid to Mortgagee, at its address listed in the Note, or at such other place, which may hereafter be designated by Mortgagee, its successors or assigns, with interest, the principal sum of _____ dollars ($_____) with final maturity, if not sooner paid, as stated in said Note unless amended or extended according to the terms of the Note executed by Mortgagor and payable to the order of Mortgagee, then these presents shall cease and be void, otherwise these presents shall remain in full force and effect.

COVENANTS OF MORTGAGOR

Mortgagor covenants and agrees with Mortgagee as follows:

Secured Indebtedness. This Mortgage is given as security for the Note and also as security for any and all other sums, indebtedness, obligations and liabilities of any and every kind arising, under the Note or this Mortgage, as amended or modified or supplemented from time to time, and any and all renewals, modifications or extensions of any or all of the foregoing (all of which are collectively referred to herein as the Secured Indebtedness), the entire Secured Indebtedness being equally secured with and having the same priority as any amounts owed at the date hereof.

(continued on next page)

Performance of Note, Mortgage, Etc. Mortgagor shall perform, observe and comply with all provisions hereof and of the Note and shall promptly pay, in lawful money of the United States of America, to Mortgagee the Secured Indebtedness with interest thereon as provided in the Note, this Mortgage and all other documents constituting the Secured Indebtedness.

Extent Of Payment Other Than Principal And Interest. Mortgagor shall pay, when due and payable, (1) all taxes, assessments, general or special, and other charges levied on, or assessed, placed or made against the Premises, this instrument or the Secured Indebtedness or any interest of the Mortgagee in the Premises or the obligations secured hereby; (2) premiums on policies of fire and other haZard insurance covering the Premises, as required herein; (3) ground rents or other lease rentals; and (4) other sums related to the Premises or the indebtedness secured hereby, if any, payable by Mortgagor.

Care of Property. Mortgagor shall maintain the Premises in good condition and repair and shall not commit or suffer any material waste to the Premises.

Prior Mortgage. With regard to the Prior Mortgage, Mortgagor hereby agrees to: (1) Pay promptly, when due, all installments of principal and interest and all other sums and charges made payable by the Prior Mortgage; (2) Promptly perform and observe all of the terms, covenants and conditions required to be performed and observed by Mortgagor under the Prior Mortgage, within the period provided in said Prior Mortgage; (3) Promptly notify Mortgagee of any default, or notice claiming any event of default by Mortgagor in the performance or observance of any term, covenant or condition to be performed or observed by Mortgagor under any such Prior Mortgage. (4) Mortgagor will not request nor will it accept any voluntary future advances under the Prior

Mortgage without Mortgagee's prior written consent, which consent shall not be unreasonably withheld.

DEFAULTS

Default. The occurrence of any one of the following events which shall not be cured within _____ days after written notice of the occurrence of the event, if the default is monetary, or which shall not be cured within _____ days after written notice, if the default is non-monetary, shall constitute an Event of Default: (1) Mortgagor fails to pay the Secured Indebtedness, or any part thereof, or the taxes, insurance and other charges, as herein before provided, when and as the same shall become due and payable; (2) Any material warranty of Mortgagor herein contained, or contained in the Note, proves untrue or misleading in any material respect; (3) Mortgagor materially fails to keep, observe, perform, carry out and execute the covenants, agreements, obligations and conditions set out in this Mortgage, or in the Note; (4) Foreclosure proceedings (whether judicial or otherwise) are instituted on any mortgage or any lien of any kind secured by any portion of the Premises and affecting the priority of this Mortgage.

Upon the occurrence of any Event of Default, the Mortgagee may immediately do any one or more of the following: (1) Declare the total Secured Indebtedness, including without limitation all payments for taxes, assessments, insurance premiums, liens, costs, expenses and attorney's fees herein specified, without notice to Mortgagor (such notice being hereby expressly waived), to be due and payable at once, by foreclosure or otherwise; (2) In the event that Mortgagee elects to

(continued on next page)

accelerate the maturity of the Secured Indebtedness and declares the Secured Indebtedness to be due and payable in full at once as provided for herein, or as may be provided for in the Note, then Mortgagee shall have the right to pursue all of Mortgagee's rights and remedies for the collection of such Secured Indebtedness, whether such rights and remedies are granted by this Mortgage, any other agreement, law, equity or otherwise, to include, without limitation, the institution of foreclosure proceedings against the Premises under the terms of this Mortgage and any applicable state or federal law.

MISCELLANEOUS PROVISIONS

Prior Liens.
Mortgagor shall keep the Premises free from all prior liens (except for those consented to by Mortgagee).

Notice, Demand and Request.
Every provision for notice and demand or request shall be deemed fulfilled by written notice and demand or request delivered in accordance with the provisions of the Note relating to notice.

Severability.
If any provision of this Mortgage shall, for any reason and to any extent, be invalid or unenforceable, the remainder of the instrument in which such provision is contained, shall be enforced to the maximum extent permitted by law.

Governing Law.
The terms and provisions of this Mortgage are to be governed by the laws of the State of _____. No payment of interest or in the nature of interest for any debt secured in part by this Mortgage shall exceed the maximum amount permitted by law.

Descriptive Headings.
The descriptive headings used herein are for convenience of reference only, and they are not intended to have any effect whatsoever in determining the rights or obligations of the Mortgagor or Mortgagee and they shall not be used in the interpretation or construction hereof.

Attorney's Fees.
As used in this Mortgage, attorneys' fees shall include, but not be limited to, fees incurred in all matters of collection and enforcement, construction and interpretation, before, during and after suit, trial, proceedings and appeals. Attorneys' fees shall also include hourly charges for paralegals, law clerks and other staff members operating under the supervision of an attorney.

Exculpation.
Notwithstanding anything contained herein to the contrary, the Note which this Mortgage secures is a non-recourse Note and such Note shall be enforced against Mortgagor only to the extent of Mortgagor's interest in the Premises as described herein and to the extent of Mortgagor's interest in any personalty as may be described herein.

IN WITNESS WHEREOF, the Mortgagor has caused this instrument to be duly executed as of the day and year first above written.

_____
Mortgagor

STATE OF)   COUNTY OF)

Subscribed and sworn before me this the _____ day of _____, 20____.

Witness my hand and seal.

_____ My commission expires:
Notary Public

There is a process that must be followed in the trustee's sale. Notification must be given to the trustor in default, and all other interested parties, and then a formal sale must be held. There is a certain amount of time between the notification and sale called the **statutory reinstatement period**, when the trustor may repay the debt against the property and reinstate the loan. Not only can the trustor make the necessary payment to satisfy the debt, but any person holding a junior lien against the property may also reinstate the loan. The reinstatement period runs from the notification period until five days before the sale. Once the reinstatement period has expired, the trustor may still redeem the property by paying off the entire loan for the house, including all interest, fees and costs associated with the trustee's sale.

A lender generally does not begin foreclosure proceedings immediately when a trustor is late or misses one payment. There is generally a grace period of 10–15 days for the trustor to make the payment and continue paying the note in good standing with the lender. One of the most important things to highlight about a foreclosure is that the lender does not want the property; he or she just wants to ensure he or she receives payment for the loan that was granted for the property to be purchased. In the event that the trustor simply cannot keep up with the payments, the lender has no choice but to foreclose. To begin foreclosure proceedings, the lender will deliver the original trust deed and note to the trustee and instruct the trustee to prepare a notice of default.

The **notice of default** must be recorded in the county recorder's office and then sent by certified mail to the trustor within 10 days after recording the notice of default. The recording with the county recorder's office must occur at least three months before the trustee's sales is held. In addition to sending a copy of the notice to the trustor, a copy of the notice of default must be sent to the trustor's successors or those with interest in the property, in addition to any junior lien holders, the State Controller and all parties requesting a copy of the notice. Anyone interested in a specific deed of trust can fill out a request for notice with the county recorder's office, and will be notified when or if a notice of default has been sent to the trustor.

The notice of default must state in **bold letters**, all caps, and in the first sentence that the property is in foreclosure due to the buyer's delinquency in payment. This is important, because if the notice of default is improperly prepared, a trustor may win a court case against the lender, even if payments have not been made.

Once the notice of default has been recorded in the county recorder's office of the county where the property is located, the trustee must wait three months before taking any further action. During these three months, the trustor may repay the debt and reinstate the note on the property. After three months have expired, the trustee may then record a notice of trustee's sale.

The notice of trustee's sale must be published in a newspaper of general circulation where the property is located, so that the general public is made aware of the sale. The notice must run once each week for 20 days, with no more than 7 days between notices. The notice of trustee's sale must also contain a property description. Finally, the notice of trustee's sale must be posted in a public place - also in the area in which the property is located.

Notice of default

- Must be recorded in the country recorder's office in the county where the property is located
- First sentence of the notice must be in bold, all caps, stating the foreclosure is due to delinquent payment of the loan
- The notice of default must be delivered to the trustor, the trustor's successors, junior lienholders, the State Controller and any other interested party requesting the notice
- Notice of default begins the 3-month period until the trustee can record the trustee's sale

As mentioned, the reinstatement period will be valid until five days before the trustee's sale. Once this period has expired, the trustor is required to pay off the entire loan, along with all costs and interest, in order to take possession of the property.

Trustee's sale

Must be recorded in the county recorder's office in the county where the property is located 3 months after the notice of default

- Must be posted in a public place
- Must be printed in a newspaper of general circulation once each week for 20 days, with no more than 7 days separating each notice
- Redemption period ends 5 days before the sale

The sale will be conducted, auction-style, in the county where the property is located. People can make a bid on the property; but, until the bidding is over and finalized, the trustor may pay the entire amount owed on the loan (including all costs to cover interest, fees and cost of the sale). If this takes place before bidding is over, the sale will end, with the trustor as official owner of the property. If this does not happen, the person who makes the highest bid will become the new owner of the property.

The auction is open to any person wishing to make a bid on the property, though all bids must be paid in cash or cashier's check. The primary lienholder or the lender may credit the bid for the amount the trustor still owes on the note. In this case, the trustor will not have to pay the money, because they hold the lien on the property. This is not attractive to a lender. They would rather get their money back than own several properties they cannot use or do not wish to own.

Once a person successfully makes a bid and makes payment for their bid on the property he or she will receive a trustee's deed to the property. The original trustor no longer has any rights or interest in the property and must vacate it. If the original trustor does not vacate the property, an unlawful detainer will be filed and the sheriff will legally remove the old trustor and his or her belongings from the property.

The proceeds from a trustee sale will first be applied to any costs or fees associated with the sale. After all fees associated with the sale are paid, the beneficiary will be paid the amount owed on the original loan for the property. After the beneficiary is paid, any junior lienholders will be paid. This will happen in the order in which the liens were recorded. Last in line for any money from the proceeds of the sale are the debtor or old trustor. After all debts have been satisfied, any remaining money is rightfully returned to the debtor.

The person who wins the bid on a property must understand that he or she is responsible for certain liens on that property, which may not have been paid off from the proceeds of the trustee sale. These liens include federal tax liens and real property taxes. Additionally, junior lienholders who stand to be repaid from the proceeds of a sale should attend the sale and ensure that the bid is high enough for the liens to be paid with the sale's proceeds. If the bids are relatively low, and it does not look like the liens will be paid, the trustor should make his or her own bid to drive up the price of the property and thereby insuring payment to him or herself.

A **judicial foreclosure** may be used to foreclose on a property in lieu of a trustee's sale. However, the process takes much longer than the three months and 21 days of a trustee's sale. In a judicial foreclosure, the trustee is not a part of the foreclosure process. Rather, a court proceeding takes place and a judge will determine who is in the wrong. The judge will also determine if there is to be a sale to repay any debts against the property. While this process generally takes longer than a trustee's sale, it might be appealing to a beneficiary, because in a judicial foreclosure, the beneficiary may seek a deficiency judgment against the trustor. Deficiency judgments are not allowed in a trustee's sale. A deficiency judgment seeks a personal payment from the trustor for all debts not covered in the sale of the property.

A judicial foreclosure utilizes a court-appointed commissioner or the sheriff to conduct the sale and ensure that all aspects of the sale are handled properly. The sheriff or commissioner will ensure the trustor vacates the property. In a judicial foreclosure, the person winning the bid for the property does not take possession of the property until the redemption period has expired, and even then only if no successors have come forward to pay the debt on the property.

Trustee Sale Procedure

- Lender notifies the trustee of the foreclosure proceedings and delivers the original note and trust deed to the trustee

- Trustee records the notice of default, and notifies the trustor and all other parties requiring notification

- Reinstatement period begins after recording of the notice of default

- Notice of the trustee's sale is recorded three months after recording the notice of default, is in place for three weeks

- Sale is held

- Trustee's deed is given to the highest bidder at the sale. All sales must be made in cash or cashier's check

Remember

Foreclosure will not eliminate the following types of liens

- Real property tax liens
- Federal tax liens

FORECLOSURE UNDER A MORTGAGE

When the borrower and lender realize that a loan is not going to be repaid because of some inability on the part of the borrower to make the payment or to sell the property to pay off the amount borrowed, foreclosure is the lender's remedy for default on the loan.

In each state, specific foreclosure laws vary, but there are three general types of foreclosure proceedings. When the security instrument (either a trust deed or mortgage) conveys a power of sale to the lender in case of default, a **nonjudicial foreclosure** is allowed. A lender must request a court-ordered sale of the property after proving that the borrower has defaulted on the terms of the loan in states recognizing judicial foreclosure. Much less common, strict foreclosure allows a lender to get title to the property immediately upon default by the borrower and either sell the property or keep it to satisfy the debt.

In any case, if there is any money left over after a foreclosure sale, the lender must return any proceeds in excess of the loan amount and certain fees to the borrower. The foreclosure process used depends primarily on whether the state uses mortgages or deeds of trust for the purchase of real property. Generally, states that use mortgages conduct judicial foreclosures; states that use deeds of trust conduct nonjudicial foreclosures. The principal difference between the two is that the judicial procedure requires court action.

Nonjudicial Foreclosure

The procedure by which the lender conducts the sale of a mortgaged property without the involvement of a court is called nonjudicial foreclosure. Also known as foreclosure by power of sale, the process may be used as long as there is a clause included in the original mortgage allowing it.

The lender directs the sale procedure to sell the property, by first filing, or recording, a notice of default in the county where the property is located. Next is a waiting period during which the borrower can redeem the property by bringing the loan current, including taxes, insurance and any fees incurred by the foreclosure. The length of the waiting period is determined by state law.

If the borrower is unable to cure the default, the lender sells the property at a public auction. If the state statute allows the borrower to redeem the property after the sale, he or she has up to a year in some cases to do so.

In some states, if the property does not sell at the public auction for the full amount of the loan, or, in other words, there is a deficient amount realized at the sale, the lender has the remedy of a court action to claim the amount of the deficiency and obtain a deficiency judgment.

Judicial Foreclosure

To foreclose in accordance with the judicial procedure, a lender must prove that the mortgagor is in default. Once the lender has exhausted its attempts to resolve the default with the homeowner, the next step is to contact an attorney to pursue court action. A judicial foreclosure requires a lawsuit on the part of the lender. The attorney contacts the mortgagor to try to resolve the default. If the mortgagor is unable to pay off the default, the attorney files a lis pendens (action pending) with the court. The lis pendens gives notice to the public that a pending action has been filed against the mortgagor. A prospective buyer for the property would then be notified of the cloud on the title and could then decide whether to proceed with the purchase. The purpose of the court action is to provide evidence of a default and get the court's approval to initiate foreclosure.

Of the two common methods of foreclosure, the judicial foreclosure is more costly and time-consuming. It may, however, provide for the recovery of that part of the loan that was not repaid by the sale of the property at a public foreclosure sale. When there is a deficient amount realized from a foreclosure sale, the lender can sue the borrower and get a deficiency judgment against all other assets of the borrower, causing the borrower to be personally responsible for repayment of the loan.

The judicial foreclosure is conducted by the county sheriff or by a referee appointed by the court. Anyone can bid on the property, for cash, including the borrower in default. In some cases, a cash deposit of 10% of the accepted bid is made at the sale, with the balance due 30 days later, upon closing. The lender who is foreclosing may bid up to the amount owed without having to pay cash if no one else makes a bid high enough.

In that case the lender would get the property back to hold or sell later, as they wish. The property would then be bank-owned or known as an **REO** or Real Estate Owned. If a buyer purchases the property for less than the total encumbrances, the junior liens go away. If the original borrower prevails in the bidding for the property, the junior liens remain on the property.

The successful bidder at the foreclosure sale, depending on which state the property is in, will get either a **referee's deed in foreclosure or sheriff's deed**, or a **certificate of sale**. The first two are special warranty deeds that give the buyer the title the borrower had at the time the original loan was made. The referee's deed and sheriff's deed are used primarily in states with no statutory redemption laws, where the buyer gets immediate possession of the property after the sale, which is final, with no redemption allowed to the buyer.

A certificate of sale is issued to the buyer at a foreclosure sale in states with statutory redemption laws. Depending on the state, the borrower has from one month to one year, or more, after foreclosure to redeem the property by paying off the judgment and reclaiming title to the property.

The buyer does not get possession of the property, in some states, until the redemption period is over.

Remember

There are three methods of foreclosure
   1. Nonjudicial foreclosure, which requires the power of sale
   2. Judicial foreclosure, which requires a court-ordered sale.
   3. Strict foreclosure, which does not involve a judicial sale and is not commonly used.

Priority of Payment
A property may be used as the security for more than one loan. There may be a second or even a third mortgage against a property. These are known as junior mortgages. This is a common practice, and poses no difficulty for the original lender as long as the borrower is willing to make the payments on all the loans and is able to do so. It becomes more than a nuisance, however, when a default occurs on one or more of the loans, and the property does not sell for an amount sufficient to cover all the loans against it at the foreclosure sale. In many foreclosures, the proceeds of the sale do not pay all the debt; therefore a fair system of priorities for paying off holders of mortgages against the property was created. The debt with the highest priority is satisfied first from the proceeds of the sale, and then the next highest priority debt is paid, then the next, and so on, until either the sale proceeds have faded to nothing or all holders of debt relating to the property are contented with their payoff.

California Real Estate Finance

Steps in a Judicial Foreclosure

1. The lender files a lawsuit against the borrower and anyone else who acquired an interest in the property after the mortgage being foreclosed was recorded.

2. The lender must show evidence of default on the loan to a court of law.

3. The lender asks for judgment instructing that the borrower's interest in the property be severed, the property be sold at public auction, and the lender be paid from the proceeds of the sale.

4. A copy of the complaint and summons is delivered to the defendants.

5. A lis pendens is filed to inform the public of pending litigation.

6. A public auction is held, at which the property will be sold to the highest bidder, who will then receive a sheriff's deed or a certificate of sale on the property.

7. Statutory redemption may be allowed, but not always.

A lender would rather be in as senior a position as possible, regarding priority of recording, for obvious reasons. Since the priority of a mortgage is determined by when it is recorded, the mortgage that is recorded first will be first in line to get paid if the borrower defaults. After that, the second mortgage to get recorded will get paid, and so on. The mortgage itself will not be identified as a first, second or third mortgage. The date and time of recording will be stamped by the county recorder on the document, and its priority will be determined by that imprint.

The logical outcome of this priority system of paying off holders of mortgages in case of foreclosure is that, sometimes, the property does not bring enough money at the foreclosure sale to satisfy all the creditors holding mortgages against the property. In those cases, the mortgages not paid off are eliminated. As a matter of fact, in some cases, there is not even enough money to pay the holder of the first mortgage off completely. That lender, then, must decide if it is worthwhile to pursue a deficiency judgment. If the amount is small enough, it probably would not be worth the cost of the lawsuit to recover the deficiency.

A majority of states allow the lender to obtain a deficiency judgment for any amount that is not recovered at the foreclosure sale. The judgment, if you recall, allows a lender to proceed against the borrower's other unsecured assets, if he or she has any.

Junior Lienholders

In a process much like what happens with a trust deed, the foreclosure sale of a property will extinguish the mortgage securing the debt to the mortgagee, or lender, and will also extinguish any junior mortgages. That means the holder of a junior lien (a second, third, etc.), in order to protect his or her interest, must make a bid for the property, or possibly lose the right to collect on the loan if the sale amount is not enough for a pay-off on all mortgages held against the property.

At this point, upon learning of the impending foreclosure on a mortgage senior to the one he or she holds, the junior lienholder has two choices: either stay silent and hope the proceeds from the foreclosure sale are enough to pay off the mortgage, or start his or her own foreclosure, which will then stop the first foreclosure that has already been filed.

If the junior lienholder chooses to file a notice of default, he or she then has the right to claim the property after the statutory time period has passed, without having to bid against other hopeful buyers at the foreclosure sale. The junior lienholder acquires the property subject to all loans senior to his or her own, with the obligation to keep them current, or face foreclosure.

The junior lienholder now owns the property, and may either keep it until the property has regained its former value, or try to sell it on the open market. Since it would not have brought enough at the foreclosure sale to pay off all liens, however, it probably still will not sell at a high enough price for the former lienholder and now owner to get the investment returned.

Notice of Default and Election to Sell Under Deed of Trust
IMPORTANT NOTICE
IF YOUR PROPERTY IS IN FORECLOSURE BECAUSE YOU ARE BEHIND IN YOUR PAYMENTS, IT MAY BE SOLD WITHOUT ANY COURT ACTION, and you may have the legal right to bring your account in good standing by paying all of your past due payments plus permitted costs and expenses within the time permitted by law for reinstatement of your account, which is normally five business days prior to the date set for the sale of your property. No sale date may be set until three months from the date this notice of default may be recorded (which date of recordation appears on this notice). This amount is _____ as of _____, and will increase until your account becomes current.

(Date)

You may not have to pay the entire unpaid portion of your account, even though full payment was demanded, but you must pay the amount stated above. However, you and your beneficiary or mortgagee may mutually agree in writing prior to the time the notice of sale is posted (which may not be earlier than the end of the three-month period stated above) to, among other things, (1) provide additional time in which to cure the default by transfer of the property or otherwise: (2) establish a schedule of payments in order to cure your default; or both (1) and (2).

Following the expiration of the time period referred to in the first paragraph of this notice, unless the obligation being foreclosed upon or a separate written agreement between you and your creditor permits a longer period, you have only the legal right to stop the sale of your property by paying the entire amount demanded by your creditor.

To find the amount you must pay, or to arrange for payment to stop the foreclosure, or if your property is in foreclosure for any other reason, contact:

_____
(Name of beneficiary or mortgagee)

_____
(Mailing address)

_____
(Telephone)

If you have any questions, you should contact a lawyer or the government agency which may have insured your loan.

Notwithstanding the fact that your property is in foreclosure, you may offer your property for sale, provided the sale is concluded prior to the conclusion of the foreclosure.

Remember, **YOU MAY LOSE LEGAL RIGHTS IF YOU DO NOT TAKE PROMPT ACTION.**

NOTICE IS HEREBY GIVEN, THAT _____ a corporation, is duly appointed Trustee under a Deed of Trust dated _____ executed by _____ as Trustor; to secure certain obligations in favor of _____

_____, as beneficiary, recorded _____ , as instrument no. _____ , in book _____ , page _____ , of Official Records in the Office of the Recorder of _____ County, California, describing land therein as:

_____ said obligations including _____ note _____ for the _____ sum of $ _____

that the beneficial interest under such Deed of Trust and the obligations secured thereby are presently held by the undersigned; that a breach of, and default in, the obligations for which such Deed of Trust is security has occurred in that payment has not been made of:

that by reason thereof, the undersigned, present beneficiary under such Deed of Trust, has executed and delivered to said duly appointed Trustee, a written Declaration of Default and Demand for Sale, and has deposited with said duly appointed Trustee, such Deed of Trust and all documents evidencing obligations secured thereby, and has declared and does hereby declare all sums secured thereby immediately due and payable and has elected and does hereby elect to cause the trust property to be sold to satisfy the obligations secured thereby.

_____

_____

Dated _____

SPACE ABOVE THIS LINE FOR RECORDER'S USE

REQUEST FOR NOTICE

UNDER SECTION 2924b CIVIL CODE

				ALL
				PIN

Escrow or Loan No.

Title Order No.

In accordance with section 2924b, Civil Code, request is hereby made that a copy of any Notice of Default and a copy of any Notice of Sale under the Deed of Trust recorded as Instrument No. _____ on _____ , in book _____ , page _____ , Official Records of _____ County, California, and describing land therein as

Executed by _____ . as Trustor.
in which _____ is named as
Beneficiary, and _____ . as Trustee.
be mailed to _____
at _____
   Number and Street

_____
   City and State

NOTICE: A copy of any notice of default and of any notice of sale will be sent to the address contained in this recorded request. If your address changes, a new request must be recorded.

Signature _____

Dated _____

State of _____CALIFORNIA_____

County of _____ } SS.

On _____ before me,

Notary Public, personally appeared _____

_____

personally known to me (or proved to me on the basis of satisfactory evidence) to be the person(s) whose name(s) is/are subscribed to the within instrument and acknowledged to me that he/she/they executed the same in his/her/their authorized capacity(ies), and that by his/her/their signature(s) on the instrument the person(s), or the entity upon behalf of which the person(s) acted, executed the instrument.

WITNESS my hand and official seal.

Signature _____

S U M M A R Y

This chapter introduced you to trust deeds and mortgages, and the many differences between the two. Many people don't realize that trust deeds are used in California as the primary security for the promissory note. With "mortgage" being such a common term, trust deeds are often referred to as "mortgages" by default.

Trust deeds and mortgages are similar in their primary purpose, but different in many ways in their function, issuance and foreclosure process. Where mortgages allow a person to seek and receive deficiency judgments in the foreclosure process, trust deeds do not. A person's personal assets will be secure if he or she holds a trust deed, since his or her other assets cannot be used to satisfy the debt.

Foreclosure procedures are only one of the areas in which mortgages and trust deeds differ, there are several other features that are markedly different between the two. They are

- Number of parties involved in the process
- Statute of limitations
- Remedies available upon default
- Conveyance of the title
- Reinstatement period
- Deficiency judgment
- Redemption period
- Procedure following satisfaction of the debt

T E R M S   A N D   P H R A S E S

Acceleration Clause   condition of a loan that states that the entire payment for the loan is due in certain circumstances (such as upon sale of the property)

Agreement of Sale   financing option in which the seller finances the property for the buyer, without giving up legal title to the property. The buyer receives possession of the property, but does not receive the title to the property until the loan is paid in full.

Alienation Clause   condition of a loan that allows the lender to require full payment of the loan in the event the property is going to be sold

Assignment of Rents   agreement between the property owner and the holder of a trust deed or loan on the property. In this case, the holder has the right to collect rents from any tenants occupying the property, as security for the loan. The holder of the loan will only receive this right if the property owner defaults on the note.

Assumption Clause   financing option where the buyer takes over the existing loan on a property and is thereby liable for the note. The seller still remains secondarily liable in the event that the buyer defaults on the loan. The buyer can only take over the existing loan if approved by the lender.

Balloon Payment   note requiring a large payment at the end of its term to cover the debt in full. This is used when only a small percentage of the principal is being covered by each of the monthly payments.

Beneficiary   lender or financial institution that provides a loan to the borrower

Collateral   object of value that is pledged as security for the purchase of another object of value. In real estate, collateral is the property that is pledged as security for the note, as evidenced by the trust deed

Contract of Sale   financing option where the seller finances the property for the buyer, but does not give up legal title to the property. The buyer receives possession of the property, but does not receive the title to the property until the loan is paid in full

Default   failure by the trustor to pay the monthly or installment payments on the promissory note for the property.

Deficiency Judgment   court ruling against a borrower for the balance of debt owed on property after foreclosure and sale of the property. Deficiency judgments can only be imposed on hard money loans involved in a judicial foreclosure

Equitable Title   interest in property held by a trustor or vendee before the entire loan has been paid off

Foreclosure   procedure a lender may take to legally sell property in default, done through court action or by a trustee's sale

Foreclosure Sale   sale that occurs when property is being foreclosed on to satisfy a debt against it

Holder   party to whom the promissory note is made payable (usually the lender)

Holder in Due Course   person who has obtained a negotiable instrument (such as a check, promissory note or any other legal tender document) in the ordinary course of business, before it is due, in good faith, for value, and without knowledge that it has been previously dishonored.

Hypothecation   process by which a borrower may use a property as collateral for a loan, yet still remain in possession of the property

Judicial Foreclosure   foreclosure by court action

Junior Trust Deed   trust deed that is recorded after the first trust deed. The junior trust deed is considered less important (or of lesser priority) than the trust deed that was recorded first.

Land Contract   financing option in which the seller finances the property for the buyer, but does not give up legal title to the property. The buyer receives possession of the property, but does not receive its title until the loan is paid in full.

Legal Title   title to property that is complete, with no encumbrances. This title may be held by a trustee in a trust deed, to be reconveyed to the trustor when the note is paid in full.

Maker   borrower who requests funds from a lender. The borrower will make a promissory note and become liable for the debt against him or her. Usually, the promissory note is accompanied by the trust deed in a real estate purchase.

Mortgage   legal document pledging property as security for a debt

Mortgagee   lender loaning the money for the purchase of real estate

Mortgagor   borrower requesting a loan to purchase real estate

Naked Legal Title   title allowing a trustee to reconvey title to property upon satisfactory payment of a debt, or foreclosure (in the event of default). This title does not grant any ownership privileges to the property.

Negotiable Instrument   any written document that may be transferred by endorsement or delivery from one party to another

Notice of Default   written notice given to the borrower, informing them him or her that he or she is delinquent on payment of the loan

Notice of Trustee's Sale   notice published regarding a trustee's sale to dispose of property in an effort to satisfy a debt against it

Novation   substitution of a new obligation for an old one

Pledge   transferring property to a lender as security for a loan. In this situation, the lender will take possession of the property.

Power of Sale   clause in a loan that allows the lender to sell a property in the event that a borrower defaults on the loan

Promissory Note   written evidence of debt and a promise a borrower makes to a lender pledging to pay back a loan

Reconveyance Deed   deed used to transfer property from a lender back to the borrower, once the loan is paid in full

Reinstate   to reactivate a loan after any default debt is paid

Release Clause   provision found in blanket loans that allows the release of certain properties after partial payment of the loan is made

Request for Notice   notice sent to all parties that have an interest, or that have requested notice, that a loan is in default

Second Trust Deed   junior trust deed, or evidence of a debt that is recorded after the original trust deed

Security   collateral used to secure a loan

Sheriff's Deed   deed given by a court to the successful bidder at a foreclosure sale

Statutory   laws created by legislation, rather than by a court judgment

Trust Deed   document where the title to property (bare legal title) will pass to a third party (called a trustee) as security for the debt

Trustee's Deed   deed given to the successful bidder at a trustee's sale

Trustee's Sale   sale of property, after foreclosure, to satisfy the debt against a property

Trustee   holds bare legal title to property where there is a deed of trust

Trustor   borrower in a trust deed

Vendee   buyer utilizing a contract of sale

Vendor   seller utilizing a contract of sale

1. Which of the following parties in a trust holds the trust deed?
   a. Trustee
   b. Beneficiary
   c. Trustor
   d. None of the above

2. The lender is the
   a. Trustor
   b. Trustee
   c. Beneficiary
   d. Both A and C

3. Who is responsible for foreclosing a property in the event of default on the loan?
   a. Trustor
   b. Trustee
   c. Lender
   d. Courts

4. Assignment of rents allows
   a. the lender to take possession of a foreclosed property and collect rent from any tenants.
   b. the owner in default to continue to collect rents from any tenants on property until all payments are caught up.
   c. the tenants of a foreclosed property to forego paying rent, as the owner no longer has control of the building.
   d. none of the above.

5. How many days does the trustor have to reinstate the promissory note before the date of the trustee's sale?
   a. 10 days
   b. 7 days
   c. 5 days
   d. 3 days

6. What or who gives the trustee the power to foreclose or reconvey the deed to property?
   a. Owner of the property
   b. Lender
   c. Trust
   d. Courts

7. A judicial foreclosure is used in which of the following situations?
   a. Trust deeds
   b. Mortgages
   c. Both A and B
   d. Neither A nor B

8. A notice of default must be sent to the trustor within how many days after it is recorded?
   a. 5
   b. 10
   c. 15
   d. 30

9. A person who purchases property at a trustee's sale will receive what kind of deed?
   a. Sheriff's deed
   b. Certificate of sale
   c. Trust deed
   d. Both A and B

10. What is the redemption period?
    a. The time during which junior lien holders or the mortgagee's successors may repurchase a property after a foreclosure sale.
    b. The act of seeking a personal judgment against the person defaulting on the promissory note.
    c. The time by which a bidder must pay the amount in full for the property he or she is purchasing.
    d. The time between the notice of sale and the actual sale of the foreclosed property.

11. A deficiency judgment is allowed in which of the following situations?
    a. With a defaulted trust deed
    b. With a defaulted mortgage
    c. Both A and B
    d. Neither A nor B

12. In a trustee's sale, which of the following parties is not required to be notified when the notice of default is recorded?
    a. Trustor
    b. Junior lien holders
    c. Beneficiary
    d. State Controller

13. When the seller makes a junior trust deed, it is sometimes called
    a. carryback
    b. foolish
    c. novation
    d. conveyance

14. A non-judicial foreclosure is also known as
    a. reconveyance.
    b. power of sale.
    c. deficiency judgment.
    d. trustee's sale.

15. How many days does the trustor have to repay the debt in order to reinstate the note on a foreclosed property?
    a. 10 days
    b. 7 days
    c. 5 days
    d. 0 days, as he or she may redeem property until the date of the sale.

16. A junior lienholder holds what type of a lien?
    a. Property tax lien
    b. Second or any subsequent trust deed
    c. Lien on personal property such as furnishings or a car note
    d. None of the above

17. Which of the following are benefits of a trust deed to the lender?
    a. No redemption after foreclosure
    b. Trust deeds never expire
    c. Short foreclosure process
    d. All of the above

18. Which of the following can be foreclosed on by either judicial action or by a trustee's sale?
    a. Trust deed only
    b. Mortgage only
    c. Both A and B
    d. Neither A nor B

19. Which of the following is not a method of foreclosure?
    a. Nonjudicial
    b. Strict
    c. Sheriff
    d. Judicial

20. Which of the following liens is not eliminated in a foreclosure?
    a. Junior lien
    b. Property tax lien
    c. First trust deed
    d. None of the above

CHAPTER

SECONDARY MORTGAGE AND TRUST DEED MARKETS

What you will learn in this Chapter

- The Secondary Mortgage Market
- Fannie Mae
- Freddie Mac
- Ginnie Mae
- Office of Federal Housing Enterprise Oversight (OFHEO)
- Electronic Underwriting System
- Real Estate Mortgage Investment Conduit (REMI)

Test Your Knowledge

1. Which of the following is not a participant in the secondary mortgage market?
   a. VA
   b. OFHEO
   c. Freddie Mac
   d. Ginnie Mae

2. Fannie Mae buys
   a. only single-family detatched residences.
   b. single family residences made up of 1–4 units.
   c. any type of residential property regardless on the number of units.
   d. any type of property.

3. The loan cap on a Fannie Mae purchase is limited to
   a. no more than 80% pf the HUD area average home price.
   b. determined every 5 years.
   c. determined annually.
   d. none of the above.

4. Which of the following is the purpose of Freddie Mac?
   a. Buy and sell conventional loans
   b. Guarantee securities issued by FHA-approved lenders
   c. Make legislative recommendations
   d. Buy securities from the general public

5. The system that is being used by Fannie Mae to process loans is
   a. REMIC.
   b. FICO.
   c. Desktop Underwriter.
   d. Loan Prospector.

6. Which is not a rule for credit scoring?
   a. Don't automatically disqualify someone because of a sub-par score
   b. Work with the applicant to clear fixable items
   c. Be aware of potential errors in electronic credit files
   d. Disregard the score factor codes for sub-par scores

7. The largest single investor in the mortgage industry today is
   a. Freddie Mac.
   b. Fannie Mae.
   c. Ginnie Mae.
   d. the VA.

INTRODUCTION

Primary lenders—usually banks and savings associations—create new real estate loans. Some of these loans are maintained by these lenders in their investment portfolios, but most are sold in the **secondary market** to Fannie Mae, Freddie Mac, and Ginnie Mae. With the funds received from these sales, primary lenders can offer more new loans. Concurrently, institutions that buy mortgages on the secondary market can then sell security interests in the pools of mortgages they have collected. Individual investors can buy fractional interests in these secondary mortgage market pools through their stockbrokers.

Mortgage holders also can collect pools by packaging FHA, DVA, or conventional mortgages and then issuing securities that represent shares in the package. Mortgage pool originators continue to receive payments from borrowers, but they pass these payments on to the investors in the pool. Such mortgage pool securities may be guaranteed by Ginnie Mae or insured by private mortgage insurance companies.

Today's almost instantaneous communications and sophisticated computers have extended the reach of the secondary mortgage market and, to various degrees, replaced the personal relationships between local lenders and borrowers. Payments that used to require a visit to the bank or at least a check sent via postal mail can now be withdrawn automatically from a borrower's checking account, for example.

Despite the reduction in personal contact however, the growth of the secondary market has resulted in greater stability and less risk for lenders and their depositors and more funds available for loans no matter what regional differences in the level of economic activity exist at a given time.

At one time, the trend was to sell fixed-rate loans to the secondary market as quickly as possible. The secondary market purchased many of these loans, but at relatively deep discounts, which meant that primary lenders often shouldered fairly substantial monetary losses to transfer the long-term risk of these mortgages. However, this strategy meant that many lenders stayed in business that would have otherwise failed— a much worse scenario for local economies.

However, selling loans as quickly as they are created is no longer as prevalent today because of the **Real Estate Mortgage Investment Conduit (REMIC)**. With REMIC, loans are now held in pools, and interests in these pools are sold as securities to public and private investors. REMIC is discussed further later in this chapter after a review of how the secondary market developed and how its various components operate.

Purpose and History

Real estate mortgage debt in the U. S., and especially in California, is at an all-time high, and does not show any signs of coming down. Population increases—both in terms of sheer numbers and in terms of migration—creates demand for housing and related development, such as nearby shopping, entertainment, and suburban offices. Furthermore, steady increases in construction costs, higher loan-to-value (L/V) ratios, and longer mortgage repayment terms have made mortgage money a hot commodity.

Earlier chapters reviewed the importance of the national secondary market for buying and selling mortgage securities and distributing available mortgage money where it is needed. The secondary mortgage market is given this name because local originators of real estate loans can sell them to "second" owners anywhere in the country and as a result, free up their own capital so they have enough money for more mortgages.. Basically, the secondary market redistributes funds from cash-rich to cash-poor locations.

This process has attempted to keep up with rapidly rising mortgage activity over the past 20 years by balancing the mortgage money available with the needs of an area and thereby stabilizing the mortgage money market. Ultimately, the secondary market reduces fluctuations in regional real estate cycles and their impacts on the construction industry and local economies.

Before the Great Depression of the early 1930s, drastic changes in economic conditions were considered a normal part of a free market system. "Laissez-faire" economists and business leaders repeated Darwin's theory of survival of the fittest as the most efficient means of distributing resources—until they too went bankrupt in the various panics that occurred with fair regularity. The social reforms of the 1930s under President Franklin D. Roosevelt involved government intervention to bring some stability to the economy and protect the jobs, savings, and overall welfare of citizens.

The long-term economic recovery of the U.S. during this time included stimulating the construction industry through the newly established **Federal Housing Administration (FHA)**. The FHA mortgage insurance program standardized credit and appraisal. The real estate securities market is based on the reliable and accepted FHA determinations of borrowers' credit and property values—both needed to estimate risk and therefore, discount rates. Furthermore, buyers of these securities knew that the FHA guaranteed all loans and would cover any defaults—another essential factor for reinstating and maintaining investors' confidence.

In 1944, the **Department of Veterans Affairs Guaranteed Loan Program** expanded the amount of low-risk mortgage securities available for investment. This expansion led to the development of a national clearinghouse for the huge number of mortgage securities traded annually. As a result, Fannie Mae emerged from relative obscurity, followed by Freddie Mac and Ginnie Mae. These three agencies facilitate the national re-distribution of real estate financing.

The primary lender of a real estate loan may be in personal contact with a borrower fairly regularly, if only to send statements and information needed for the borrower's income tax return, among other communications. However, it is very likely that the original lender actually sold the promissory note portion of the loan to another investor quite a while ago. Even so, the lender often continues to service the loan for its entire term or until the property is sold, and the new owners' mortgage is held elsewhere.

The sales and purchases of real estate promissory notes make up the secondary mortgage market. The secondary market is an opportunity for institutions and individuals to invest money in real estate, much as they would invest in the stock and bond markets. In the next section, the federal agencies primarily involved in the secondary mortgage market are discussed.

The primary agencies involved in the Secondary Mortgage Market are

- **Federal National Mortgage Association (Fannie Mae)**
- **Government National Mortgage Association (Ginnie Mae)**
- **Federal Home Loan Mortgage Corporation (Freddie Mac)**
- **Office of Federal Housing Enterprise Oversight (OFHEO)**

FANNIE MAE

Fannie Mae (www.fanniemae.com) was created in 1938 to serve as a secondary market for FHA-insured and VA-guaranteed loans. In later years, Fannie Mae's authority was expanded to allow it to offer conventional loans, as well. Fannie Mae currently buys properties financed through FHA, VA, graduated payment mortgages, adjustable-rate mortgages, and conventional fixed rate first (and some second) mortgages for properties consisting of 1 to 4 units.

Loans meeting Fannie Mae's criteria are called **conforming loans**. The dollar amount is determined every year; in 2006, the limit is $417,000 for single-family residences in the continental U. S.; limits on these loans are higher in Alaska, Hawaii, Guam, and the U.S. Virgin Islands. Also, higher limits exist for 2, 3, and 4-family units.

Fannie Mae buys a group of mortgages from a lender in exchange for mortgage-backed securities that represent undivided interest in the group of loans. The lender keeps these securities or sells them into the secondary mortgage market. Fannie Mae guarantees the payment of both interest and principal of these loans to whomever holds the note, no matter whether he or she is the original lender or an investor.

History of Fannie Mae

In order to encourage investors to buy FHA-insured mortgages on the secondary market, the Reconstruction Finance Corporation (RFC), a financial agency established by President Franklin D. Roosevelt, was charged in 1938 with organizing, funding, and managing the Federal National Mortgage Association, which later wound up with the abbreviation, Fannie Mae. With the initial capital of $10 million provided by the RFC, and with the authority to issue notes when more funds were needed, Fannie Mae started granting direct loans for the construction of rental housing under FHA Section 207 and purchasing FHA-insured mortgages from all qualified sellers. Fannie Mae purchased these mortgages at par; in other words, the agency paid mortgage holders the full face value for their securities, without any discount. These mortgages would not have sold through the usual channels for full par value; Fannie Mae thus became an immediate and attractive source of cash for holders of FHA-insured mortgage loans. FHA programs were guaranteed success as a result, and the amount of capital available for making more FHA mortgages was replenished by the secondary market purchases. Approved lenders selling mortgages to Fannie Mae were allowed to continue to service these loans for a small fee.

In 1948, Fannie Mae's scope was expanded to include purchasing loans to military veterans guaranteed by the Department of Veterans Affairs. Fannie Mae's mortgage holdings increased dramatically, and in 1950, it became part of the Housing and Home Finance Agency, which coordinated federal home financing activity. Also in 1950, the U.S. Congress authorized $250 million in funding for Fannie Mae to purchase eligible mortgages; Fannie Mae was also authorized to offer its bonds to private investors.

Fannie Mae and the Charter of 1954

In 1954, Fannie Mae was rechartered and tasked with setting up a national secondary mortgage market clearinghouse to be financed with private capital. Fannie Mae was authorized to sell its mortgages and purchase new insured or guaranteed FHA and DVA securities. Reorganized as a corporate entity, Fannie Mae proceeded to issue preferred stock to the U.S. Treasury and common stock to mortgage security dealers in who participated in Fannie Mae programs. Actually, these mortgage security dealers were *required* to purchase Fannie Mae stock in order to continue to trade in the secondary market. Most Fannie Mae stock, however, was owned by the Treasury until a 1968 reorganization made Fannie Mae a private corporation.

The 1954 Charter Act authorized Fannie Mae to

- Operate the national secondary mortgage market to provide liquidity for mortgage investments and improve the distribution of funds for real estate finance

- Handle management and liquidity duties for controlling the orderly repayments and foreclosures of FHA and DVA mortgages acquired before 1954

- Provide special assistance in supervising housing loans created under emergency public aid programs

Fannie Mae and the Secondary Mortgage Market

Each function had separate assets and borrowing authority. In addition to raising funds from stock sales, Fannie Mae was permitted to sell credit obligations to the public or the Treasury as needed to accomplish its tasks. At the same time however, the 1954 Charter stopped Fannie Mae from making any more direct loans. Furthermore, Fannie Mae was no longer to purchase mortgages at par, but at whatever discounted price would yield a reasonable rate of return. This new profit orientation was consistent with the eventual goal of reorganizing Fannie Mae as a private corporation. As of 1954, Fannie Mae no longer was required to purchase every mortgage submitted, but only those mortgages that met its standards for marketability. Now, Fannie Mae could impose its own criteria on lenders.

This new state of affairs sometimes created animosity among mortgage originators. They argued that one federal agency—Fannie Mae—should not reject loans that met other agencies'—FHA and DVA—standards. Fannie Mae responded by pointing out that FHA and DVA standards for credit and appraisal were minimums, and all mortgages submitted to Fannie Mae should meet Fannie Mae's standards for quality, yield, and risk. As a result, the quality and stability of guaranteed and insured government loans went up in order to meet Fannie Mae's requirements.

Servicing the mortgages bought by Fannie Mae remained in the hands of the loan originator/ seller, who received a fee to do this. The fee was a percentage of the mortgage balance, and many originators received significant income this way.

Furthermore, financial fiduciaries, mortgage bankers, and mortgage brokers also received income from origination and collection fees as well as from interest charged on loans—if they held them instead of selling them. Now, as then, the profits of mortgage bankers who issue most of the FHA and DVA loans granted are particularly tied to the volume of loans they make. By selling these mortgages at par, or even below par, to Fannie Mae, originators of FHA and DVA loans can obtain more cash for making additional loans, further increasing their profits from origination fees as well as continuing to take in fees for servicing the earlier loans, along with newer ones.

After the Charter of 1954, Fannie Mae sold its mortgages in open-market transactions. Purchasers now had to pay current prices for the securities. This operation also correlated with the profit motives of this quasi-government agency/corporate entity. Since 1954, sales of Fannie Mae mortgages have varied over the years, with peak sales occurring when other investment opportunities are less attractive or unavailable.

Fannie Mae's Management and Liquidation Duties
In the 1954 charter, Fannie Mae was tasked with supervising the collection of payments from mortgages it had bought before 1954. Originally, Fannie Mae had been established in the 1930s to provide a federal guarantee that FHA and DVA mortgages would not default in order to attract investors to buy mortgage-backed securities. At that time, Fannie Mae was not as profit-motivated in its early years as it became later, so many mortgages bought between the 1930s and 1954 did not meet the agency's new standards. These older mortgages were segregated for collection and retirement, and problem mortgages were dealt with individually and liquidated if necessary.

Fannie Mae and Emergency Public Aid Programs
Fannie Mae was empowered to purchase mortgages issued to finance houses under emergency circumstances. For example, Fannie Mae purchased many FHA and DVA loans created under the Emergency Housing Act of 1958, which was passed to stimulate the construction industry and help offset a recession that occurred at that time. Fannie Mae also purchased mortgages granted under various urban renewal projects. It also bought mortgages on properties reconstructed after floods and tornadoes, properties located in areas where loans were particularly difficult to obtain, and properties identified by the President and Congress as requiring special attention.

Fannie Mae and the Housing and Urban Development Act of 1968
The Housing and Urban Development Act of 1968 changed Fannie Mae again. Based on its successful operations as a quasi-public, for-profit corporation, Fannie Mae was reorganized as a completely private corporation. All stock in Fannie Mae owned by the U.S. Treasury was redeemed and a similar amount of over-the-counter common stock was offered to the general public. Fannie Mae now was a privately owned corporation subject to corporate income tax, although it still was sponsored by the federal government.

Today, Fannie Mae is governed by a 15-member board of directors each serving for one year. Ten of the members are elected by Fannie Mae stockholders. The other five are appointed by the President, and represent the construction, real estate, and finance industries. The Fannie Mae board of directors seeks advice from an eight-member General Advisory Committee, established in 1959. Its members are largely from the housing and real estate financing industries. The secretary of HUD must approve Fannie Mae's policies on borrowing, liquidity, and paying dividends.

As a result of the 1968 restructuring, Fannie Mae continued to operate the secondary mortgage market, including retaining all assets and liabilities related to that function., Fannie Mae was also established as a private corporation dealing in mortgage securities. It no longer was required to deal with pre-1954 mortgages or special assistance programs. These functions were reassigned to the new Government

National Mortgage Association (Ginnie Mae), an agency of the U.S. Department of Housing and Urban Development (HUD).

The 1968 reorganization was aimed at improving Fannie Mae's participation in the secondary mortgage market and encouraging new money to enter the real estate mortgage market. Fannie Mae continues to meet these objectives successfully. With the 1968 changes, Fannie Mae could purchase mortgages at a premium and also buy securities issued by Ginnie Mae, thus contributing to the support of this new agency. Fannie Mae also expanded its borrowing power by floating securities backed by specific blocks of mortgages in its portfolio.

The **Emergency Home Finance Act** of 1970 gave Fannie Mae additional authority to purchase conventional mortgages, significantly expanding its influence on real estate financing in the U.S. Fannie Mae could also buy and sell mortgage loans issued for the hospital construction or modernization.

Fannie Mae's Administered Price System

Before 1983, Fannie Mae had bought mortgages in a free-market-system auction. Fannie Mae bought the lowest-priced loans—those with the deepest discounts—offered by lenders. In February, 1983, this system was replaced by an **administered price system**, in which Fannie Mae adjusts its required yields daily depending on market factors and its financial needs.

Lenders now call a special rate line to get current yield quotes and place orders to sell. Lenders may order a mandatory commitment, by which delivery of loans to Fannie Mae is guaranteed, or a standby commitment, by which the lender has the option of delivering the loans or not, depending on the price at time of delivery.

Fannie Mae's Stricter Standards of the 1980s

In the 1980s, a large number of foreclosures led Fannie Mae to require stricter underwriting standards for borrowers to qualify for loans that could be sold in the secondary market. The borrower's debt-to-income ratio could be no more than 36% of stable monthly income from all sources. The debt variable in the ratio is the sum of all housing costs plus any long-term installment debt payments, such as car loans. Under special circumstances, for example, with low-income or first-time homebuyers, this ratio may be as high as 43%. It can go to 50% for a Fannie Mae Streamlined Purchase Money Mortgage Option 2.

Fannie Mae's Special Programs

Today, Fannie Mae is the largest investor in home mortgages, providing financing for single-family, multifamily, and community development lending. In 1991, **"Opening Doors to Affordable Housing"** was established by Fannie Mae as a commitment to offering financing to the "underserved" market of low- to moderate-income families, minorities, immigrants, and families living in distressed inner-city communities. In 1994, Fannie Mae said it would offer $1 billion in targeted housing financing by the year 2000 through the "Opening Doors" program. That goal was achieved eight months ahead of schedule in 1999. In 2000, Fannie Mae started offering another $2 billion through the program that will continue until 2010.

Other Fannie Mae programs include

- **Community Home Buyer**, which requires only a 5% down payment; borrowers must attend a homebuyer education class

- **Flex 97** affordable housing loan program, which requires only a 3% down payment for qualified borrowers; funds can come from gifts, loans from family members, cash assistance from an employer, or other sources—and not just the borrower's personal funds.

To maintain the flow of funds available for the purchase of mortgage loans from the private market, Fannie Mae issues securities backed by pools of mortgage loans called **mortgage-backed securities**, which are sold on the open market.

Fannie Mae's Web site (www.fanniemae.com) includes information on its home improvement loans and energy conservation loans, as well as mortgage loans.

F R E D D I E   M A C

Freddie Mac (www.freddiemac.com) was created in 1970, because mortgage funds available to consumers were in short supply. Freddie Mac buys loans and then sells them on the secondary mortgage market to provide additional funds for borrowers and investors. Freddie Mac loans are restricted to the same limits as Fannie Mae. Freddie Mac also issues stock to the general public, much like Fannie Mae.

Very tight credit in 1969 and 1970 resulted in the passage of the Emergency Home Finance Act of 1970, which established, among other things, the **Federal Home Loan Mortgage Corporation (FHLMC)**, now known as Freddie Mac. This agency was set up specifically to provide a secondary mortgage market for the savings and loan associations that are members of the Federal Home Loan Bank System.

Organization of Freddie Mac
In 1968, business and industry were expanding and with that, demands for operational loans were increasingly urgent. At the same time, the federal government refinanced a large number of long- and short-term Treasury debt instruments. Both of these conditions, occurring almost simultaneously, drained available reserves in the economy. Meanwhile, the Federal Reserve, trying to prevent what they saw as a super-inflationary spiral, slowed the printing of money. As a result, money became scarce and interest rates went up. Yields on short-term securities climbed to higher levels than long-term ones, a situation that economists call an inverted yield curve. Money was withdrawn from savings accounts all around the country to purchase these high-yield financial

vehicles that did not require a long-term investment. In other words, these investments were still relatively liquid, despite their high returns.

Hardest hit in this depletion of conventional bank savings accounts—called disintermediation—were savings and loan associations. They soon had no funds with which to make new mortgage loans. In fact, the monthly payments on existing loans barely covered daily cash operating requirements because those loans had been made at the lower interest rates of previous years. Meanwhile, depositors were withdrawing their cash and not making significant deposits anymore because of the availability of higher yielding money market investments.

To reduce the impact of this major cash flow situation, Freddie Mac came on the scene with an initial subscription of $100 million from the 12 Federal Home Loan district banks. Under the direction of three members of the Federal Home Loan Bank Board, Freddie Mac raised additional funds by floating its own securities, backed by its own mortgage pools and guaranteed by Ginnie Mae.

In 1989, Freddie Mac became an independent stock company, directly competing with Fannie Mae. Freddie Mac is governed by an 18-member board, 13 of whom are elected by the stockholders and five appointed by the President. It has a line of credit with the U.S. Treasury, giving it the same status as Fannie Mae. Both HUD and the Treasury provide overall supervision to Freddie Mac.

Operations of Freddie Mac
Freddie Mac purchases conventional loans, as well as FHA-insured and DVA-guaranteed loans, from savings associations all over the country, which is of significant help to the thrifts particularly when money is tight. These savings institutions handle **conventional mortgages** primarily, and these are not backed by any federal or state insurance or guarantee program. Freddie Mac accepts **convertible mortgages**, that is, loans with adjustable rates of interest that can be converted to fixed rate loans during their terms.

Freddie Mac's commitments to purchase are made at specific discounts and/or interest rates and for various types of mortgages. Fees are charged accordingly. All loans submitted to Freddie Mac must have closed within one year of their sale.

Credit Standards of Freddie Mac
Freddie Mac's "**Gap Ratio**" credit standard for qualifying loan applicants is a useful benchmark for potential homebuyers. The gap ratio is the difference between the applicants' monthly debt-payment-to-income ratio and monthly housing-expense-to-income ratio. The gap between these two ratios should be no more than 15% as points. This standard recognizes the impact of applicants' credit card balances, car loan payments, student loans, and other revolving credit payments on their ability to repay their mortgage loans.

For example, if a couple's housing expense is 31% of monthly income, and their monthly revolving credit payments total 19% of monthly income, their total monthly debt-to-income ratio is 50%. That total when considered alone may not always result in these applicants being denied a loan. However, in this case, their total revolving debt load is more than a 15% addition to their housing debt load; that is the reason the loan is denied.

Potential Competitive Difficulties: Freddie Mac vs. Fannie Mae
U.S. banks and other major lenders have in recent years voiced concern that Freddie Mac and Fannie Mae might move into the loan origination business, which has always been the lenders' guarded turf. In June, 2005, The Heritage Foundation said that Fannie Mae and Freddie Mac controlled half of the residential real estate mortgages outstanding, which was estimated to total more than $9 trillion. The U.S. Congress has been working on new statutes to control the activities of Fannie Mae and Freddie Mac, but legislation has not been passed to date.

G I N N I E   M A E

Ginnie Mae (www.ginniemae.gov) offers high yield, low-risk, guaranteed securities. Ginnie Mae does not buy securities as Fannie Mae does. Rather, it guarantees securities already issued by FHA-approved home lenders. Investors who purchase the FHA loans in the secondary mortgage market are thus guaranteed to receive their investment back including interest, minus any fees charged by Ginnie Mae. This means that if an investor purchases a loan, and the borrower is late on a payment, Ginnie Mae will make the payment to the investor who holds the note. This assures investors that they will always be paid on time.

Created in 1968 as a wholly-owned government corporation under the Urban Development Act, Ginnie Mae is an agency of the **Department of Housing and Urban Development (HUD)**. Since then, Ginnie Mae has expanded its activities in the secondary mortgage market, and today, it has a great deal of influence in stabilizing the national real estate financial market.

Securities Pools of Ginnie Mae
Backed by the credit of the U.S. government and funded by the borrowing power of the U.S. Treasury, Ginnie Mae guarantees timely payments of principal and interest by issuers of securities to the holders of those securities. This guarantee means that qualified mortgage originators along with authorized dealers in approved mortgages can raise additional capital for making loans by pledging a pool of their existing loans as collateral for a securities issue. The Ginnie Mae-backed guarantee is essentially an alternative to selling the mortgages. The loan originators continue to collect servicing fees, but now they have additional funds to lend. The securities buyers also benefit from Ginnie Mae's guarantee in that they know they will receive their shares of monthly mortgage payments even if a borrower defaults on a loan.

For example, an individual investor purchases a fractional number of securities from the Ginnie Mae pool. A $200,000 purchase means that the investor would "own" $200,000 worth of a large pool of mortgages. The investor would receive a proportionate share of the payments made by borrowers collected in the pool, an amount sufficient to pay at least the principal and interest due on the $200,000 invested.

One Ginnie Mae program calls for mortgages to have homogeneous interest rates and finance similar types of properties. The pool of these mortgages has a value of at least $2 million and backs up a securities issue equaling the total value of the pool. The collateral pool contains eligible mortgages not more than one year old (or two years for multifamily mortgages), for identifiable properties. The mortgages were taken out by real people who make regular monthly payments. Another Ginnie Mae program does not require that the pooled mortgages be homogeneous. Their interest rates may vary by 1%. The securities backed by these mortgage pools and guaranteed by Ginnie Mae are registered and issued in requested denominations.

There are three general types of mortgage-backed securities

1. **Straight pass-throughs**

2. **Modified pass-throughs**

3. **Fully modified pass-throughs**

Straight pass-through securities guarantee a monthly interest payment to the securities owner, regardless of whether the entire principal and interest payment was received from the mortgage pool. Fully modified pass-through securities guarantee a monthly principal and interest payment, no matter what the actual payment collected totals.

Ginnie Mae charges issuers of securities a $500 application fee and a premium for its guarantee based on the outstanding balance of the securities at the end of each month. Most mortgage-backed securities pools follow the Ginnie Mae process, even private ones that have been set up in recent years.

Ginnie Mae and Fannie Mae in Tandem Plan

The Fannie Mae-Ginnie Mae **tandem plan** combines Fannie Mae's secondary market activities with Ginnie Mae's guaranteed backing of mortgage securities. The tandem plan offers lenders special assistance when money is tight, and discounts for mortgages are high. Although Ginnie Mae can operate in tandem with any qualified mortgage financier, this agency primarily performs these functions with Fannie Mae.

The tandem plan is used for high-risk mortgages. Fannie Mae commits to an originator of such mortgages to purchase the loans at normal market rates. Ginnie Mae then guarantees to Fannie Mae that Ginnie Mae will buy the mortgages from Fannie Mae at par value. The originator sells the mortgages to Fannie Mae at market value, and Ginnie Mae makes up the discount difference between par value and market rates. As a result, Fannie Mae continues to purchase loans and maintains its profit orientation by depending on Ginnie Mae to subsidize any large discounts resulting from the loan's high degree of risk.

The tandem plan increases Ginnie Mae's special assistance financing—one of the tasks it took over after the 1968 Fannie Mae restructuring. Fannie Mae funds actually back the mortgage. Ginnie Mae makes up only the discount. So, more funds are available to finance special assistance projects.

OFFICE OF FEDERAL HOUSING ENTERPRISE OVERSIGHT

The Office of Federal Housing Enterprise Oversight (**OFHEO**), www.ofheo.gov) makes legislative recommendations to enhance Fannie Mae and Freddie Mac programs. OFHEO conducts audits of Fannie Mae and Freddie Mac, so it can make recommendations to the Congress when these programs are under consideration.

Overview

Fannie Mae

- Issues stock to general public
- Issues mortgage-backed securities

Ginnie Mae

- Guarantees securities issued by FHA-approved lenders

Freddie Mac

- Issues stock to general public
- Buys and sells conventional loans

Office of Federal Housing Enterprise Oversight

- Conducts audits of Fannie Mae and Freddie Mac
- Makes legislative recommendations

ELECTRONIC UNDERWRITING SYSTEMS

Today, automation and computerization are significantly changing how the mortgage finance industry works. A major example is **automated underwriting**, an electronic underwriting system currently offered by Fannie Mae that objectively and accurately predicts the risks of lending to specific borrowers.

Fannie Mae's Desktop Underwriter system analyzes borrowers' credit and the property's value and provides lenders with an opinion of the risk level they would incur if they lend these borrowers mortgage money on this property. The system's "opinion" is based on information submitted on the loan application, and lenders receive it between 1 and 30 minutes after inputting the data. Fannie Mae must receive verification from loan originators before full approval. Usually, originators fax information, such as a prospective borrower's pay stubs, two years of W2 income tax forms, and three monthly bank statements, to Fannie Mae.

Loan approval standards built into the automated underwriting systems were specified by the **Mortgage Industry Standard Maintenance Organization (MISMO)**, a subsidiary of the **Mortgage Bankers Association**, and adopted by the mortgage banking industry in July 2001. Almost all mortgage companies now use some form of automated underwriting. Close to 60% use Fannie Mae's Desktop Underwriter or Freddie Mac's Loan Prospector. Common underwriting standards simplify and speed up electronic mortgage application and reduce costs.

Fannie Mae and Freddie Mac also provide a means for automated home appraisals, involving statistical models to compute values in seconds. The system looks at sales prices of homes in a neighborhood on various databases and compares the property under appraisal to them. Fannie Mae's appraisals are free; Freddie Mac charges $50 to $200 for an appraisal.

Credit scoring is one of the underpinnings of automated mortgage approval. Credit scoring objectively determines credit risk of a specific borrower based on the probability that he or she will repay the debt. Credit scores are calculated by a formula that weights payment history, balance of outstanding debt, credit history, types of credit held, and number of credit inquiries, among other factors. Credit scores are considered more fair and objective than earlier methods of determining a person's credit worthiness because personal characteristics such as age, race, gender, religion, national origin, marital status, current address, or whether the borrower was ever on welfare do not enter the equation. Applicants' credit information on which these scores are based is collected by three major credit information repositories: Experian, Equifax, and Transunion.

According to the **Fair, Isaac & Co. (FICO)** test, loan applicants who always pay their bills on time receive the highest credit scores of 700 to more than 800. Applicants who do not pay their bills on time receive scores of 400 to 620. So, it is important for young people just starting to use credit to realize the impact of how they handle it from the beginning. Their behavior regarding credit now can affect their ability to obtain mortgages in the future and how high an interest rate they will pay. Borrowers can check the effect of their credit scores on interest rates at the Fair, Isaac & Co. Web site, www.myfico.com. If borrowers do not know their credit scores, they can obtain that information from the lender or from Fair, Isaac & Co. for a fee.

It is important to note that some misuse of credit scoring has occurred, thus it is recommended that lenders remember the following

- Do not automatically disqualify someone simply based on a subpar score; credit scores may not be used to "single out" or prevent low-to-moderate-income borrowers from receiving mortgages.

- Double check electronic credit files because errors are common.

- If an applicant has a subpar score, examine the score factor codes carefully and work with the applicant to remove "fixable" items.

REAL ESTATE MORTGAGE INVESTMENT CONDUIT—REMIC

The **Real Estate Mortgage Investment Conduit (REMIC)**, in place since January 1, 1987, enables lenders to pool real estate loans as collateral covering the sale of securities to institutional and private investors, thus providing them with addition funds so they can offer more loans.

Legislation establishing the REMIC removed federal tax law obstacles to issuing and investing in residential and commercial mortgage-backed securities. A REMIC holds mortgages and issues securities representing interests in those mortgages. Because the REMIC is exempt from federal income tax, the income from the mortgages is taxable only to the holders of the REMIC securities, eliminating the double taxation that previously made these types of securities less attractive. Similar securities before the advent of REMIC were taxed both at the pool level and at the investor level.

Essentially, a REMIC is a conduit that holds fixed mortgage pools that back securities. The collateral for the securities is the cash flow in the form of regular mortgage payments by borrowers. Today, REMIC is the structure for mortgage securitization and has been extremely successful in opening general capital markets to real estate borrowers.

Through the REMIC structure, issuers can set up classes of securities called **tranches** that meet the needs of groups of investors and respond to market conditions. Issuers set up a series of tranches, with payments from the mortgage pool allocated sequentially to each class. A tranche receives principal payments only after the principal on the previous class (tranche) has been paid. In other words, the higher the tranche is, the shorter is its term to maturity.

Some tranches are "stripped" into their **interest-only (IO)** or **principal-only (PO)** components. These sorts of derivative securities generate trading and hedging opportunities based on the uncertain repayment feature of mortgage securities. With strips, the cash flows from a mortgage pool are divided. The IO strips receive only the interest components of the payments, and the PO strips receive only the part of the payment going to principal. When interest rates fall and mortgage payments accelerate, IO strips decrease in value because their holders will not receive as much interest over the life of the securities than they originally anticipated. At the same time, PO strips go up in value because the holders of those securities will get principal payments at a faster rate. When interest rates rise, the opposite situation occurs.

The **Commercial Mortgage-Backed Securities pool (CMBS)** is a popular REMIC because until its advent, commercial loan originators had no option but to keep these loans in their own portfolios. There was no Fannie Mae or Freddie Mac for commercial real estate lending. Usually, very large commercial real estate loans had to be divided among several lenders to spread the risk.

S U M M A R Y

Because credit worthiness of borrowers and collateral evaluation have been relatively standardized, trading in securities that are backed by mortgages has become common and attractive to investors. Loan originators sell mortgages to second owners who invest in them nationwide, and as a result, capital is freed up, enabling the lenders to make more loans.

Besides the original secondary market for only FHA and DVA loans, today conventional mortgages can be bought and sold on the secondary market. These loans can be mortgages on single-family homes, condominiums, multifamily buildings, and even commercial developments. The federally established agency/corporations Fannie Mae, Freddie Mac, and Ginnie Mae redistribute funds from cash-rich regions of the country to cash-poor areas through their operations on the secondary market.

Fannie Mae was formed in 1938 as a federal agency involved in purchasing and managing FHA-insured loans. Today, however, Fannie Mae is a private, for-profit corporation dealing in every type of real estate mortgage loan. To raise funds for purchase mortgages, Fannie Mae charges lenders fees and can borrow from the U.S. Treasury. Recently Fannie Mae was authorized to sell its own securities and is expanding its scope and policies in response to the current active real estate market.

Ginnie Mae, created in 1968, remains a wholly owned government corporation under HUD. Ginnie Mae participates in the secondary market through its mortgage-backed securities pools and the tandem plan. Ginnie Mae guarantees the payment of principal and interest to investors in securities backed by homogeneous mortgage pools collected by qualified mortgage originators.

The tandem plan connects Fannie Mae's secondary market activities with Ginnie Mae's role of guaranteeing loans to stabilize the national money market. Ginnie Mae does most of its tandem activities with Fannie Mae, although Ginnie Mae can team up with any qualified financier. More than any other federal government-instituted method, the secondary mortgage market has reduced fluctuations in regional real estate cycles and their impact on the construction and other industries and the U.S. economy as a whole. Fannie Mae, Freddie Mac, and Ginnie Mae enable local lenders to sell their loans and increase their cash flow so they can make more loans available and also increase their placement and service fees.

Electronic underwriting is revolutionizing mortgage financing, because an analysis of a borrower's credit worthiness and the value of property as collateral for a mortgage is available within minutes of submitting a loan application. Fannie Mae's Desktop Underwriter and Freddie Mac's Loan Prospector programs are used extensively by lenders today. Furthermore, the foundation of these systems is built-in standardized credit scoring, which provides objective assessments of the probability of loan repayment, regardless of the borrower's personal background. The best credit scores of 700 or more qualify borrowers for the loans with the lowest interest rates because these borrowers present the least risk to the lenders.

The Real Estate Mortgage Investment Conduit (REMIC) expands secondary mortgage market activities by enabling pooled mortgages to be securitized. These pools back securities, and the payments on the mortgages are the collateral for the securities. The REMIC offers classes (tranches) of mortgage pools to investors and essentially makes the U.S. mortgage loan market limitless in potential scope. The Commercial Mortgage-backed Securities pool is a special REMIC that serves the secondary market for commercial and multifamily loans.

TERMS AND PHRASES

Administered Price System   Fannie Mae securities purchasing procedure where required yields are adjusted daily to reflect financial market factors

Conventional Mortgages   mortgage loan made without any additional guarantees for repayment, such as FHA insurance, DVA guarantees, or private insurance; usually given at an 80% loan-to-value (L/V) ratio

Convertible Mortgages   borrower can change to a fixed rate at any time during the life of an adjustable-rate loan

Credit Scoring   used in electronic underwriting to analyze a borrower's credit

Desktop Underwriter   Fannie Mae's electronic system for qualifying borrowers

Disintermediation   rapid withdrawal of money from savings accounts to invest in higher-yield instruments

Electronic Underwriting System   using the Internet to analyze data to qualify a borrower's credit and the property's value

Fair, Isaac & Co.   company which originated credit scoring

Loan Prospector   Freddie Mac's electronic underwriting source

Multi-class Mortgage Securities   short-term or long-term mortgage securities, with or without pass-through privileges

Par   face value of a bond or security

Pass-Throughs   payment on securities sold in the secondary market that are sent directly to the investors

Primary Lenders   originators of real estate loans

Real Estate Mortgage Investment Conduit (REMIC)   multi-class securities that hold real estate mortgages and issue securities representing interests in these mortgages

Secondary Mortgage Market   source to which originators of loans may sell them, freeing funds for continued lending; aids in distributing mortgage funds on a national level from money-rich to money-poor areas

Securitization   pooling of real estate mortgages and trust deeds to act as collateral for the sale of securities

Tandem Plan   investment plan combining Fannie Mae secondary market activities with Ginnie Mae guarantees

Tranche   portion or class of a multi-class security

C H A P T E R   Q U I Z

1. Which primary participant in the secondary mortgage market guarantees investors that they will receive payment for the security they hold by making late payments for the borrower, if necessary?
    a. Ginnie Mae
    b. Fannie Mae
    c. Freddie Mac
    d. Office of Federal Housing Enterprise Oversight

2. New real estate loans are created by
    a. primary lenders.
    b. Ginnie Mae.
    c. Freddie Mac.
    d. Fannie Mae.

3. Today, most loans created by the various fiduciary sources will be
    a. warehoused.
    b. kept in the lender's portfolio.
    c. sold in the secondary market.
    d. refinanced.

4. The secondary mortgage market is made up of
    a. small loans made by lending institutions.
    b. private investors.
    c. the sale of real estate promissory notes.
    d. None of the above

5. Which of the following is not a participant in the secondary mortgage market?
    a. the VA
    b. OFHEO
    c. Freddie Mac
    d. Ginnie Mae

6. Fannie Mae buys
   a. only single-family detached residences.
   b. single family residences made up of 1-4 units.
   c. any type of residential property regardless on the number of units.
   d. any type of property.

7. The loan cap on a Fannie Mae purchase is
   a. no more than 80% of the HUD area average housing price.
   b. determining ever 5 years.
   c. determined annually.
   d. $500,000.

8. Which of the following is the purpose of Freddie Mac?
   a. Buy and Sell conventional loans
   b. Guarantee securities issued by FHA approved lenders
   c. Make legislative recommendations
   d. Buy securities from the general public

9. The system that is being used by Fannie Mae to process loans is
   a. REMIC.
   b. FICO.
   c. Desktop Underwriter.
   d. Loan Prospector.

10. Which is not a rule for credit scoring?
    a. Don't automatically disqualify someone because of a sub-par score
    b. Work with the applicant to clear fixable items
    c. Be aware of potential errors in electronic credit files
    d. Disregard the score factor codes for sub-par scores

11. The largest single investor in the mortgage industry today is
    a. Freddie Mac.
    b. Fannie Mae.
    c. Ginnie Mae.
    d. the VA.

12. Which of the following is exempt from federal income tax?
    a. REITs.
    b. MISMOs.
    c. REMICs.
    d. FHLMCs.

13. Freddie Mac is governed by an 18-member board of directors. Who elects these members?
    a. Stockholders of Freddie Mac
    b. President of the United States
    c. Congress
    d. Both A and B

14. Fannie Mae is able to maintain the flow of funds available for the purchase of mortgage loans from the private market by issuing
    a. bonds.
    b. stocks.
    c. mortgage-backed securities.
    d. none of the above.

15. The flex 97 affordable housing loan program is part of
    a. Fannie Mae.
    b. Freddie Mac.
    c. Ginnie Mae.
    d. REIT.

16. Fannie Mae uses an electronic underwriting program achieving an estimated loan approval within 60 seconds to 30 minutes. In addition to this electronic underwriting system, the originator of the loan must also fax which the following alternative verification information
    a. three years of W2s.
    b. 2 monthly bank statements.
    c. pay stubs.
    d. all of the above.

17. Which credit scores qualify for the best interest rate loans?
    a. 710+
    b. 620-710
    c. 520-620
    d. Any score over 500

18. Freddie Mac was created in
    a. 1938.
    b. 1970.
    c. 1968.
    d. none of the above.

19. The tandem plan combines
    a. Ginnie Mae and Freddie Mac.
    b. Freddie Mac and Fannie Mae.
    c. Ginnie Mae and Fannie Mae.
    d. Ginnie Mae and REMIC.

20. Which of the following is not a credit reporting agency?
    a. Experion
    b. Equifax
    c. Transunion
    d. FICA

7

MORTGAGE LENDERS

What you will learn in this Chapter

- Institutional Lenders

- Non-Institutional Lenders

Test Your Knowledge

1. What conditions caused the restructuring of real estate finance and mortgage options available to consumers?
   a. Disintermediation
   b. High interest rates
   c. Short money supply
   d. All of the above

2. What is the minimum number of investors required for a REIT?
   a. 100
   b. 75
   c. 125
   d. 50

3. Commercial banks receive their funding from what source?
   a. Checking accounts
   b. Certificates of Deposit
   c. Other intermediaries
   d. All of the above

4. Disintermediation occurred when
   a. people took their money out of Savings and Loan Associations and deposited it into savings accounts at commercial banks
   b. people began depositing their money into Savings and Loan Associations for the high rate of return they promised.
   c. people took their money out of Savings and Loan Associations to deposit it into investments with higher rates of interest.
   d. people began investing in real estate.

5. Which one of the following methods is NOT used by the Fed to regulate the nation's money supply?
   a. Reserve requirements
   b. Open market operations
   c. Sell loans on the secondary mortgage market
   d. Change the discount rate

6. The reserve requirement the Fed requires is
   a. a percentage of deposits.
   b. allowed to be loaned out to customers.
   c. may be raised or lowered.
   d. Both A and C

7. The process whereby a mortgage company will use funding from a commercial bank to make a loan, with the intention of selling that loan to an investor, is called
   a. warehousing.
   b. origination.
   c. secondary mortgage market.
   d. None of the above

The lender will screen applicants, verify their veteran status, and process the loan if the candidate meets all qualifications. The Department of Veterans Affairs does not need to approve any applications. Interested candidates request a Certificate of Eligibility from their VA office before filling out the loan application. This certificate will indicate the amount of the loan guarantee, or their **veteran's entitlement**.

VA loans may be used for the purchase of property, construction, repairs to a property, or improvements to a property. The loan must be used for property consisting of 1 to 4 units, or a condominium. Residential complexes with more than four units will not qualify for a VA-guaranteed loan.

The Veterans Administration does not make loans. It guarantees loans made by an approved institutional lender, much like the FHA. The main differences between the two government programs are that only an eligible veteran may obtain a VA loan, and the VA does not require a down payment up to a certain loan amount. Both programs were created to assist people in buying homes when conventional loan programs did not fit their needs.

These loans are made by a mortgage lender, such as a mortgage company, savings and loan or bank. The VA's guaranty on the loan protects the lender against loss if the payments are not made, and is intended to encourage lenders to offer veterans loans with more favorable terms. The amount of guaranty on the loan depends on the loan amount and whether the veteran used some entitlement previously.

With the current maximum guaranty, a veteran who hasn't previously used the benefit may be able to obtain a VA loan up to $417,000 with no down payment in 2006, depending on the borrower's income level and the appraised value of the property. A local VA office can provide more details on guaranty and entitlement amounts.

The loan guarantee amount is based on the size of the loan. A veteran is able to use this loan only once in his or her lifetime. If a veteran uses only a portion of his or her entitlement, he or she may use the remaining portion on a separate loan at a later date. There are, however, certain exceptions to this rule. For example, if a veteran has sold the property, and the VA-guaranteed loan is paid in full; if the Department of Veteran's Affairs is released from the original loan; if any losses suffered by the Department of Veteran's Affairs are paid in full; or if the property is transferred to another veteran with loan guarantee benefits. In these cases, the veteran is entitled to increase the loan guarantee amount to the full amount of his or her entitlement.

A veteran must possess a **Certificate of Eligibility**, which is available from the Veterans Administration, before applying for a VA loan, The certificate will show the veteran's entitlement, or right to obtain the loan.

If a veteran decides to sell his or her home, the VA requires a release from personal liability to the government to be signed prior to the sale of the home. If this release is not completed, the veteran remains responsible for the property. Additionally, the release

Mobile homes fall under a separate category. A mobile home must measure at least 400 square feet to qualify as a property for purchase with a VA-guaranteed loan. Single-wide mobile homes have a maximum financing term of 15 years and 32 days. Double-wide mobile homes have a maximum financing term of 20 years and 32 days. VA-guaranteed loans do not require a down payment, provided that the estimate of reasonable value does not exceed the VA loan guarantee; however, the lender may require a down payment. This is negotiated directly with the lender. If the purchase price of a property is more than the reasonable value, a VA-guaranteed loan may still be used, as long as the buyer pays the difference between the reasonable value and the purchase price in cash at closing.

In the event that a veteran has a difficult time paying the loan, and defaults for a period of three months, a notice of default is given to the Department of Veterans Affairs, alerting them to the situation. The VA will then aid the veteran in making the necessary payments, and counsel him or her on how to keep on track with future payments.

Five Easy Steps to a VA Loan

1. Apply for a **Certificate of Eligibility**. A veteran who doesn't have a certificate can obtain one easily by completing VA Form 26-1880, Request for a Certificate of Eligibility for VA Home Loan Benefits, and submitting it to one of the Eligibility Centers with copies of his or her most recent discharge or separation papers covering active military duty since September 16, 1940, which show active duty dates and type of discharge.

2. Decide on a home the buyer wants to acquire, and sign a purchase agreement.

3. Apply to a VA-approved mortgage lender for the loan. While the appraisal is being done, the lender (mortgage company, savings and loan, bank, etc.) can be gathering credit and income information. If the lender is authorized by the VA to do automatic processing, upon receipt of the VA appraisal the loan can be approved and closed without waiting for VA's review of the credit application. For loans that must first be approved by VA, the lender will send the application to the local VA office, which will notify the lender of its decision.

4. The lender orders an appraisal, known as Certificate of Reasonable Value (CRV), from VA. A loan can't exceed the value established by the CRV. Most VA regional offices offer a "speed-up" telephone appraisal system.

5. The loan closes, and the buyer moves in.

A major benefit of a loan guaranteed by the Veterans Administration is that no down payment is required for some VA loans. There is a maximum loan amount allowed for a no-down-payment transaction, and a formula to establish the amount of down payment for a larger loan amount.

If a veteran sells his or her home, and the buyer gets a new loan which pays off the old VA loan, the veteran may restore eligibility and apply for a new VA loan. If a veteran sells his or her home and the buyer takes it "subject to" the existing VA loan, the veteran remains personally liable for the loan. A VA loan is a purchase-money loan that may result in a deficiency judgment in the case of foreclosure, and the original borrower (the veteran) would be liable for the deficient amount.

Maximum loan amounts vary in different areas of the state depending on local economies. There is no maximum sales price a veteran may pay. Certain specific criteria apply to these loans, however. All property secured by a VA loan must be owner-occupied. Points charged to the seller, and interest rates, are subject to change depending on economic conditions. No prepayment penalty is allowed on a VA loan. The seller usually pays loan discount points, unless the loan is a refinance.

There are a variety of loan types available, including fixed-term loans, adjustable-rate loans, and graduated payment loans.

VA Financing
Millions of veterans and service personnel are eligible for VA financing.
Even though many veterans have already used their loan benefits, it may be possible for them to buy homes again with VA financing using remaining or restored loan entitlement.

- Before arranging for a new mortgage to finance a home purchase, veterans should consider some of the advantages of VA home loans.

- Most importantly, no down payment is required in most cases.

- Loan maximum may be up to 100% of the VA-established reasonable value of the property. Due to secondary market requirements, however, loans generally may not exceed $417,000 (2006 maximum).

- Flexibility of negotiating interest rates with the lender

- No monthly mortgage insurance premium to pay

- Limitation on buyer's closing costs

- An appraisal that informs the buyer of property value

- Thirty-year loans with a choice of repayment plans
    - ❖ Traditional fixed payment (constant principal and interest; increases or decreases may be expected in property taxes and homeowner's insurance coverage)
    - ❖ Graduated Payment Mortgage (GPM)—low initial payments which gradually rise to a level payment starting in the sixth year
    - ❖ Growing Equity Mortgage (GEM)—in some areas; gradually increasing payments with all of the increase applied to principal, resulting in an early payoff of the loan

- For most loans for new houses, construction is inspected at appropriate stages to ensure compliance with the approved plans, and a 1-year warranty is required from the builder warranting that the house is built in conformity with the approved plans and specifications. In those cases where the builder provides an acceptable 10-year warranty plan, only a final inspection may be required

- An assumable mortgage, subject to VA approval of the assumer's credit

- Right to prepay loan without penalty

- The VA performs personal loan servicing and offers financial counseling to help veterans avoid losing their homes during temporary financial difficulties.

Overview

- VA loans provide a guarantee to the lender that it will receive the loan guarantee amount based on the selling price of the home

- Lenders fill out all applications and submit them to the Department of Veteran's Affairs

- An approved VA appraiser must be used to arrive at the amount of the certificate of reasonable value

- There are 4 different loan types that may be used: fixed-term loans; adjustable-rate mortgage; growing equity mortgage, and graduated payment mortgage

- VA-guaranteed loans for property consisting of 1 to 4 units (or condominiums) may be financed for up to 30 years and 32 days.

- Single-wide mobile homes may be financed for up to 15 years and 32 days, while double-wide mobile homes may be financed for up to 20 years and 32 days

- There is no down payment required for a VA-guaranteed loan

California Veterans Farm and Home Purchase Program (Cal-Vet)

California Veterans Farm and Home Purchase Program, or Cal-Vet (www.cdva.ca.gov/calvert) is a full-service lender for veterans. Cal-Vet authorizes, processes, funds and services all loans it administers. The program was developed in 1921, to assist veterans in purchasing both homes and farms. There are no outside funds involved in the Cal-Vet programs; all the money that is used for these loans comes from voter-approved bonds issued by the legislature.

The California Department of Veterans Affairs will buy a property from its seller, and sell the property to an interested, qualified veteran. The title will remain with the California Department of Veterans Affairs until the note has been paid in full, though the borrower holds equitable title and may take possession of the property immediately. Veterans may use the Cal-Vet program to purchase an existing home or farm, finance a land purchase to build a new home, remodel a home purchased as-is, or make home improvements.

Veterans eligible for the Cal-Vet program must be purchasing a property in California, and must also be California residents. They may not have taken a previous benefit from another state and must have served at least 90 days active service duty and received an honorable discharged or discharged under honorable conditions in order to qualify.

There is a maximum amount of money available to each applicant for a VA-guaranteed loan. This loan maximum works well in nearly every California market, and is higher than some other government loan programs

Cal-vet loans require a down payment of 5% of the selling price. All applicants wishing to participate in a Cal-Vet loan must have applied for the loan before the purchase of property was made. The veteran has an obligation to apply for life insurance, with the Department of Veterans Affairs as beneficiary, to pay off the debt in case of the veteran's death.

Remember

The recipient of a Cal-Vet loan will not receive title to the property until the loan is paid in full.

The good news about Cal-Vet is the money a veteran can save with low interest rates, low down payment and easier qualification. Best of all, this program is available to a qualified veteran at no cost to California taxpayers. Here are some of the attractive features of the Cal-Vet loan

- Low interest rate
- Even lower rate for qualified first-time home buyers
- Low down payment
- Subsequent eligibility—use the loan again
- Home and loan protection plans

Interest Rates

Interest rates for new loans are reviewed frequently to ensure that the rates offered are below market. Interest rates are subject to change without notice. Current rates are posted on the Cal-Vet website. A borrower's rate is locked in as of the date he or she applies, and if rates are reduced while the loan is being processed, the veteran will receive the benefit of the lower rate. While technically this is a flexible rate, there is a 1/2% cap on increases during the term of the loan.

Low Down Payment

The veteran's out-of-pocket investment is minimal, with a low down payment requirement. A borrower can invest as little as 2 or 5% of the purchase price or appraised value, whichever is less, as the down payment.

Loan Fees

Cal-Vet obtains a loan guaranty on all loans, using either a guaranty from the United States Department of Veterans Affairs or private mortgage insurance. A borrower also will be charged a loan origination fee (common with most loans) of 1% of the loan amount. This fee must be paid in escrow.

No Monthly Private Mortgage Insurance Premium

Most traditional lenders require a Private Mortgage Insurance (PMI) Premium on loans that exceed an 80% loan-to-value ratio. Cal-Vet helps veteran-borrowers by charging a guarantee fee at the close of escrow, which eliminates the monthly PMI premium.

Expanded Eligibility

Most veterans planning to buy a home in California are eligible; there is no prior residency requirement. Eligible veterans must meet federal rules regarding the use of the bond funds. Cal-Vet has several bond fund sources for veterans who served during a wartime era, regardless of when they served. Veterans whose service was during peacetime are eligible, but must meet the requirements for use of Revenue Bonds funds. Veterans must have received a discharge under honorable conditions, and provide a copy of their DD-214 or release from active duty. If a veteran is currently serving on active duty, he or she can provide a Statement of Service to verify qualifying dates and character of service.

Reusable Loans

A veteran may obtain a new Cal-Vet loan each time he or she decides to purchase a different residence. It may be used again and again as long as the previous loan has been paid off.

Home and Loan Protection Plans

In an effort to ensure that a veteran's investment is safe and sound, Cal-Vet provides comprehensive protection for a veteran and his or her family. No other lender offers protection against natural disasters like Cal-Vet. While thousands of Californians have lost everything in natural disasters like floods and earthquakes, Cal-Vet loan holders have full replacement cost coverage for their homes, keeping disaster in check. A Cal-

Vet home-owner is fully protected against floods and earthquake damage with a Cal-Vet financed home. Cal-Vet's deductible is a low $500 on flood claims, and $500 or 5% of the coverable loss (whichever is greater) on earthquake and mudslide claims. The Cal-Vet loan also includes fire and hazard insurance coverage. There is guaranteed replacement cost coverage on the home, with low premiums and a $250 deductible. With the Cal-Vet loan a veteran receives limited guaranteed life insurance in an amount sufficient to make the principal and interest payments for 1 to 5 years, depending on his or her health status at the time the loan is originated. Optional coverage is offered by the insurance carrier, including additional life insurance for the veteran, life insurance for the veteran's spouse, and disability insurance. Applicants must be under the age of 62 when their loan is funded to receive the life insurance coverage.

Loan Processing

A veteran may process the loan through the local Cal-Vet office or with a Cal-Vet approved mortgage broker. A real estate agent or broker may coordinate the entire process with Cal-Vet, just as they would do with loans from other lenders. Loan processing functions have been centralized to provide consistent and timely processing. Cal-Vet commonly closes most loans within 30 days from receipt of the application.

Overview

- Cal-Vet loans are funded, serviced, processed and authorized in-house.

- Eligibility requirements state that veterans must have served active duty for 90 days and have been honorably discharged.

	FHA	VA	Cal-Vet
Type of Property	Dwellings consisting of one to four units	Dwellings consisting of one to four uits	One unit dwellings or farms
Borrower Eligibility	All U.S. Residents	U.S. Veterans	California Veterans
Maximum Loan Amount	See website for current maximums	None, but loan based on max. entitlement would be $417K including fees. (max. amt. can change yearly)	See website for current maximums
Maximum Purchase Price	None	None	None
Down Payment	At least 3% of acquisition cost	At the discretion of the lender	5%
Discount Points	Yes	Yes	No
Type of Loan	Variety of fixed and variable-rate loans	Fixed rate; GEM; GPM	Variable rate, others possible
Interest Rates	Negotiated	Negotiated	Set by Cal-Vet; can change annually
Maximum Loan Terms	30 years;35 years for new construction; less for mobile homes	30 years; less for mobile homes	30 years
Prepayment Penalty	None	None	None
Secondary Financing	Not at time of sale	Not at time of sale	Yes

P R I V A T E   M O R T G A G E   I N S U R A N C E

Private Mortgage Insurance (PMI) is extra insurance that lenders require from most homebuyers who obtain loans that are more than 80% of their new home's value. In other words, buyers with less than a 20% down payment are normally required to pay PMI.

Benefits of PMI
PMI plays an important role in the mortgage industry by protecting a lender against loss if a borrower defaults on a loan, and by enabling borrowers with less cash to have greater access to homeownership. With this type of insurance, it is possible for a borrower to buy a home with as little as a 3% to 5% down payment. This means that a consumer can buy a home sooner without waiting years to accumulate a large down payment.

New PMI Requirements

The **Homeowner's Protection Act (HPA) of 1998**, requires lenders or servicers to provide certain disclosures concerning PMI for loans secured by the consumer's primary residence and obtained on or after July 29, 1999. The HPA also contains disclosure provisions for mortgage loans that closed before July 29, 1999. In addition, the HPA includes provisions for borrower-requested cancellation and automatic termination of PMI.

Why a Change in PMI Requirements?

In the past, most lenders honored consumers' requests to drop PMI coverage if their loan balance was paid down to 80% of the property value and they had a good payment history. However, consumers were responsible for requesting cancellation, and many consumers were not aware of this possibility. A consumer had to keep track of the loan balance to know if there was enough equity, and then had to request that the lender discontinue requiring PMI coverage. In many cases, people failed to make this request even after they became eligible, and they paid unnecessary premiums ranging from $250 to $1,200 per year for several years. With the new law, both consumers and lenders share responsibility for how long PMI coverage is required.

The Homeowner's Protection Act (HPA) of 1998

Generally, the HPA applies to residential mortgage transactions obtained on or after July 29, 1999, but it also has requirements for loans obtained before that date. This law does not cover VA and FHA government-guaranteed loans. In addition, the law has different requirements for loans classified as "high-risk."

Although the HPA does not provide the standards for what constitutes a "high risk" loan, it permits Fannie Mae and Freddie Mac to issue guidance for mortgages that conform to secondary market loan limits. Fannie Mae and Freddie Mac are corporations chartered by Congress to create a continuous flow of funds to mortgage lenders in support of home ownership. As of January 1, 2006 mortgages in amounts of $417,000 or less are considered **conforming loans**. For non-conforming mortgages, the lender may designate mortgage loans as "high risk."

The following are the four requirements for a transaction to be considered a residential mortgage.

1. A mortgage or deed of trust must be created or retained.

2. The property securing the loan must be a single-family dwelling.

3. The single-family dwelling must be the primary residence of the borrower.

4. The purpose of the transaction must be to finance the acquisition, initial construction or refinancing of that dwelling.

How Does a Borrower Cancel or Terminate PMI?

Under the Homeowners Protection Act (HPA), a borrower has the right to request cancellation of PMI when he or she pays down a mortgage to the point that it equals 80% of the original purchase price or appraised value of the home at the time the loan was obtained, whichever is less. The borrower also needs a good payment history, meaning that he or she has not been 30 days late with the mortgage payment within a year of the request, or 60 days late within 2 years. The lender may require evidence that the value of the property has not declined below its original value, and that the property does not have a second mortgage, such as a home equity loan.

Automatic Termination

Under HPA, mortgage lenders or servicers must automatically cancel PMI coverage on most loans once a borrower pays down the mortgage to 78% of the value, as long as the borrower is current on the loan. If the loan is delinquent on the date of automatic termination, the lender must terminate the coverage as soon thereafter as the loan becomes current. Lenders must terminate the coverage within 30 days of cancellation or the automatic termination date, and are not permitted to require PMI premiums after this date. Any unearned premiums must be returned to the borrower within 45 days of the cancellation or termination date.

For high-risk loans, mortgage lenders or servicers are required to automatically cancel PMI coverage once the mortgage is paid down to 77% of the original value of the property, provided the borrower is current on the loan.

Final Termination

Under HPA, if PMI has not been cancelled or otherwise terminated, coverage must be removed when the loan reaches the midpoint of the amortization period. On a 30-year loan with 360 monthly payments, for example, the chronological midpoint would occur after 180 payments. This provision also calls for the borrower to be current on the payments required by the terms of the mortgage. Final termination must occur within 30 days of this date.

What Disclosures Does the Homeowners Protection Act (HPA) Require?

Loans Obtained on or After July 29, 1999

The HPA has established three different times when a lender or servicer must notify a consumer of his or her rights. Those times are at loan closing, annually, and upon cancellation or termination of PMI.

The content of these disclosures varies depending on whether

1. PMI is "borrower-paid PMI" or "lender-paid PMI"

2. the loan is classified as a "fixed rate mortgage" or "adjustable rate mortgage"

3. the loan is designated as "high risk" or not

At loan closing, lenders are required to disclose all of following to borrowers

- The right to request cancellation of PMI and the date on which this request may be made

- The requirement that PMI be automatically terminated and the date on which this will occur

- Any exemptions to the right to cancellation or automatic termination

- A written initial amortization schedule for fixed rate loans

Annually, a mortgage loan servicer must send borrowers a written statement that discloses

- The right to cancel or terminate PMI

- An address and telephone number to contact the loan servicer to determine when PMI may be canceled

When the PMI coverage is canceled or terminated, a notification must be sent to the consumer stating that

- PMI has been terminated, and the borrower no longer has PMI coverage

- No further PMI premiums are due

The obligation for providing notice of cancellation or termination is with the servicer of the mortgage.

For Loans Obtained Before July 29, 1999

An annual statement must be sent to consumers whose mortgages were obtained before July 29, 1999. This statement should explain that under certain circumstances PMI may be canceled (such as with consent of the mortgagee). It should also provide an address and telephone number to contact the loan servicer to determine whether PMI may be canceled. The HPA's cancellation and automatic termination rules do not apply to loans made before July 29, 1999.

Although parts of this law apply only to loans obtained on or after July 29, 1999, many lenders report that they plan to follow the HPA's requirements for both new and existing loans. Making a call to your mortgage loan servicer will help you understand exactly how the law applies to you and your mortgage.

What if the Value of the Home Has Increased?

When making mortgage payments, most of the payments during the first few years consist of interest. Therefore, it can take 10 to 15 years to pay down a loan to reach 80% of the loan value. If the home prices in the area are rising quickly, the borrower's property value may increase, so that the borrower can reach the 80% mark a lot faster. The property value could also increase due to home improvements that the borrower makes to the home.

If a borrower thinks that the home value has increased, he or she may be able to cancel PMI on the mortgage. Although the law does not require a mortgage servicer to consider the current property value, a borrower should contact the lender to see if there is willingness to do so. Also, a borrower should be sure to ask what documentation may be required to demonstrate the higher property value.

S U M M A R Y

In this chapter we learned about the different federal and state agencies that play a role in keeping real estate finance ethical and feasible for borrowers. We also learned of the different federal and state agencies that aid in guaranteeing and insuring loans to keep a lender's investment safe while helping the borrower to secure the loan they need to purchase property. We outlined special programs for those persons serving in the military, as well as the requirements of such programs. Additionally, we looked at mortgage insurance and private mortgage insurance and their requirements.

T E R M S   A N D   P H R A S E S

Adjustable Rate Mortgage (ARM)   type of loan which allows its interest rate to fluctuate with market conditions. When the national interest rate goes up, so does the interest rate on the note (and vice versa). Payment of the note will fluctuate with changes in the interest rate.

Variable Rate Mortgage (VRM)   mortgage in which the interest rates may vary, depending on the national interest rate which in turn alters the amount of each monthly payment.

C H A P T E R   Q U I Z

1. What is the purpose of a FHA loan?
    a. To guarantee the loan
    b. To insure the loan
    c. Both A and B
    d. Neither A nor B

2. Who or what funds Cal-Vet loans?
    a. Voter-approved bonds
    b. Outside funding
    c. California Department of Veterans Affairs

d. Traditional banks and mortgage companies

3. Under a VA-guaranteed loan, for how long may a traditional single-family dwelling be financed?
   a. 25 years
   b. 20 years
   c. 35 years
   d. 30 years

4. Which one of the following loan types is not allowed when using a VA guaranteed loan?
   a. Fixed-term
   b. Seller-financed loan
   c. Adjustable-rate mortgage
   d. Graduated payment mortgage

5. Which of the following is not a type of default insurance?
   a. Self-insurance
   b. Partial coverage insurance
   c. Third party guaranty insurance
   d. Full coverage insurance

6. With self-insurance, the entire risk falls with
   a. lender.
   b. buyer.
   c. seller.
   d. seller and the buyer.

7. Coinsurance differs from partial coverage insurance in what way?
   a. No difference in coverage, just variations in policy requirements.
   b. Partial coverage covers a percentage of loss; coinsurance covers both a portion of loss and a part of loss incurred beyond the insured amount.
   c. Coinsurance covers a percentage of loss; partial coverage covers a percentage of the loss and an additional portion of loss incurred beyond the insured amount.
   d. Partial insurance only covers a portion of the loss; coinsurance covers the entire loss.

8. Any person may qualify for which type of government-guaranteed loan?
   a. FHA
   b. VA
   c. Cal-Vet
   d. Any of the above

9. In an FHA guaranteed loan, who pays for the Mutual Mortgage Insurance?
   a. Lender

    b.   Federal government

    c.   Borrower

    d.   Seller

10. A graduated payment mortgage

    a.   allows the buyer to pay only a percentage of the interest on the note for the first five years. .

    b.   increases the borrower's monthly payment after 5 years until the borrower has paid the note in full

    c.   both A and B.

    d.   neither A nor B.

11. A borrower interested in an FHA loan will apply directly to

    a.   the Federal Housing Administration.

    b.   the Department of Housing and Urban Development.

    c.   an approved lender.

    d.   either A or C.

12. Who is eligible for a VA loan?

    a.   Any person

    b.   Any person who has served in the United States military

    c.   Only those persons honorably discharged from military service and or their spouses.

    d.   Only active servicemen or women.

13. A VA loan requires what percentage of down payment?

    a.   0%

    b.   2%

    c.   5%

    d.   15%

14. Which of the following is not acceptable form of financing for a VA loan?

    a.   Fixed Term

    b.   Growing equity mortgage

    c.   Adjustable-rate mortgage

    d.   Wrap around trust deed

15. VA loans will cover a mobile home as long as

    a.   it is at least a "double-wide" mobile home.

    b.   it is off the chassis and permanently attached to a lot.

    c.   the home is 350 square feet or more.

    d.   None of the above

16. in 2006, a VA loan may not exceed

    a. $378,000.

    b. $417,000.

    c. $463,000.

    d. $504,000.

17. Cal-Vet benefits may be extended to

     a. an active or formerly active duty service man or woman.

     b. an honorably discharged service man or woman.

     c. a disabled service man or woman.

     d. all of the above.

18. Cal-Vet loans
     a. do not have a maximum amount.
     b. are tied to the HUD area average housing price.
     c. are based on maximums set in the bonds used to finance these loans.
     d. have maximums based on Ginnie Mae guarantees.

19. The maximum purchase price that can qualify for a Cal-Vet loan is
     a. unlimited.
     b. $322,700.
     c. $300,000.
     d. $70,000.

20. Private mortgage insurance is generally required when
     a. when borrowers finance 70% of their home.
     b. when borrowers finance more than 80% of their home.
     c. when borrowers finance 50% to 75% of their home.
     d. for any note amount.

9

CONSUMER PROTECTION

What you will learn in this Chapter

- What to Know About Creditors

- Federal Consumer Protection Laws

- Fair Housing

- State Laws

Test Your Knowledge

1. The Fair Housing Act protects people from all of the following except
    a. redlining
    b. blockbusting
    c. discrimination based on age
    d. landlords refusing to rent to a person with bad credit

2. What federal law expanded the 1866 Civil Rights Act to include more than just discrimination on the basis of race?
    a. Jones v. Mayer
    b. Fair Housing Act
    c. Unruh Act
    d. Civil Rights Act of 1968 and 1988

3. Which state law protects citizens against discrimination when seeking a private residence, whether a single-family home or an apartment?
    a. Unruh Civil Rights Act
    b. California Civil Code Section 54-55.1
    c. California Fair Employment and Housing Act
    d. Housing Financial Discrimination Act

4. Which of the following is NOT considered one of the five most important disclosures under the Truth in Lending Act?
    a. Annual percentage rate
    b. Finance charge
    c. Total amount of payments
    d. Right to rescind

5. Regarding age, which of the following is a false statement?
    a. The creditor may favor candidates 62 or older based on a credit-scoring system.
    b. A creditor may favor candidates under 35 based on a credit-scoring system.
    c. The borrower is too young to sign contracts if he or she is younger than 18.
    d. A creditor may consider a borrower's age if he or she is close to retirement and his or her income may drop upon retirement.

6. Which of the following is a way to build a good credit rating?
    a. Open a checking or savings account
    b. Obtain a credit card or charge card, and make all payments on time
    c. Secure a loan with a co-signer
    d. All of the above

7. Which of the following are allowed on a high rate, high fee loan?
    a. Balloon payments
    b. Default interest rates higher than the pre-default rate
    c. Rebates of interest
    d. Consolidation of two periodic payments or more

INTRODUCTION

The Consumer Credit Protection Act of 1968—which launched Truth in Lending disclosures—was landmark legislation. For the first time, creditors had to state the cost of borrowing in common language so that the consumer could figure out what the charges are, compare costs, and shop for the best credit deal.

Since 1968, credit protections have multiplied rapidly. The concepts of "fair" and "equal" credit have been written into laws that prohibit unfair discrimination in credit transactions, require that consumers be told the reason when credit is denied, let borrowers find out about their credit records, and set up a way for consumers to settle billing disputes.

Each law was meant to reduce the problems with, and confusion about, consumer credit, which—as it became more widely used in our economy— also grew more complex. Together, these laws set a standard for how individuals are to be treated in their financial dealings.

WHAT TO KNOW ABOUT CREDITORS

Creditors look for an ability to repay debt and a willingness to do so—and sometimes for a little extra security to protect their loans. They speak of the "Three Cs of Credit": **capacity, character and collateral**.

Three Cs of Credit
• capacity
• character
• collateral

Capacity   Can the borrower repay the debt? Creditors ask for employment information: the borrower's occupation, how long he or she has worked there, and for what earnings. They also want to know what the borrower's expenses are: how many dependents there are, whether the borrower pays alimony or child support, and the amount of any other obligations.

Character   Will the borrower repay the debt? Creditors will look at the borrower's credit history: the amount of money owed, the frequency of borrowing, the timeliness of paying bills, and a pattern of living within one's means. Creditors also look for signs of stability: how long the borrower has lived at the present address, whether he or she owns or rents the home, and the length of present employment.

Collateral   Is the creditor fully protected if the borrower fails to repay? Creditors want to know what the borrower may have that could be used to back up or secure a loan, and any other resources the borrower has for repaying debt other than income, such as savings, investments or property. Creditors use different combinations of these facts to reach their decisions. Some set unusually high standards; others simply do not make certain kinds of loans. Creditors also use different rating systems. Some rely strictly on their own instinct and experience. Others use a "credit-scoring" or statistical system to predict whether the borrower is a good credit risk. They assign a certain number of points to each of the various characteristics that have proved to be reliable signs that a borrower will repay. Then they rate the borrower on this scale.

Different creditors may reach different conclusions based on the same set of facts. One may find the applicant an acceptable risk, whereas another may deny the loan.

Information the Creditor Can't Use

The Equal Credit Opportunity Act does not guarantee that an applicant will get credit. The borrower must still pass the creditor's tests of credit-worthiness. But the creditor must apply these tests fairly and impartially. The act bars discrimination based on age, gender, marital status, race, color, religion and national origin. The act also bars discrimination because the applicant receives public income, such as veteran's benefits, welfare or social security, or because he or she exercises rights under federal credit laws, such as filing a billing error notice with a creditor. This protection means that a creditor may not use any of these grounds as a reason to

- Discourage a consumer from applying for a loan

- Refuse a consumer a loan if qualified

- Lend a consumer money on terms different from those granted another person with similar income, expenses, credit history and collateral

- Close an existing account

Although creditors may not discriminate on the basis of national origin, they may consider a borrower's immigration status when making a loan decision.

Special Rules

Rules for creditworthiness have changed dramatically over the past 35 years, and consumers can hardly be blamed for their ignorance regarding their rights when borrowing money. Consumer protection has become a complex matter, with myriad laws to defend everyone's right to equal protection under those laws.

Age

In the past, many older persons have complained about being denied credit because they were over a certain age. Or when they retired, they often found their credit suddenly cut off or reduced. So the law is very specific about how a person's age may be used in credit decisions.

A creditor may ask borrowers their age, but if they are old enough to sign a binding contract (usually 18 or 21 years old depending on state law), a creditor may not

- Turn down a borrower or offer a borrower less credit or less favorable credit terms because of his or her age.

- Ignore a borrower's retirement income in evaluating the application.

- Close a borrower's credit account or require a borrower to reapply for it because he or she has reached a certain age or retired.

- Deny a borrower credit or close a borrower's account because credit life insurance or other credit-related insurance is not available to a person of a certain age.

Creditors may "score" a borrower's age in a credit-scoring system, but if a borrower is 62 or older, he or she must be given at least as many points for age as any person under 62.

Because individuals' financial situations can change at different ages, the law lets creditors consider certain information related to age, such as how long until a borrower will retire or how long a borrower's income will continue. An older applicant might not qualify for a large loan with a very low down payment and a long term, but might qualify for a smaller loan with a larger down payment and a shorter term. Remember that although declining income may be a handicap if a borrower is older, he or she can usually offer a solid credit history to his/her or their advantage. The creditor has to consider all the facts and apply the usual standards of creditworthiness to every borrower's particular situation.

Public Assistance

A borrower may not be denied credit just because he or she receives social security or public assistance, such as Temporary Assistance to Needy Families (TANF). But as is the case with age, certain information on this source of income could clearly affect creditworthiness. A creditor may consider such things as how old a borrower's dependents are (because a borrower may lose benefits when he or she reaches a certain age) or whether a borrower will continue to meet the eligibility requirements for receiving benefits. This information helps the creditor determine the likelihood that a borrower's public assistance income will continue.

Housing Loans

The Equal Credit Opportunity Act covers a borrower's application for a mortgage or home-improvement loan. The act bars discrimination because of characteristics such as a borrower's race, color, gender or because of the race or national origin of the people in the neighborhood where a borrower lives or wants to buy a home. Creditors may not use any appraisal of the value of the property that considers the race of the people in the neighborhood.

Also, a borrower is entitled to receive a copy of an appraisal report that he or she paid for in connection with an application for credit, provided the borrower makes a written request for the report.

Gender Discrimination

Both men and women are protected from discrimination based on gender or marital status. But many of the law's provisions were designed to stop particular abuses that generally made it difficult for women to get credit. For example, denying credit or offering less favorable credit terms based on the misperception that single women ignore their debts when they marry, or that a woman's income " doesn't count" because she'll stop work to have and raise children, is unlawful in credit transactions .

The general rule is that a female borrower may not be denied credit because she is a woman or because she is married, single, widowed, divorced or separated. Here are some important protections.

Gender and Marital Status   Usually, creditors may not ask a borrower's gender on an application form (one exception is on a loan to buy or build a home). A borrower does not have to use Miss, Mrs., or Ms. with her name on a credit application. But in some cases, a creditor may ask whether she is married, unmarried or separated (unmarried includes single, divorced and widowed).

Childbearing Plans   Creditors may not ask about a woman's birth-control practices or plans to have children, and they may not assume anything about those plans.

Income and Alimony   The creditor must count all of a woman's income, even income from part-time employment. Child support and alimony payments are a source of income for many women. A woman doesn't have to disclose these kinds of income, but if she does, creditors must count them.

Telephones   Creditors may not consider whether a woman has a telephone listing in her name, because this factor would discriminate against many married women. (However, you may be asked if there's a telephone in your home.)
A creditor may consider whether income is steady and reliable, so a woman must be prepared to show that she can count on uninterrupted income, particularly if the source is alimony payments or part-time wages.

Her Own Account   Many married women once were turned down for credit in their own names, or their husband had to cosign an account—that is, agree to pay if the wife didn't—even when a wife made sufficient income to easily repay the loan herself. Single women couldn't get loans because they were thought to be less reliable than other applicants. Women now have the right to their own credit, based on their own credit records and earnings. Their own credit means separate accounts or loans in their own names, not joint accounts with their husbands or duplicate cards on husbands' accounts.

Here are the rules

- Creditors may not refuse to open an account because of gender or marital status.

- A woman can choose to use her first name and maiden name (Mary Smith), her first name and husband's last name (Mary Jones), or a combined last name (Mary Smith-Jones).

- If she is creditworthy, a creditor may not require her husband to cosign her account, with certain exceptions when property rights are involved.

- Creditors may not ask for information about a woman's husband or ex-husband when she applies for her own credit based on her own income, unless that income is alimony, child support, or separate maintenance payments from a spouse or former spouse.

This last rule, of course, does not apply if a woman's husband is going to use the account or be responsible for paying the debts on the account or if a woman lives in a community property state. (Community property states are Arizona, California, Idaho, Louisiana, Nevada, New Mexico, Texas, Washington and Wisconsin.)

Change in Marital Status   Married women have sometimes faced severe hardships when cut off from credit after their husbands died; single women have had accounts closed when they married, and married women have had accounts closed after a divorce. The law says that creditors may not make a woman reapply for credit because she marries or becomes widowed or divorced. Nor may they close a woman's account or change the terms of her account on these grounds. There must be some sign that her creditworthiness has changed. For example, creditors may ask a woman to reapply if she relied on her ex-husband's income to get credit in the first place.

Setting up her own account protects a woman by establishing her own history of how she handles debt. She can rely on this record if her financial situation changes or if she becomes widowed or divorced. When a woman plans to get married and will take her husband's surname, she should write to her creditors and tell them she wants to keep a separate account.

Application Denied
Remember, a borrower's gender or race may not be used to discourage the individual from applying for a loan. And creditors may not hold up or otherwise delay an application on those grounds. Under the Equal Credit Opportunity Act, a borrower must be notified within 30 days after making an application whether the loan has been approved or not. If credit is denied, the notice must be in writing, and it must explain the specific reasons that a borrower was denied credit, or tell the borrower of the right to ask for an explanation. A borrower has the same rights if an active account is closed.

If consumers are denied credit, they should find out why. They may have to ask the creditors for this explanation. It may be that the creditor thinks the borrower has requested more money than can be repaid from current income. It may be that a borrower has not worked or lived long enough in the community. A consumer can discuss terms with the creditor and ways to improve creditworthiness.

Building a Good Record
A borrower's first attempt to get credit may mean facing a common frustration: sometimes it seems a borrower has to already have credit in order to get credit. Some creditors will look only at a borrower's salary and job and the other financial information on the application. But most also want to know about a borrower's track record in handling credit, namely how reliably the person has repaid past debts. They turn to the records kept by credit bureaus or credit-reporting agencies, whose business is to collect, store and report information about borrowers that is routinely supplied by many lenders. These records include the amount of credit a borrower has received and how faithfully it was repaid.

Here are several ways a borrower can begin to build a good credit history

- Open a checking account or a savings account or both. These do not begin a borrower's credit file, but may be checked as evidence that he or she has money and knows how to manage it. Cancelled checks can be used to show that a borrower pays utilities or rent bills regularly, a sign of reliability.

- Apply for a department store credit card. Repaying credit card bills on time is a plus in credit histories.

- Ask whether funds may be deposited with a financial institution to serve as collateral for a credit card; some institutions will issue a secured credit card, with a credit limit usually no greater than the amount on deposit.

- If a borrower is new in town, write for a summary of any credit record kept by a credit bureau in the former town.

- If a borrower doesn't qualify on the basis of his or her own credit standing, ask to have someone cosign the application.

- If a borrower is turned down, find out why and try to resolve any misunderstandings.

Maintaining Complete and Accurate Credit Records
Mistakes on a borrower's credit record can cloud future credit. A consumer's credit rating is so important; the individual should make sure that credit bureau records are complete and accurate. The Fair Credit Reporting Act says that a borrower must be told what's in the credit file and have any errors corrected.

Negative Information
If a lender refuses a borrower credit because of unfavorable information in his or her credit report, the borrower has the right to get the name and address of the agency that keeps the report. Then, the borrower may request information from the credit bureau,

either by mail or in person. The borrower may not get an exact copy of the file, but he or she will learn what's in the report. The law also says that the credit bureau must help the borrower interpret the data in the report, because the raw data may take experience to analyze. If a borrower is questioning a credit refusal made within the past 60 days, the bureau cannot charge a fee for explaining the report.

If a borrower notifies the bureau about an error, generally the bureau must investigate and resolve the dispute within 30 days after receiving the notice. The bureau will contact the creditor who supplied the data and remove any information that is incomplete or inaccurate from the credit file. If a borrower disagrees with the findings, he or she can file a short statement (100 words) in the record, giving the borrower's side of the story. Future reports to creditors must include this statement or a summary of it.

Old Information

Sometimes credit information is too old to give a good picture of a borrower's financial reputation. There is a limit on how long certain information may be kept in the file.

- Bankruptcies must not be reported after 10 years. However, information about any bankruptcies at any time may be reported if a borrower applies for life insurance with a face value over $150,000, for a job paying $75,000 or more, or for credit with a principal amount of $150,000 or more.

- Suits and judgments paid, tax liens, and most other kinds of unfavorable information must not be reported after 7 years.

- A borrower's credit record may not be given to anyone who does not have a legitimate business need for it. Stores to which a borrower is applying for credit may examine the record; curious neighbors may not. Prospective employers may examine a borrower's record with his or her permission.

Filing a Complaint with Federal Enforcement Agencies

If a borrower has a complaint about a bank or other financial institution, the Federal Reserve System may be able to help. The Federal Reserve System investigates consumer complaints received against state-chartered banks that are members of the system. Complaints about these types of banks will be investigated by one of the 12 Federal Reserve Banks around the country. The Federal Reserve will refer complaints about other institutions to the appropriate federal regulatory agency and let the consumer know where the complaint has been referred. Or a consumer may write directly to the appropriate federal agency by referring to the listing later in this chapter. Many of these agencies do not handle individual complaints; however, they will use information about a consumer's credit experiences to help enforce the credit laws.

When writing to the Federal Reserve, a consumer should submit the complaint— and it should be in writing—to the Division of Consumer and Community Affairs, Board of Governors of the Federal Reserve System, Washington, DC 20551. Be sure to provide the complete name and address of the bank, a brief description of the complaint, and any documentation that may help to investigate the complaint. Do not send original documents, send only copies; and remember to sign and date the letter. The Federal Reserve will acknowledge the complaint within 15 business days, letting the consumer know whether a Federal Reserve Bank will investigate the complaint or whether the complaint will be forwarded to another federal agency for attention.

For complaints investigated by the Federal Reserve (those involving state-chartered member banks), the Reserve Bank will analyze the bank's response to the complaint to ensure that the consumer's concerns have been addressed, and will send the consumer a letter about the findings. If the investigation reveals that a Federal Reserve regulation has been violated, the Reserve Bank will inform the consumer of the violation and the corrective action the bank has been directed to take.

Although the Federal Reserve investigates all complaints about the banks it regulates, it does not have the authority to resolve all types of problems, such as contractual or factual disputes or disagreements about bank policies or procedures. In many instances, however, if a consumer files a complaint, a bank may voluntarily work with the consumer to resolve the situation. If the matter is not resolved, the Federal Reserve will advise the consumer whether he or she should consider legal counsel to resolve the complaint.

FEDERAL CONSUMER PROTECTION LAWS

The sweeping influence of the federal government in housing issues has provided a healthy background for the inspiring story of the persistent growth of private ownership of real property in the United States. Because laws requiring fair and equal treatment of all consumers have been passed, more people are able to buy their own homes now than in any time in history.

Equal Credit Opportunity Act (ECOA)

The **Equal Credit Opportunity Act** (www.lawdog.com/equal2/ec1.htm) protects people from discrimination when applying for a loan. Under this act, no person may be discriminated against based on their sex, religion, race, color, age, marital status, national origin or on the grounds of receiving public funds from welfare. Every buyer is assured that he or she will be treated fairly, without discrimination, when going through the loan application process for a home or for other credit.

The Equal Credit Opportunity Act (ECOA) ensures that all consumers are given an equal chance to obtain credit. This doesn't mean all consumers who apply for credit get it. As discussed earlier, factors such as income, expenses, debt, and credit history are considerations for creditworthiness. The law protects a borrower when dealing with any creditor who regularly extends credit, including banks, small loan and finance companies, retail and department stores, credit card companies and credit unions. Anyone involved in granting credit, such as real estate brokers who arrange financing, is covered by the law. Businesses applying for credit also are protected by the law.

Equal Opportunity Credit Act Guidelines

- Borrowers are not required to answer questions regarding birth control practices or methods or whether they plan on starting a family.

- Borrowers may be asked if they are married; however, a lender is not allowed to ask if a borrower is divorced or widowed.

- Borrowers must be notified within 30 days if they qualify for the loan for which they applied. If the borrower is denied for the loan, the lender must supply the reason(s) for the denial of the loan.

- Borrowers are not required to reveal any information regarding receipt of child support or alimony. Those borrowers who must pay child support or alimony may be asked about it, as it pertains directly to the borrower's income versus obligations. Such obligations may be a determining factor in whether a borrower can make the necessary payment on a loan.

- Borrowers who have a poor credit rating due to sharing a joint account with another person may provide information showing that the delinquent account is through the fault of another person, and not their own.

Under ECOA, when a borrower applies for credit, a creditor may not

- Discourage the borrower from applying because of sexual orientation or gender, marital status, age, race, national origin, or because borrower receives public assistance income.

- Ask the borrower to reveal sex, race, national origin or religion. A creditor may ask a borrower to voluntarily disclose this information (except for religion) if applying for a real estate loan. This information helps federal agencies enforce anti-discrimination laws. A borrower may be asked about his or her residence or immigration status.

- Ask if the borrower is widowed or divorced. When permitted to ask marital status, a creditor may only use the terms "married", "unmarried" or "separated."

- Ask about the borrower's marital status if he or she is applying for a separate, unsecured account. A creditor may ask you to provide this information if you live in community property states, such as Arizona, California, Idaho, Louisiana, Nevada, New Mexico, Texas, Washington and Wisconsin. A creditor in any state may ask for this information if the borrower is applying for a joint account or one secured by property.

- Request information about the borrower's spouse, except when the spouse is applying with the borrower, a spouse will be allowed to use the account, the borrower is relying on a spouse's income or on alimony or child support income from a former spouse, or if the borrower resides in a community property state.

- Inquire about the borrower's plans for having or raising children.

- Ask if the borrower receives alimony, child support, or separate maintenance payments, unless he or she is first told there is no need to provide this information if not relying on these payments to get credit. A creditor may ask if the borrower has to pay alimony, child support or separate maintenance payments.

Under ECOA, when deciding to give a borrower credit, a creditor may not

- Consider the borrower's sex, marital status, race, national origin or religion.

- Consider whether the borrower has a telephone listing in his or her name. A creditor may consider whether the borrower has a phone.

- Consider the race of people in the neighborhood where the borrower wants to buy, refinance or improve a house with borrowed money.

- Consider the borrower's age, unless

  o The borrower is too young to sign contracts, generally younger than 18 years of age

  o The borrower is 62 or older, and the creditor will favor the applicant because of age

  o It's used to determine the meaning of other factors important to credit worthiness. For example, a creditor could use the borrower's age to determine if income might drop because of retirement.

  o It's used in a valid scoring system that favors applicants age 62 and older. A credit-scoring system assigns points to answers provided to credit application questions. For example, length of employment might be scored differently depending on the person's age

Under ECOA, when evaluating a borrower's income, a creditor may not

- Refuse to consider public assistance income the same way as other income.

- Discount income because of the borrower's sex or marital status; for example, a creditor cannot count a man's salary at 100 percent and a woman's at 75 percent. A creditor may not assume a woman of childbearing age will stop working to raise children.

- Discount or refuse to consider income because it comes from part-time employment or pension, annuity or retirement benefits programs.

- Refuse to consider regular alimony, child support or separate maintenance payments. A creditor may ask the borrower to prove receiving this income consistently.

Under ECOA, a borrower also has the right to

- Have credit in one's own birth name (Mary Smith), own first name and spouse's last name (Mary Jones), or own first name and a combined last name (Mary Smith-Jones).

- Get credit without a cosigner, if the borrower meets the creditor's standards.

- Have a cosigner other than a borrower's husband or wife, if one is necessary.

- Keep his or her own accounts after a name change, marital status change, reaching a certain age, or retiring, unless the creditor has evidence that the borrower is not willing or able to pay.

- Know whether the borrower's application was accepted or rejected within 30 days of filing a complete application.

- Know why an application was rejected. The creditor must give the borrower a notice that tells either the specific reasons for the rejection or the borrower's right to learn the reasons within 60 days.

- Get acceptable reasons for rejection. Acceptable reasons include: "Your income was low," or "You haven't been employed long enough." Unacceptable reasons are: "You didn't meet our minimum standards," or "You didn't receive enough points on our credit-scoring system." Indefinite and vague reasons are illegal, so ask the creditor to be specific.

- Find out why the borrower was offered less favorable terms than he or she applied for—unless the borrower accepts the terms. Examples of less favorable terms include higher finance charges or less money than you requested.

- Find out why the borrower's account was closed or why the terms of the account were made less favorable, unless the account was inactive or delinquent.

Remedy for Discrimination If consumers can prove that creditors have discriminated against them for any reason prohibited by this act, they may sue, as an individual, for actual damages plus punitive damages—that is, damages of up to $10,000 for the fact that the law has been violated. In a successful lawsuit, the court will award the consumer court costs and a reasonable amount for attorney's fees. Class action suits are also permitted.

If a consumer suspects discrimination, he or she should

- Complain to the creditor. Make it known the consumer is aware of the law. The creditor may find an error or reverse the decision.

- Check with the state Attorney General to see if the creditor violated state equal credit opportunity laws. The state may decide to prosecute the creditor.

- Bring a case in federal district court. If the borrower wins, he or she can recover damages, including punitive damages. The borrower also can obtain compensation for attorney's fees and court costs.

- Join with other borrowers and file a class action suit. A borrower may recover punitive damages for the group of up to $500,000 or 1% of the creditor's net worth, whichever is less.

- Report violations to the appropriate government agency. If a borrower is denied credit, the creditor must supply the name and address of the agency to contact. While some of these agencies don't resolve individual complaints, the information provided helps them decide which companies to investigate. A list of agencies follows.

If a retail store, department store, small loan and finance company, mortgage company, oil company, public utility, state credit union, government lending program, or travel and expense credit card company is involved, contact

Consumer Response Center
Federal Trade Commission
Washington, DC 20580
The FTC cannot intervene in individual disputes, but the information provided may indicate a pattern of possible law violations that require action by the Commission.

If the complaint concerns a nationally chartered bank (National or N.A. will be part of the name), write to

Comptroller of the Currency
Compliance Management
Mail Stop 7-5
Washington, DC 20219

If the complaint concerns a federally chartered credit union, write to
National Credit Union Administration
Consumer Affairs Division
Washington, DC 20456

If the complaint concerns a federally chartered or federally insured savings and loan association, write to

Office of Thrift Supervision
Consumer Affairs Program
Washington, DC 20552

Complaints against all kinds of creditors can be referred to:
Department of Justice
Civil Rights Division
Washington, DC 20530

If the complaint concerns a state-chartered bank that is insured by the Federal Deposit Insurance Corporation but is not a member of the Federal Reserve System, write to

Federal Deposit Insurance Corporation
Consumer Affairs Division
Washington, DC 20429

Equal Credit Opportunity Act—Regulation B:

Regulation B was issued by the Board of Governors of the Federal Reserve System to implement the provisions of the **Equal Credit Opportunity Act (ECOA)**. The law was enacted in 1974 to make it unlawful for creditors to discriminate in any aspect of a credit transaction on the basis of sex or marital status. In 1976, through amendments to the Act, it also became unlawful to discriminate on the basis of race, color, religion, national origin, age, receipt of public assistance and the good faith exercise of rights under the Consumer Credit Protection Act.

The primary purpose of the ECOA is to prevent discrimination in the granting of credit, by requiring banks and other creditors to make extensions of credit equally available to all creditworthy applicants—with fairness and impartiality, and without discrimination on any prohibited basis. The regulation applies to consumer credit and other types of credit transactions.

Real Estate Settlement Procedures Act (RESPA)

The Real Estate Settlement Procedures Act (RESPA) requires that lenders make certain disclosures to borrowers utilizing a federal mortgage loan or loan program. Any sale of property of 1 to 4 units using these loans must be accompanied by the appropriate disclosures. Federal mortgage loan or loan programs affected by the Act include the following

- Loans made by a lender insured by FDIC or another federal agency

- Loans financed through a federal agency such as the Federal Housing Administration (FHA) or through the Department of Veteran's Affairs (VA)

- Loans sold in the secondary mortgage market to Fannie Mae, Ginnie Mae or Freddie Mac

Lenders are required to supply every applicant with all disclosures and material. If there is more than one person applying for a loan, each applicant must receive his or her own copy of all disclosures. The lender must send the applicants all material no later than three days after the application has been received.

This law protects consumers from abuses during the residential real estate purchase and loan process, and enables them to be better-informed shoppers by requiring that they be given disclosure of the costs of settlement services.

The Real Estate Settlement Procedures Act applies to all federally-related mortgage loans used to purchase or refinance real property improved with buildings of 1 to 4units, provided the property includes the principal residence of the borrower. These include most purchase loans, assumptions, refinances, property improvement loans, and equity lines of credit.

The U.S. Department of Housing and Urban Development's (HUD) Federal Housing Administration (FHA) administers several regulatory programs to ensure equity and efficiency in the sale of housing. HUD's Office of Consumer and Regulatory Affairs, Interstate Land Sales/RESPA Division, is responsible for enforcing RESPA. The Real Estate Settlement Procedures Act (RESPA) applies to almost all mortgage loans and lenders, not just FHA-insured mortgages.

Disclosures at the Time of Loan Application: When a potential homebuyer applies for a mortgage loan, the lender must give the buyer

- A Special Information Booklet, which contains consumer information on various real estate settlement services.

- A Good Faith Estimate of settlement costs, which lists the charges the buyer is likely to pay at settlement and states whether the lender requires the buyer to use a particular settlement service.

- A Mortgage Servicing Disclosure Statement, which tells the buyer whether the lender intends to keep the loan or to transfer it to another lender for servicing, and also gives information about how the buyer can resolve complaints.

- If the borrowers don't get these documents at the time of application, the lender must mail them within 3 business days of receiving the loan application. If the lender turns down the loan within 3 days, however, then RESPA does not require the lender to provide these documents.

The RESPA statute does not provide an explicit penalty for the failure to provide the Special Information Booklet, Good Faith Estimate or Mortgage Servicing Statement. However, bank regulators may choose to impose penalties on lenders who fail to comply with federal law.

Disclosures Before Settlement (Closing) Occurs

- An Affiliated Business Arrangement Disclosure is required whenever a settlement service refers a buyer to a firm with which the service has any kind of business connection, such as common ownership. The service usually can not require the buyer to use a connected firm.

- A preliminary copy of a HUD-1 Settlement Statement is required if the borrower requests it 24 hours before closing. This form gives estimates of all settlement charges that will need to be paid, both by buyer and seller.

Disclosures at Settlement

- The HUD-1 Settlement Statement is required to show the actual charges at settlement.

- An Initial Escrow Statement is required at closing or within 45 days of closing. This itemizes the estimated taxes, insurance premiums, and other charges that will need to be paid from the escrow account during the first year of the loan.

Disclosures after Settlement

- An Annual Escrow Loan Statement must be delivered by the servicer to the borrower. This statement summarizes all escrow account deposits and payments during the past year. It also notifies the borrower of any shortages or surpluses in the account and tells the borrower how these can be paid or refunded.

- A Servicing Transfer Statement is required if the servicer transfers the servicing rights for a loan to another servicer.

Along with these disclosures, RESPA protects consumers by prohibiting several other practices.

- Kickbacks, fee-splitting, and unearned fees: All persons are prohibited from giving or accepting a fee, kickback, or anything of value in exchange for referrals of settlement service business involving a federally related mortgage loan, which covers almost every loan made for residential property. RESPA also prohibits fee-splitting and receiving unearned fees for services not actually performed. Violations of these RESPA provisions can be punished with criminal and civil penalties.

- Seller-required title insurance: A seller is prohibited from requiring a home buyer to use a particular title insurance company. A buyer can sue a seller who violates this provision.

- Limits on escrow accounts: A limit is set on the amount that a lender may require a borrower to put into an escrow account to pay taxes, hazard insurance and other property charges. RESPA does not require lenders to impose an escrow account on borrowers, but some government loan programs or lenders may require an escrow account. During the course of the loan, RESPA prohibits a lender from charging excessive amounts for the escrow account, and each year the lender must notify the borrower of any escrow account shortage and return any excess of $50 or more.

Persons who believe a settlement service provider has violated RESPA in an area in which HUD has enforcement authority may wish to file a complaint. The complaint should outline the violation and identify the violators by name, address and phone number. Complainants should also provide their own name and phone number for follow-up questions from HUD. Requests for confidentiality will be honored. Complaints should be sent to

Director, Interstate Land Sales / RESPA Division
Office of Consumer and Regulatory Affairs
U.S. Department of Housing and Urban Development
Room 9146 451 7th Street SW
Washington, DC 20410

Truth in Lending Act Regulation Z

The Federal Reserve Board created the Truth in Lending Act (simply called Regulation Z), which requires creditors to disclose various credit terms to the borrower. This allows the borrower to make an informed decision between the different creditors and/or sources of available credit.

Creditors are those who extend credit or make loans to borrowers (more than 25 times each year for non-secured loans; 5 times each year for those loans requiring real property as security for the loan). A written arrangement, outlining payment amount, timing and other terms of the loan is required. A creditor is allowed to charge interest on the loan, provided that the interest on the loan is payable in four installments and that there is written agreement to these terms. It is important to note that the person arranging credit is not the creditor. Rather, the institution, or actual person making the loan, is the creditor. For example, a loan officer at Wells Fargo Bank is not a creditor; Wells Fargo Bank is the creditor.

There are certain transactions that are exempt from the Truth in Lending Act. These transactions are commercial, agricultural or business loans. Loans made for more than $25,000 are exempt from Regulation Z, unless the loan is a purchase money loan (where the loan must be secured by real or personal property) and the borrower plans to use the property as his or her primary place of residence. Any loans made to purchase, maintain or improve a rental property fall under different regulations and rules. If this rental property will be owner-occupied within one year the following rules apply

- Loans made to acquire rental property consisting of one or more units are considered business loans, and are regulated as such

- Loans made to improve or maintain a property consisting of four or more units are also considered business loans and are regulated as such

Any loans acquired for the purpose of purchasing, maintaining or improving a rental property which will not be owner-occupied will always be considered a business loan.

Customers who have decided not to go ahead with the purchase of a property may cancel the loan. This is known as the **right to rescind**. A borrower has three days to cancel any loan involving a security interest in the borrower's principal residence. The three-day period will end at midnight on the third business day. The following events must occur for the borrower to rescind

- Use of the transaction

- Borrower has received the truth in lending disclosure statement

- Borrower has received notice of the right to rescind

The right to rescind does not apply to the following situations

- Refinancing a loan secured by property which is not occupied by the owner
- Residential purchase money, first mortgage, or trust deed loans
- Borrower refinances a loan, and no new funds are advanced to the borrower

In emergency situations, the right to rescind may be waived so that the lender can fund the borrower's loan as fast as possible. Such situations may occur when closing needs to happen at a specific time for the purchase contract to be accepted.

There are certain disclosures required by Regulation Z. All disclosures must be grouped together, with the information set off by a box apart from the rest of the information on the loan. A different type style, bold type, or a different color background is also required, so that the disclosures will clearly stand out. These disclosures must be made before the transaction is completed (which is generally before closing). Usually, this disclosure statement will be delivered to the borrower at the same time as the loan commitment information is sent. This is normally after the loan has been approved, but before the loan has been funded.

The required disclosures pertain to financial information. It is necessary to state the following: the name of the creditor, the description of the security interest, the amount of money to be financed, the finance charge associated with the loan, the annual percentage rate, the total amount of the payments, and the total sales price. The borrower must be informed of any prepayment penalties, rebates or late payment charges, so that there are no surprise charges associated with an early payoff or a late payment. When insurance is not a requirement of the loan, and the borrower wishes to obtain insurance on the item to be purchased, the borrower must sign a request for insurance. When a signature is not required, the borrower's initials must be placed on the document.

Five most important disclosures
• Amount to be financed
• Finance charge
• Annual percentage rate
• Total amount of the payments
• Total sales price (for any credit sales)

As we learned in another chapter, loans may be assumable when the borrower wishes to sell the property to another buyer. A borrower in a residential mortgage transaction must be informed of whether or not this is possible with their loan. This should be included in the disclosure statement.

Regulation Z also governs the types of advertisements that may be made for loans. In any advertisement, the ad must state the annual percentage rate of the loan, along with its payment terms. Specific information regarding the different forms of adjustable rate loans must also be included in the advertisement.

The **Truth in Lending Act (TILA)**, Title I of the Consumer Credit Protection Act, is aimed at promoting the informed use of consumer credit by requiring disclosures about its terms and costs. The Truth in Lending Act requires disclosure of the **finance charge** and the **annual percentage rate**—and certain other costs and terms o f credit—so that a consumer can compare the prices of credit from different sources. It also limits liability on lost or stolen credit cards. In general, this regulation applies to each individual or business that offers or extends credit when: that credit is offered or extended to consumers; the credit is subject to a finance charge or is payable by a written agreement in more than four installments; the credit is primarily for personal, family or household purposes; and the loan balance equals or exceeds $25,000.00 or is secured by an interest in real property or a dwelling.

TILA is intended to enable the customer to compare the cost of cash versus credit transaction and the difference in the cost of credit among different lenders. The regulation also requires a maximum interest rate to be stated in variable rate contracts secured by the borrower's dwelling, imposes limitations on home equity plans that are subject to the requirements of certain sections of the act, and requires a maximum interest rate that may apply during the term of a mortgage loan. TILA also establishes disclosure standards for advertisements that refer to certain credit terms.

The federal Truth in Lending Act was originally enacted by Congress in 1968 as a part of the Consumer Protection Act. The law is designed to protect consumers in credit transactions by requiring clear disclosure of key terms of the lending arrangement and all costs. The law was simplified and reformed as a part the Depository Institutions Deregulations and Monetary Control Act of 1980. The Truth in Lending Act is important for small businesses involved in consumer credit transactions or consumer leasing.

Regulations   The law has been implemented by the Federal Reserve Board through two key regulations. Regulation Z explains how to comply with the consumer credit parts of the law. This law applies to each individual or business that offers or extends consumer credit if four conditions are met.

- The credit is offered to consumers.
- Credit is offered on a regular basis.
- The credit is subject to a finance charge (i.e. interest), or must be paid in more than four installments, according to a written agreement.
- The credit is primarily for personal, family or household purposes.
- If credit is extended for business, commercial or agricultural purposes, Regulation Z does not apply.

Regulation M includes all the rules for consumer leasing transactions. This law applies to contracts in the form of a bailment or lease where the use of personal property is primarily for private, family or household purposes. The lease period must exceed 4 months, and the total contractual obligations must not exceed $25,000, regardless of whether the lessee has the option to purchase the property at the end of the lease term.

Home Mortgages   One of the biggest lending transactions any individual is likely to enter is borrowing to purchase a home. These transactions have become more complicated in recent years. Historically, someone trying to buy a home had very few options. Often, only a traditional 30-year loan was available. Now, loans of various duration and interest rate variations are available to every home buyer. The Federal Reserve Board and the Federal Home Loan Bank Board have published a book entitled *Consumer Handbook on Adjustable Rate Mortgages* to help consumers understand the purpose and uses of adjustable rate mortgage loans. Regulation Z requires that creditors offering adjustable rate mortgage loans make this booklet, or a similar one, available to consumers.

Disclosure   Disclosure is generally required before credit is extended. In certain cases, it must also be made in periodic billing statements. Regulation M includes similar rules for disclosing terms when leasing personal property for personal, family or household purposes, if the obligations total less than $25,000. In general, disclosure is required before any **closed-end credit transaction** is completed. There is an exception made when credit is extended over the telephone or by the mail. In those cases, a disclosure may be made after the fact. Disclosure is also required before the first transaction under an **open-end account**, and again at the time the periodic billing statement is sent.

The term "closed-end credit transaction" is defined by exclusion. That is, it includes any credit arrangement (either a consumer loan or credit sale) that does not fall within the definition of an open-end credit transaction. Open-end credit includes credit arrangements like revolving credit cards, where the borrower (that is the credit card holder) is not required to pay off the principal amount within any particular period of time. Rather, the borrower is simply charged interest periodically, and is usually only required to make some minimum payment.

The "term credit" sale means a sale in which the seller is the creditor: that is, the amount of the purchase price is financed by the seller. This includes any consumer lease, unless the lease is terminable without penalty at any time by the consumer, or when

- The consumer agrees to pay an amount substantially equal to, or more than, the total value of the property or services involved

- The consumer has the opportunity to purchase the property for at least nominal consideration

Under Regulation Z, disclosure must be made of the following important credit terms.

Finance charge   The most important disclosure made about a loan is the amount charged to the consumer for the credit.

Annual percentage rate   This is the measure of the cost of the credit which must be disclosed on a yearly basis. The method for calculating this rate is determined by the underlying transaction.

Amount financed   The amount that is being borrowed in a consumer loan transaction, or the amount of the sale price in a credit sale.

Total of payments   Includes the total amount of the periodic payments by the borrower/buyer.

Total sales price   Total cost of the purchase on credit, including the down payment and periodic payments.

Evidence of compliance with the Truth-in-Lending requirements must be retained for at least 2 years after the date of disclosure. Disclosures must be clear and conspicuous and must appear on a document that the consumer may keep.

Home Ownership and Equity Protection Act of 1994 (HOEPA)   This law deals with high-rate, high-fee mortgage loans that are refinanced or home equity installment loans. The law addresses certain deceptive and unfair practices in home equity lending. It amends the Truth in Lending Act (TILA), and establishes requirements for certain loans with high rates and/or high fees. The rules for these loans are contained in Section 32 of Regulation Z, which implements the TILA, so the loans are also called **Section 32 Mortgages**. Here's what loans are covered, the law's disclosure requirements, prohibited features, and actions a borrower can take against a lender who is violating the law.

What Loans Are Covered? A loan is covered by the law if it meets the following tests

- For a first-lien loan (the original mortgage on the property), the annual percentage rate (APR) exceeds by more than eight percentage points the rates on Treasury securities of comparable maturity

- For a second-lien loan (a second mortgage), the APR exceeds by more than 10 percentage points the rates in Treasury securities of comparable maturity

- The total fees and points payable by the consumer at or before closing exceed the larger of $488 or 8 % of the total loan amount. (The $488 figure is for 2003. This amount is adjusted annually by the Federal Reserve Board, based on changes in the Consumer Price Index.) Credit insurance premiums for insurance written in connection with the credit transaction are counted as fees.

The rules primarily affect refinancing and home equity installment loans that also meet the definition of a high-rate or high-fee loan. The rules do not cover loans to buy or build a home, reverse mortgages, or home equity lines of credit (similar to revolving credit accounts).

What Disclosures Are Required? If a loan meets the above tests, a borrower must receive several disclosures at least three business days before the loan is finalized. The lender must give the borrower a written notice stating that the loan need not be completed, even though he or she has signed the loan application and received the required disclosures. The borrower has three business days to decide whether to sign the loan agreement after receiving the special Section 32 disclosures.

The notice must warn the borrower that, because the lender will have a mortgage on that home, the borrower could lose the residence and any money put into it if he or she fails to make payments.

The lender must disclose the APR, the regular payment amount (including any balloon payment where the law permits balloon payments, discussed below), and the loan amount (when the amount borrowed includes credit insurance premiums, that fact must also be stated). For variable rate loans, the lender must disclose that the rate and monthly payment may increase, and state the amount of the maximum monthly payment.

These disclosures are in addition to the other TILA disclosures that the borrower must receive no later than the closing of the loan.

What Practices Are Prohibited? The following features are banned from high-rate, high-fee loans

- All balloon payments—where the regular payments do not fully pay off the principal balance and a lump sum payment of more than twice the amount of the regular payments is required—for loans with less than 5-year terms. There is an exception for bridge or swing loans of less than 1 year used by consumers to buy or build a home. In that situation, balloon payments are not prohibited.

- Negative amortization, which involves smaller monthly payments that do not fully pay off the loan and that cause an increase in the total principal debt.

- Default interest rates higher than pre-default rates

- Rebates of interest upon default calculated by any method less favorable than the actuarial method

- A repayment schedule that consolidates more than two periodic payments that are to be paid in advance from the proceeds of the loan

- Most prepayment penalties, including refunds of unearned interest calculated by any method less favorable than the actuarial method. The exception is if

- The lender verifies that the total monthly debt (including the mortgage) is 50% or less of the borrower's monthly gross income
- The borrower gets the money to prepay the loan from a source other than the lender or an affiliate lender
- The lender exercises the penalty clause during the first 5 years following execution of the mortgage

- A due-on-demand clause. The exceptions are if
  - There is fraud or material misrepresentation by the consumer in connection with the loan
  - The consumer fails to meet the repayment terms of the agreement
  - There is any action by the consumer that adversely affects the creditor's security

Creditors also may not

- Make loans based on the collateral value of the secured property without regard to the borrower's ability to repay the loan. In addition, proceeds for home improvement loans must be disbursed either directly to the borrower, jointly to the borrower and the home improvement contractor, or, in some instances, to the escrow agent.

- Refinance a HOEPA loan into another HOEPA loan within the first 12 months of origination, unless the new loan is in the borrower's best interest. The prohibition also applies to assignees holding or servicing the loan.

- Wrongfully document a closed-end, high-cost loan as an open-end loan. For example, a high-cost mortgage may not be structured as a home equity line of credit if there is no reasonable expectation that repeat transactions will occur.

How Are Compliance Violations Handled? A borrower may have the right to sue a lender for violations of these new requirements. In a successful suit, the borrower may be able to recover statutory and actual damages, court costs and attorney's fees. In addition, a violation of the high-rate, high-fee requirements of the TILA may enable the borrower to rescind (or cancel) the loan for up to 3 years.

Other Features of the Truth in Lending Act   The Truth in Lending Act has other important features. If credit terms are advertised, the law requires disclosure of key lending terms. Also, the law gives the consumer the right to rescind certain credit transactions within a short period, such as home equity loans.

To assist creditors, sellers and lessors, the Federal Reserve Board has provided a series of model disclosure forms and clauses for Regulation Z and Regulation M. Copies of these regulations and model forms may be found at most public libraries and law school libraries. Regulation Z is in the Code of Federal Regulations at 12 C.FR. Part 226. Regulation M is also in the Code of Federal Regulations at 12 C.FR. Part 213. (The librarian can use these citations to locate these regulations.)

The penalties for failure to comply with the Truth in Lending Act can be substantial. A creditor who violates the disclosure requirements may be sued for twice the amount of the finance charge. In the case of a consumer lease, the amount is 25% of the total of the monthly payments under the lease, with a minimum of $100 and a maximum of $1,000. Costs and attorney's fees may also be awarded to the consumer. A lawsuit must be begun by the consumer within a year of the violation. However, if a creditor sues a consumer more than a year after a violation date, violations of the Truth in Lending Act can be asserted as a defense.

Violations   The number of violations appears to be increasing; the penalties for violations are minimal. Moreover, many builders and lenders apparently do not understand the rules. It remains to be seen whether the Federal Trade Commission or the Federal Reserve Board will commence an enforcement program.

Real Estate Brokers Not Credit Arrangers   Regulation Z, promulgated by the Federal Reserve Board under the Truth in Lending Act, classifies mortgage lenders as "arrangers of credit." Thus, lenders must fill out settlement disclosure statements at all real estate closings. Are real estate brokers "credit arrangers" when they close a contract sale, or an assumption sale, or some other seller-financed sale? Must they fill out Truth in Lending disclosure statements? The answer is that real estate brokers have been generally exempt from this burden from the outset of Regulation Z. However, as special financing has become so common, the Federal Reserve Board began to look again at real estate brokers. Finally, the Board tentatively announced an amendment to Regulation Z that would have redefined "credit arranger" to include brokers on seller-financed sales. Because of protests, the Fed held up the amendment until Congress reviewed the question.

Congress finally settled the issue in favor of real estate brokers. The Depository Institutions Deregulation Act of 1982 prevents the Fed from assigning "arranger of credit" status to real estate brokers in seller-financed transactions. This means that brokers will remain generally exempt from the "credit arranger" rules of Regulation Z as before.

Of course, it does not mean that just because a broker has a real estate license, he or she is now automatically exempt from Regulation Z. If that broker has customarily financed sales and lent mortgage funds, he or she has been an arranger of credit the same as any other mortgage lender, and must continue to comply with Regulation Z, just as in the past. The new act simply keeps Regulation Z from being extended to real estate brokers who have heretofore been exempt.

Rights to Financial Privacy Act   provides that customers of financial institutions have a right to expect that their financial activities will have a reasonable amount of privacy from federal government scrutiny. The act establishes specific procedures and exemptions concerning the release of the financial records of customers, and imposes limitations on and requirements of financial institutions prior to the release of such information to the federal government.

Expedited Funds Availability Act requires all banks, savings and loan associations, savings banks, and credit unions to make funds deposited into checking, share draft and NOW accounts available according to specified time schedules and to disclose their funds availability policies to their customers. The law does not require an institution to delay the customer's use of deposited funds, but instead limits how long any delay may last. The regulation also establishes rules designed to speed the return of unpaid checks.

Fair Debt Collection Practices Act is designed to eliminate abusive, deceptive and unfair debt collection practices. It applies to third-party debt collectors or those who use a name other than their own in collecting consumer debts. Very few commercial banks, savings banks, savings and loan associations, or credit unions are covered by this act, since they usually collect only their own debts. Complaints concerning debt collection practices generally should be filed with the Federal Trade Commission.

The Federal Trade Commission Act requires federal financial regulatory agencies to maintain a consumer affairs division to assist in resolving consumer complaints against institutions they supervise. This assistance is given to help get necessary information to consumers about problems they are having, in order to address complaints concerning acts or practices which may be unfair or deceptive.

Home Equity Loan Consumer Protection Act requires lenders to disclose terms, rates and conditions (APRs, miscellaneous charges, payment terms, and information about variable rate features) for home equity lines of credit with the applications and before the first transaction under the home equity plan. If the disclosed terms change, the consumer can refuse to open the plan and is entitled to a refund of fees paid in connection with the application. The act also limits the circumstances under which creditors may terminate or change the terms of a home equity plan after it is opened.

Home Mortgage Disclosure Act (HMDA) requires certain lending institutions to report annually on their originations and acquisitions of home purchase and home improvement loans as well as applications for such loans. The type of loan and location of the property, as well as the race or national origin, sex, and income of the applicant or borrower are reported. Institutions are required to make information regarding their lending available to the public and must post a notice of availability in their public lobby. Disclosure statements are also available at central depositories in metropolitan areas. This information can help the public determine how well institutions are serving the housing credit needs of their neighborhoods and communities.

Home Mortgage Disclosure Act Aggregation Project
Using loan data collected from each covered institution, the **Federal Financial Institutions Examination Council (FFIEC)** prepares disclosure statements and various reports for individual institutions in each metropolitan statistical area (MSA), showing lending patterns by location and age of housing stock, and income level, sex and racial characteristics of borrowers. The disclosure statements and reports are made

available to the public at central depositories located in each MSA. Requests for the list of central depositories should be forwarded to the FFIEC.

Federal Financial Institutions Examination Council
2100 Pennsylvania Avenue, NW
Suite 200
Washington, DC 20037

The Council is a formal interagency body empowered to prescribe uniform principles, standards, and report forms for the Federal examination of financial institutions by the Board of Governors of the Federal Reserve System (FRB), the Federal Deposit Insurance Corporation (FDIC), the National Credit Union Administration (NCUA), the Office of the Comptroller of the Currency (OCC), and the Office of Thrift Supervision (OTS), and to make recommendations to promote uniformity in the supervision of financial institutions.

National Flood Insurance Act
National Flood Insurance is available to any property holder whose local community participates in the national flood control program by adopting and enforcing flood plain management. Federally regulated lenders are required to compel borrowers to purchase flood insurance in certain designated areas. Lenders also must disclose to borrowers whether their structure is located in a flood hazard area.

Credit Practices Rule   prohibits lenders from using certain remedies, such as confessions of judgment, wage assignments, and nonpossessory, non-purchase money security interests in household goods. The rule also prohibits lenders from misrepresenting a cosigner's liability, and requires that lenders provide cosigners with a notice explaining their credit obligations as a cosigner. It also prohibits the pyramiding of late charges, or the allowing the charges to grow exponentially.

Electronic Fund Transfer Act   provides consumer protection for all transactions using a debit card or electronic means to debit or credit an account. It also limits a consumer's liability for unauthorized electronic fund transfers.

The Interstate Land Sales Full Disclosures Act   protects consumers from fraud and abuse in the sale or lease of land. It requires land developers to provide each purchaser with a disclosure document called a **Property Report**. The Property Report contains relevant information about the subdivision, and must be delivered to each purchaser before the signing of the contract. The act and regulations require also that certain provisions be included in the contract of sale, to protect consumers from fraud and abuse in the sale or lease of land.

Fair Credit Reporting Act (FCRA)
One of the most important laws protecting consumers' identity and credit information is the **Fair Credit Reporting Act**. Designed to promote the accuracy, fairness and privacy of the information collected and maintained by credit reporting agencies, the

FCRA gives consumers specific rights.

The Fair Credit Reporting Act establishes procedures for correcting mistakes on a person's credit record, and requires that a consumer's record only be provided for legitimate business needs. It also requires that the record be kept confidential. A credit record may be retained 7 years for judgments, liens, suits, and other adverse information except for bankruptcies, which may be retained 10 years. If a consumer has been denied credit, a cost-free credit report may be requested within 30 days of denial.

A consumer may sue any credit-reporting agency or creditor for breaking the rule about who may see his or her credit records or for not correcting errors in a credit file. Again, a consumer is entitled to actual damages, plus punitive damages that the court may allow if the violation is proved to have been intentional. In any successful lawsuit, a consumer will also be awarded court costs and attorney's fees. A person who obtains a credit report without proper authorization, or an employee of a credit-reporting agency who gives a credit report to unauthorized persons, may be fined up to $5,000 or imprisoned for 1 year or both.

Consumers must be told if personal credit information is used against them. If a consumer is denied credit, employment or insurance because of information in the credit report, the denying party must alert the consumer and provide the name, address and phone number of the credit reporting agency used to support the denial.

A consumer has access to his or her file. Upon request, a credit reporting agency must give a consumer the information in the file and a list of everyone who has requested it within a certain time period. There is no charge if the consumer has been denied credit, employment or insurance because of items in the file (if a request is made within 60 days). In addition, a consumer is entitled to one free report every 12 months if unemployed or on welfare, or if there is proof that a report is inaccurate.

A consumer can dispute inaccurate information. A credit reporting agency must investigate items that a consumer reports as inaccurate. The consumer will receive a full copy of the investigation report. If the dispute is not settled to his or her satisfaction, the consumer may add a statement to the report. Inaccurate information must be corrected or deleted. Credit reporting agencies are required to remove or correct inaccurate or unverified information. They are not required to remove accurate data unless it is outdated.

Access to a consumer's file is limited. Only people and institutions with needs recognized by the FCRA may legally gain access to a file. This normally includes creditors, government agencies, insurers, employers, landlords and some businesses. A consumer can remove his or her name from credit reporting agency lists used for unsolicited credit and insurance offers. Unsolicited offers must include a toll-free phone number where the consumer can call to be removed from credit reporting agency lists.

The Community Reinvestment Act is intended to encourage depository institutions to help meet the credit needs of the communities in which they operate, including low-

and moderate-income neighborhoods. It was enacted by the Congress in 1977 and is implemented by **Regulation BB**.

Evaluation of CRA Performance   The CRA requires that each depository institution's record in helping meet the credit needs of its entire community be evaluated periodically. That record is taken into account in considering an institution's application for deposit facilities.

Neither the CRA nor its implementing regulation gives specific criteria for rating the performance of depository institutions. Rather, the law indicates that the evaluation process should accommodate an institution's individual circumstances. Nor does the law require institutions to make high-risk loans that jeopardize their financial safety. To the contrary, the law makes it clear that an institution's CRA activities should be undertaken in a safe and sound manner.

F A I R   H O U S I N G

Over the past 140 years, as home ownership has become a reality for many Americans, the process has not always been fair to everyone. There is no area where the country has experienced more growing pains than in the area of discrimination and prejudice.

Over the years, however, laws have been created to make the housing market equitable, leveling the playing field for all Americans. Many of these laws have been aimed at discriminatory practices in the sale, financing and rental of houses. Since discrimination on the basis of race, creed, gender or national origin is not in the public interest, not to mention morally wrong, the federal government has taken an active role in the prohibition of discriminatory housing practices.

1866 Civil Rights Act
The 1866 Civil Rights Act prohibits discrimination against persons based on race in any property transaction. This act was basically ignored until 1968, when the United States Supreme Court Case of Jones v. Mayer upheld the 1866 Civil Rights Act and the 13th amendment to the United States Constitution which banned slavery.

Civil Rights Act of 1968 and 1988 Amendments Act
In leasing or selling residential property, the **Civil Rights Act of 1968** expands the definition of categories protected from discrimination to include not only race, but national origin, color and religion. The **Fair Housing Amendments Act of 1988** (effective March 12, 1989) further broadens the categories to include age, sex and handicapped status. Under these laws, real estate offices are required to display fair housing posters. Any complaints must be filed with HUD.
Fair Housing Act
The Civil Rights Act of 1968 and the 1988 Amendments Act changed the original Civil Rights Act. The Amendment made it illegal to discriminate against people purchasing homes, or leasing property, based on race alone. It is now illegal to discriminate against a possible buyer or tenant because of their national origin, religion, age, sex, color or handicapped status.

The **Fair Housing Act** protects people from the following actions

- Sellers refusing to sell property to qualified buyers

- Landlords refusing to rent property to qualified renters

- Landlords treating two separate applicants differently for housing for any discriminatory reason

- Financial firms treating applicants differently in connection with rates or loan terms and conditions

- Discrimination in property advertisements

- Restricting tenants from the enjoyment or exercise of their rights under the act

- Blockbusting

- Redlining

- Brokers denying services to any group due to discrimination based on race, sex, religion, color, handicap, presence or absence of children or national origin

It is HUD's responsibility to enforce fair housing laws. If a person feels he or she has been discriminated against, he or she may take up the grievance with HUD, or may elect to have his or her case heard in a U.S. District Court. Penalties for those found guilty of discriminatory practices range from $10,000 (for the first offense), to $50,000 (for the third offense). The party discriminated against will have damages awarded, with all other monies paid to the federal government. Those who willfully fail to give information or evidence or who give false information in a fair housing investigation will be charged with criminal penalties and a fine of up to $100,000.

Protection for People with Disabilities protects people who have a physical or mental disability that restricts one or more life activities. Handicaps include mental illness, AIDS, blindness, hearing impairment, mental retardation and mobility limitations.

Senior Citizen Exemptions
There are certain exemptions to the fair housing rules regarding housing for senior citizens. It is allowable to discriminate based on age in housing when the housing is intended for senior citizens only, provided the housing can meet the needs of the seniors living there. The following list is a list of criteria that makes senior housing exempt from the prohibition against discrimination based on familial status

- The housing is intended for persons 62 years of age or over

- Housing provides for the social and physical needs of seniors

- Policies and procedures of the housing complex demonstrate the intent to provide housing for persons 55 years of age or over

- Housing is a federal program, designed specifically to assist senior citizens.

- Housing unit is intended and operated for persons at least 55 years of age

- 80% of the units are occupied by persons 55 years of age or over

Significant Recent Changes in the Fair Housing Act of 1988 In addition to expanding the number of protected classes and creating new enforcement procedures, the 1988 amendments to the Fair Housing Act also created an exemption to the provisions barring discrimination on the basis of familial status for those housing developments that qualified as housing for persons age 55 or older.

Fair Housing Assistance Program

The **California Fair Employment and Housing Act** (formerly called the **Rumford Act**) prohibits discrimination in the sale or rental of property. This law also covers discrimination in financing homes. Discrimination in sale, rental or financing based on race, color, marital status, ancestry, religion, sex or national origin is strictly prohibited, and any grievances must be reported directly to the state Department of Fair Employment and Housing.

Housing Financial Discrimination Act (or the **Holden Act**) prohibits lenders from discriminating against a loan applicant based on the location, neighborhood or other characteristic of the property to be financed. Denying a loan based on the aforementioned factors would meet the definition of **redlining**. The exception is if it is proven that the loan is a risky one that the bank or lender would refuse anyway. Any violations based on the Housing Financial Discrimination Act should be reported directly to the state's Secretary for Business and Transportation.

The Fair Housing Initiatives Program   established by the Housing and Community Development Act of 1987 (HCD Act of 1987) and was amended by the HCD Act of 1992. FHIP provides funding to public and private entities formulating or carrying out programs to prevent or eliminate discriminatory housing practices. Through four distinct categories of funding, FHIP supports projects and activities designed to enhance compliance with the act and substantially equivalent state and local laws prohibiting housing discrimination. These activities include programs of enforcement, voluntary compliance, and education and outreach. The program provides a coordinated approach to

- Further the purposes of the Fair Housing Act

- Guarantee the rights of all Americans to seek housing in an open market free of discrimination

- Inform the American citizenry of its rights and obligations under the Fair Housing Act.

Enforcement of the Fair Housing Act   HUD has had a lead role in the administering the Fair Housing Act since its adoption in 1968. The 1988 amendments, however, have greatly increased the Department's enforcement role. First, the newly protected classes have proven to be significant sources of new complaints. Second, HUD's expanded enforcement role took the Department beyond investigation and conciliation into the mandatory enforcement area.

The Fair Housing Act gives HUD the authority to hold administrative hearings, unless one of the parties elects to have the case heard in U.S. District Court and to issue subpoenas. The Administrative Law Judge in these proceedings can issue an order for relief, including actual damages, injunctive or other equitable relief, and penalties.

Complaints filed with HUD are investigated by the **Office of Fair Housing and Equal Opportunity (FHEO)**. If the complaint is not successfully conciliated, then FHEO determines whether reasonable cause exists to believe that a discriminatory housing practice has occurred. Where reasonable cause is found, the parties to the complaint are notified by HUD's issuance of a Determination, as well as a Charge of Discrimination, and a hearing is scheduled before a HUD administrative law judge. Either party—complainant or respondent—may cause the HUD-scheduled administrative proceeding to be terminated by electing instead to have the matter litigated in federal court.

Whenever a party has so elected, the Department of Justice takes over HUD's role as counsel seeking resolution of the charge on behalf of aggrieved persons, and the matter proceeds as a civil action. Either form of action is subject to review in the U.S. Court of Appeals.

The penalties range from up to $10,000 for a first violation, to up to $50,000 for the third violation and those thereafter. The penalties are paid to the federal government. The damage payments go to the proven victims.

The act adds criminal penalties of a $100,000 maximum fine and imprisonment as sanctions against people who willfully fail to give information and evidence or who willfully give false information in a fair housing investigation or proceeding.

The Age Discrimination Act of 1975 prohibits discrimination on the basis of age in programs and activities receiving federal financial assistance. The act, which applies to all ages, permits the use of certain age distinctions and factors other than age that meet the act's requirements. The Age Discrimination Act is enforced by the Civil Rights Center.

The Age Discrimination in Employment Act of 1967 (ADEA) protects certain applicants and employees 40 years of age and older from discrimination on the basis of age in hiring, promotion, discharge, compensation, or terms, conditions or privileges of employment. The ADEA is enforced by the **Equal Employment Opportunity Commission (EEOC)**.

Title II of The Americans with Disabilities Act of 1990 (ADA)

Title II of the ADA prohibits discrimination against persons with disabilities in all services, programs and activities made available by state and local governments. The Department of Justice (DOJ) has coordination authority for the ADA. The DOJ regulations cover all state and local governments, and extend the prohibition of discrimination in federally-assisted programs established by **Section 504** of the **Rehabilitation Act of 1973** to all activities of state and local governments, including those that do not receive federal financial assistance.

HUD is the designated agency for all programs, services and regulatory activities relating to state and local public housing and housing assistance and referrals. In addition, HUD has jurisdiction over a state or local government activity when HUD has jurisdiction under Section 504 of the Rehabilitation Act of 1973.

The Architectural Barriers Act of 1968 requires buildings and facilities that are constructed by or on behalf of or leased by the United States, or buildings financed, in whole or in part, by a grant or loan made by the United States to be accessible to persons with mobility impairments. The Architectural and Transportation Barriers Board (ATBCB) has coordination authority for the ABA.

S T A T E   L A W S

Many state laws also provide rights and remedies in consumer financial transactions. Unless a state law conflicts with a particular federal law, the state law usually will apply. Some states have usury laws, which establish maximum rates of interest that creditors can charge for loans or credit sales. The maximum interest rates vary from state to state and depend upon the type of credit transaction involved.

Complaint Filing Process

If the consumer has a complaint against a financial institution, the first step is to contact an officer of the institution and attempt to resolve the complaint directly. Financial institutions value their customers and most will be helpful. If the consumer is unable to resolve the complaint directly, the financial institution's regulatory agency may be contacted for assistance.

The agency will usually acknowledge receipt of a complaint letter within a few days. If the letter is referred to another agency, the consumer will be advised of this fact. When the appropriate agency investigates the complaint the financial institution may be given a copy of the complaint letter.

The complaint should be submitted in writing and should include the following

- Complainant's name, address, and telephone number
- The institution's name and address
- Type of account involved in the complaint—checking, savings, or loan—and account numbers, if applicable

- Description of the complaint, including specific dates and the institution's actions (copies of pertinent information or correspondence are also helpful)

- Date of contact and the names of individuals contacted at the institution with their responses

- Complainant's signature and the date the complaint is submitted to the regulatory agency

The regulatory agencies will be able to help resolve the complaint if the financial institution has violated a banking law or regulation. They may not be able to help where the consumer is not satisfied with an institution's policy or practices, if no law or regulation was violated. Additionally, the regulatory agencies do not resolve factual or most contractual disputes.

The following information will help in determining which agency to contact.

National Bank   If the word "National" appears within a bank's name, or the initials "N.A." appear after the name, contact Comptroller of the Currency.

State-Chartered Bank, Member of the Federal Reserve System   Two signs will be prominently displayed on the door of the bank or in the lobby. One will say "Member, Federal Reserve System." The other will indicate deposits are insured by the Federal Deposit Insurance Corporation and/or "Deposits Federally Insured to $ 100,000—backed by the Full Faith and Credit of the United States Government." The word "National" does not appear in the name; the initials "N.A." do not appear after the name. Contact Federal Reserve Board for federal laws; State Banking Department for state laws.

State Non-Member Bank or State-Chartered Savings Bank Federally Insured
A sign will be prominently displayed at each teller station that indicates deposits are insured by the Federal Deposit Insurance Corporation and/or "Deposits Federally Insured to $100,000—backed by the Full Faith and Credit of the United States Government." There will not be a sign saying "Member, Federal Reserve System." The word "National" or the initials "N.A." will not appear in the name. Contact Federal Deposit Insurance Corporation for federal laws; State Banking Department for state laws.

Federal Savings and Loan Association or Federal Savings Association Federally Insured   Usually, the word "Federal" will appear in the name of a savings and loan association or its name will include initials such as "FA", which indicates its status as a federal savings and loan association. A sign will be prominently displayed at each teller station that says "Deposits Federally insured to $100,000— Backed by the Full Faith and Credit of the United States Government." Contact Office of Thrift Supervision.

Federal Savings Bank Federally Insured   Generally, the word "Federal" appears in the name of the savings bank or its name includes the initials such as "FSB" which indicate its status as a federal savings bank. A sign will be prominently displayed at each teller station that says "Deposits Insured to $ 100,000—Backed by the Full Faith and Credit of the United States Government." Contact Office of Thrift Supervision.

State-Chartered Federally Insured Savings Institution   There will be a sign prominently displayed at each teller station that says "Deposits Federally insured to $100,000—Backed by the Full Faith and Credit of the United States Government." Agency to Contact: Office of Thrift Supervision.

State Chartered Banks or Savings Institutions without Federal Deposit Insurance Institution has none of the above described characteristics. Contact State Banking Department for state laws; Federal Trade Commission for federal laws.

Federally Chartered Credit Union   The term "Federal Credit Union" appears in the name of the credit union. Contact National Credit Union Administration.

State-Chartered, Federally Insured Credit Union   A sign will be displayed by stations or windows where deposits are accepted indicating that deposits are insured by NCUA. The term "Federal Credit Union" does not appear in the name. Contact state agency that regulates credit unions or Federal Trade Commission.

State-Chartered Credit Unions without Federal Insurance   The term "Federal Credit Union" does not appear in the name. Contact state agency that regulates credit unions or Federal Trade Commission.

Other   Institutions have none of the characteristics described. Contact the appropriate state agency for state laws, and the Federal Trade Commission for federal laws.

S U M M A R Y

This chapter introduced you to the consumer credit protection and the mandatory disclosures that must be given to all persons borrowing money. Before the laws originated for consumer credit protection, lenders could operate any way they saw fit, with no accountability when it comes to discrimination.

With the new laws, there should be less confusion regarding credit, how it is used in our economy, and the laws governing discrimination. This chapter is important for you to understand so you can be a reliable and accurate resource for your client regarding any questions they may have regarding the financing of their new home.

T E R M S   A N D   P H R A S E S

Blockbusting   causing people to move out of a neighborhood because another group of people are moving in, causing a perception of lower home values

Redlining   discriminating against a loan applicant based on the location, neighborhood or other characteristic of the property to be financed

C H A P T E R   Q U I Z

1. What federal law expanded the 1866 Civil Rights Act to include more than just discrimination on the basis of race?
    a. Jones v. Mayer
    b. Fair Housing Act
    c. Unruh Act
    d. Civil Rights Act of 1968 and 1988

2. The act of getting people to sell their homes in an area by telling them a minority group is moving in is called
    a. steering.
    b. redlining.
    c. panic selling.
    d. blockbusting.

3. Which state law protects citizens against discrimination when seeking a private residence, whether a single-family home or an apartment?
    a. Unruh Civil Rights Act
    b. California Civil Code Section 54-55.1
    c. California Fair Employment and Housing Act
    d. Housing Financial Discrimination Act

4. Which one of the following categories is NOT protected from discrimination under the Equal Credit Opportunity Act?
    a. sex
    b. color
    c. religion
    d. sexual orientation

5. Under the truth in lending act, how many days does a buyer have to rescind a loan?
    a. 1
    b. 3
    c. 5
    d. 10

6. Which of the following is NOT considered one of the five most important disclosures under the Truth in Lending act?
    a. Annual percentage rate
    b. Finance charge
    c. Total amount of payments
    d. Right to rescind

7. The three "C's" include all of the following except
    a. collateral.
    b. credit.
    c. character.
    d. capacity.

8. At what age does a credit score change based on age?
    a. 58
    b. 60
    c. 62
    d. None of the above

9. Who or what agency enforces the fair housing laws?
    a. HUD
    b. CAR
    c. California Supreme Court
    d. NAR

10. The Fair Housing Act protects people from all of the following except
    a. redlining
    b. blockbusting
    c. discrimination based on age
    d. landlords refusing to rent to a person with bad credit

11. The Truth In Lending act is also called
    a. RESPA
    b. HUD
    c. Regulation Z
    d. Regulation B

12. The Age Discrimination In Employment Act protects people who are
    a. 40 or older.
    b. 45 or older.
    c. 50 or older.
    d. 53 or older.

13. If a consumer feels he or she has been discriminated against, he or she should
    a. complain to the creditor.
    b. join others and file a class action suit (if applicable).
    c. check with the state attorney general.
    d. All of the above.

14. Regarding age, which of the following is a false statement?
    a. The creditor may favor candidates 62 or older based on a credit-scoring system.
    b. A creditor may favor candidates under 35 based on a credit-scoring system.
    c. The borrower is too young to sign contracts if he or she is younger than 18.
    d. A creditor may consider a borrower's age if he or she is close to retirement and his or her income may drop upon retirement.

15. Which of the following is a false statement?
    a. Creditors must include public assistance as valid income.
    b. Creditors must include retirement or pension as valid income.
    c. Creditors may exclude alimony or child support as valid income.
    d. Creditors may not consider men and women's salaries to be different.

16. Good credit is important to obtain. Which of the following is a way to build a good credit rating?
    a. Open a checking or savings account
    b. Obtain a credit card or store charge card, making all payments on time
    c. Secure a loan with a co-signer
    d. All of the above

17. The Federal Deposit Insurance Corporation insures accounts up to
    a. $50,000.
    b. $100,000.
    c. $200,000.
    d. $350,000.

18. Which of the following is not one of the most important disclosures regarding Regulation Z?
   a. Total amount of the payments including interest
   b. Amount to be financed
   c. Name of the creditor
   d. Annual percentage rate

19. When filing a complaint, which of the following is not necessary?
   a. Institution's name and address
   b. Complainant's name, address and telephone number
   c. Description of the complaint
   d. Amount of grievance if applicable

20. Which of the following are allowed on a high rate, high fee loan?
   a. Balloon payments
   b. Default interest rates higher than the pre-default rate
   c. Rebates of interest
   d. Consolidation of two periodic payments or more

10

A P P R A I S A L

What you will learn in this Chapter

- Definition

- Value

- Principles of Valuation

- The Appraisal Process

- Reconciliation

- Obtaining an Appraisal License

Test Your Knowledge

1. Which one of the following is not considered a reason for obtaining an appraisal of property?
    a. Taxation
    b. Insurance
    c. Financing and credit
    d. Fair market value

2. Which one of the following terms best fits the definition "The price a property would bring if freely offered in an open market with both a willing seller and buyer?"
    a. Market value
    b. Utility value
    c. Market price
    d. Objective value

3. A development where all the homes are constructed in a similar architectural style, of similar age, and built out of similar materials, to keep the value of the homes high, best illustrates the principle of
    a. contribution.
    b. conformity.
    c. balance.
    d. highest and best use.

4. Which of the following is NOT one of the three appraisal techniques used to determine the value of a property?
    a. Sales comparison approach
    b. Cost approach
    c. Square foot method
    d. Income capitalization approach

5. An appraiser is required to take continuing education classes every
    a. year.
    b. 2 years.
    c. 3 years.
    d. 4 years.

6. Which of the following are considered examples of physical deterioration?
    a. Termite damage
    b. Damage from severe weather
    c. Damage from normal wear and tear
    d. All of the above

7. Which of the following is NOT an appraisal report form?
    a. Short form
    b. Final conclusion
    c. Letter form
    d. Narrative

INTRODUCTION

If you have ever looked for property, whether a home, an income property (such as a duplex or apartment complex) or a building for office space, you probably have a good idea of how much property costs in your community, neighborhood or region of the state. But have you ever wondered how this value is determined? Why is a 2,000 square foot home in Santa Monica worth so much more than an equally large home in Fresno or Bakersfield? How does an appraiser know the difference between homes, or how to price them accordingly?

This chapter will introduce you to the appraisal process. The appraisal process is a detailed, data-driven process, which results in an estimated opinion. This opinion is based on all the facts gathered regarding the property in question, as well as all comparable properties surrounding the property in question.

We will first describe for you an appraisal, followed by the concept of value. Following that, we will outline the different forces that determine or influence value. After you are fully exposed to value and the forces driving it, we will more closely examine the basic concept of the chapter: the appraisal process. We will discuss the steps an appraiser takes to determine a property's value, the different appraisal methods an appraiser can use, and the process an appraiser goes through when analyzing a site. Finally, you will learn the steps necessary to become an appraiser.

The appraisal process is very important for a real estate agent to understand, as clients may ask you for your opinion on a property's value. A real estate professional must understand the concepts of appraisal to give an accurate opinion, or to explain how the appraiser arrived at his or her estimate of value on the property in question.

DEFINITION

Real estate appraisal is an appraiser's estimate of what a property is worth in an open market. This worth is estimated or measured based on a monetary value. This value measures the present worth of rights a homeowner may gain, as well as any future benefits that will come from ownership of the specific piece of property. It is important to understand that while there are guidelines for appraising property, the final number that the appraiser arrives at is simply an estimate, or opinion. Appraisals are also useful to determine the worth of a property for insurance or investment purposes. The appraisal can indicate a property's type and condition, its usefulness for a specific purpose, or its highest and best use.

An appraisal is an unbiased estimate or opinion of the property value on a given date. **Value** is the present worth of rights to future benefits that come from property ownership. An appraiser gives his or her opinion of value in a written statement called an **appraisal report**. It is the conclusion of the appraiser's research and analysis of all relevant data regarding the subject property.

The process by which the appraiser arrives at the estimate involves a series of steps. First, the appraiser will inspect the property, to obtain a solid visual idea of its physical location, condition and amenities. Next, the appraiser will compile a variety of data regarding the property, its location or area, and other important data necessary to arrive at an estimate. After this, the appraiser will consider the current market forces and local market conditions which may make the property more or less desirable at a given time, given its location. Finally, the appraiser will determine the value, or estimate, of what he or she believes the appropriate property value, given the current market. The data collected and factors considered may vary, depending on the purpose(s) of the appraisal.

Appraisers are generally third parties, with no direct interest in the property. It is important for an appraiser to be unbiased in determining the value of the property, to determine its true worth. They must appraise without the emotion a seller may have, or the motivation a buyer may have, regarding the property. Experienced, professional appraisers are trained extensively in this process. They operate with an ethical, unbiased opinion, to correctly measure all influences determining the value of a property. Again, it is important that the appraiser be a neutral party, uninfluenced by the specific interests of either the buyer or seller.

An appraiser's final value will be a dollar value, indicating the property's market value on that specific day in that specific market. There are five main reasons for making an appraisal. Each one may result in different prices for the same property, even on the same day. The five reasons for obtaining an appraisal value are: to transfer property from one person to another; for financing and credit purposes; for tax reasons; for condemnation, and for insurance. When making an appraisal, it is important for the appraiser to know the specific reason the appraisal is being made, as this could drastically change the value of the appraisal.

Five reasons for an appraisal

- Transfer property from one party to another
- Financing and credit
- Tax
- Condemnation
- Insurance

VALUE

The price that a specific piece of real estate (whether land, house or building), or its land and all structures on it would bring in an open market where there is a willing buyer and seller is called **market value**. This figure is based on what a person is willing to pay for a specific property, given its utility or value. The market value is subjective, depending on the buyer, the purposes for which the property might be used, and other market conditions.

There are certain kinds of property sales that do not constitute an open market sale. Such sales are said to occur through **default**. Examples of such sales are foreclosure, bankruptcy, divorce, death, or any other special circumstance causing the sale of property. An appraiser would not consider the price paid for these properties (many of which may be sold at an auction or for less than the actual value of the home) a measure of market value.

There are five assumptions that can be made regarding open market sales

- The buyer and seller are willingly acting in their own interest
- The property has been on the real estate market for a reasonable length of time, given its specific property type.
- There has been full disclosure to both the buyer and seller, with a knowledgeable decision being made, taking into account the property's defects and assets
- No unusual circumstances exist
- Normal financing is available to the buyers who qualify and normal financing is used to purchase the property

Even though market value is the price that a property could bring in an open market with both a willing buyer and seller, the market price does not necessarily mirror the accurate market value. Market price is the price at which property actually sold. So, while market price is the actual price for which the property sold, market value is the price for which it "should" have sold. It is important to understand that market price is not always a lower amount than market value. It is possible, in a very hot market, or in an extremely desired location, for the market price to be well above market value.

When thinking about value and cost or price, it is important for you to understand that realistic and/or human factors play an important role in determining the worth of a property. For example, a home may appraise for $400,000, and could easily bring in that amount. However, the seller may be going through a bitter divorce, and needs to sell the property immediately. In this case, the seller is very motivated, and under a lot of pressure to sell the property in order to divide up marital assets. If a first-time homebuyer comes along and makes a bid of $370,000 (which is $30,000 under its market value), the bid has a good chance of being accepted, because of the seller's personal circumstances. So, the market value compared to the market price is not equal. This example serves to demonstrate that value is not always going to be the same as the cost or price of a property, although it certainly may be the same in other situations.

All properties have a **utility value**, which is the usefulness of property for a specific purpose. A piece of farmland in California's Central Valley, hundreds of miles away from a major metropolitan area, has high utility value to a farmer, but a low utility value for a real estate developer looking to build a 60-story skyscraper for office space.

As we have seen from some of the examples given, cost is not an essential element in determining value. What one person finds valuable, another may not; still another might determine it priceless. Market value only represents the amount for which a property can be sold in the current market given all present conditions. This can be determined by data, and is thus called the **objective value**.

Value is subjective, but it is a present factor with future anticipated utility or enjoyment. There is also an anticipated profit associated with value. **Price** is the amount of money that is paid for an object. **Cost** represents the expenses that were incurred when producing an object. These costs could be in the form of labor, materials, or any other sacrifices that had to be made in order to acquire the property.

> **Remember**
> - Market value is what a property should sell for in an open market
>
> - Market price is the actual amount of money for which a property sold
>
> - Utility value is the usefulness of a property for a specific purpose to a specific person
>
> - Objective value is similar to market value, as it can be determined by current data
>
> - Cost represents the amount of money it takes to produce something
>
> - Price represents what a person paid for a good or service
>
> - Value is defined as the present enjoyment, with consideration of future anticipated profits

There are four basic elements that must be present for an object to have value, easily remembered by the acronym **DUST**, which stands for **demand, utility, scarcity** and **transferability**.

A market will only exist when there is demand for a product, and the scarcer the product is, the higher the demand will be. Once a person acquires a product that is scarce, and thus holds value, it is important for this product to be able to be transferred to someone else in exchange for money or other desired goods. Finally, utility will also determine the usefulness of a product. Utility, coupled with scarcity, will also increase the value of a product.

Four elements of value

- Demand
- Utility
- Scarcity
- Transferability

An appraiser must take all of these elements into consideration when determining the value of a property. Is the property going to be used for its intended purpose, thus increasing its utility? Are there several similar properties in the neighborhood, or is this one unique, thus increasing the scarcity of the property? Is the title to the property clear of any encumbrances, or, will the transfer of property include a long closing period affecting the ease of transferability of the property? Once each of these elements has been considered, an appropriate value can be determined for a specific property.

Just as there are elements that determine value, there are also forces and other factors that determine the value of property. There are four main forces, as well as geographical, physical and governmental sub-factors, that determine value. The four main forces influencing value are **economic influences, social standards, environmental and physical conditions**, and **political regulations**.

Four of determining value

- Economic influences
- Social standards
- Environmental and physical conditions
- Political regulations

Economic influences include factors such as the availability of money or credit in a certain community, price levels, tax base, interest rates, and wages. Additionally, the rate of new development, building, industrial and commercial health also plays a role in economic influences. One economic influence that may not be as obvious is the amount and type of natural resources in an area. An area rich in natural resources generally has a lot of industry, tourism, or other means of creating a healthy, local economy.

Social standards do not mean mental or behavioral characteristics, so much as demographics. Some of the social standards used in determining value for an area include marriage rate, birth rate, death rate, and divorce rate for a community. Population is also a factor, as the growth or decline of population in an area may be indicative of the economic health of the community.

Environmental and physical conditions are more obvious factors in determining the value of a property. In California, property tends to be more expensive if it is closer to water, or at a higher elevation. So naturally oceanfront property will have more value than property 50 miles inland. Property on a hill, with canyon views, will have more value than a home nestled in a valley and surrounded by other homes, with no view. Other environmental factors that influence value include climate, topography, soil type, and, as mentioned earlier in this example, proximity to mountains and oceans. Some of the other environmental or physical conditions considered when determining property values are access to shopping, availability of public transportation, school districts, local conveniences, entertainment, and access to houses of worship.

Political regulations are the fourth and final element in determining a property's value. An example of this type of force is a community's economic base. Things like rent control, zoning regulations or building codes may also have in influence in the value of property in a community or area.

Other factors influencing value include the following

- **Shape** of a lot, with irregular-shaped plots both more difficult and more expensive to develop.

- **Topography** of the land, which influences the cost to develop a site. Houses or buildings built on a hillside, or in the mountains, will be more expensive than those built on flat, level surfaces.

- **Location** is perhaps the most important factor in determining value. Is it an oceanfront property? Does it have commanding views of the valley from atop a hill or mountain? Is it nestled next to a lake or river? Or is it located in the middle of the desert? The phrase "location, location, location" really does describe the three most important things to consider when shopping for property.

- **Directional growth**, which describes the direction in which a city or town is growing. Is the city growing to the north or south? Or is it simply expanding all over? The new growth area of a city tends to already have a higher value, or will increase in value much more quickly than other areas.

- **Obsolescence** describes external influences or economic changes which may decrease the usefulness of the property, decreasing its value.

- **Utility** of the property, as a property that cannot be used for its intended purpose will decrease in value. Factors affecting utility may include building restrictions or zoning ordinances.

- The **business climate** of an area, whether healthy or stagnant, will either increase or decrease the value of a property. If a home or business is located in a bustling area, full of shopping, office space, medical centers and wholesale and industrial areas, its value will increase.

- **Corner influence**, which describes the physical location of a home or business on a city block. A corner lot increases the frontage of a building. This is great for businesses who want more exposure. However, it decreases privacy for a home. Corner lots are generally larger, but can incur more maintenance costs.

- **Directional exposure** does not seem to be an important condition; however, a southern or western exposure is ideal for businesses, as those storefronts are generally in the shade. Most customers will walk on the shady side of the street, and the storefronts and windows will be clearly visible, without glare from the sun.

- **Size** of the property will obviously determine value. The larger a property, the more valuable it is in the given market.

- **Through streets** and **width of sidewalks or streets** can affect value. In a residential area, it is more desirable to live on a dead-end street or cul-de-sac, as there will be less traffic and noise. Meanwhile, a business thrives from the traffic and exposure brought by a busy street.

- **Assemblage** or **plottage**, in which plots of land are placed together to create one larger plot owned by one single person, can create a more valuable piece of property.

Appraisers must take many factors or forces driving market value into account when arriving at their evaluation of property. It is important for an appraiser to look for all of these factors or conditions early on in the appraisal process, so he or she can calculate the most accurate value figure possible. The real estate market is constantly evolving. An area considered desirable today may not be sought-after tomorrow. Meanwhile, an area considered run down or undesirable may provide a great opportunity for purchase property at a low price, with monies left over for renovation and creation of a very nice space. The following concepts are just a few factors that an appraiser must take into account when appraising a property.

The principle of **supply and demand** describes the availability of property to purchase, versus the number of individuals interested in purchasing that particular type of property. When there is high demand for a specific type of property or home in a certain neighborhood, and the supply of such properties is short, the property will be purchased at a premium. When the opposite happens, and there is low demand for the property, prices will drop a bit. A market in **equilibrium** occurs when the supply of property meets the demand for property.

A property's **highest and best use** refers to the best way to utilize the land. Generally, the highest and best use of land takes into account the most profitable way to utilize the land, as well as whether it is legally and physically possible to utilize the land in the desired way. When property is being redeveloped, any existing structures will also be considered. Will it be cost effective to renovate the structures? Will demolishing the property be more expensive than leaving it alone? Questions such as these must be asked when finding the land's best and most profitable use.

Keeping land in **balance** is important. Balance simply means that the land uses result in the highest profit possible for that specific use. It also can refer to the proximity of businesses, shopping and medical facilities to homes and housing developments.

The presence of similar buildings in a specific area promotes **conformity**. When each building on an industrial campus or each home in a housing development is constructed out of similar materials, with similar architecture or are of similar age, they exhibit conformity. Generally speaking, conformity in a residential neighborhood keeps property values high.

The **principle of substitution** is important to appraisers, as this is the most common way to determine value for similar properties. When a home in a particular area is put on the market for sale, an appraiser uses the principle of substitution by projecting the established property's value onto the property that has come up for sale. Of course, the appraiser will need to conduct a thorough appraisal of the new property, but having a reference point regarding where the current property market in an area is a good place to begin the appraisal process.

Most people who purchase real estate **anticipate** gaining future benefits from the property in the future. This may be as simple as expecting property values in the neighborhood to rise, anticipating the creation of equity in the home, or believing that an up-and-coming area will be developed as expected (creating a new hip area to live, higher property values, and high demand for property in the area).

A building's value can be affected in a positive or negative way with regards to the buildings surrounding it. This theory is described as the principle of **progression and regression**. If a nice home is situated in an area with homes of lesser value, or with homes that are not as physically appealing, the price of the nicer home will decrease to a lower level than if it were located in a different neighborhood with similar homes. This is regression. Progression is just the opposite; a home in a nice area, with other homes of higher value, will have a higher value than the same home in another area.

Changes, whether subtle or drastic, can raise or decrease the value of property. There are four types of changes which can affect the value of property. These factors are

- Physical
- Economic
- Social
- Political

A **physical change** could be a natural disaster, such as a landslide, mudslide, earthquake or fire. Any one of these changes could damage property, decreasing its value. A physical change can negatively impact property value, but it may also increase property value. A property bordering a river or stream can benefit from the gradual building up of the land, increasing the area's land mass. **Economic forces** affecting an area could include transportation, the economy or the job market. Positive economic forces raise property value, while negative economic forces decrease its value. **Social forces** are our lifestyle and choices. The level of education in a community, the size of its families, if any, what people do in their leisure time, or the general age range of a community will create a desirable or undesirable location, depending on the person seeking property. **Political forces** include zoning and building codes. If zoning codes are very restrictive, they may decrease a property's utility, thus decreasing its value.

Homeowners are constantly making improvements to their homes. The addition of a swimming pool, remodeling of a bathroom, removing of carpet and installment of hardwood floors are all improvements to a home, which may contribute to the home's value. In an appraisal, the appraiser will determine if the improvements make a **contribution** to the overall value of the home, or if such improvements raise the value of the property.

Every area will experience a much scripted, predictable **life cycle**. When an area is first being developed, it will see a growth period. New houses are being constructed in a very clean and fresh neighborhood. The growth period will naturally reach an equilibrium point, when the neighborhood does not see any more growth. The homes are maintained, but there is no new construction. After the equilibrium, the area will experience a decline, where properties are worth less, and may be showing their age. Eventually, there will be a revitalization stage, where new homebuyers, younger buyers or investors will purchase property to fix and either sell, or live in themselves. Getting new, younger buyers into an area will help revitalize it.

Competition is the theory that too much competition is not good for a property's value, but a healthy level will keep value high. For example, if there are more office spaces in an area than demand for them, the price for which an office will be rented will be less than if there were equilibrium, or if there was more demand (renters) than supply (space).

PRINCIPLES OF VALUATION

A real estate agent or a professional appraiser must know the following basic principles of valuation before assigning value to any property.

Principle of Conformity
When land uses are compatible and homes are similar in design and size, the maximum value is realized.

Principle of Change
Cities and neighborhoods are always changing, and individual homes within those neighborhoods reflect that change. An appraiser must be aware of trends that affect the value of real estate. Economic, environmental, government and social forces are always dynamic, causing changing values in real property.

Principle of Substitution
The basis of the appraisal process, this principle is the foundation of estimating the value of real property. Explained simply, value is set by the cost of getting an equally desirable substitute. An owner cannot expect to sell for more than someone would ordinarily pay for a similar property, under similar conditions.

Principle of Supply and Demand
Increasing supply or decreasing demand will reduce the price in the market. Reducing supply or increasing demand will raise the price in the market. The less there is of something, the higher the cost; the more there is, the lower the cost.

Principle of Highest and Best Use
This principle is based on the reasonable use of real property, at the time of the appraisal, which is most likely to produce the greatest net return to the land and/or the building over a given period of time. Evaluating the highest and best use includes assessing buyers' reasons for buying, the existing use of the property, the permitted use, zoning, benefits of ownership, the market's behavior, and community or environmental factors.

Principle of Progression
A lesser-valued property will be worth more because of the presence of greater-valued property nearby.

Principle of Regression
A greater-valued property will be worth less because of the presence of a lower valued property nearby.

Principle of Contribution
The worth of an improvement is what it adds to the entire property's market value, regardless of the actual cost of the improvement. A remodeled attic may not contribute its entire cost to the value of the property, but a new family room could increase the value of the house by more than the cost to build it. This principle must be kept in mind by homeowners who want to change the character of their house in such a way that it no longer fits in the neighborhood. The cost of the improvement may not add to the value if the house is overbuilt for the area.

Principle of Anticipation
Future benefits to be derived from a property will probably increase the value. An appraiser estimates the present worth of future benefits when he or she assigns a value based on anticipated returns.

Principle of Competition

When considerable profits are being made, competition is created. When there is a profitable demand for homes, there will be competition among builders. The supply would then increase in relation to the demand, bringing lower selling prices and unprofitable competition, leading to more decline in supply.

Principle of Balance

When contrasting, opposing or interacting elements are in balance in a neighborhood or area, value is created. A careful mix of varying land use creates value also. Over-improvement or under-improvement will cause imbalance.

Principle of the Three-Stage Life Cycle

All neighborhoods change. They start out as young, dynamic areas, and eventually disintegrate in the process of passing years. All property goes through three distinct stages.

Growth and decline is normal in all areas, and many times it can be reversed just as it reaches the last stages. For example, when a lovely neighborhood grows to be old and worn out, young families may choose to move in and completely restore the process of change. They start the life cycle of the neighborhood all over again with development.

THE APPRAISAL PROCESS

The appraisal process is carried out in steps. Before the appraiser can determine the value of any property, a series of questions must be identified and then answered. The appraiser will conduct research in the following order

- State the problem
- List all data needed to solve the problem and sources from which the data can be gathered
- Gather and verify all necessary data
- Determine the highest and best use of the property
- Make an estimation of the value of the land itself
- Estimate the value of the property by utilizing each of the three appraisal approaches
- Reconcile the estimated value of the property for a final value estimation (taken from one or a combination of more than one of the appraisal methods)
- Create the final report of the value estimate

The first step every appraiser must take, in order to know what direction their appraisal process will follow, is to identify the problem, or identify the property to be appraised and the purpose of the appraisal. Is the appraisal for a home currently being sold? Is it for an income property being sold and then rented? Or is it for new construction?

Value will be determined by the rights that come with a property. If a single-family home in the middle of a neighborhood was purchased with the intent to convert it into a 6-unit apartment building, but zoning laws prohibit such a conversion, the value to the buyer will be very low. However, if a family of 6 needed a larger home, and was interested in the same property because it has 6 bedrooms and lots of space, the value to the buyer will be much higher.

The next step an appraiser must take is to list the data needed and the sources from which this data can be obtained. Upon determining what data must be collected, the appraiser must gather the data on the highest and best use of the property. The data gathered must include more than just a visual site inspection on the home. There must be data gathered for the general region, the city and the neighborhood in which the property is located. This data is considered the general data. After the general data is gathered, the appraiser must gather specific data on the site or property itself. This data includes the location of the site, the lot on which it is located and any nearby buildings. Lastly, the appraiser needs to collect data for each individual appraisal technique. This data will include sales data for similar properties, cost data, and income and expense data for similar properties.

Data to Gather

General Data
- National, regional, city and neighborhood data

Specific Data
- Site, lot and buildings or improvement data

Data for each appraisal approach
- Sales data, cost data and income and expense data

The type of property that will be appraised will determine the different types of data to be collected. For example, if the property for sale is a single-family home, data on other homes in the area may be collected. Residential or income properties, on the other hand, would require collection and analysis of different data. The appraiser in this situation may seek out data on income or expenses of similar income properties.

Data can be easily obtained through many sources. General data can be gathered through government publications, general newspapers, or magazines. Regional data, such as data for an area like the San Francisco Bay area, Central Valley, or Southern California, can be gathered from regional planning commissions, government agencies or monthly bank summaries. (A major component of value, after all, is determined by demand. Subsequently, the level of income or wealth of an area will determine the consumer purchasing power. This is an important component in determining value on a regional basis.) Community data can be gathered from city government agencies, the Chamber of Commerce, City Planning Commissions, banks and real estate boards. Neighborhood data is gathered by conducting personal inspections. An appraiser can also consult with local real estate agents or builders. The appraiser is looking for the age and cosmetic appearance of the neighborhood and the proximity of the community to services (such as health providers, schools, business, transportation, recreation and houses of worship). An appraiser will also note any negative influences present (such as crime and social hazards) and any physical or social influences (such as development or the possibility of future development).

A site analysis will provide the appraiser with accurate and sufficient information regarding the condition of the lot, site and structure(s) that could not otherwise be determined by conducting a search through the MLS, Chamber of Commerce, County Recorder's office or any other agency search. The appraiser can see the lot size, shape, layout and position on the block. The appraiser can also see the type and condition of the home or structure and materials, which aids in producing a much more accurate appraisal of value.

There are six different lot types, all of which play a part in determining value. The six lot types are **cul-de-sac, corner lot, interior lot, flag lot, T-intersection**, and **key lot**. The cul-de-sac is located at the end of what is, essentially, a dead end street. The lot is shaped like a piece of pie, with the narrow section of the lot facing the street, while the back of the lot is the wide end. A corner lot has a frontage facing two streets. This can be desirable for storeowners who want maximum exposure for their business, but it may be a deterrent for homeowners, as it reduces privacy. In addition, facing two streets increases the amount of traffic noise. An interior lot is the most common type of lot, with neighbors on each side and a frontage toward the street. The flag lot physically looks like a flag on a pole. There is no frontage to the street, except for a long, narrow drive accessing the property. There is usually another lot in front of the flag lot. A T-intersection is a lot where one street dead-ends into another. Essentially, there are two streets affecting this lot; the street that dead-ends with the oncoming headlights and the street running parallel to the lot. Finally there is the key lot, which is immediately in front of the flag lot and surrounded by several back yards. It has the least amount of privacy from neighbors.

The next several pages show some of the factors that appraisers consider when describing and evaluating property.

Location and Types of Lots

1. *Cul-de-sac*

   A **Cul-de-sac** is sometimes known as a dead-end street. It is a street that has only one way in and the same way out. This may be desirable because of the privacy and quiet, but the lot may be oddly pie-shaped if it is on the turn-around section of the street.

2. *Corner lot*

   A **Corner Lot** is found at the intersection of two streets. It may be desirable because of its accessibility, but may also be noisy and expensive to maintain because of the increased frontage.

3. *Key lot*

   A **Key Lot**, so named because it resembles a key fitting into a lock, is surrounded by the back yards of other lots. It is the least desirable because of the lack of privacy.

4. *T-intersection lot*

   A **T-Intersection Lot** is one that is fronted head-on by a street. The noise and glare from headlights may be detractors from this type of lot.

5. *Interior lot*

   An **Interior Lot** is one that is surrounded by other lots, with a frontage on the street. It is the most common type lot and may be desirable or not, depending on other factors.

6. *Flag lot*

   A **Flag Lot** looks like a flag on a pole. The pole represents the access to the site, which is usually located to the rear of another lot fronting a main street.

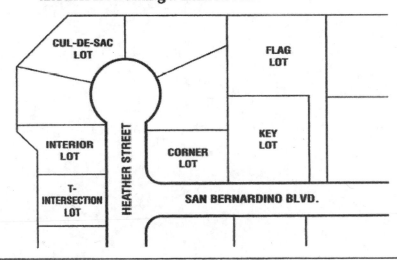

Roof Types

Dust Pan or Shed Dormer

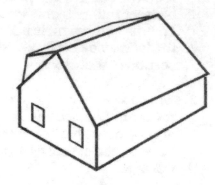

Gable

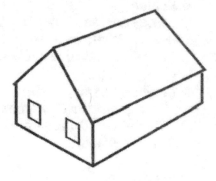

Hip

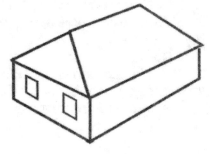

Flat

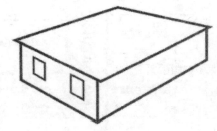

Roof Types

Single Dormers

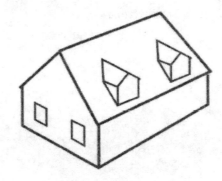

Gambrel

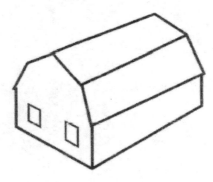

Mansard

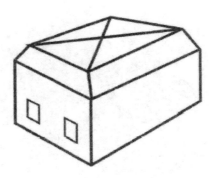

Pyramid

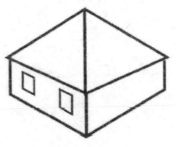

House Styles

Mediterranean

Ranch

Split Level

Townhouse

Victorian

House Styles (continued)

Cape Cod

Colonial

Contemporary

English Tudor

1. Anchor bolt—Attaches mud sill to foundation; embedded in concrete foundation

2. Bracing—Diagonal board nailed across wall framing to prevent sway

3. Building paper—Waterproof paper used between sheathing and roof covering

4. Closed sheathing—Foundation for exterior siding; boards nailed to studding

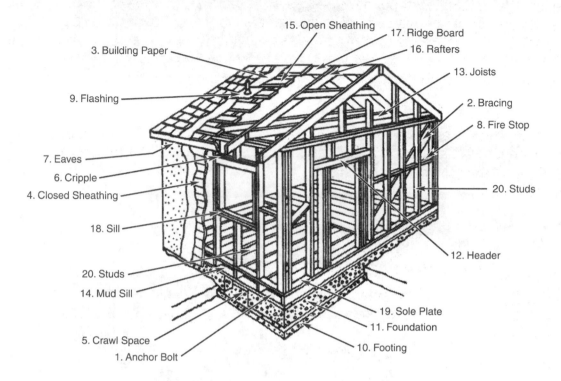

5. Crawl space—Area between floor and ground under the house

6. Cripple—Stud above or below a window opening or above a doorway

7. Eaves—Part of roof that hangs over the exterior walls

8. Fire stop—Boards nailed between studs to block the spread of fire in the walls

9. Flashing—Sheet metal that keeps the water out

10. Footing—Extended part of foundation

11. Foundation—Base of house; usually concrete

12. Header—The board over a doorway or window opening

13. Joists – Boards supporting floors or ceilings (A board supporting them is a girder.)

14. Mud Sill – Redwood board that is fastened with bolts to the foundation

15. Open sheathing – Boards nailed to rafters to form foundation for the roof

16. Rafters – slanted boards that support the roof boards and shingles

17. Ridge board – Highest part of the frame building

18. Sill – Board along the bottom of window or door opening

19. Sole plate – Support for studs

20. Studs – Vertical 2"x4" boards in the walls spaced 16" on center

Some of the physical factors an appraiser will inspect when conducting the site inspection include the shape of the lot, its topography and soil conditions, corner influence, relations of the site to other properties, landscaping and other improvements, availability of public utilities, and encroachments from neighboring properties. Property is more valuable if it is closer to the front of the lot, closer to the street, than if it is to the rear of the lot. The lot is divided up into quarters, with the front quarter worth 40% of the total value; the quarter immediately behind the front is worth 30% of the total value, followed by 20% and 10% of the total values, respectively. This is sometimes referred to as the 4-3-2-1 rule. This makes it clear why commercial properties prefer corner lots, as the frontage of a store facing the street means it will be seen first and more often by customers.

Now that the appraiser has gathered the data, it is time to determine which appraisal method or technique to use in appraising the property. The three different appraisal techniques that an appraiser may use are the sales comparison, the cost approach, and the income capitalization approach.

The Three Appraisal Techniques

- The sales comparison approach evaluates descriptions of recently sold comparable properties.

- The cost approach analyzes building cost data.

- The income capitalization approach requires income and expense data on the building that may be purchased, as well as other comparable properties nearby.

An appraiser must determine which of the three methods to use in determining the value of a given property. Not all methods are appropriate for every appraisal, but each of the methods has an important component that adds to the final appraisal value. At the end of the appraisal process, the appraiser weighs each of the different methods and decides which one most accurately represents the value of the property in question. The appraiser will then reconcile his or her findings in the form of a **final property value**.

Sales Comparison Approach

The sales comparison approach is not only the easiest appraisal technique; it is also the most widely used most appropriate method for arriving at the value of residential property. The sales comparison approach is referred to as the **market data approach**, the **market comparison approach** or the **paired sales approach**.

The basis of the sales comparison approach is the principle of substitution. An appraiser will find several recently sold properties with comparable characteristics to the home being appraised. These homes must offer comparable amenities to the property in question and must have been sold within the past six months. Basic qualities to look for in a comparable property are location, square footage, number of bedrooms, number of bathrooms, number of other rooms such as formal dining room or entertaining space, age of the home, its architectural style, and the financing terms.

An appraiser will then analyze each of the individual sales, to determine what differences, if any, exist between the properties. The appraiser must make the necessary **adjustments** based on those differences. An adjustment is the addition or subtraction of value on the property being appraised. If there are similar properties that have been sold after the six months prior to the appraisal of the subject property, the appraiser may allow for an adjustment for this as well. It is important to understand when it is appropriate to add value, and when it is appropriate to subtract value. If the subject property has additional features or amenities not shared by the comparable property value must be added to the adjustment portion of the equation. If the comparable property has features or amenities not present in the subject property, value will be subtracted from the adjustments.

Once the appraiser has analyzed all of the individual comparable properties, he or she will make a determination of value of the subject property. This process, if you think in terms of a mathematical equation, would look like this

Sales Price of Similar Properties + / - Adjustments = Subject Property Value

> *Example*
> *Several properties in the Smiths' neighborhood have sold within the past 3 months, and now the Smiths plan on selling their home. An appraiser has determined that the home next door is comparable to the Smiths' own home. This home sold for $320,000. The Smith's home has the same number of bedrooms and bathrooms, same size entertaining space for company, and is roughly the same square footage as the neighboring property. The only difference is that the Smith's home has a heated pool in the back yard, whereas the neighboring home did not. The appraiser determines that the heated pool adds an additional $11,000 to the Smiths' property, and determines the appropriate value for the Smiths' home, using the following equation*
>
> *$320,000 + $11,000 = $331,000*
>
> *The adjusted price of the neighboring property is $331,000, which is the most accurate estimate of what the Smiths' home is worth.*

An appraiser is able to make adjustments for most situations. However, there is one scenario for which it is nearly impossible to make an adjustment. If the comparable home's transaction was not an "arm's-length" transaction, it would be impossible to make an adjustment. An arm's-length transaction is when the home is being sold by a willing seller, and purchased by a willing buyer. If the property was sold under any other circumstances, such as a divorce or foreclosure sale, the sale price may not represent what the home could bring in an open market. Thus, an appraiser would have a hard time making an adjustment for such an issue.

As a real estate agent you have a very important tool at your disposal: your own records. No doubt, there will be a history of homes sold through your office in the same neighborhood as your new listing. So, a quick search of office records will give you a good place to begin an appraisal of your new listing. Additionally, if you are an independent broker and do not have records of any other properties sold in a specific neighborhood, you can always use other resources close at hand. The MLS system, for example, will provide very helpful information regarding similar properties in the same neighborhood. You may also check with the county recorder's office for any recently-recorded transactions.

Practice Problem

You are to determine the market value of your home.
Your home is a two-story brick home with 4 bedrooms, three bathrooms, a formal living room, family room, formal dining room, eat-in kitchen and detached 3-car garage. You have recently replaced all appliances, but will still offer a warranty to the buyer for all major mechanical issues on these appliances. All homes to which you will compare your own are 2-story brick homes, with similar rooms and cosmetic appeal on the outside.

Differences in homes
The dark-colored brick home only has 2.5 bathrooms.
The light-colored brick home has a fireplace in the master bedroom.
The grey-colored brick home is being offered without a home warranty.
It is determined that the extra half-bath your home has is worth $4,300; the fireplace in the master bedroom is worth $3,300; and the home warranty is worth $750.

The dark-colored brick home sold for $300,000; the light-colored brick home sold for $315,000; and the grey-colored brick home was sold for $305,000.

Complete the chart based on the given information

	Dark-colored brick	Light-colored brick	Grey-colored brick
Sales Price	$300,000	$315,000	$305,000
Adjustment Variables			
Half Bath			
Fireplace			
Home Warranty			
Total Adjustments			
Adjusted Value			

Agents who are not appraisers can offer a competitive market analysis to their clients in order to assist the clients in selling their home. One major difference between the competitive market analysis and an appraisal is that the competitive market analysis does not include the agent's opinion of value. An agent can assist the buyer or seller in determining the fair market value of a property, but will not assign a specific value to that property per se. The most important source of information for a competitive market analysis is the MLS. The MLS will list properties that are currently available, properties, which have just been sold and properties that were previously listed but not sold. The MLS will also provide details such as the number of days a property has been on the market, its neighborhood, its amenities and other important features.

A competitive market analysis will aid the seller in determining a fair asking price for the given market. An MLS history may indicate the number of days a certain priced property lasted on the market. A higher-priced property may take longer to sell, while a more competitively priced property may be sold in a very short amount of time. The buyer can benefit from this analysis as well, as he or she may get an idea of what price offer to make, as well as the chance of having the offer accepted.

Cost Approach
In the cost approach, the appraiser looks at two factors: the cost for reproducing the subject property, and the value of the land. When determining the final property value, the accrued depreciation must also be taken into account. The mathematical equation of the cost approach might look like this

Cost to Build A New Structure—Accrued Depreciation + Land Value = Property Value
The cost to rebuild a new structure in the same style as the old is called the **reproduction cost**. In a reproduction cost, the builder will use the same design as well as the same materials as were used in the original structure, so, if we want to determine the cost of reproducing a 100-year old structure, the new structure must be identical to the old, and use the same materials in its construction. The **replacement cost** is similar to the reproduction cost, except the replacement cost factors in the use of modern materials, design and building methods. The replacement structure will not have identical specifications to the one it is replacing, but will be similar.

The reproduction or replacement cost can be determined by four different methods:
- Square-foot method
- Quantity-survey method
- Unit-in-place cost method
- Index method

The **square foot method** estimates the cost of construction to replace a structure. It is the most common method used, and is simple to calculate. The square footage of the building in question will be compared to other structures with the same square footage. The cost per square foot will be used to determine the cost of the subject building. (The **cubic-foot method** may also be used. In this method, the height of the building will also be taken into account.)

The **quantity survey method** estimates all labor and materials, which go into the construction of the property. Very specific items such as overhead, insurance, contractor's profit and other direct costs will be added into the cost. This is an uncommon method of determining the replacement cost, as it is very time-consuming.

The **unit-in-place cost method** takes into account the different costs for various components of a building and then adds them all together. For example, the cost of the walls, heating or air conditioning units, and flooring are all calculated on a square-footage basis and added together to determine the replacement cost. This is the most detailed method of estimating value; but it is time consuming and sometimes impractical.

The **index method** is relatively simple. The appraiser takes the cost of the original building and multiplies that number by a factor that represents the increase or decrease in building expenses. This will determine the change in costs from area to area and from time period to time period.

Land value is determined through the **sales comparison approach**. An appraiser can consult the county recorder to see land values for similar lots in the neighborhood. The appraisal procedure will basically follow the equation above. First, the land value will be estimated based on the comparable land sales (or the sales comparison approach). Second, the appraiser will determine the cost of existing buildings, based on a replacement or reproduction basis. After the value of the buildings if they were to be rebuilt has been determined, the amount of accrued depreciation will be estimated. This depreciation is taken on all improvements to the lot; the lot itself will not depreciate. Next, an appraiser subtracts the accrued depreciation from the replacement cost of the buildings to estimate the depreciated value of the structures. Finally, the estimated depreciated value for the structures is added to the land value. This number is the appraiser's opinion of the estimated value of the property.

The cost method assumes that the property is already being used for the highest and best use possible. This means that the property is very specialized, and most likely would not be considered for any other use. For example, an investor who is looking to buy property for office space would most likely not purchase a school or hospital. In the event that a school or hospital was being sold, the new owner would most likely continue using the structure in its intended manner.

Remember

The cost method assumes that structures are already being used for the highest and best use possible, and are most likely highly specialized (or very specific purpose) buildings or properties.

Depreciation is the loss in value regardless of cause. Depreciation can be the result of deterioration of the structure (because the technology is old and may not be effective). It usually represents the estimate between the current cost of replacement of the entire structure and the estimated value of the existing structure. The three main types of depreciation are

1. **Physical Depreciation** may result from wear and tear or negligence. Natural factors, such as termites, rot, or weather may also add to the physical depreciation. This type of depreciation may or may not be correctable.

2. **Functional Obsolescence** refers to the actual function of a structure. Poor design or out-of-date equipment, as well as changes of style, advancements of technology and utility demand, will contribute to the functional obsolescence of a structure. Depending on the severity, this type of depreciation may or may not be correctable.

3. **Economic Obsolescence** refers to depreciation due to outside forces acting on the structure. Social and economic forces can create this type of depreciation. Zoning changes, oversupply of property, decreased demand, recession, or governmental restrictions will also create this type of depreciation, which is usually not correctable.

Depreciation is generally computed in one of two ways: **straight-line** and **observed condition** methods. The straight-line depreciation method allows a certain value of depreciation to be subtracted on a yearly basis, and that number will stay constant for the life of the structure. This method is perhaps the simplest type of depreciation to understand.

Every building has an economic life, which is the period of time, measured in years, which the building can be used for its intended purpose. The value of the building is divided by this economic life, and the resulting figure will be the amount of depreciation which can be deducted each year. There are situations, however, where the building is maintained exceptionally well, or the technological advancements used in building the structure were well ahead of their time. Thus, the effective age is now longer than the estimated calendar age of the property. For instance, if the economic life is estimated at 35 years, the actual effective age may be 40 years.

> *Example:*
> *The effective age of a building is 35 years, while the cost to build that structure was $200,000. What is the depreciation per year on the building?*
> *$200,000 / 35 years = $5,714.29 per year*

The observed condition depreciation method requires an appraiser to deduct a loss of value for each individual depreciable item. This will not take into account those items that are curable or incurable.

Curable items are damages or problems that can be economically cured. If there is damage to a building that is not economically feasible to cure, it is considered incurable. Minor earthquake damage or other such problems are certainly curable, while economic obsolescence is generally incurable.

An appraiser will figure the entire amount of depreciation on a building, based on three depreciation factors, and add them together, and once the physical, functional and economic obsolescence have been added together, that number is then subtracted from the reproduction cost to find the total value of the building or structure.

Income Capitalization Approach
The income capitalization approach first requires the appraiser to break down the appraisal process and determine the property's potential gross income. When determining the potential gross income of a property, the appraiser must add all sources of income for the property. For example, this income may come from rents, money collected from any vending or laundry machines, or other revenue-producing sources.

Next, the appraiser needs to estimate the property's **market rent**, which is similar to the market price of a property for sale. It represents the amount of rent the property is capable of generating in an open market. Rent received for the property is referred to as **contract rent**, which is usually not the same dollar amount as the market rent.

The appraiser must also figure in the vacancy and collection losses. This loss is figured because not every unit in a building is full at all times. There is also the possibility that some tenants will be late on their monthly payments. The appraiser must estimate any anticipated losses on one of these forms, and subtract this amount from the gross income to arrive at the effective gross income of the property.

Taking it one step further, operating expenses are subtracted from the effective gross income. The resulting number is the net operating income. A capitalization rate is then applied to the net operating income to arrive at an estimate of market value for the building. The capitalization rate (cap rate) is the property owner's annual expected rate of return. This cap rate can be represented as the relationship between the net operating income from the property and the property's market value. The mathematical equation might look like this

$$\text{Net Operating Income} / \text{Value} = \text{Capitalization Rate}$$
$$\text{And}$$
$$\text{Capitalization Rate} \times \text{Value} = \text{Net Operating Income}$$
$$\text{And}$$
$$\text{Net Operating Income} / \text{Capitalization Rate} = \text{Value}$$

The income capitalization approach appears quite complicated, and certainly requires a lot of data before a property value can be estimated. There are other situations where a property may not have been purchased as an income property, but ends up as such. For example, a single-family residence may have been originally purchased with the original intention of occupation by a family. However, when the family learns they are being transferred to another state due to job responsibilities, they decide to remain the owners of the home, and rent it out to another family. In this case, a less complicated method (called the **gross income multiplier**) of determining value may be used. This value is determined by the sale prices of similar properties being rented. We divide the sales price of the similar property by the amount of rent it produces to arrive at the gross income multiplier. The mathematical equation might look like this

$$\text{Sales Price} / \text{Gross Income} = \text{Gross Income Multiplier}$$

An appraiser should compare several properties to determine the most appropriate multiplier for the subject property. The actual property value of the subject property will be determined by multiplying the gross income multiplier by the projected income expected. That mathematical equation might look like this

$$\text{Gross Income} \times \text{Gross Income Multiplier} = \text{Market Value}$$

It is important to note that while the gross income multiplier is simple to understand and use, it fails to take into account all variables that the income capitalization rate will cover.

R E C O N C I L I A T I O N

The final step in an appraisal is the appraisal report. The appraiser examines the values from each of the appraisal methods and determines which value is most appropriate for the property being appraised. Different properties benefit from different appraisal methods. In general, single-family dwellings will most likely utilize the market comparison approach. New or specialized buildings will most likely use the cost approach, while rental properties (whether industrial, commercial or residential) will most likely use the income approach. Once the value is determined, the appraiser will prepare the final report. An appraiser can report his or her opinion of value in one of three ways: through **letter form**; through **short form**; or through **narrative**.

The letter form report contains a brief description of the property in question, the type of value sought, the purpose of conducting the appraisal, the date on which the value was assigned, the final opinion of value, and the appraiser's signature. This type of report is generally used when the client is familiar with the area and does not need a lot of supporting information or data regarding the area.

A check sheet between two and eight pages is called the short form report. It is a very brief report that includes all necessary or important information regarding the property.

The narrative report is a very extensive and detailed report. All of the information included in the short form report and the letter form is included in the narrative report. This is in addition to computations, the reasons for those computations, value inclusions, maps, photographs, charts and plot plans. This type of report is prepared for those clients who are not familiar with an area, or for court cases in which a detailed amount of data is required.

The appraisal report should contain the final conclusion of value, the date the value was assigned to the property, the date the report was prepared, a description of the property (whether a brief or extensive description), information on the city and neighborhood, a description of the appraisal method used to arrive at the final value, certification, and the signature of the appraiser.

OBTAINING AN APPRAISAL LICENSE

Appraisers in the state of California must be licensed if they are to appraise properties that will be financed or guaranteed through federal or federally sponsored programs. This means that persons utilizing an FHA loan, veterans using a VA or Cal-Vet loan, and persons using banks that are federally insured or backed must use a licensed appraiser when getting an appraisal on the property in which they are interested. Every licensed appraiser must take an approved continuing education class every four years to keep his or her license current and valid. It is important to note that banks require an appraisal of a property for funding purposes. So, whether an appraiser is licensed or not, an appraisal is usually necessary before a bank will fund a loan.

Appraisers may work for themselves, for an appraisal company or a bank, for a mortgage company, or for another financial institution that issues and funds loans. A **fee appraiser** is an appraiser who is independently employed and charges a fee to appraise a property. This appraisal amount will be the individual fee appraiser's opinion of the property's value. Other types of appraisers must also be licensed. An appraiser working for a bank, mortgage company, or other financial institution will need to be licensed, as the bank will fund federally sponsored loans or federally guaranteed loans. Appraisers working for a bank, mortgage company, financial institution, or on staff at an appraisal firm will be considered employees of those organizations, not as independently employed persons.

UNIFORM RESIDENTIAL APPRAISAL REPORT   File No.

Property Address 4807 Catalpa Road	City Woodview State CA Zip Code 90000
Legal Description Attached	County Delta
Assessor's Parcel No. 6412-028-007	Tax Year XXXX R.E. Taxes $ Prop. 13 Special Assessments $ 465

Borrower	Current Owner		Occupant ☐ Owner ☐ Tenant ☒ Vacant
Property rights appraised ☒ Fee Simple ☐ Leasehold		Project Type ☐ PUD ☐ Condominium (HUD/VA only)	HOA $ /Mo.
Neighborhood or Project Name Forest Glen		Map Reference	Census Tract
Sale Price $	Date of Sale	Description and $ amount of loan charges/concessions to be paid by seller	
Lender/Client		Address	
Appraiser		Address	

Location	☐ Urban ☒ Suburban ☐ Rural	Predominant occupancy	Single family housing	Present land use %	Land use change
			PRICE $ (000)	AGE (yrs)	
Built up	☒ Over 75% ☐ 25-75% ☐ Under 25%				One family 100%	☒ Not likely ☐ Likely
Growth rate	☐ Rapid ☒ Stable ☐ Slow	☒ Owner	90 Low 7	2-4 family	☐ in process
Property values	☒ Increasing ☐ Stable ☐ Declining	☐ Tenant	120 High 7	Multi-family	To:
Demand/supply	☒ Shortage ☐ In balance ☐ Over supply	☐ Vacant (0-5%)	110 Predominant 7	Commercial	
Marketing time	☒ Under 3 mos. ☐ 3-6 mos. ☐ Over 6 mos.	☐ Vacant (over 5%)			( )

Note: Race and the racial composition of the neighborhood are not appraisal factors.

Neighborhood boundaries and characteristics: The Forest Glen neighborhood is bounded on the east by the Village of Willow; south, 40th Street; west, Grand Street; north, Park District land.

Factors that affect the marketability of the properties in the neighborhood (proximity to employment and amenities, employment stability, appeal to market, etc.): The City of Woodview has remained attractive to newcomers from in-state and out-of-state because of its proximity to Bay City and diversity of employment opportunities. Houses in the price range offered by Forest Glen have benefitted from their relative affordability in the greater metropolitan area.

Market conditions in the subject neighborhood (including support for the above conclusions related to the trend of property values, demand/supply, and marketing time -- such as data on competitive properties for sale in the neighborhood, description of the prevalence of sales and financing concessions, etc.): The market is stable, with property values slowly but steadily increasing. Typical financing is the conventional mortgage, at interest rates from 7 to 8-1/4%, with as much as 95% of purchase price financed. Financing concessions are unusual.

Project Information for PUDs (if applicable) -- Is the developer/builder in control of the Home Owners' Association (HOA)? ☐ Yes ☐ No
Approximate total number of units in the subject project _____. Approximate total number of units for sale in the subject project _____
Describe common elements and recreational facilities:

Dimensions 65' x 130'	Topography	Level
Site area 8,450 sq. ft.	Corner Lot ☐ Yes ☒ No Size	8,450 SF/Typical
Specific zoning classification and description R-2, Single-family residential	Shape	Rectangular
Zoning compliance ☒ Legal ☐ Legal nonconforming (Grandfathered use) ☐ Illegal ☐ No zoning	Drainage	Appears adequate
Highest & best use as improved ☒ Present use ☐ Other use (explain)	View	Neighborhood
	Landscaping	Average

Utilities	Public	Other	Off-site improvements Type	Public	Private		
Electricity	☒		Street	Asphalt	☒		Driveway Surface Asphalt
Gas	☒		Curb/gutter	Concrete	☒		Apparent easements Utilities
Water	☒		Sidewalk	Concrete	☒		FEMA Special Flood Hazard Area ☐ Yes ☒ No
Sanitary sewer	☒		Street lights		☒		FEMA Zone _____ Map Date _____
Storm sewer	☒		Alley				FEMA Map No.

Comments (apparent adverse easements, encroachments, special assessments, slide areas, illegal or legal nonconforming zoning use, etc.): Underground electric and telephone lines; no other easements or encroachments evident.

GENERAL DESCRIPTION		EXTERIOR DESCRIPTION		FOUNDATION		BASEMENT		INSULATION	
No. of Units	1	Foundation	Concrete	Slab		Area Sq. Ft.		Roof	☐
No. of Stories	1	Exterior Walls	Stucco	Crawl Space	Conc. walls	% Finished		Ceiling 6"	☒
Type (Det./Att.)	Detached	Roof Surface	Asph. Shingle	Basement		Ceiling		Walls 6"	☒
Design (Style)	Ranch	Gutters & Dwnspts.	Galv./paint	Sump Pump		Walls		Floor	☐
Existing/Proposed	Existing	Window Type	Aluminum	Dampness		Floor		None	☐
Age (Yrs.)	7	Storm/Screens	Aluminum	Settlement		Outside Entry		Unknown	☐
Effective Age (Yrs.)		Manufactured House		Infestation					

ROOMS	Foyer	Living	Dining	Kitchen	Den	Family Rm.	Rec. Rm.	Bedrooms	# Baths	Laundry	Other	Area Sq. Ft.
Basement												
Level 1		1	1	1		1		3	2		6 clos.	
Level 2												

Finished area above grade contains: 7 Rooms; 3 Bedroom(s); 2 Bath(s); 1,950 Square Feet of Gross Living Area

INTERIOR	Materials/Condition	HEATING		KITCHEN EQUIP.		ATTIC		AMENITIES		CAR STORAGE:	
Floors	Vinyl/cpt/oak/Avg.	Type	FA	Refrigerator	☒	None	☐	Fireplace(s) # 1	☒	None	☐
Walls	Dryw/paint/paper/Avg.	Fuel	Gas	Range/Oven	☒	Stairs	☐	Patio	☐	Garage	# of cars
Trim/Finish	Pine/Avg.	Condition	Very good	Disposal	☒	Drop Stair	☒	Deck	☐	Attached	☐
Bath Floor	Ceramic/Avg.	COOLING		Dishwasher	☒	Scuttle	☐	Porch	☐	Detached	2
Bath Wainscot	Ceramic/Ave.	Central	Yes	Fan/Hood	☒	Floor	☐	Fence Rear	☒	Built-In	☐
Doors		Other		Microwave	☐	Heated	☐	Pool	☐	Carport	☐
		Condition	Good	Washer/Dryer	☐	Finished	☐			Driveway	Asphalt

Additional features (special energy efficient items, etc.): 6" insulation above ceiling and behind drywall.

Condition of the improvements, depreciation (physical, functional, and external), repairs needed, quality of construction, remodeling/additions, etc.: The subject shows evidence of normal wear and tear only. Physical deterioration is estimated at 10%, with no sign of functional or external obsolescence. Overall property condition is good.

Adverse environmental conditions (such as, but not limited to, hazardous wastes, toxic substances, etc.) present in the improvements, on the site, or in the immediate vicinity of the subject property: No adverse conditions on or near the property were noted by the appraiser during a routine property inspection.

Freddie Mac Form 70 6-93   10 CH.   PAGE 1 OF 2   Fannie Mae Form 1004 6-93

UNIFORM RESIDENTIAL APPRAISAL REPORT File No.

Property Description

Property Address 4807 Catalpa Road		City Woodview	State CA	Zip Code 90000
Legal Description Attached			County Delta	
Assessor's Parcel No. 6412-028-007		Tax Year XXXX R.E. Taxes $ Prop.13	Special Assessments $ 465	
Borrower	Current Owner		Occupant ☐ Owner ☐ Tenant ☐ Vacant	
Property rights appraised ☒ Fee Simple ☐ Leasehold	Project Type ☐ PUD ☐ Condominium (HUD/VA only)	HOA$ /Mo.		
Neighborhood or Project Name Forest Glen		Map Reference	Census Tract	
Sales Price $	Date of Sale	Description and $ amount of loan charges/concessions to be paid by seller		
Lender/Client		Address		
Appraiser		Address		

Location	☐ Urban ☒ Suburban ☐ Rural	Predominant occupancy	Single family housing PRICE $(000) / AGE (yrs)	Present land use %	Land use change
Built up	☒ Over 75% ☐ 25-75% ☐ Under 25%	☒ Owner	90 Low 7	One family 100%	☒ Not likely ☐ Likely
Growth rate	☐ Rapid ☒ Stable ☐ Slow	☐ Tenant	120 High 7	2-4 family	☐ In process
Property values	☒ Increasing ☐ Stable ☐ Declining	☐ Vacant (0-5%)	Predominant	Multi-family	To:
Demand/supply	☒ Shortage ☐ In balance ☐ Over supply	☐ Vacant (over 5%)	110 7	Commercial	
Marketing time	☒ Under 3 mos. ☐ 3-6 mos. ☐ Over 6 mos.		( )	( )	

Note: Race and the racial composition of the neighborhood are not appraisal factors.

Neighborhood boundaries and characteristics: The Forest Glen neighborhood is bounded on the east by the Village of Willow; south, 40th Street; west, Grand Street; north, Park District land.

Factors that affect the marketability of the properties in the neighborhood (proximity to employment and amenities, employment stability, appeal to market, etc.): The City of Woodview has remained attractive to newcomers from in-state and out-of-state because of its proximity to Bay City and diversity of employment opportunities. Houses in the price range offered by Forest Glen have benefitted from their relative affordability in the greater metropolitan area.

Market conditions in the subject neighborhood (including support for the above conclusions related to the trend of property values, demand/supply, and marketing time -- such as data on competitive properties for sale in the neighborhood, description of the prevalence of sales and financing concessions, etc.): The market is stable, with property values slowly but steadily increasing. Typical financing is the conventional mortgage, at interest rates from 7 to 8-1/4%, with as much as 95% of purchase price financed. Financing concessions are unusual.

Project Information for PUDs (if applicable) -- Is the developer/builder in control of the Home Owners' Association (HOA)? ☐ Yes ☐ No
Approximate total number of units in the subject project _____. Approximate total number of units for sale in the subject project _____.
Describe common elements and recreational facilities:

Dimensions 65' x 130'		Topography Level
Site area 8,450 sq. ft.	Corner Lot ☐ Yes ☒ No	Size 8,450 SF/Typical
Specific zoning classification and description R-2, Single-family residential		Shape Rectangular
Zoning compliance ☒ Legal ☐ Legal nonconforming (Grandfathered use) ☐ Illegal ☐ No zoning		Drainage Appears adequate
Highest & best use as improved ☒ Present use ☐ Other use (explain)		View Neighborhood

Utilities	Public	Other	Off-site Improvements Type	Public	Private			
Electricity	☒		Street Asphalt	☒	☐	Landscaping	Average	
Gas	☒		Curb/gutter Concrete	☒	☐	Driveway Surface	Asphalt	
Water	☒		Sidewalk Concrete	☒	☐	Apparent easements Utilities		
Sanitary sewer	☒		Street lights	☒	☐	FEMA Special Flood Hazard Area ☐ Yes ☒ No		
Storm sewer	☒		Alley			FEMA Zone _____ Map Date _____		
						FEMA Map No.		

Comments (apparent adverse easements, encroachments, special assessments, slide areas, illegal or legal nonconforming zoning use, etc.): Underground electric and telephone lines; no other easements or encroachments evident.

GENERAL DESCRIPTION	EXTERIOR DESCRIPTION	FOUNDATION	BASEMENT	INSULATION
No. of Units 1	Foundation Concrete	Slab	Area Sq. Ft.	Roof ☐
No. of Stories 1	Exterior Walls Stucco	Crawl Space Conc. walls	% Finished	Ceiling 6" ☒
Type (Det./Att.) Detached	Roof Surface Asph. Shingle	Basement	Ceiling	Walls 6" ☒
Design (Style) Ranch	Gutters & Dwnspt. Galv./paint	Sump Pump	Walls	Floor ☐
Existing/Proposed Existing	Window Type Aluminum	Dampness	Floor	None ☐
Age (Yrs.) 7	Storm/Screens Aluminum	Settlement	Outside Entry	Unknown ☐
Effective Age (Yrs.)	Manufactured House	Infestation		

ROOMS	Foyer	Living	Dining	Kitchen	Den	Family Rm.	Rec. Rm.	Bedrooms	# Baths	Laundry	Other	Area Sq. Ft.
Basement												
Level 1		1	1	1		1		3	2		6 clos.	
Level 2												

Finished area above grade contains: 7 Rooms; 3 Bedroom(s); 2 Bath(s); 1,950 Square Feet of Gross Living Area

INTERIOR	Materials/Condition	HEATING		KITCHEN EQUIP.	ATTIC		AMENITIES		CAR STORAGE:	
Floors	Vinyl/cpt/oak/Avg.	Type PA	Refrigerator ☒	None ☐		Fireplace(s) # 1 ☒		None ☐	
Walls	Dryw/paint/paper/Ag.	Fuel Gas	Range/Oven ☒	Stairs ☐		Patio		Garage # of cars	
Trim/Finish	Pine/Avg.	Condition Very go	Disposal ☒	Drop Stair ☒		Deck		Attached	
Bath Floor	Ceramic/Avg.	COOLING	Dishwasher ☒	Scuttle ☐		Porch		Detached 2	
Bath Wainscot	Ceramic/Ave.	Central Yes	Fan/Hood ☒	Floor ☐		Fence Rear ☒		Built-In	
Doors		Other	Microwave ☐	Heated ☐		Pool		Carport	
		Condition Good	Washer/Dryer ☐	Finished ☐				Driveway Asphalt	

Additional features (special energy efficient items, etc.): 6" insulation above ceiling and behind drywall.

Condition of the improvements, depreciation (physical, functional, and external), repairs needed, quality of construction, remodeling/additions, etc.: The subject shows evidence of normal wear and tear only. Physical deterioration is estimated at 10%, with no sign of functional or external obsolescence. Overall property condition is good.

Adverse environmental conditions (such as, but not limited to, hazardous wastes, toxic substances, etc.) present in the improvements, on the site, or in the immediate vicinity of the subject property: No adverse conditions on or near the property were noted by the appraiser during a routine property inspection.

There are three types of appraisal licenses: **a licensed appraiser, certified residential appraiser**, and **certified general appraiser**.

A licensed appraiser can appraise a residential property consisting of 1 to 4 units up to a value of $1 million (if appraising a non-complex property) and up to $250,000 (if appraising a complex property or non-residential property).

Certified residential appraisers may also appraise residential units consisting of 1 to 4 units. However, there is no dollar value or complexity limit on the properties they can appraise. A certified residential appraiser may appraise non-residential properties valued up to $250,000.

Certified general appraisers may appraise any property, regardless of complexity, dollar amount or property type. More information can be obtained by visiting the website www.OREA.CA.Gov/html/lic_reqmts.shtml

Three types of appraisers

- Licensed appraiser
- Certified residential appraiser
- General appraiser

S U M M A R Y

Appraisals are necessary for all real estate transactions, and it is important for the appraiser to be as accurate in his or her estimation as possible. Accuracy is likely when an appraiser utilizes all the tools available for analyzing a property. Appraisals are also important for other reasons, such as determining the tax base for a region, for insurance premiums, or for determining the best and highest use of property.

Appraisers are in search of the market value of property. The way market value is determined is by weighing demand for the property, the utility the property can provide, the scarcity of the specific type of property, and the transferability of the property. Appraisers can based their opinion on a property's value on the day they inspect the property or on any time in the recent past.. However, an appraiser cannot predict or forecast the value of a property in the future.

Appraisers have several factors or principles they must analyze, or take into account when making an appraisal. There will be several forces, constantly changing, which determine the value of a property at a given moment. Ignoring any one of these factors, or forgetting to factor it into the final equation, may yield an incorrect value estimate.

Appraisers can use the comparison approach, cost approach or income capitalization approach when determining the value of a property. Each approach is appropriate for specific appraisals, and not all methods will work for every appraisal situation. The appraiser needs to determine the reason for the appraisal, and then utilize the necessary appraisal approach. Generally speaking, the sales comparison approach is the best method when finding the value for residential property; the cost approach is useful for new construction; and the income capitalization approach is appropriate to use when determining the value of income or commercial property.

There are three different types of appraisers. Some appraisers are more restricted than others in their expertise or types of properties they are able to evaluate. Appraisers who are dealing with federally backed or funded loans must be licensed, though this is not the case for independent appraisers who are not appraising a property for a federally backed loan.

T E R M S   A N D   P H R A S E S

Accrued   amount that accumulates over time

Accrued Depreciation   difference between the cost to replace a property and that property's current appraised value.

Actual Age   real age of a building

Actual Depreciation   depreciation that occurs as a result of physical, functional or economic forces

Anticipation   principle that a property will offer future benefits, which tend to increase the present value of the property

Appraisal   person's opinion of how much a property is worth, supported by factual data, collected for a specific date in time

Appraisal Report   formal, written report, stating an appraiser's estimate of a property's value

Appreciation   property's increase in value over time, resulting in equity

Balance   principle that combines different land uses that will result in the highest overall value of a property

Book Depreciation   accounting principle referring to an allowance a homeowner can take to recover invested capital in a home

Book Value cost of a property when it was purchased, plus any improvements made, and minus any depreciation which has accrued

Capital Improvements improvements made to property to increase the useful life of the property or increase the property's value

Capitalization process of calculating the present worth of a property on the basis of its capacity to continue to produce an income stream

Capitalization Rate rate of interest considered a reasonable return on an investment, used in the process of determining value based on net operating income; the yield necessary to attract investment. Capitalization rate is also referred to as the cap rate.

Competitive Market Analysis informal estimate of market value, performed by a real estate agent usually for the buyer or the seller, utilizing the sales history of nearby properties and usually expressed as a range of the possible market values for the property

Comps term used in the real estate profession by both appraisers and real estate agents to refer to two properties that are similar or comparable

Conformity real estate principle that states that buildings or home values will be highest when all properties, buildings or homes in the area are similar in construction, age and materials used

Contract Rent amount of rent agreed to by a tenant and landlord

Contribution principle determining that a feature or item is valued in proportion to its total contribution to the overall value of the property, not by its cost alone

Corner Lot property at the intersection of two streets with neighbors only on one or two sides of the property, rather than neighbors on three or four sides of the property

Cost amount of money that must be spent to obtain materials and labor; the measure of something given up or sacrificed to obtain something else

Cost Approach method of appraising property in which value is assigned based on the present-day cost of replacing all buildings or structures on the property, less any depreciation

Cul-De-Sac street in the shape of a closed loop

Deferred Maintenance failure of a building owner or supervisor to properly maintain the structure

Demand economic concept measuring the consumer's desire to obtain goods or services

Depreciation   loss in value

Economic Life   period of time over which an improved property will yield a return on investment in the form of rent or usefulness

Effective Age   cosmetic appearance of a building or structure based on its use, rather than its actual chronological age

Effective Gross Income   actual income from all sources, less any collectable losses or vacancies

External Obsolescence   property's loss in value due to outside causes, whether economic or environmental

Fair Market Value   price a property would receive if it was offered in an open real estate market with both a willing buyer and seller ready to make the appropriate transaction

Federally Related Transaction   any transaction, loan or other financial course of action involving a bank, lending institution or other financial organization that is federally insured or backed in some way

Flag Lot   lot that does not have a side facing the street (with the exception of an access drive). The lot looks like a flag on a pole, with the narrow access drive forming the pole portion and the flag portion representing the actual lot itself.

Front Footage   width of a property facing the street

Gross Rent   income received from a rental unit before any expenses are figured or deducted from the total amount

Highest and Best Use   best way to use property to gain the most profit, the best legal use of property or the most physically feasible use of property to maximize its potential

Improvements   any fixtures, buildings or structures added to a lot

Income Capitalization Approach   appraisal method where the net operating income of property is divided by its expected rate of return (capitalization rate) to arrive at an estimate of market value

Index Method   method of estimating building reproduction costs by multiplying the original cost of the building by a factor that represents the percentage change in construction costs from the time of construction to the time of valuation

Interior Lot   lot surrounded by properties on both sides, with one side having its frontage on the street

Market Rent   amount of rent a property should bring in if it were offered in an open market

Market Value   highest amount of money a property would bring in if it were offered in an at-arms-length transaction in an open market

Net Income   amount of income that remains after all operating expenses have been subtracted from the gross income

Observed Condition Method   method whereby depreciation is calculated by estimating the loss in each individual structure

Physical Deterioration   loss of property value by physical wear and tear on a structure

Plottage (Assemblage)   combining multiple plots of land under one ownership to increase the total value of the combined lots

Potential Gross Income   maximum amount of income a property is capable of generating

Price   amount of money paid for a desired good or service

Progression   idea that a building or home of lesser value has its value increased by being near or next to a building(s) or home(s) of higher value

Quantity Survey Method   one way of estimating building reproduction costs by making an accurate itemization of all construction costs through the addition of both direct costs (raw materials and labor) and indirect costs (such as permits, overhead or profits).

Reconciliation   appraisal method analyzing the appraisal value figured by each of the three appraisal methods to arrive at the market value of a property.

Regression   idea that a building's or home's value will decline if the building(s) or home(s) around it are of lesser value

Replacement Cost   cost of replacing buildings using current prices, materials and labor

Reproduction Cost   cost of reproducing a building to make it look as it was originally built in a previous time period, using similar building materials and methods but current prices

Revitalization   act of new buyers moving into a run-down or impoverished area and fixing up homes and buildings

Sales Comparison Approach   or market data approach, is an appraisal method in which the sale prices of comparable structures are analyzed and adjusted to reflect differences between the comparables and the subject property.

Scarcity   an element of value that affects the demand for a product

Site   geographical positioning of a lot or parcel of land in a neighborhood

Site Value   value for a specific lot or parcel of land as it is positioned in a neighborhood

Square Foot Method   appraisal tool for figuring the reproduction cost of a structure by multiplying the current cost per square foot of a comparable building and comparing that to the number of square feet in the subject building

Straight Line Method   depreciating a building or structure at a steady rate over the life of the structure

Substitution   present cost of acquiring an equally valuable property compared to constructing a new building

Supply and Demand   economic principle outlining the amount of goods and services available compared to consumers' desire to obtain those goods and services. Generally speaking, the scarcer a good or service, the higher the demand will be, thus dictating a higher premium or price. The opposite is true for goods or services with low scarcity.

T-Intersection   lot that is situated at the end of a street, which will not continue as a through street. The physical shape of the two streets forms a "T"; headlights and traffic noise may be a problem for such a property location, particularly for private property such as a home.

Transferability   ease with which a property may be transferred from one owner to another; used to determine value; high transferability = high value

Utility Value   usefulness of a property to a potential or current owner

Unit-In-Place Method   way to estimate a building's reproduction cost by adding the construction cost per unit of measure of each of the separate parts of the subject property

Utility Value   usefulness of a particular property to a potential or current owner

Vacancy Factor   percentage of a building's square footage that remains unrented over a period of time

Value   amount of one good or service that must be traded to obtain another good or service of equal usefulness or benefit

1. Which one of the following is not considered a reason for obtaining an appraisal of property?
   a. Taxation
   b. Insurance
   c. Financing and credit
   d. Fair market value

2. Which best describes the appraisal process?
   a. Appraisal is a mathematical science by which the appraiser determines the exact dollar amount a property is worth
   b. Appraisal is the process by which the appraiser arrives at an estimate of the property's present worth
   c. Appraisal is the process by which the appraiser arrives at the exact worth of a property
   d. None of the above

3. There are certain types of sales that would not determine, or represent, the fair market value of a property. Which one of the following is NOT one of these special circumstances?
   a. Death
   b. Divorce
   c. Cash Sale
   d. Bankruptcy

4. Which one of the following terms best fits the definition "The price a property would bring if freely offered in an open market with both a willing buyer and seller?"
   a. Market value
   b. Utility value
   c. Market price
   d. Objective value

5. The amount of money for which a property actually sold is its
   a. market value.
   b. utility value.
   c. market price.
   d. objective value.

6. Which of the following is not a necessary element of value?
   a. Price
   b. Cost
   c. Both A and B
   d. Neither A nor B

7. Which one of the following is NOT one of the forces affecting value of property?
    a. Economic influences
    b. Political regulations
    c. Environmental and physical conditions
    d. Scarcity

8. The desirability of having a south or west-facing front describes which of the following factors?
    a. Exposure
    b. Corner influence
    c. Shape
    d. Location

9. A development where all homes are constructed with similar architectural style, of similar age and built from similar materials (e.g., all brick, or all adobe style) to keep the value of the homes high, best illustrates the principle of
    a. contribution.
    b. conformity.
    c. balance.
    d. highest and best use.

10. Which of the following characteristics does NOT determine a property's highest and best use?
    a. Most profitable use
    b. Physically possible use
    c. Regression
    d. Legally permissible use

11. Which one of the following factors is not a factor affecting the market value of property?
    a. Age of home
    b. Anticipation
    c. Supply and demand
    d. Conformity

12. Which of the following is NOT one of the three appraisal techniques used to determine the value of a property?
    a. Sales comparison approach
    b. Cost approach
    c. Square foot method
    d. Income capitalization approach

13. An appraiser must gather which of the following types of data when arriving at the value of a property?
    a. Regional
    b. City
    c. Neighborhood
    d. All of the above

14. An appraiser is required to take continuing education classes every
    a. year.
    b. 2 years.
    c. 3 years.
    d. 4 years.

15. The sales comparison approach is based on what factors?
    a. Sales of other homes in the neighborhood
    b. Cost of replacing the home
    c. Cost of building a new home
    d. None of these

16. Which of the following is considered physical deterioration?
    a. Termite damage
    b. Damage from severe weather
    c. Damage from normal wear and tear
    d. All of the above

17. Which one of the following is NOT an appraisal report form?
    a. Short form
    b. Final conclusion
    c. Letter form
    d. Narrative

18. When is the cost approach most appropriately used in appraising a property's value?
    a. When determining the value of a new structure or very specialized structure, such as a church or hospital
    b. When determining the value of a single-family dwelling
    c. When determining the value of an income property
    d. None of the above

19. Of the four methods used to estimate the cost of a new building, which is the most detailed account of the value?
    a. Square-foot method
    b. Index method
    c. Unit-in-place cost method
    d. Quantity survey method

20. What are the two methods of computing depreciation?
    a. Straight line and effective age
    b. Observed condition and economic life
    c. Economic life and straight line
    d. Straight line and observed condition

11

LOAN TERMS AND PAYMENTS

What you will learn in this Chapter

- Different Types of Mortgage Loans and Interest Rates

- Alternative Payment Plans

- Variations in Loan Formats

Test Your Knowledge

1. If a seller finances a junior trust deed to the buyer of his or her property, what options does the buyer have regarding the loan?
   a. The seller may carry the note until it is paid in full
   b. The seller may sell the note at a lower rate to a mortgage broker.
   c. He or she may force the buyer into paying the note back earlier than originally planned, because he or she needs the money for a new car
   d. Both A & B

2. The Graduated Rate Mortgage is also known as
   a. a flexible rate mortgage.
   b. an adjustable rate mortgage
   c. a step-up mortgage.
   d. none of the above.

3. Which of the following loans allows individual properties to be released from the responsibilities of the loan, provided there is a sufficient payment?
   a. Blanket loan
   b. Wrap-around loan
   c. Open-ended loan
   d. Unsecured loan

4. An index is
   a. another name for interest.
   b. another name for the prime rate.
   c. the starting point of a borrower's applicable interest rate for an adjustable rate mortgage.
   d. the amount an adjustable rate mortgage may increase or decrease.

5. The shared appreciation mortgage usually involves the borrower and what other party to share in the increase of value in the property?
   a. Co-signer
   b. Lender
   c. Builder
   d. None of the above

6. Loans which allow for a borrower to secure additional funds from a lender under the terms of an original note are called
   a. open-end loans.
   b. construction loans.
   c. blanket loans.
   d. all of the above.

7. The wrap-around trust deed
   a. takes priority to the original loan.
   b. allows the seller to retain the title to the home.
   c. allows the seller to finance the buyer, providing a loan covering all payments including the first or any subsequent trust deed.
   d. usually has a lower interest rate than a traditional loan.

INTRODUCTION

A number of real estate financing problems can be overcome by applying one of the tools currently available to lenders. Adjustable payments and/or interest rates and "wrapping a wrap," real estate loans can be adapted to meet the needs of borrower and investors. This chapter looks at ways of varying mortgages, trust deeds, and land contracts to meet the requirements of borrowers and lenders.

DIFFERENT TYPES OF MORTGAGE LOANS AND INTEREST RATES

In a fixed-rate conventional loan instrument, two factors do not change for the life of the loan—the interest rate and repayment term. This standard loan may also be called a budget loan if, along with principal and interest, funds needed to pay property taxes and insurance are included in the monthly payment. Accrued interest due is credited first to the borrower's account, with the remainder of the payment allocated to principal, taxes, and insurance, according to a pre-set formula. As a result, the borrower starts building equity in the property by paying something toward principal with every payment.

Although most real estate loans follow this formula, alternative payment plans are increasingly popular. With these alternatives, borrowers may qualify for larger loans or take advantage of payment flexibility that allows them to protect or increase other assets. At the same time, lenders receive returns on a par with current interest rates and avoid the problems associated with low-cost loans in their portfolios.

The Graduated Payment Adjustable Mortgage, also known as a flexible rate mortgage, defers part of the principal until the end of the loan. The payments for the first few years of the loan's term are lower than payments of the final years, enabling borrowers who anticipate salary increases in the future to purchase property now, and defer some of the principal payments until later. Interest and some payment toward principal are still made with each payment; but the amount of principal paid is adjusted from the beginning of the loan to the end of the loan.

The GPM helps people purchase homes by significantly reducing payments in the early years of a loan. Payments increase gradually until they total enough to fully amortize the loan over its remaining life. Buyers therefore obtain homes with mortgage payments they can afford, and lenders charge the prevailing interest rate.

Furthermore, a GPM may allow early payments that actually do not fully cover even the interest due. This negative amortization or deferred interest is offset by increasing the principal amount. The FHA 245 program and the Department of Veterans Affairs graduated payment plan are two deferred interest payment plans in use.

Adjustable-Rate Mortgages (ARMs)

The interest rates on variable rate mortgages/adjustable rate mortgages (ARMs) fluctuate with market interest rates. When interest rates rise, interest on the loan reflects the increase, and the monthly payment goes up. Similarly, decreases in market interest rates lead to decreased monthly payments. In addition, the term of the loan may change. Usually, a cap on the number of percentage points of fluctuation is part of the loan agreement.

Borrowers should consider the factors below when evaluating ARMs or variable-rate mortgages

- **Note Rate (Contract Rate)** The original interest rate charged to the borrower; it is listed on closing documents.

- **Payment Rate** Sometimes lower than the note rate, this means that early payments on the loan will be lower than later ones. The difference is paid by the borrower as additional funds required at closing (a buy-down) or via special terms with the lender.

- **Qualifying Rate** Because ARM interest rates fluctuate, the interest rate at which a borrower is qualified can be difficult to specify. If the original ARM rate is low but expected to rise soon, the risk question revolves around whether the borrower can make the higher payments.

Freddie Mac's (FHLMC) loan underwriting rule says that borrowers putting up less than a 20% down payment and seeking a 2% annual rate-capped loan must qualify at the maximum interest rate expected in the second year, based on the current loan note rate—and not the potentially lower payment rate.

Borrowers should question incentives offered by some lenders who may advertise below-market rates available for a short time. At the end of the initial period, the interest rate is automatically increased. For example, if the special offer rate is 5.25%, on a 30 year, $150,000 mortgage, the monthly payment is about $828.00. However, the payment increases to $900.00 per month when the interest rate reverts to the market rate of 6%. That means that the borrower must be able to pay about $72.00 more per month, or $864 per year.

Index The indexed interest rate sets the floor for determining the interest rate offered to a borrower. Lenders use indexes that borrowers can easily find information about that are also not under the lender's control. Some indexes are more volatile than others. The following indexes are used frequently

- Six-month, three-year, and five-year Treasury bill rates
- Eleventh District Federal Home Loan Bank cost of funds
- LIBOR (London (London International Bank Overnight Rate)
- National average contract interest rate on conventional home loans
- National median cost of funds to federally insured savings institutions
- New CD-ARMs issued by Fannie Mae and tied to the average CD interest rate

Margin Each lender adds a marginal percentage to the index at every ARM adjustment period to determine the new interest rate to charge the borrower. Lenders set different margins based on their estimated expenses and profit goals. Fannie Mae's ARM interest rate adjustments are based on the following calculations

- Six-month Treasury bill rate + 1.60 = interest rate

- Three-year Treasury notes + 1.70 = interest rate

- Five-year Treasury notes + 1.90 = interest rate

Interest Rate Cap Most variable rate loans include an annual cap to the interest rate or the note, but not on the buy-down rate. The cap limits interest rate increases or decreases to a specified range of percentage points over a given time. These caps vary among lenders and usually range from 1% to 2% per year. Some lenders also include a life-of-the-loan cap of up to 6%. Interest rate caps protect borrowers from major raises in payment amounts.

Payment Cap Lenders may also cap annual payments instead of interest rates. The most common payment cap is 7.5% of the initial payment. This means that if the initial ARM payment is $900.00 per month in principal and interest, the monthly payment cannot go up or down more than $67.50 per month in any year during the life of the loan. Payment caps may be combined with life-of-the-loan caps,

It should be pointed out that while interest caps offer borrowers protection, payment caps without corresponding interest caps can result in negative amortization. In other words, the unpaid interest portion would be added to the outstanding balance of the loan, making the loan amount bigger than it should be at that point in its repayment. If negative amortization occurs, the total unpaid balance of the loan cannot exceed 125% of the original amount. If negative amortization results in a loan greater than 125% of the original, the loan would have to be recast, with the remaining loan balance after negative amortization, the remaining term of the loan, and the market interest rate then in effect as the characteristics. Bottom line, the borrower would now have a mortgage with considerably higher monthly payments. So, borrowers need to make sure they do not agree to terms that could put them in this position.

Prepayment penalty Fortunately, today most variable-rate loans do not impose a prepayment penalty. Without this penalty, borrowers can more readily refinance and obtain a fixed-rate mortgage when they want to do so. Some lenders offer a variable-rate loan that can convert to a fixed-rate loan after the first adjustment period.

Disclosure All ARMs offered by federally insured lending institutions must comply with strict disclosure rules. Regulation Z (Truth-in-Lending law) requires that borrowers considering ARMs receive

- A descriptive brochure

- Details on the specific loan program

- Examples based on a $10,000 loan that show payment and loan balance changes as index interest rates have fluctuated historically

Shared Appreciation Mortgage (SAM)

Used for many years for commercial property development, the SAM, also known as a participation mortgage, is now available for single-family homes and condominiums. SAMs allow lenders to share in the appreciated value of the collateral property. For example, under a SAM, lenders reduce interest rates on loans in exchange for one-third to one-half of the property's increase in value over 5 to 7 years. The borrower keeps total ownership of the property, but the note accompanying the mortgage or trust deed details the partnership arrangement. Borrowers are expected to refinance the property at the end of the partnership period and give the lender his or her share of the appreciated value.

Obviously, for the lender, a SAM makes sense only if the appreciation exceeds the lost interest. Borrowers usually are required to use the property as their primary residence during the term of the contract. If the property is sold or leased, the appreciation comes due in full immediately.

Pledged Account Mortgage (PAM)

With a PAM loan, borrowers pay graduated payments; lenders receive fixed and level payments; and sellers receive the full selling price at closing. Property buyers make down payments directly to lenders, who deposit this money into savings accounts. The lenders then make loans for 100% percent of the property's selling price, thus cashing out the seller. The buyer-borrower's monthly payments are set up on a graduated schedule. A regular amount is withdrawn from the savings account funded by the down payment and added to the mortgage payment. This process continues for 3 to 5 years until the savings account is emptied. Now, the borrower starts paying the full monthly payment, which usually covers the amortization of the loan balance.

Buydown

In this variation of the PAM, the home seller, builder, buyer, and any other third parties pay the lender a lump sum at loan origination, which is used to supplement the buyer's monthly payments during the loan's early years.

As an example, say a buyer puts 10% down on a new $200,000 home and finances the balance, $190,000, at an interest rate of 7% for 30 years. The builder agrees to pay to the lender 2% of the interest for the first year and 1.5% the second year, resulting in a savings to the homebuyer of about $6,650 over the two years.

Under Fannie Mae's buydown plan, the buyer's monthly payments cannot go up more than 7.5% per year or more than 15% from one year to the next. Also, the builder or other entity selling the home cannot reduce (buy down) the buyer's effective interest rate by more than 3% each year.

FIXED/ADJUSTABLE RATE NOTE

(One Year Treasury Index - Rate Caps)

THIS NOTE PROVIDES FOR A CHANGE IN MY FIXED INTEREST RATE TO AN ADJUSTABLE INTEREST RATE. THIS NOTE LIMITS THE AMOUNT MY ADJUSTABLE INTEREST RATE CAN CHANGE AT ANY ONE TIME AND THE MAXIMUM RATE I MUST PAY.

_____ , _____   _____ , _____
[Date]   [City]   [State]

_____
_____
[Property Address]

1. BORROWER'S PROMISE TO PAY

In return for a loan that I have received, I promise to pay U.S. $ _____ (this amount is called "Principal"), plus interest, to the order of the Lender. Lender is _____
_____
_____ .

I will make all payments under this Note in the form of cash, check or money order.

I understand that the Lender may transfer this Note. The Lender or anyone who takes this Note by transfer and who is entitled to receive payments under this Note is called the "Note Holder."

2. INTEREST

Interest will be charged on unpaid principal until the full amount of Principal has been paid. I will pay interest at a yearly rate of _____ %. The interest rate I will pay may change in accordance with Section 4 of this Note.

The interest rate required by this Section 2 and Section 4 of this Note is the rate I will pay both before and after any default described in Section 7(B) of this Note.

3. PAYMENTS

(A) Time and Place of Payments

I will pay principal and interest by making a payment every month.

I will make my monthly payments on the first day of each month beginning on _____ ,
_____ . I will make these payments every month until I have paid all of the principal and interest and any other charges described below that I may owe under this Note. Each monthly payment will be applied as of its scheduled due date and will be applied to interest before Principal. If, on _____ , _____ , I still owe amounts under this Note, I will pay those amounts in full on that date, which is called the "Maturity Date."

I will make my monthly payments at _____
_____

or at a different place if required by the Note Holder.

(B) Amount of My Initial Monthly Payments

Each of my initial monthly payments will be in the amount of U.S. $ _____ .
This amount may change.

(C) Monthly Payment Changes

Changes in my monthly payment will reflect changes in the unpaid principal of my loan and in the interest rate that I must pay. The Note Holder will determine my new interest rate and the changed amount of my monthly payment in accordance with Section 4 of this Note.

4. ADJUSTABLE INTEREST RATE AND MONTHLY PAYMENT CHANGES

(A) Change Dates

The initial fixed interest rate I will pay will change to an adjustable interest rate on the first day of _____ , _____ , and the adjustable interest rate I will pay may change on that day every 12th month thereafter. The date on which my initial fixed interest rate changes to an adjustable interest rate, and each date on which my adjustable interest rate could change, is called a "Change Date."

(B) The Index

Beginning with the first Change Date, my adjustable interest rate will be based on an Index. The "Index" is the weekly average yield on United States Treasury securities adjusted to a constant maturity of one year, as made available by the Federal Reserve Board. The most recent Index figure available as of the date 45 days before each Change Date is called the "Current Index."

If the Index is no longer available, the Note Holder will choose a new index that is based upon comparable information. The Note Holder will give me notice of this choice.

(C) Calculation of Changes

Before each Change Date, the Note Holder will calculate my new interest rate by adding _____ _____ percentage points (_____ %) to the Current Index. The Note Holder will then round the result of this addition to the nearest one-eighth of one percentage point (0.125%). Subject to the limits stated in Section 4(D) below, this rounded amount will be my new interest rate until the next Change Date.

The Note Holder will then determine the amount of the monthly payment that would be sufficient to repay the unpaid principal that I am expected to owe at the Change Date in full on the Maturity Date at my new interest rate in substantially equal payments. The result of this calculation will be the new amount of my monthly payment.

(D) Limits on Interest Rate Changes

The interest rate I am required to pay at the first Change Date will not be greater than_____ % or less than _____%. Thereafter, my adjustable interest rate will never be increased or decreased on any single Change Date by more than_____ percentage points (_____ %) from the rate of interest I have been paying for the preceding 12 months. My interest rate will never be greater than _____ %.

(E) Effective Date of Changes

My new interest rate will become effective on each Change Date. I will pay the amount of my new monthly payment beginning on the first monthly payment date after the Change Date until the amount of my monthly payment changes again.

(F) Notice of Changes

The Note Holder will deliver or mail to me a notice of any changes in my initial fixed interest rate to an adjustable interest rate and of any changes in my adjustable interest rate before the effective date of any change. The notice will include the amount of my monthly payment, any information required by law to be given to me and also the title and telephone number of a person who will answer any question I may have regarding the notice.

5. BORROWER'S RIGHT TO PREPAY

I have the right to make payments of Principal at any time before they are due. A payment of Principal only is known as a "Prepayment." When I make a Prepayment, I will tell the Note Holder in writing that I am doing so. I may not designate a payment as a Prepayment if I have not made all the monthly payments due under the Note.

I may make a full Prepayment or partial Prepayments without paying any Prepayment charge. The Note Holder will use my Prepayments to reduce the amount of Principal that I owe under this Note. However, the Note Holder may apply my Prepayment to the accrued and unpaid interest on the Prepayment amount before applying my Prepayment to reduce the Principal amount of this Note. If I make a partial Prepayment, there will be no changes in the due dates of my monthly payments unless the Note Holder agrees in writing to those changes. My partial Prepayment may reduce the amount of my monthly payments after the first Change Date following my partial Prepayment. However, any reduction due to my partial Prepayment may be offset by an interest rate increase.

6. LOAN CHARGES

If a law, which applies to this loan and which sets maximum loan charges, is finally interpreted so that the interest or other loan charges collected or to be collected in connection with this loan exceed the permitted limits, then: (a) any such loan charge shall be reduced by the amount necessary to reduce the charge to the permitted limit; and (b) any sums already collected from me which exceeded permitted limits will be refunded to me. The Note Holder may choose to make this refund by reducing the Principal I owe under this Note or by making a direct payment to me. If a refund reduces Principal, the reduction will be treated as a partial Prepayment.

7. BORROWER'S FAILURE TO PAY AS REQUIRED

(A) Late Charges for Overdue Payments

If the Note Holder has not received the full amount of any monthly payment by the end of _____ calendar days after the date it is due, I will pay a late charge to the Note Holder. The amount of the charge will be _____ % of my overdue payment of principal and interest. I will pay this late charge promptly but only once on each late payment.

(B) Default

If I do not pay the full amount of each monthly payment on the date it is due, I will be in default.

(C) Notice of Default

If I am in default, the Note Holder may send me a written notice telling me that if I do not pay the overdue amount by a certain date, the Note Holder may require me to pay immediately the full amount of Principal that has not been paid and all the interest that I owe on that amount. That date must be at least 30 days after the date on which the notice is mailed to me or delivered by other means.

(D) No Waiver By Note Holder

Even if, at a time when I am in default, the Note Holder does not require me to pay immediately in full as described above, the Note Holder will still have the right to do so if I am in default at a later time.

(E) Payment of Note Holder's Costs and Expenses

If the Note Holder has required me to pay immediately in full as described above, the Note Holder will have the right to be paid back by me for all of its costs and expenses in enforcing this Note to the extent not prohibited by applicable law. Those expenses include, for example, reasonable attorneys' fees.

8. GIVING OF NOTICES

Unless applicable law requires a different method, any notice that must be given to me under this Note will be given by delivering it or by mailing it by first class mail to me at the Property Address above or at a different address if I give the Note Holder a notice of my different address.

Unless the Note Holder requires a different method, any notice that must be given to the Note Holder under this Note will be given by mailing it by first class mail to the Note Holder at the address stated in Section 3(A) above or at a different address if I am given a notice of that different address.

9. OBLIGATIONS OF PERSONS UNDER THIS NOTE

If more than one person signs this Note, each person is fully and personally obligated to keep all of the promises made in this Note, including the promise to pay the full amount owed. Any person who is a guarantor, surety or endorser of this Note is also obligated to do these things. Any person who takes over these obligations, including the obligations of a guarantor, surety or endorser of this Note, is also obligated to keep all of the promises made in this Note. The Note Holder may enforce its rights under this Note against each person individually or against all of us together. This means that any one of us may be required to pay all of the amounts owed under this Note.

10. WAIVERS

I and any other person who has obligations under this Note waive the rights of Presentment and Notice of Dishonor. "Presentment" means the right to require the Note Holder to demand payment of amounts due. "Notice of Dishonor" means the right to require the Note Holder to give notice to other persons that amounts due have not been paid.

11. UNIFORM SECURED NOTE

This Note is a uniform instrument with limited variations in some jurisdictions. In addition to the protections given to the Note Holder under this Note, a Mortgage, Deed of Trust, or Security Deed (the "Security Instrument"), dated the same date as this Note, protects the Note Holder from possible losses that might result if I do not keep the promises that I make in this Note. That Security Instrument describes how and under what conditions I may be required to make immediate payment in full of all amounts I owe under this Note. Some of those conditions are described as follows:

(A) Until my initial fixed interest rate changes to an adjustable rate under the terms stated in Section 4 above, Uniform Covenant 18 of the Security Instrument shall read as follows:

Transfer of the Property or a Beneficial Interest in Borrower. As used in this Section 18, "Interest in the Property" means any legal or beneficial interest in the Property, including, but not limited to, those beneficial interests transferred in a bond for deed, contract for deed, installment sales contract or escrow agreement, the intent of which is the transfer of title by Borrower at a future date to a purchaser.

If all or any part of the Property or any Interest in the Property is sold or transferred (or if Borrower is not a natural person and a beneficial interest in Borrower is sold or transferred) without Lender's prior written consent, Lender may require immediate payment in full of all sums secured by this Security Instrument. However, this option shall not be exercised by Lender if such exercise is prohibited by Applicable Law.

If Lender exercises this option, Lender shall give Borrower notice of acceleration. The notice shall provide a period of not less than 30 days from the date the notice is given in accordance with Section 15 within which Borrower must pay all sums secured by this Security Instrument. If Borrower fails to pay these sums prior to the expiration of this period, Lender may invoke any remedies permitted by this Security Instrument without further notice or demand on Borrower.

(B) When my initial fixed interest rate changes to an adjustable interest rate under the terms stated in Section 4 above, Uniform Covenant 18 of the Security Instrument described in Section 11(A) above shall then cease to be in effect and Uniform Covenant 18 of the Security Instrument shall instead read as follows:

Transfer of the Property or a Beneficial Interest in Borrower. As used in this Section 18, "Interest in the Property" means any legal of beneficial interest in the Property, including, but not limited to, those beneficial interests transferred in a bond for deed, contract for deed, installment sales contract or escrow agreement, the intent of which is the transfer of title by Borrower at a future date to a purchaser.

If all or any part of the Property or any Interest in the Property is sold or transferred (or if Borrower is not a natural person and a beneficial interest in Borrower is sold or transferred) without Lender's prior written consent, Lender may require immediate payment in full of all sums secured by this Security Instrument. However, this option shall not be exercised by Lender if such exercise is prohibited by Applicable Law. Lender also shall not exercise this option if: (a) Borrower causes to be submitted to Lender information required by Lender to evaluate the intended transferee as if a new loan were being made to the transferee; and (b) Lender reasonably determines that Lender's security will not be impaired by the loan assumption and that the risk of a breach of any covenant or agreement in this Security Instrument is acceptable to Lender.

To the extent permitted by Applicable Law, Lender may charge a reasonable fee as a condition to Lender's consent to the loan assumption. Lender may also require the transferee to sign an assumption agreement that is acceptable to Lender and that obligates the transferee to keep all the promises and agreements made in the Note and in this Security Instrument. Borrower will continue to be obligated under the Note and this Security Instrument unless Lender releases Borrower in writing.

If Lender exercises the option to require immediate payment in full, Lender shall give Borrower notice of acceleration. The notice shall provide a period of not less than 30 days from the date the notice is given in accordance with Section 15 within which Borrower must pay all sums secured by this Security Instrument. If Borrower fails to pay these sums prior to the expiration of this period, Lender may invoke any remedies permitted by this Security Instrument without further notice or demand on Borrower.

WITNESS THE HAND(S) AND SEAL(S) OF THE UNDERSIGNED.

_____ (Seal)   _____ (Seal)
                                        -Borrower   -Borrower

_____ (Seal)   _____ (Seal)
                                        -Borrower   -Borrower

_____ (Seal)   _____ (Seal)
                                        -Borrower   -Borrower

                                                                                    (Sign Original Only)

MULTISTATE FIXED/ADJUSTABLE RATE NOTE - ONE YEAR TREASURY INDEX - Single Family - Fannie Mae Uniform Instrument

DOCPREP SERVICES, INC. FORM - MS3522N-3569   Page 5 of 5   Form 3522 1/01

Renegotiable Rate Mortgage (RRM)

The RRM—or rollover loan or bullet loan—also offers flexible payment schedules and interest rates. Loans with terms of up to 30 years are made with monthly payments as if they were set up to amortize conventional mortgages. But call dates in the note can specify that in 5, 10, or 15 years, borrowers must refinance to meet the balances due. At the refinancing point, lenders can reexamine the condition of the collateral property and the borrower's finances. Furthermore, the lender can adjust the interest rate to reflect market conditions and charge new loan placement fees.

Lease Option

In this alternative, a lease on a property is set up so a tenant has an option to purchase it at the end of the lease. Often, some part of the rent already paid is credited to the purchase.

Lease-Purchase

A lease-purchase contract includes an agreement on the part of the tenant—not just an option—to buy the property, with some part of the rent paid applied to the purchase price.

Zero Percent Financing (ZPF)

In this alternative, sellers offer property at no interest on the contract. Buyers are usually required to make down payments of 20 to 30% of the selling price. Balances are paid in 36, 48, or 60 equal, monthly, principal-only payments, thus amortizing the debt. The IRS imputes a 10% interest rate to both seller and buyer for deduction purposes. Borrowers usually must have stellar credit ratings to qualify for these sorts of loans.

Growing Equity Mortgage (GEM)

The GEM is a variation on the ZPF involving a graduated payment plan in which only the principal portion of the mortgage increases over time. As a result, the loan matures sooner.

Biweekly Loan

Although it requires more record-keeping on the part of the lender—which was much more difficult before computers took over this task—the biweekly loan enables borrowers to amortize mortgages significantly more quickly. Each year, borrowers make 26 regular payments of one-half the monthly payment each. Essentially, as a result, the borrower makes one half of a monthly payment more than if he or she were paying the mortgage off monthly. The extra payment can reduce a 30-year loan to one that is paid off in slightly more than 20 years.

Biweekly loans are popular also because they correspond to biweekly payrolls. In other words, most people are paid biweekly, so a biweekly mortgage payment is easier to remember.

Reverse Annuity Mortgage (RAM)

Reverse annuity mortgages are basically the opposite of a conventional home loan. In a reverse annuity mortgage, money is drawn against the equity owners have in property they have owned for many years—(original mortgages may have been paid off for some time). Retirees who have lived in their homes for many years and whose incomes are relatively fixed are the primary customers for RAMs. They can supplement their incomes by collecting monthly payments against their homes. According to financial counselors, it is people older than 70 who get the most benefit from RAMs,

Generally, this money does not have to be repaid until the owner dies or sells the property. At that point, the accumulated debt to the bank is paid, and any funds over that amount are given to the sellers or to their estates or heirs.

In an RAM, the property is pledged as collateral to a lender, who sends monthly checks to the borrower until an agreed upon loan amount has been reached. The home owner pays nothing because the increasing loan balance includes both the funds advanced (principal) and interest on the outstanding balance. When the borrower (owner) has received the pre-set maximum loan amount, he or she must begin to repay the loan, which may, in some cases, mean that the property must be sold.

The age at which borrowers apply for reverse mortgages is a major factor in the amount of money they receive, and interest rates are higher than conventional mortgages. The American Association of Retired Persons (AARP) reports that while the minimum age to get a reverse mortgage is 62, the average is 76. Life expectancy, which of course, changes with how old the borrower is currently, limits the amount the person can borrow. A borrower of 70 with $100,000 equity in a home receives $272.00 per month with an FHA-insured reverse mortgage at 10% interest. If the borrower is 80 years old, the monthly check is $453.00

RAMs are available from the following lenders

- The U.S. Housing and Urban Development Department (HUD) insures loans by homeowners at least 62 years of age through three loan plans

  1. **Tenure loan**, in which a lender makes monthly payments for as long as the owners occupy the residence

  2. **Term loan**, in which a lender makes monthly payments for a specified number of years

  3. **Line-of-credit loan**, in which owners can draw against the credit provided the cumulative draws plus accrued interest are less than the principal loan limit

- The Capital Holding Corporation of Louisville, Kentucky, one of this nation's largest insurance companies, offers a RAM program to residents of Washington D.C., Baltimore, and Louisville who are at least 65 years old, with homes valued at between $75,000 and $300,000. Monthly income is provided for as long as the borrowers remain in their homes and/or up to 12 months after the owner moves to a nursing home. The interest rate varies annually based on two points above the 10-year U.S. Treasury bond rate. The repayment made to the lender, after the owners die or sell their property, is the smallest of three amounts

1. The accumulated loan balance

2. The actual sale price of the home

3. The projected home value based on the home's initial value adjusted by annual changes in the consumer price index (CPI) plus 1.3%. This amount is based on a national average annual real estate appreciation value used for more than 30 years

- The Providential Home Income Plan, Inc., of San Francisco, California, offers lifetime payment RAMs of $200 to $2,000 or more monthly for as long as borrowers live in their homes. Repayments are deferred until the homeowners' death or when they move from and/or sell their houses. Repayments total the funds advanced, interest, plus a previously agreed-to amount based on a proportion of the home's potential appreciation during the loan term.

Convertible Loans
With convertible loans, borrowers can convert ARMs to conventional fixed-rate loans. Borrowers can choose when to convert. This type of loan is attractive especially when interest rates are relatively volatile.

Fannie Mae Resale/Refinance Program
Used when borrowers' loan interest rates are lower than market rates, the Fannie Mae refinancing program offers a **blended rate** to borrowers who agree to secure a new Fannie Mae loan and pay off their current loans. To calculate a blended rate, Fannie Mae adds the old and new rates and the old and new loan balances and comes up with a weighted average rate that is fair to both the borrower and the lender. This program helps borrowers refinance existing loans and cash out some of their equity on the property. Borrowers must meet all Fannie Mae's underwriting guidelines.

Fannie Mae Senior Housing Opportunities Program
This special program for citizens older than 62 years offers financing options for the following living arrangements

- An accessory apartment: a private unit in a single-family home, providing the senior with an independent and private living arrangement with assurance of nearby assistance if needed.

- Cottage housing: a separate, self-contained unit built on the lot of an existing home, generally that of a relative, providing the senior with privacy and assurance of nearby assistance if needed.

- Home sharing: a single-family home that has been converted into no more than four living units meeting Fannie Mae standards.

- Sale-leaseback arrangement: seniors sell their homes to investors, often relatives, and then lease them back. To qualify, income from part-time work, pensions, Social Security, interest, dividends, and other sources must meet Fannie Mae's usual requirements. Monthly lease payments cannot exceed 28% of the borrowers' monthly gross income. The borrowers' total debt, including the monthly payments, may not exceed 36% of their gross income.

Fannie Mae Two-Step Mortgage Plan

The Fannie Mae two-step mortgage is a hybrid of a fixed-rate and adjustable-rate loan. The two-step requires a 10% down payment and offers interest rates at least three-eighths of 1% lower than market rates for a 30-year fixed-rate loan. The lower rate is in effect for seven years and then is automatically adjusted just one time for the balance of the loan period. The new rate is based on the 10-year Treasury bond rate, but has a maximum 6% cap. No additional fees are charged when the mortgage is converted.

Customized Mortgages

Historically, "**prime lenders**" offered borrowers one rate and only one rate. Borrowers who could not qualify for loans from prime lenders turned to "**subprime lenders**"—and usually higher interest rates. Today however, customized loans are offered throughout the mortgage industry with rate arrangements and fee reductions to attract borrowers with all levels of financial wherewithal. On the other hand, some major lenders hesitate to enter this market and offer these sorts of loans because lower-income borrowers may be at a disadvantage if they take on loans other than conventional ones with their tried-and-true requirements.

V A R I A T I O N S   I N   L O A N   F O R M A T S

The note and mortgage, deed of trust, and land contract can be used to solve almost every real estate financing problem. Terms and conditions can be altered to meet individual requirements, and changes can be made to these three lending instruments to provide financing, no matter how unique the situation. Some alternative forms of these basic financing instruments are described in the next pages.

Open-End Loans

Also known as a mortgage or deed of trust for future advances, an **open-end loan** allows borrowers to get additional funds from a lender under the terms specified in the original loan. Often, these funds represent principal already paid by the borrower, so the situation is similar to taking out a second mortgage—but at the rate of interest on the original loan. As a result, the loan's term is extended, and borrowers may not have to deal with the hassle and expense of refinancing. The funds advanced are repaid by either extending the term of the loan or increasing monthly payments by an amount that maintains the original amortization schedule. The interest rate can be adjusted, and the lender usually charges a fee for this service.

If the borrower uses the funds received from securing an open-end loan to buy personal property, and if this personal property is added to the loan's collateral, then the open-end loan converts to a **package mortgage** (see more information on this subject later in this chapter).

Farmers often use open-end loans for seasonal operating expenses. Builders use them as construction loans. Advances from these loans, called draws, are made at specific times as construction progresses. Furthermore, brokerage houses are also offering customers an open-end loan so they can draw down a line of credit that is collateralized by the equity they have in their homes.

One legal issue associated with open-end loans is preserving the priority of the existing note on a property against any possible intervening liens. In California, obligatory future funds advances under the terms of an existing loan have been determined to have priority over intervening liens. For example, the advances made under construction loans with specific patterns of draws have priority over a mechanic's liens that have been filed since the last advance.

However, nonobligatory future advances do not have priority over intervening liens, according to California state law. Thus, the legal security of the future advances made under the terms of an existing **mortgage or trust deed** may not be enforceable against debts incurred by the borrower in the intervening time. So, if the terms of the loan do not obligate a lender to make specific future advances, the lender should protect the priority of the advances by determining whether any intervening liens exist, before making the advances. Prevailing practice in making these loans in the first place does not require a title search, but nevertheless, the lender is legally bound to any liens of which outside notice has been made.

Furthermore, under the Uniform Commercial Code (UCC) adopted in most states, any personal property security agreements made in California for the purchase of fixtures on the collateral property have a priority lien over future advances made under the original loan. As an example, consider a homeowner who signs a financing contract with the Peerless Heating and Cooling Company to buy and install a central air conditioning system in June. Six months later, in December, the homeowner secures an advance on his open-end loan to build an addition to the home. The central air conditioning is now a fixture on the property, and the HVAC company's lien takes priority over any future advances made by the lender who holds the open-end loan.

One question needing to be resolved in an open-end loan is what loan terms prevail for the repayment of the future advances. Do the terms of the original agreement continue to be used, or are new terms that reflect the current market put in force?

If new funds are lent to the borrower under existing terms, then the payments being made by the borrower will not be sufficient to repay the loan plus the advances in full in the same time period specified in the original note. Also, interest rates when advances are made may be very different from when the loan originated. However, if market conditions have changed little, then the advances could be repaid within the same term as the original loan by adding slightly to the monthly payment.

Of course, market conditions usually vary. Most open-end loans carry provisions for altering payments and interest rates if the borrower requests additional funds under the loan. Under these circumstances, the lender of the open-end loan can adjust interest rates and payment schedules to reflect current market conditions. Also, most open-end lenders are allowed to review the borrower's credit scores, reevaluate the collateral property, check the property's title for intervening liens, and charge the borrower fees for doing all this. Basically, when a borrower requests advances, the open-end loan can be recast entirely; the loan is refinanced by the same lender—who keeps a good investment in his or her portfolio.

Construction Loans

Also called an **interim financing instrument**, a **construction loan** is a form of open-end loan that finances the costs of labor and materials as they are used during construction of a new building. An interim loan usually covers financing from the point when construction begins until it is replaced by more permanent financing when construction is complete. The unique character of these sorts of loans stems from the fact that the building pledged as collateral for the loan does not yet exist when the loan originates. The land on which the building will be constructed is the only collateral of value at the loan's origination. So, lenders of construction loans usually require additional protection from the risk of default.

To ensure this protection, funds from the loan are paid to the builder in installments at specific milestones of the project, not in a lump sum at the beginning. The full amount of the loan is committed at the start of construction, however, so the builder knows the funds will be forthcoming as the project progresses. Essentially, the outstanding loan balance grows with the increasing value of the collateral. To obtain a construction loan, the borrower, who may be the owner, the builder, or both, submits construction plans and specifications to a loan officer for analysis, usually at a commercial bank or savings association. Based upon the total value of the land and the planned building, lenders make commitments for usually 75% of that total value. The amount thus committed should be enough to cover construction costs with the remaining 25% of the value considered equity in the land underneath the building.

Commercial banks and savings associations require that the land be lien-free so the construction loan holds first priority position. If the lot is encumbered by an already existing loans or leases, whoever holds those loans, leases, or liens must subordinate their interests to the lien of the construction loan before it can be granted.

Construction loans are available for projects of all sizes. Usually a one-time, 1% placement fee is charged at the loan's origination. Interest rates are usually two or three points above the prime rate charged to top-rated borrowers. Interest rates and placement fees vary depending on business cycles, borrowers' credit ratings, and individual cases.

The disbursement of funds from a construction loan usually follows one of two basic patterns. The disbursement schedule may involve a series of **draws** as construction progresses. In a five-stage plan, an interim financier distributes 20% of the funds each time the building progresses another one-fifth of the way toward completion. The final payment may be withheld until all payments for labor and materials are made, to make sure no liens are attached to the property. Each contractor and subcontractor on the job will be required to submit a lien waiver. The final loan installment may also be held back until the builder receives a certificate of completion and approval for occupancy issued by a building inspector from a municipal agency.

Interest is charged on these funds only after they are disbursed following an inspection of the building's progress. Lenders keep careful records of the interest as it begins to be added to the loan installment staring with the disbursement date. Accumulated interest and the entire construction loan principal are usually paid in full within a relatively short time after the building is completed. Then, under usual circumstances, permanent, long-term financing is secured to replace the construction loan. Also, usually, the borrower has arranged for such long-term financing early in the project. Borrowers may also submit all bills for subcontracted labor and materials to their lenders, who then pay these bills and charge the loan account. This disbursement plan means the lender has more oversight and can make sure that intervening mechanic's liens are not charged against the project, that is, that the construction loan retains highest priority.

Disbursement of the funds in a construction loan as draws or payments by the lender results in the value of the collateral more or less equaling the loan amount outstanding at any given time during the project. If a default occurs, the lender can foreclose and recover the collateral in its unfinished condition. The property and its partially finished building can then be sold as is, or the lender can arrange for its completion by another builder so as to recover the investment.

Lender Protection in Construction Loans
No insurance plans guarantee payments on construction loans. Many construction lenders require that borrowers take out a completion bond from an insurance company that stipulates the lender as the primary beneficiary. The bond covers the total construction cost, and is exercised only if the builder cannot complete the job. If this happens, the lender can use the bond proceeds to arrange for the completion and sale of the property and thereby recover funds already advanced. However, small building companies may not qualify for bonding simply based on the current project and must pledge other assets as collateral to meet the bonding requirement to obtain a construction loan.

Construction loans usually have short terms, 6 to 12 months for a house and up to three years for larger projects. The construction loan lender is paid in full at the end of the term of the construction loan. Obviously, this lender focuses on ensuring in advance that this final payment is secure and will be paid on time. At the same time, the borrower is equally focused on this same issue and is also anxious to be relieved of the interest that must be paid, as it substantially reduces profits. So, permanent, long-term mortgages are arranged before the project starts in order to pay back the interim financier when the project is completed. Thus, builders submit plans and specifications to the potential long-term lender before the construction starts—as well as to the interim financier. If the builder's application for long-term financing is approved, the interim lender is notified in writing of the details of the **standby commitment**. Then the interim lender can go forward with the construction loan because he or she knows that payment in full will be tendered at the completion of the construction.

Of most significance in these transactions is that the long-term lender's requirements must be met before the permanent loan is funded. These requirements vary, but are likely to include meeting all local building codes and conforming exactly to the plans and specifications submitted, among other items. One very important requirement for permanent financing found in the standby commitments of large projects is that the building constructed be leased to its breakeven point. So, for an office building, enough tenants need to have already signed leases before the building can be occupied so that their rents at least enable the builder to pay all costs involved in running the building, including the loan payments. Many long-term lenders do not approve standby loan commitments until the breakeven number of tenants have committed to leasing space in the building. Leases are essentially collateral pledged to ensure that principal and interest payments, along with property taxes, hazard insurance premiums, and maintenance costs are all covered—in other words, the costs of running the building to at least break even.

Advance leases on some projects must be upwards of 85% of total occupancy to meet lender requirements. **Rent-up ratios** (the occupancy rate needed to break even) vary, depending on loan terms, taxes, and insurance and maintenance costs.

Marketing programs to attract tenants are a part of every large commercial real estate project. Owners cannot postpone this effort until after the building is ready for occupation, but rather, intensely look for tenants before and during construction. National retail chains with good credit ratings are contacted and encouraged with all sorts of incentives to commit to leasing space in a new shopping center just in the planning stages, for example. These "anchor" stores' rent is often enough to enable the project to break even.

Lenders rent-up requirement can make or break developers' projects on the drawing board. Because market conditions are always in flux, the predicted breakeven point might go up without much warning, and so, permanent financing to cover the construction loan might not be forthcoming. Permanent lenders can also hold back some part of the long-term loan until a new, higher rent-up requirement is met.

If this occurs, interim lenders of construction loans are in a tight spot. They expect to receive their payback of the total proceeds of the construction loan from the permanent lender. Sometimes, interim lenders hold back part of the construction loan in these circumstances—often the final draw. Another possibility is to require borrowers to obtain a letter of credit or second loan equal to the money held back by the permanent lender.

The interim lender's holding back part of the construction loan results in a gap in the financing structure. If a second loan is acquired by the builder to fill this gap, the interest rate is usually higher than the construction loan, because the second loan is a relatively risky proposition. If additional tenant commitments result in meeting the rent-up requirements, the permanent lender then covers the entirety of the long-term financing, and all lien-holders are paid in full. However, if the builder cannot rent-up to the breakeven point, the project may fail. In this case, the lender of the loan filling the gap either loses the investment or must take over a failing project—and neither scenario is optimal, to say the least.

Standby Commitments for Financing Construction

Especially in overbuilt markets, builders may face restrictions in obtaining loans for acquisition, development, and/or construction, even for well-conceived, substantiated projects. One way of dealing with these circumstances is to obtain a standby takeout commitment. This instrument is funded only if a permanent lender cannot be found to finance the long-term loan to cover the completed project. Standby takeout commitments come in three forms

1. In a Regular Standby, the lender agrees to take out the construction lender by funding a 3 to 5-year permanent loan in exchange for a substantial fee and high interest rate. Credit companies are common sources for regular standby loans

2. In a Suicide Standby, the lender agrees to fund the commitment only under very difficult terms and high interest rates to discourage the borrower. Obviously, a suicide standby is used rarely and only in extreme circumstances

3. In a Purchase Standby, insurance companies, pension funds, and/or other equity buyers offer to purchase the project after completion for a predetermined price, which is typically 100% of the construction cost, including the developer's fees. As a result, developers know that, at worst, everyone will be paid, although they will no longer own the building or participate in its potential income

Sources of Funds

The short term of construction loans matches investment profiles of commercial banks, and they are heavily involved in this type of financing. In addition, some financial firms that usually deal in long-term loans also offer such interim financing. For example, some lenders provide construction loans and then simply convert these to permanent loans for qualified borrowers. These lenders have available loan packages especially developed for this market called **construction/permanent loans**.

Gap financing better matches the lending profiles of both real estate trusts and private companies. Permanent long-term takeout loans correlate better with the investment interests of savings institutions and life insurance companies. So, all types of fiduciaries can be involved in financing different stages of construction. Moreover, mortgage banking or mortgage brokerage companies can coordinate all these various lenders to ensure that the project progresses smoothly toward realization.

Blanket Loans

Blanket loans cover multiple pieces of property. Builders seek these loans when constructing new condominium or home developments to be eventually sold to individual consumers. **Blanket loans** typically include a clause releasing individual houses or properties one at a time at their sale. When released, the house no longer is covered by the blanket loan. Basically, the **release clauses** provide a way the builder can relinquish ownership of individual parcels of property.

Usually, in exchange for a designated repayment—such as the long-term residential mortgage of a new homeowner—specific properties are freed from the lien of a blanket loan. Without a release clause, payment in full of the entire loan balance would be required before any part of the development could be sold lien-free.

Another possibility is to sell part of the land covered by a blanket loan without paying off the portion covering the land being sold. However, this can cause much difficulty for someone who buys a small parcel because if payments on the blanket loan are not made on time by the developer, the owner of this small parcel may see his or her property taken over in a foreclosure. Unfortunately, many land promotion developments work this way—without release clauses—and individual buyers wind up with a very high risk investment.

Responsible land developers include special recognition clauses in their financing that protect individual owners of small parcels of the property. These clauses say that if a default occurs with a resultant foreclosure, the lender of the underlying loan recognizes and protects the rights of each individual lot owner. California requires full disclosure of the physical attributes of the land involved in such developments, plus full descriptions of all financing terms. These disclosure requirements follow federal government rules on interstate land sale promotions.

Participation Loans

The three types of participation loans are

1. A partnership of several lenders
2. A team of several borrowers
3. A partnership between a lender and a borrower

Partnerships of Lenders

In a partnership of lenders, more than one lender owns the instrument financing a real estate project. This participation loan is usually used to finance large projects, and each lender advances a share of the funds required and receives a proportionate share of the payments.

Ginnie Mae mortgage-backed securities are a form of participation finance. Many individual investors, large and small, purchase shares in a designated pool of loans, and Ginnie Mae guarantees repayment of principal and interest on these shares. **Real Estate Mortgage Trusts (REMTs)** also offer loan partnerships. Using the pool of funds received from the sale of these beneficial interests, mortgage trust managers invest in real estate loans and distribute the profits according to a prearranged formula. Because REMTs are privately owned, the REMT managers are able to invest in higher risk loans, such as junior loans or gap financing. If financial conditions are less than optimal however, REMTs can inadvertently be converted to **REITs (Real Estate Investment Trusts)** when foreclosures on delinquent borrowers result in the investors owning the properties that they had financed.

Partnerships of Borrowers (Cooperatives/Condominiums)

Participation loans can involve a number of borrowers who share responsibility for a single loan on a multifamily property. For example, in the years after World War II, cooperative apartments were promoted in major cities such as Chicago, Los Angeles, New York, and Philadelphia, in response to rising rents. These buildings were basically financed by all the people who lived in the apartments sharing responsibility for the loan.

Cooperative ownership can take three forms: trust, corporate, or individual. In a **trust cooperative**, legal ownership of the property is give to a trust company that issues beneficial participation certificates to the purchasers. Ownership of these certificates includes the right to lease a unit in the building subject to the rules and regulations of the project. Property management is the responsibility of the trust's officers.

A **corporate cooperative** places ownership in a corporation that issues stock to purchasers, giving them the right to lease a unit from "their" corporation. Property management is the responsibility of a board of directors elected by the stockholders—the people leasing the units.

Individual cooperative ownership includes tenancy in common and condominium ownership. As a **tenant in common**, a buyer of a property receives a deed for a proportionate undivided interest in the entire property, along with the right to occupy a specific unit. The major weakness of the tenancy in common form is that each participant in such a cooperative depends on all the other owners to avoid defaulting on the loan. Financially irresponsible tenants or units empty for significant time periods result in financial strains on the other tenants—who are liable for the full loan payments. By contrast, in **condominium ownership**, participants hold fee simple absolute title to their individual units and are responsible only for their own mortgages or trust deeds. So, condominium ownership eliminates the problems associated with cooperatives.

Partnerships of Lenders and Borrowers

This type of loan participation arises when a lender becomes an owner of a project that will be financed by a loan from that lender. Lenders may accept a higher loan-to-value (L/V) ratio, lower the interest rate, or make other concessions in exchange for an ownership interest in the project as a condition for issuing the loan commitment. The lender's ownership percentage can range from 5% to 50% or more, thus making the lender a partner in the development as well as its financial backer. The shared appreciation mortgage (SAM) is a form of participation financing used for single-family homes and condominiums.

Convertible Participating Loans

Hybrid financing availability has risen along with increasing volatility in some real estate markets, and some lenders now offer participation and convertible loans. As it has been described earlier, participation loans are debt with some equity characteristics. The debt component is a fixed-interest loan made at lower-than-market rates. The equity component is the share in the property's appreciation that the lender receives in exchange for the favorable terms on the debt component. A convertible loan also has a rate of interest below market rates. At this type of loan's maturity, the lender can convert the debt to a 50% interest in the property ownership. However, even though the lower interest rate is advantageous, the developer's overall cost of capital with hybrid loans is significantly higher than with conventional financing. So, hybrid loans are usually only attractive when market conditions close the doors on standard methods.

Leasehold Lending

Since colonial times, in the city of Baltimore and other parts of Maryland, a real estate financing system of "ground rents" has been common. Landowners gave perpetual leases called **ground rents** to tenants who pledged their interests in the property to obtain funds to build improvements on the land. The owner, or lessor, retained title to the land and received an annual rent from the tenant, or lessee, who possessed the land and could use it as he or she desired.

However, the fact that these leases were perpetual led to a good deal of difficulty for both the lessors and the lessees. Lessees could never acquire title to the land, and had to negotiate with the lessor to determine who was liable for the property. In 1884, the Maryland legislature passed a law requiring that ground leases held for more than 15 years provide the lessee with an option to purchase the property.

Pennsylvania had a similar system of land rents, but here tenants could obtain title on a land contract on which payments were made "forever." However, in 1885, the Pennsylvania legislature prohibited the use of contracts that required payments in perpetuity and required terminating dates and redemption rights for the tenant.

Today, Maryland and Pennsylvania financial institutions grant loans with a tenant's lease-hold interest as collateral, with the ground rent as a prior lien. If the tenant-borrower defaults, the lender takes over the position of the borrower under terms of the ground rent contract.

Leasehold Loan Expansion

The ground rent system did not become popular in other parts of the country as they developed In the 19th century, land west of the Mississippi River was easy to buy because the federal government was eager to encourage western settlement. Other financing methods and sources developed to support this exploration, growth, and settlement.

But leasehold lending still exists, and the history of ground rents in the original colonies provided a foundation, understanding, and confidence in this system. Tenants pledge their leasehold interests as collateral for improvement loans, some of which are eligible for FHA and DVA insurance and guarantees. National banks are authorized to make such loans provided that the lease term extends beyond the expiration of the leasehold loan. The DVA, for example, guarantees leasehold loans to be repaid 15 years before the expiration of the ground lease. The FHA insures only loans issued on property with 99-year leases. In California, the Irvine Ranch Corporation granted 75-year leases on single-family home lots.

Subordination

Major sources of leasehold loans are life insurance companies, mutual savings banks, and commercial banks. The fiduciary lender must have the first priority lien position so full title to the collateral property can be secured if default occurs. To ensure this position, a leasehold loan arrangement usually includes the landlord's pledge of the legal fee simple rights in the property and the tenant's pledge of the improvements as collateral for the loan. The landlord's pledge is called **subordination**. As a result, if a default occurs that leads to foreclosure, the lender is protected because he has the legal right to recover both the land and the improvements.

Credit Loans

In rare exceptions, the landlord is not required to pledge the land or subordinate the legal fee to the lender. These situations usually involve tenant-developers with extremely strong credit—so strong that the value of the collateral that would be pledged is negligible compared to the net worth of the tenant. For example, when Kroger or Wal-Mart wants to obtain financing to build stores, processing plants, or warehouses, these companies obtain funds simply on signature and the pledge of the leasehold interests if the company builds on leased land. Landowners, in this case, would not need to participate in these financial arrangements. **Credit loan** is the name for this type of finance, where loans are issued on the credit of the borrower.

Credit loans are highly leveraged commercial mortgages of usually 80% to 100% of the property's market value. The net lease between a high-credit corporation as lessee and an investor as lessor is the key instrument in the credit tenant loan. The initial lease term must be at least as long as the loan term, usually between 20 and 25 years. The rent paid by the lessee under a credit tenant lease must be absolutely net; the tenant pays all taxes except income tax, all insurance premiums, repair and maintenance costs, capital replacement costs, and all other operational costs. Because the net lease rather than the property is the primary collateral for the loan, the lender requires that the mortgage is subordinated to the lease. If a foreclosure occurs, the lease survives, and the lender is protected.

Commercial Leasehold Insurance

Many commercial property lenders require that this insurance is obtained before they issue a loan for large rental development projects to a tenant-borrower. If the tenant-developer plans to lease out the improvements under construction, this insurance guarantees rental continuity from the project's tenants. With AAA-rated commercial tenants, lenders would probably not require **commercial leasehold insurance**.

However, in developments lacking in enough such highly rated tenants to satisfy a lender's rent-up requirements, leasehold insurance is required for the rents of the lower-rated tenants. As a result, both the developer and the subordinated landowner are protected, and the lender's security requirements are met.

The largest company offering this product is **Commercial Leasehold Insurance Corporation (CLIC)**, a wholly owned subsidiary **of Mortgage Guaranty Insurance Corporation (MGIC).** CLIC insurance covers tenants in shopping centers, office buildings, and industrial developments who do not have prime-rated credit. Various plans are available that guarantee an insured tenant's rental payments. An additional benefit for the developer who buys commercial leasehold insurance is the screening process used by the insurance company in its underwriting. If the insurance company refuses to write a policy on a prospective tenant, the developer has a warning of that tenant's poor credit rating.

Package Loans

Package loans are secured by more than just the property financed. The **package loan** may require as collateral the property, buildings on it, and also fixtures attached to the property and/or personal property (such as a car or truck)—whatever is necessary to secure the loan.

Items such as heating systems, plumbing fixtures, lighting fixtures, and central air systems, because they are physically attached and integrated into the real estate, are real property that is automatically included in the loan. Other fixtures are not usually considered real property, including stoves and ranges, ovens, refrigerators, freezers, dishwashers, and carpets. However, these items may be included in a home purchase financing agreement to attract buyers. These appliances and other items enable the home buyers to stretch the payments for these items over the entire term of a real estate loan instead of paying for them immediately or taking out a shorter term consumer installment loan.

When California adopted the Uniform Commercial Code dealing with financing personal property, the state instituted the filing of financing statements with the Secretary of State. Local filing at a county recorder's office may also be necessary for certain types of collateral, such as farm equipment or crops. Later filings must also occur at the same place where the original filing was made so notice is given of the continuing basis of the financing. Such documents may include Statements of Continuation, Termination, Release, Assignment, and Amendment. Financing statements are effective for specified time periods, often five years in length. These must be renewed or they automatically lapse.

Package loans are increasingly popular in the U.S. because as a result, home buyers do not have to make separate payments for fixtures and other items, plus payments are lower compared to the relatively high interest rates for short-term personal property financing. Furthermore, TRA '86 allows homeowners to deduct interest payments on home loans from their income taxes, but consumer loan interest is not tax deductible.

So, many commercial rental properties, including condominiums, apartments, offices, and healthcare facilities, are specifically designed to qualify for package financing.

In this type of real estate financing, old items that are no longer functioning as well as they should be must be replaced to keep the value of the collateral equivalent. However, when such new replacement items are financed through retailers, they are no longer available as collateral for the original loan. If the package loan financier refuses to release these personal properties from the blanket lien, borrowers may find themselves with several useless items, such as no- longer functioning washing machines or torn-up carpeting stored in their basements or attics—or in remote storage units that require monthly rent payments. Furthermore, for a package loan to be worthwhile for the lender, only real property should be considered as collateral. Most personal property that can be included in a package loan is really too easily removed from the site if a default occurs.

Loans for Mobile Homes

The primary question related to financing mobile homes is whether the collateral—the mobile home—is real property or personal property. This decision is needed to determine what type of financing is proper.

A travel trailer attached to a vehicle by a hitch or placed on the bed of a pickup truck or a bus-like motor home is obviously personal property. They can be moved with relatively ease and are not tied down in some way to a parcel of land. If you purchase these items, even though their prices are significant, they will be financed by a personal property debt instrument, and interest payments will not be tax deductible unless they are used for business.

Mobile homes that are greater in length than travel trailers and motor homes, but that still can be attached to a "regular" vehicle by a hitch and parked temporarily at rental-trailer parks are also viewed as personal property and financed similarly to motor homes and travel trailers.

However, larger mobile homes—sometimes called "manufactured homes"—that are sold as prefabricated portable housing units fall into a different category. These units are usually—and legally—moved only by professional movers. They are permanently attached to specific lots in rental parks for long periods of time. Sometimes, they are installed on property owned by the mobile home owner. Under these conditions that involve the permanent connection of the mobile home to a plot of land, the borrower needs to apply for real estate financing.

While all mortgage types can be used to finance both the mobile home and its lot, the repayment term is usually shorter than for single-family or multifamily residential real estate. Many lending institutions have some reluctance to finance mobile homes for long periods of time, even though their construction has improved considerably over the years. Furthermore, mobile homes typically depreciate a good deal during the first few years after their manufacture—similarly to vehicles. So, few mobile home loans terms are longer than 15 years, although in recent years, newer "doublewides" that are permanently tied down to fixed foundations have been financed for up to 30 years. Also, these loans may qualify for FHA or DVA financing provided title insurance is secured.

The California Department of Housing and Community Development (HCD) requires the registration and licensing of all mobile homes—except those affixed to a foundation. Only some travel trailers are now registered with the Department of Motor Vehicles.

Purchase-Money Mortgages

In a purchase-money mortgage, the seller makes the loan, as opposed to a bank or mortgage company. The loan is secured by a standard mortgage or deed of trust, but the loan does not have to conform to financial industry standards of loan-to-value ratios, interest rates, or credit qualifications of the borrower, among others. Yes, the seller takes on the entire risk of the loan, but this type of financing may be justifiable if the sale would not go forward otherwise or if it means that the seller receives a larger price for the property. Furthermore, depending on the financial situation of the seller, it might be advantageous for income tax purposes not to receive the purchase price as a lump sum, but rather in installments over the term of the loan.

Hard-Money Loans

A hard-money loan is a first mortgage or trust deed executed in exchange for cash. Hard-money loans are usually junior liens given to private mortgage companies for cash so borrowers can buy personal property or pay for some major service, such as medical assistance or property remediation. The borrower's existing equity in the property is pledged as collateral for this loan.

Bridge Loans

Bridge loans are equity loans to cover some specific need, usually for only a short time. A "classic" bridge loan would cover property borrowers want to buy while they are still waiting to sell another property, the proceeds from which will eventually be used to pay the bridge loan. Payments on bridge loans usually cover only the interest, with balloon payments at their stop dates.

Wrap-around Encumbrances/All-Inclusive Trust Deeds (AITD)

Wrap-around loans are another way to finance property. Sometimes these loans are called an all-inclusive trust deed (AITD). A wrap-around loan usually consists of both the existing note held by the seller, and the new loan secured by the buyer. The new loan "wraps around" the existing loan, and one payment is made to cover both loans. One loan consumes all the present encumbrances of the property plus the amount of the new loan.

Because this is not a blanket loan or open-ended loan, there is a hierarchy which makes the AITD subordinate to any previously recorded trust deed on the property. If the property should be foreclosed, any previous trust deeds must be paid first (even though the wrap-around loan is making the payments for these loans). One difference regarding the AITD loan versus other financing is that, with an AITD loan, the buyer receives the title to the property at closing. Usually an AITD is utilized when a seller and buyer are both financing a property. In a traditional loan assumption or when the seller carries back a note on the property, the buyer takes a loan to cover the cost of the existing loan plus the difference in the sale price of the home. The seller benefits from this situation, because he or she receives the full price for the home. The buyer generally benefits through a lower down payment, and also does not have to endure the traditional qualifying process to obtain the loan.

The AITD includes the unpaid principal balance of the existing loan plus the amount of the new loan being made by the seller to the buyer. The seller continues to make payments on the loan that he or she has taken out from his or her financial institution, while the buyer makes payments to the seller for the AITD. Of course, payment from the buyer will be enough to cover the original loan plus a higher interest rate to the seller. This is in concert with the additional money borrowed from the seller to cover the difference between the original trust deed and the selling price of the property.

While this type of loan seems like a great idea for a buyer, there are situations when it simply does not work out as well. If a seller needs to cash out of a loan for the purchase of another property, or for any other reason, he or she is not able to do so with an AITD loan. The seller is obligated to repay the entire original note to the lender that is wrapped around by the loan they have provided to the buyer. Some loans contain a due-on-sale clause, meaning the seller would not be able to wrap around a loan to the existing loan, as the original loan must be paid off when the home is sold. If there is no **due-on-sale clause**, the lender may have to approve the wrap-around loan, and there are some cases when the buyer may not qualify (for example, because of their credit score or debt-to-asset ratio). In a market with high interest rates, an AITD may not be the best choice, because the buyer ends up paying a much higher rate than the current market demands for the wrap-around loan. This higher rate is, however, financially attractive to the seller.

The buyer typically does not make payments directly to the seller, although in theory that is what is happening. Instead, the buyer will usually make payments to a collection company, which will then distribute the money to the appropriate parties. The original lender will receive a monthly payment, while the seller will receive the amount predetermined by the contract. This is done to protect the buyer from mismanagement on the seller's behalf, and to ensure that the original note is being paid according to the promissory note's terms and conditions. This protects all parties involved, and ensures that this type of financing remains feasible and functional.

Wrap-around loan/All-inclusive trust deed

- Seller finances the buyer by providing a loan encompassing all payments to the first or subsequent trust deeds.

- Buyer's payment to the seller includes the payment on the original loan, plus the higher interest rate, as well as the difference between the principal owed on the first note and the amount of the sale price of the home.

- Wrap-around loan is subordinate to the original loan.

- Buyer takes the title to the home.

- Buyer makes payments to a collection company ensuring that all funds are distributed to the appropriate parties.

S U M M A R Y

Today, a number of variations on the conventional mortgage loan have enabled the real estate financing industry to expand its scope considerably. The following innovative payment and interest systems are available to borrowers

- With variable-rate mortgage loans (VRMs) and variable payment plan loans, such as the graduated payment mortgage (GPM), lenders can alter interest rates and payment terms to meet prospective borrowers' needs.

- With a shared appreciation mortgage (SAM), the lender receives some part of the value appreciation of the collateral along with the interest payments on the loan.

- With a pledged account mortgage (PAM), borrowers make lower payments during the first few years of the loan; sellers receive cash for their properties as they would with a conventional loan; and lenders make profitable loans as well as hold subsidy funds from the borrowers in reserve accounts.

- With a renegotiable rate mortgage (RRM, also called a rollover or bullet loan), the amortization period is 30 years to reduce the monthly payment, but the loan actually comes due in full sooner—in 3, 5, 10, or 15 years. When the loan comes due, it is usually renewed at current interest rates.

- With a lease option, or lease-purchase, tenants have the right to buy the property that they have occupied, usually with rental payments counting against the purchase price.

- With, zero percent financing (ZPF), all payments are deducted from the principal balance.

- With a growing equity mortgage (GEM), payments increase gradually by an amount that is applied against the principal, which substantially shortens the amortization period. With a biweekly payment loan, a variation on the GEM, borrowers make 26 payments of one-half the conventional monthly payment each. This pattern correlates to the usual biweekly payroll schedule of most borrowers—which is convenient—plus it shortens the amortization period of the loan significantly.

- With a reverse annuity mortgage (RAM), senior citizens with considerably equity in their homes pledge their property as collateral and receive monthly payments from lenders until a predetermined total is reached. Then the loan must be repaid, usually by selling the property.

- With convertible loans, borrowers can switch their adjustable-rate mortgages to fixed-rate ones to reduce the uncertainty of rising interest rates and unaffordable payments.

The most common open-end loan is a construction loan, in which the increasing value of the collateral as it is built is matched by the incremental accumulation of funds received from the lender. However, loans that are not for construction can also be arranged so borrowers receive predetermined advances from lenders. Usually, the funds received are equivalent to the principal already paid on the loans. Borrowers of open-end loans have their credit reviewed and the collateral reevaluated periodically by their lenders. Often, after these reviews, interest rates are changed, escrow fees charged, and new payment schedules arranged.

Construction loans finance the cost of labor and materials during building. The funds lent correlate with the growing value of the collateral building. Usually, the borrower draws funds according to a predetermined schedule. Construction loans have terms of 1 to 3 years, depending on the size of the project. This interim financing is repaid by a permanent long-term loan arranged when the project is started but issued only after construction is complete.

With a blanket mortgage, more than one property is pledged as collateral. The federal government sometimes places a blanket lien on all property, real and personal, of a delinquent taxpayer, for example. More commonly, blanket loans are used in land development projects with release clauses enabling the developer/borrower to have portions of the collateral released from the loan as, for example, individual homebuyers purchase homes in the development. Each piece of property is released from the blanket loans as the lender receives payments that reduce the balance of the blanket loan.

With partnership financing, ownership is set up among two or more lenders issuing a single loan, usually for a large commercial real estate development, such as a shopping center, office building, plant, or warehouse. Borrowers may also form a partnership and share responsibility for a single loan; this is the arrangement in cooperative apartment buildings. Participation finance also occurs when a lender secures equity in a real estate project that he or she is also financing, that is, when the lender becomes both the financier of a project and one of its owners.

With leasehold loans, a tenant's leasehold interest in a property is pledged for financing improvements to the property. Usually, these loans are issued only for property covered by a very long-term lease, one that is longer than the term of the loan, in order to reduce the lender's risk.

Lenders may also require that landowners subordinate their legal fee simple interest in the property to the new leasehold loan. Under these circumstances, if default occurs, the lender can take ownership of the property.

With a package loans, personal property of the borrower as well as the real property are included under the lien. With package loans, borrowers may also purchase expensive personal property items, such as appliances and HVAC units, and pay for them over the entire term of the loan, instead of securing short-term, higher interest financing for these items. Also, with package loans, builders of new homes can include major appliances in their offers, for example—which may be attractive inducements especially to younger buyers.

A large mobile home permanently fixed to the ground is considered real property and can be financed by a mortgage, deed of trust, or contract for deed. Smaller units that can be hitched to a standard vehicle and moved relatively easily, on the other hand, are deemed personal property and are financed the way any personal property is covered. Some mobile home loans are insured by FHA or guaranteed by DVA.

With a purchase-money loan, the seller finances the sale of a property, and receives mortgage payments from the borrower. A hard-money loan is an equity loan of funds for whatever purpose the borrower has. A wraparound loan is junior financing that covers an existing financial instrument.

T E R M S   A N D   P H R A S E S

Adjustable Rate Mortgage (ARM)   loan with a flexible interest rate that increases or decreases with market interest rate changes

Balloon Payment   note requiring a large payment at the end of its term to cover the debt in full, and is used when only a small percentage of the principal is being covered by each of the monthly payments

Blanket Loan   loan covering several properties whereby each individual property can be released by paying a specific amount on the loan

Collateral   object of value that is pledged as security for the purchase of another object of value, which, in real estate, is the property that is pledged as security for the note as evidenced by the trust deed

Default   failure by the trustor to pay the monthly or installment payments on the promissory note for the property purchased

Equity   value in a property (or the appreciated value of the property over what is owed on the loan) after all the debts have been paid off

Graduated Payment Adjustable Mortgage   financing option where the loan installment payment gradually increases during the life of the loan, until it eventually levels off

Hard Money Loan   type of trust deed or loan given in exchange for cash that the borrower can utilize for any purpose; it need not be used to purchase property.

Holder   party, usually the lender, to whom the promissory note is made payable

Home Equity Loan   loan made to homeowners against the equity built up in their homes; generally it does not exceed 80 to 90% of the equity in the home.

Interest   cost a lender charges when lending money to a borrower

Junior Trust Deed   trust deed that is recorded after the first trust deed. The junior trust deed is considered less important (or of lesser priority) than the trust deed that was recorded first

Mortgage   legal document pledging property as security for a debt

Open-Ended Loan   financing option whereby the borrower is allowed to request additional funds secured by one existing trust deed

"Or More" Clause   clause in a note that allows a borrower to pay off the funds early, incurring no penalties

Package Loan   financing option where a loan can be secured not only by property, but by personal property or the fixtures attached to that property

Principal   amount of a loan, not including the interest

Promissory Note   written promise or evidence of debt that a borrower makes to a lender pledging to pay back the loan

Purchase Money Loan   loan made specifically for the purchase of real estate

Reverse Annuity Mortgage   financing option that allows a person to borrow money against the equity in his or her home. This type of loan is attractive to retired people on fixed incomes who own their homes as a means to supplement their income. The loan will not have to be paid off until a later date such as upon death of the homeowner, or when the home is sold.

Second Trust Deed   junior trust deed, or evidence of a debt that is recorded after the original trust deed

Security   collateral used to secure a loan

Shared Appreciation Mortgage – A financing option where the borrower and lender agree to share a percentage of the appreciation of a home as security for the loan.

Trust Deed   document where the title to property (bare legal title) will pass to a third party (called a trustee) as security for the debt

Variable Rate Mortgage   loan with a flexible interest rate that increases or decreases when market interest rates change

Wrap-Around Loan   financing option in which a new loan is placed in a secondary position. The new loan includes both the unpaid principal balance of the first loan as well as whatever sums are loaned by the lender. Wrap-around loans are sometimes called all-inclusive trust deeds.

C H A P T E R   Q U I Z

1. If a seller finances a junior trust deed to the buyer of his or her property, what options does the buyer have regarding the loan?
    a. He or she may carry the note until it is paid in full.
    b. He or she may sell the note at a discounted rate to a mortgage broker.
    c. He or she may force the buyer into paying the note back earlier than originally planned, because he or she needs the money for a new car.
    d. Both A & B

2. The Graduated Rate Mortgage is also known as
    a. a flexible rate mortgage.
    b. an adjustable rate mortgage.
    c. step up mortgage.
    d. none of the above.

3. Balloon payments
   a. are used on hard money loans.
   b. require a large final payment to completely repay the debt.
   c. require a 90–150 day notice from the lender to the borrower that the payment is forthcoming.
   d. all of the above.

4. Sellers who finance a buyer with a wrap-around loan typically do which of the following?
   a. Carry back a note on the property
   b. Charge the buyer a higher interest rate then he or she currently pays on the original trust deed.
   c. Collect the money directly from the buyer for the AITD
   d. Require a high down payment from the buyer

5. Which of the following loans allow individual properties to be released from the responsibilities of the loan, provided there is a sufficient payment?
   a. Blanket loan
   b. Wrap-around loan
   c. Open-ended loan
   d. Unsecured loan

6. Which of the following mortgage types best describe a loan similar to the wraparound loan or all-inclusive trust deed?
   a. Graduated payment adjustable mortgage
   b. Rollover mortgage
   c. Shared appreciation mortgage
   d. Contract of Sale

7. What is the term for selling a property at market value, below what is owed on the loan?
   a. Short Pay
   b. Walk away
   c. Foreclosure
   d. Trustee's sale

8. In a graduated payment mortgage
   a. the last few years of payments will be lower than the first.
   b. the first few years of payments will be lower than the last.
   c. the payment arrangements are ideal for people getting ready to retire as they might anticipate a lower income in the future.
   d. none of the above.

9. In an adjustable rate mortgage, an increase in interest rates will
   a. cause an increase in the payments.
   b. cause a decrease in the payments.
   c. cause no change to the payments.
   d. either A or B, depending on the prime rate.

10. An index is
   a. another name for interest.
   b. another name for the prime rate.
   c. the starting point of a borrower's applicable interest rate for an adjustable
   d. rate mortgage.

11. An adjustable rate mortgage will also have what feature?
   a. Interest rate cap
   b. Payment cap
   c. Margin
   d. All of the above

12. The shared appreciation mortgage traditionally involves the borrower and what other party to share in the increase of value in the property?
   a. Co-signer
   b. Lender
   c. Builder
   d. None of the above

13. Which of the following is not considered one of the innovative payment plans?
   a. Lease-purchase
   b. Wraparound trust deed
   c. Growing equity mortgage
   d. Zero percent financing

14. A lease-purchase is the same as an option to purchase.
   a. True
   b. False

15. A reverse annuity mortgage
   a. offers an adjustable interest rate.
   b. has the same requirements as a traditional home loan.
   c. does not require any payments until the allowed stipulated balance has been achieved.
   d. is ideal for young families.

16. Loans which allow a borrower to secure additional funds from a lender under the terms of an original note are called
   a. open-end loans.
   b. construction loans.
   c. blanket loans.
   d. all of the above.

17. The best way to describe a construction loan is
   a. temporary.
   b. permanent.
   c. fixed.
   d. variable.

18. Open-end loans are ideal for
    a. builders or construction companies.
    b. farmers.
    c. investors.
    d. both A and B.

19. Mobile homes can be financed like traditional real property when
    a. they are still attached to their chassis and mobile.
    b. they are attached to a pick-up truck.
    c. they are permanently attached to a foundation.
    d. All of the above

20. The wraparound trust deed
    a. takes priority to the original loan.
    b. allows the seller to retain the title to the home.
    c. allows the seller to finance the buyer, providing a loan encompassing all payments including the first or any subsequent trust deed.
    d. usually has a lower interest rate than a traditional loan.

12

PROCESSING
THE
LOAN

What you will learn in this Chapter

- Qualifying the Title

- Preparing Closing Statements

Test Your Knowledge

1. What documentation notifies any interested party of another's interest in the same property?
   a. Recordation
   b. Recorded deed
   c. Recorded mechanic's lien
   d. Recorded collateral

2. Risks such as forgeries, incompetency of involved parties, and surveying errors are covered under
   a. a standard title insurance policy.
   b. an expanded title insurance policy.
   c. every title insurance policy issued.
   d. construction insurance.

3. A survey will reveal which of the following?
   a. Encroachments
   b. Easements
   c. Errors in legal descriptions
   d. All of the above

4. Which of the following is not a required disclosure in the transfer disclosure statement?
   a. Flooding drainage or drainage issues near or affecting the property
   b. Disclosure of a death due to AIDS
   c. Easements, common drives or shared walks or fences with neighbors
   d. Zoning violations and insufficient setbacks

5. Pest inspection reports are divided into how many different portions?
   a. 1
   b. 2
   c. 4
   d. 5

6. The environmental hazard disclosure requires sellers of property to disclose which of the following?
   a. Formaldehyde
   b. Lead-based paint
   c. Termites
   d. Underground storage tanks

7. Before the transfer of title to a condominium, the seller must provide the buyer with
   a. a copy of the subdivision restrictions.
   b. a financial statement of the homeowner's association.
   c. a written statement from the homeowner's association regarding any unpaid assessments if any.
   d. all of the above.

INTRODUCTION

Steps involved in processing a request for a loan include searching the property's title and collecting and preparing the many closing documents. If a loan is approved for a specific property and the title search uncovers a lien that could prevent the property transfer, the collateral for that loan—the property—is no longer completely available. The loan process is stopped and is not restarted until the lender is assured all transactions regarding the property were recorded and documented legally and no liens remain that must be addressed.

This chapter takes you through the title search process, after which the title examiner issues a report clearing the title and notifying the lender that the property transfer can proceed unencumbered. Disclosures that must be made are also reviewed, along with how a loan is closed and the property transferred.

QUALIFYING THE TITLE

During the loan approval process, loan processors obtain title reports on the collateral property to be financed. A full title report includes a survey, a physical inspection of the collateral, and a records search to determine whether any interests in the property exist that would prevent a straightforward transfer. Usually, property interests are perfected by the filing and recording of standard notices. In this way, a deed, once recorded, provides notification to the general public that a grantee has the legal fee title to the property. A recorded mechanic's lien is an example of a notice of someone's interest in the property that would prevent transfer.

These records, called constructive notices, present facts related to the property that are matters of public record. Title examiners review these records as part of their determination as to whether the current owner of the property has clear title and can therefore, transfer its ownership.

Other notices regarding real estate transactions can be provided verbally or in writing by the parties to the transaction—the buyer, the seller, and the lender. This type of communications is called actual notice, and includes information about the rights of property owners and information revealed under California disclosure rules—which are described later in this chapter.

In California, you can ensure that the property you are considering purchasing has good title by obtaining an abstract and opinion of title or by purchasing title insurance. The title report resulting from either of these methods gives the loan officer and the lender's attorney all information recorded on the legal status of the property, along with any interests uncovered by constructive notice. The title search is usually a requirement for loan approval, and has as its primary purpose the further reduction in the risk the lender is taking in making this investment.

Abstract and Opinion of Title

An **abstract** is a summary of the recorded history of a property. The abstract takes all the records that the search has uncovered and presents that information in a formal report. Abstracts list each transaction related to the property in chronological order as it was recorded.

Abstracts used to be given to the buyer by the seller of a property after all transactions that occurred during the seller's ownership were added. The abstract and the deed to the property were given to the buyer for approval before closing. The buyer's attorney indicated approval verbally, by an informal note, or by formal title opinion in writing. Essentially, the buyer's attorney accepted liability if anything ever came to light in the future that could result in future losses for the buyer.

However, today, the abstract is not considered an official document because it does not disclose any hidden title hazards. The title examiner is responsible only for an accurate review of all the recorded documents pertaining to the property. If the loan officer requires more analysis, a lawyer specializing in this field is retained to provide it. The loan officer is thus apprised of any problems in the title based on the information in the abstract, If the lender requires further protection against potential title problems or errors in the abstract, title insurance must be secured, which provides a guarantee against such defects. Neither the examiner nor the lawyer providing the opinion offer such a guarantee.

Title Insurance

The title insurance industry has grown rapidly, largely because the real estate market in the U.S. has become national in nature, with loans being made locally, but often sold to another mortgage institution far from the originator and the actual property. Title companies today combine the abstracting process with insurance that guarantees the accuracy of the title search. The assets of the insurance company back up its guarantees, which are legally represented in a title insurance policy. Title insurance companies operate under the jurisdiction of the Insurance Commissioner of California.

In California, title insurance policies are of two types

- **California Land Title Association (CLTA), covering the value of the property**
- **American Land Title Association (ALTA), covering the loan amount**

Standard title insurance can also cover unusual risks, such as forgeries, lack of competency in the parties involved in the property transfer, questionable legal status of parties involved in loan negotiations, surveying errors, and other title defects. Other risks may be covered by special endorsements to the insurance policy, such as protection against recorded easements or liens, rights of parties in possession of the property, mining claims, water rights, and other items. Expanded ALTA policy coverage is generally required by secondary mortgage market investors.

Technology is enabling title insurance companies to lower costs and offer faster service by electronic information transfer that reduces the time and staff needed to perform title searches. Title companies are also expanding their services in order to increase revenue streams by providing property appraisals, flood plain certification, and credit reporting, among others.

Title Faults

If the title examiner finds a fault in the title (also called a cloud), the loan process stops and is not resumed until the fault is cleared to the satisfaction of the lender. Faults, or clouds, include unsatisfied mechanics' liens, income tax liens, property tax liens, encroachments, and zoning violations. Sometimes the borrower's name is not legally correct on the deed. The deed may have a faulty acknowledgment or does not include the appropriate signatures. The abstractor/examiner's job is to uncover and report on all the inaccuracies and problems that can exist in the title history of a property—and there can be many because real estate ownership transfer is complex, and records are not always well kept.

If title faults cannot be removed by ordinary means, the seller of the property or the borrowers may have to file suit to "**quiet title**." In this case, a judge removes or changes damaging faults in a title based on the evidence submitted. Then, and only then, does the loan process resume. The sale of foreclosed property is one time when title searches can be particularly complex, and very careful examinations and documentation are essential.

Surveys

A survey of the property is sometimes required by lenders as a condition for a loan. Newer subdivisions are usually described by licensed and registered surveyors and engineers, but homes in these subdivisions may have had additions built onto them or their lots otherwise changed since the original survey. In addition, older properties may not meet current setback restrictions required in current zoning laws. In other cases, subdivisions may have been rearranged or lot sizes further divided, and encroachments or easements may now be issues that need addressing.

PREPARING CLOSING STATEMENTS

Once the borrower's credit has been approved, the collateral's appraisal accepted, and the title search completed to the lender's satisfaction, the lending institution's loan committee approves the loan, and the loan officer starts preparing the closing documents indicating all charges and credits. Documents include at least the promissory note, the deed of trust or mortgage, and the truth-in-lending disclosure statement. Other documents, depending on the jurisdiction and any special loan circumstances, may also be prepared.

In California, the actual closing is usually handled by an independent, separate company, such as an escrow or title company, although some banks and mortgage companies may have their own escrow departments. Sellers, borrowers, and lenders are notified of the time and place of the closing, which can occur at the lending institution or the escrow or title company office. All these parties provide their documents, checks, and other material to whomever is handling the closing. Borrowers usually feel that they have signed their names more times than they ever did in their lives when they are finished with closing. When all documents have finally been signed, the deed is transferred and recorded. The seller receives payment, and the loan process is complete.

Required Disclosures in California Real Estate Closings

California and its Department of Real Estate require a number of disclosures in the never-ending goal of providing consumers with information to inform and protect them in dealing with often unfamiliar processes related to real estate transactions.

Real Estate Transfer Disclosure Statement

There are many physical features and issues regarding a property, which a seller must disclose to a buyer. If there are too many defects in a property, a buyer may not be interested in the property, but nevertheless the buyer should be made aware of these problems before making an offer. Not making these disclosures is against real estate law, as the buyer has the right to rescind the offer with no penalty if the proper disclosures are not made. Any seller of a one-to-four unit home or dwelling must deliver a disclosure to potential buyers regarding the property's structure and condition. This requirement is extended to the transfer of property by sale, exchange, installment land sale contract, and lease with an option to purchase or other option to purchase, or a ground lease coupled with improvements. There may be **Local Opinion Transfer Disclosure Statements** required or provided for neighborhoods, cities or counties that would disclose special local facts regarding the property. The following are facts that must be disclosed to a buyer of property by the seller or the seller's agent

- The age, condition, and any defects, malfunctions or problems with the structural component of the home which includes plumbing, electrical, heating, and other mechanical components or systems

- Easements and/or common drives, walks or fences shared with neighbors

- Additional rooms added to the property after it was originally built, and whether or not these rooms had the necessary building permits for construction.

- Flooding drainage or soil problems on, near, or in any way affecting the property

- Major damage to the structure or property caused by fire, earthquake or landslide

- Whether the property is located on a known earthquake fault line or within a known fault zone

- Citations against the property, lawsuits against the owner affecting the transferability of the property, or other legal issues with the current owners and property

- Homeowner's association dues and deed restrictions, or common area problems which may result in a special assessment

- Zoning violations, such as nonconforming uses or insufficient setbacks

Certain transfers are exempt from the requirement to provide a Transfer Disclosure Statement

- When property is transferred from one co-owner to another
- Sale by the state controller for unclaimed property
- The first sale of a residential property within a subdivision, where a copy of a public report is delivered to the buyer or where such a report is not required
- In a foreclosure sale
- Selling to or buying from any government entity
- A court-ordered transfer by a fiduciary in the administration of a probate estate or a testamentary trust
- Selling property to a spouse or to another related person resulting from a judgment of dissolution of a marriage, or a legal separation, or in a property settlement agreement.
- Sale of property due to failure to pay taxes

If a buyer does not receive the necessary disclosure document on a property in the allotted time, he or she may terminate the offer to purchase the property. The intention to terminate must be made either 3 days in person, or 5 days after a deposit has been given to United States Postal Services. A written notice of termination must reach the seller or the seller's agent. The time by which the Transfer Disclosure Statement must be delivered varies depending on the type of transfer. If the transfer is a regular sale, then the Transfer Disclosure Statement must be delivered before the transfer of title. If the transaction is a lease option or a ground lease with improvements, the Transfer Disclosure Statement must be delivered before execution of the contract.

The seller, the seller's agent, or any agent working in cooperation with the seller's agent is responsible for preparing the Transfer Disclosure Statement. This same person is in charge of delivering the disclosure to the buyer. In the event that there are multiple agents working with the seller, the agent who obtained the offer will be responsible for creating and delivering the Transfer Disclosure Statement.

Inspections may limit the liability of the seller and his or her agents. Inspections such as a land survey, pest inspection, roof inspection, plumbing inspection, geologic inspection or general contractor's opinion of the structure will give the buyer a better idea of the condition of the property. The seller's liability is limited, because any problems with the structure will be discovered in these inspections, and the buyer will not run into any surprises with the property. If there has been a violation of the law regarding the structure, it will not invalidate the property transfer. However, the seller will most likely be held responsible for fixing the problem, or may be held liable for any damages suffered by the buyer.

Delivery of Structural Pest Control Inspection and Certification Reports

California does not require a **structural pest control inspection** in the transfer of real property. Financing firms or buyers, on the other hand, might require that a pest control inspection be completed before a loan can be financed, or as a condition to purchase the home. If a pest inspection is required, it must be made as soon as possible after learning that it is required. Before the title is transferred or the execution of the sales contract occurs, the buyer must receive a copy of the pest report. The person conducting the report must also state in writing whether or not wood-destroying termites were visible. This report and written statement must be prepared by a licensed or registered structural pest-control company.

The pest inspection must be divided into two portions. The first portion will outline any existing damage or infestation, while the second portion of the report will outline the probability of other damage or infestation unseen by the inspector. The real estate agent who obtained the offer on the property is also responsible for obtaining the report and delivering it to the buyer. This occurs unless the seller has given written directions regarding the delivery of the report to another agent (such as the buyer's agent). The report may be delivered to the buyer in person or by mail, and the agent who obtains the report must keep it in his or her files for three years.

Disclosure of Geological Hazards and Special Studies Zones

The earth is a dynamic medium on which we live. Each day, there are geological changes to the surface of the earth, as well as changes happening within its core. Some of these geological changes require disclosures, while others do not. The geological changes that require disclosures are those that pose a potential major hazard from phenomena such as earthquakes, flooding, landslides, erosion and expansive soils. One specific condition requiring a disclosure is **fault creep**, or stress to the land caused by the shaking of an earthquake. Soil plays a major factor in fault creep. Softer soils or sediments that are looser tend to magnify an earthquake. Harder sediment, such as rock, will mask an earthquake. It is important for a new homebuyer to understand the type of soil his or her home sits on and the possible repercussions of this soil type during an earthquake. Proximity to the fault line will also play a big part in what happens during an earthquake. The closer a property is to the fault line; the more severe an earthquake's effects will be for the property. Again, this is something that must be disclosed to a homebuyer.

The State Division of Mines and Geology offers maps that show which areas of the state are susceptible to fault creep. These maps may also show areas that have had landslides in the past and/or are possibly susceptible to future landslides. For disclosure purposes, sellers and the agents working with them usually rely on maps offered by the state Division of Mines and Geology as the basis for the necessity of disclosure. For new construction, however, most structures designed for inhabitation are subject to the findings and recommendations of a **geologic report**. This report is prepared by a geologist or soils engineer registered in, or licensed by, the state of California.

Under the **Alquist-Priolo Special Studies Zones Act**, a seller who sells real estate, the seller's real estate agent, or any other cooperating agents must disclose the fact that a home sits in a **special studies zone**. This disclosure must be made on the Transfer Disclosure Statement, the Local Option Real Estate Transfer Disclosure Statement, or in the purchase agreement.

There are certain situations in which property is excluded from the requirements of the special studies zone. These circumstances are

- Alterations worth less than 50% of the total value of the structure

- Structures in existence prior to May 4, 1975

- Single-family, wood-frame or steel structures not over two stories high provided the dwelling is not part of a development consisting of four or more dwellings

- Single-family, wood-frame or steel-frame structures for which geologic reports have been approved, to be built in subdivisions authorized by the Subdivision Map Act

- Conversions of existing apartments into condominiums: it must be disclosed that the property is located within a delineated special-studies zone

An additional piece of literature for potential buyers is the "**Homeowner's Guide to Earthquake Safety**," distributed by the Seismic Safety Commission. This is not a disclosure, but it is a public brochure to encourage awareness of geologic and seismic hazards throughout the entire state of California. It outlines the related structural and nonstructural hazards, as well as recommendations for mitigating the hazards of an earthquake. The guide states that safety and damage prevention cannot be guaranteed with respect to major earthquakes, but precautions (such as retrofitting) can be undertaken to reduce the risk of damage. If a buyer of real property receives a copy of the "Homeowner's Guide," the seller is not required to provide any additional information regarding geologic and seismic hazards. Sellers and real estate agents must, however, disclose that the property is in a special studies zone and that there are known hazards in the area.

The delivery of the "Homeowner's Guide to Earthquake Safety" is required in transactions where there is a transfer of real property, those involving a residential dwelling built before January 1, 1960, and those consisting of one-to-four units (any of which are conventional, light-frame construction). It is also required in real estate transfers of any masonry building with wood-frame floors or roofs built before January 1, 1975. The transfers that are exempt from the Real Estate Transfer Disclosure Statement are also exempt from these rules about earthquake disclosures.

The bottom line is that full disclosure is required for all material facts regarding a special studies zone, local ordinances, or known structural deficiencies affecting the property. Buyers or agents may be responsible for further inquires of appropriate governmental agencies. The obligation of the buyer or the buyer's agent to make additional inquiries does not eliminate the duty of the seller's agent to make a diligent inquiry to identify the location of the real property in relationship to a defined special studies zone.

Environmental Hazard Disclosure

Sellers of property who are aware of chemical or environmental hazards are responsible for disclosing this fact to a prospective buyer, under the California Real Estate Transfer Disclosure Statement. It also requires sellers to disclose the presence of asbestos, formaldehyde, radon gas, lead-based paint, fuel or chemical storage tanks, contaminated soil, water, mold or any other hazardous substances. A landlord or owner of nonresidential property must also disclose any of these hazards to tenants or a person who leases space in the building. Sellers and property owners who do not give proper disclosures will be held liable (perhaps in the form of civil penalties) for any damages caused by these hazards.

Proposition 65 states that certain businesses may not knowingly and intentionally expose any individual to a cancer-causing agent, chemical or reproductive toxin without first giving clear warning to any person present in or using the space. You will recall warning signs at filling stations stating that one or more chemicals present in gas or at the filling station may cause cancer. These signs are required by law to be posted, giving consumers proper warning to proceed at their own risk. Recent laws have also included asbestos disclosure requirements for owners of commercial buildings built before 1979.

In addition to posted signs in commercial spaces, the Department of Real Estate, in conjunction with the Office of Environmental Health Hazard Assessment, has developed a booklet to help educate and inform consumers about environmental hazards that may affect real property. This booklet explains common environmental hazards and describes the risks involved with each of the hazards. The hazards discussed in the booklet include asbestos, radon gas, lead and formaldehyde. If a buyer has been given this booklet, the seller and the seller's agents are not required to provide any further information on the possibility of such hazards. If the seller is aware that one or more of these hazardous agents are present at the time of sale, this must be disclosed.

Energy Conservation Retrofit and Thermal Insulation Disclosure

Energy conservation is a present concern for the growing population of California, due to the state's limited resources. State law requires a minimum energy conservation standard for all new construction. If these minimum standards are not met, a building may not receive the building permit needed to go forward with construction. Besides the state standard, local standards are often imposed for further energy conservation measures on new and existing homes. These conservation goals can be met if homes are retrofitted before being sold. A seller of property must disclose to buyers the existence of state and local requirements for energy conservation. In addition to this disclosure, federal law requires sellers of new homes to disclose the type, thickness and R-value of the insulation which has been or will be used in each part of the house.

Special Flood Hazard Area Disclosure and Responsibilities of the Federal Emergency Management Agency (FEMA)

The Federal Emergency Management Agency (FEMA) creates **flood hazard boundary maps**, which identify general flood hazard zones in a community. These maps show areas of minimal risk, or areas that face risk of flooding every 500 years. There are also areas of moderate flood hazard, which have a possibility of flooding every 100–500 years. Special flood zones are labeled for those areas which have the possibility of flooding every 100 years. This flood information is very useful for insurance companies when determining where more probable flood zones are located.

A seller of property within a special flood zone or a flood hazard zone must disclose this information to the buyer, because federal law requires the buyer to obtain flood insurance in order to secure financing for a property. The cost of flood insurance will vary, depending on the flood zone in which the property is located. So, it is important for the buyer to contact the insurance company, to determine what kind of policy is necessary for financing.

Local Requirements Resulting from City and County Ordinances

Each city, county or community has its own ordinances for land use, zoning requirements, building codes, fire, health and other safety codes and regulations. These ordinances, or requirements regarding how to remain in compliance with the laws, as well as who these laws will affect, must be disclosed by the seller and the seller's agents to any prospective buyer of the property. Buyers may be deterred from purchasing property if its use is restricted. This is imperative for the buyer to know before the transaction is complete.

Foreign Investment in Real Property Tax

Under federal law, if a buyer purchases property from a foreign seller, the buyer must withhold and send the Internal Revenue Service (IRS) 10% of the gross sales price. As with most other disclosures, there are exemptions to this rule, as well. To be sure you are following the law correctly, it is advisable to contact the IRS and consult them regarding the transaction. Further assistance may be sought from a CPA, attorney, or tax advisor.

Exemptions are given for people investing in property sold by foreign sellers if any of the following conditions are met

- Seller has a non-foreign affidavit and U.S. taxpayer I.D. number

- A qualifying statement has been obtained through the IRS, stating that arrangements have been made for the collection of, or exemption from, the tax

- Sales price does not exceed $300,000

- Buyer intends to reside on the property as his or her main residence

Foreign Investment Real Estate Tax

Title 26, U.S. Code Section 1445 requires that foreign buyers of a property costing more than $300,000 must withhold 10% of the gross purchase price and send it to the IRS. U.S. resident aliens are exempt from this requirement.

Condominium Disclosure Documents

In the sale of a condominium property, the seller must give the buyer the following documents

- Governing rules of the condominium association

- Subdivision restrictions, including any occupancy limitations based on age

- Most recent financial statement of the homeowner's association

- Amount of any unpaid assessments

Disclosures for Real Estate Loans

Within 72 hours of applying for a loan, borrowers must receive a form approved by Commissioner of the California Department of Real Estate that includes

- The expected maximum amount to be paid by the borrower to obtain the loan, including fees for the appraisal, settlement, credit report, title insurance, and notary service

- The total commission to be paid to the lender for services, including points, origination fees, bonuses, and other charges

- An estimate of the funds to be paid by the borrower for mortgage payments, property insurance premiums, and property taxes

- Federal Reserve Board publication, "Consumer Handbook on Adjustable-Rate Mortgages," if the loan is an adjustable-rate contract

- Information required under Federal Truth-in-Lending (Regulation Z) regulations; Real Estate Settlement Procedures Act (RESPA); Equal Credit Opportunity Act (ECOA); and Housing Financial Discrimination Act (the Holden Act)

Costs of Obtaining a Real Estate Loan

The following descriptions of various costs involved in securing a real estate loan are not exhaustive; neither are all the following costs incurred with every real estate loan. Local conditions, specific properties, and loan terms determine just which costs borrowers must pay.

Placement or Origination Fees

Most lenders charge a fee of 1% to 3% of the total loan amount to cover the costs of handling the process of issuing a new loan. Covered by this fee are the services of the loan officer and others involved in the process, plus any materials used.

Points (Discount Fees)

Often, **points** are paid by the borrower at closing. Each point equals 1% of the loan amount. Points are funds paid up front that reduce the risk of the lender when making a loan at a lower-than-market interest rate or to a borrower with less-than-stellar credit, among other reasons. In addition, points can be charged by lenders to raise the effective yield on the loan, based on the current supply of and demand for money. Points are less often charged when money is easier to obtain, but can be as high as 4% of the loan amount in a tight money market.

Impound Requirements

Lenders often require borrowers to pay monthly installments on their annual property insurance and property taxes along with their mortgage principal and interest payments; this is called **impounding.** The insurance and tax payments are held by the lender in an **escrow** (non-interest-bearing) account, and when insurance and taxes are due, they are paid by the lender directly to the insurance company and taxing authority. Usually, borrowers who make down payments of less than 20% are required to pay their insurance premiums and taxes this way. In some cases, lenders may reduce the interest rate by some fraction of a point if borrowers agree to add installment payments of taxes and insurance to their monthly mortgage payments and to allow the lender to automatically remove the full monthly payment directly from the borrower's checking account.

At closing, to set up these escrow accounts and ensure that the lender has enough funds to cover any upcoming insurance or tax payments, borrowers must provide funds to "prime" these impounded payments. The actual amount depends on when the closing occurs relative to when insurance and tax payments are due.

Interest Adjustments

Although not required, many mortgage payments are due on the first or fifteenth day of the month; sometimes the borrower's preferences are taken into account. Mortgage payments are made in arrears; in other words, the payment made on February 1 covers the interest on the loan for the month of January. Usually, the borrower's first payment on the loan is not due until a month after the loan has closed, although this depends on the closing date. As a result of these varying dates, loan interest is usually determined from the closing date and is charged to the borrower to set up a standard pattern of payments.

The Truth-in-Lending law (Regulation Z) requires that lenders inform borrowers as to the true interest charges, known as the **annual percentage rate (APR).** This figure is the sum of the loan placement fees, points, and certain other costs along with the interest rate.

Prepayment Penalties

If a prepayment penalty exists on a current loan, and this loan is paid off with funds from a buyer who has obtained a new loan, the seller is charged with the penalty. Prepayment penalties are often waived if an existing loan is refinanced by the same lender.

Title Insurance Premiums

As discussed earlier, most lenders require title insurance. When a new loan is involved in a property sale, two title insurance policies are required. The **owner's title policy** is for the full purchase price, and is issued in the new owner's name. Often, the seller pays the premium for this title policy.

The second title insurance policy is called **mortgagee's title insurance**, and this policy is issued in the lender's name. The borrower pays this premium, which is a relatively small amount because this policy is issued simultaneously with the owner's policy, and the coverage is only for the duration and amount of the loan. Mortgagee's title insurance is usually an **American Land Title Association (ALTA)** policy, which offers the most comprehensive coverage to the lender, not to the property owner. If claims are made under a mortgagee's title insurance policy, they are usually for only the remaining balance of the loan.

Title insurance premiums are paid only once, and cover the beneficiaries as long as they own the property or the loan is in existence. When a property is sold again and/or the loan is repaid, new policies are issued to cover the new situation.

Mortgage Insurance Premiums (MIPs)

When FHA or private mortgage insurance is required, the borrower pays the premium at closing, or, with an FHA loan, the fees may be added to the loan amount. Private mortgage insurance companies may require a one-time insurance premium or a monthly payment for a number of years. If the borrower makes less than a 20% down payment, private mortgage insurance may be required until the borrower's total equity in the property equals 20% of the purchase price.

Life Insurance Premiums

Occasionally, borrowers voluntarily take out a life insurance policy naming the lender as beneficiary to ensure that the balance of the loan is paid if the borrower dies. Known as a **decreasing term policy**, this insurance makes the property "free and clear," so the family of the borrower is not liable for the mortgage in the event or his or her death. Usually, these premiums are paid along with monthly principal and interest payments.

Additional Charges

Costs of securing a credit report, appraisal, survey, attorney's title opinion, and other services are charged to the borrower and are due at closing. Sometimes, borrowers and sellers share certain costs, such as escrow fees, title policies, and recording charges.

Other Requirements

When new or remodeled houses in urban renewal are sold, documents indicating that these properties meet all housing codes and are ready for occupancy may be required. Also, property that the U.S. Army Corps of Engineers has designated as flood-prone must be covered by flood insurance.

Costs of Obtaining DVA Loans

No commission or brokerage fees are charged to veterans with DVA loans, although lenders may charge reasonable closing costs to that borrower. Under these circumstances, closing costs may include

- Charges for a DVA certificate of reasonable value
- Credit report
- Title evidence
- Survey
- Recording fees

As in conventional loans, lenders may also require veterans to pay advances to set up escrow accounts for taxes and insurance. In DVA loans, 1% of the loan amount is the maximum placement fee that can be charged, and closing costs, impound funds, and placement fees may not be included in the loan amount, that is, they must be paid separately at closing.

S U M M A R Y

After a borrower applies for a loan, the loan officer starts the processes of title search and preparation of closing statements.

In a title search, an examiner reviews all matters of public record related to the property and verifies that no interests, faults, or defects in the title exist that could interfere with the transfer of ownership and with the loan as receiving the highest priority in the event of default. The borrowers' rights to borrow against the property must be irrefutable. The status of the lender must be of the highest priority. Any faults on the title must be cleared before a loan can be issued.

After the title search, the examiner prepares an opinion of the condition of the title for approval by the borrowers and their attorneys. Borrowers then pay for title insurance to protect the lender against unforeseen claims against the property.

For closing, an escrow officer prepares statement specifying all charges and credits associated with the transaction. The lender is charged for the entire loan amount. Borrowers are charged for interest to date and all costs incurred in securing the loan, which may include points, origination fees, recording fees, collection charges, escrow fees, and the mortgagee's title insurance premium.

When all charges and credits have been approved and all loan documents signed, notarized, and recorded, the proceeds of the loan are distributed to the sellers and/or the holders of their mortgages, and the file is closed.

TERMS AND PHRASES

Abstract   process of reviewing all recorded transactions in the public record to determine whether any title defects exist that could interfere with the clear transfer of ownership of the property

ALTA Policy   American Land Title Association insurance policy covering the loan amount on property

California Land Title Association (CLTA)   insurance policy covering the value of the property being sold from sellers to buyers

Closing Statements   document which details the final financial settlement between a buyer and seller, and the costs paid by each party

Cloud   invalid encumbrance on real property

Constructive Notice   expresses reservations of pertinent facts that are usually matters of record

Disclosures   statement to a potential buyer listing information relevant to a piece of property, such as the presence of radon or lead paint

Impounds   portion of the monthly mortgage payment that is placed in an account and used to pay for hazard insurance, property taxes, and private mortgage insurance

Mortgagee's Title Insurance   required by lenders on some loans to protect lenders from a possible default. Most conventional loans with down payments or home equity percentages that are less than 20 percent of the home value require private mortgage insurance (PMI).

Origination Fee   fee charged by most lenders to cover the direct costs of arranging the loan

Point   dollar amount equal to 1% of the loan amount, and may be paid by the borrower at the time the loan is made to get a lower interest rate. Lenders offer various rate/point combinations.

Suit to Quiet Title   submitting appropriate evidence to the court and allowing judge to remove or modify an otherwise damaging fault in a title

Title Insurance   title insurance company's written commitment to insure title to the property, subject to the conditions and exclusions shown on the binder

C H A P T E R   Q U I Z

1. Which of the following is not a component of a full title report?
    a. Physical inspection of the collateral property
    b. Survey
    c. Borrower's credit check
    d. Search of the records of past documentation or interests to the collateral

2. What documentation notifies any interested party of another's interest in the same party?
    a. Recordation
    b. Recorded deed
    c. Recorded mechanic's lien
    d. Recorded collateral

3. Which of the following methods assure a property's good title?
    a. Abstract and Opinion of Title
    b. Title insurance
    c. Recorded deed
    d. Both A and B

4. An abstract of title will
    a. show any hidden title hazards.
    b. show all recorded instruments pertinent to the property.
    c. be accepted as an official document.
    d. both A and C.

5. Who renders an opinion of title's condition based on the abstract report?
   a. An attorney
   b. A judge
   c. The California Department of Real Estate
   d. California Association of Realtors

6. There are how many different types of title insurance in California?
   a. 1
   b. 2
   c. 3
   d. 5

7. The value of the property exchanged between buyers and sellers is covered by
   a. the California Land Title Association.
   b. the American Land Title Association.
   c. both A and B.
   d. neither A nor B.

8. Risks such as forgeries, incompetency of involved parties, and surveying errors are covered under
   a. a standard title insurance policy.
   b. an expanded title insurance policy.
   c. every title insurance policy issued.
   d. construction insurance.

9. An error or issue regarding the title to property is called a
   a. fault.
   b. cloud.
   c. mistake.
   d. both A and B.

10. A survey will reveal which of the following?
    a. Encroachments
    b. Easements
    c. Errors in legal descriptions
    d. All of the above

11. Which of the following is not a mandatory disclosure in a real estate transaction?
    a. Condominium Documents Disclosure
    b. Foreign Real Estate Tax
    c. Lead paint disclosure
    d. Local requirements resulting from city and county ordinances

12. Which of the following is not a required disclosure in the transfer disclosure statement?
   a. Flooding drainage or drainage issues near or affecting the property
   b. Disclosure of a death due to AIDS
   c. Easements, common drives or shared walks or fences with neighbors
   d. Zoning violations and insufficient setbacks

13. Which group is exempt from providing a transfer disclosure statement?
   a. The transfer of property from one co-owner to another
   b. The sale of property in a foreclosure sale
   c. Selling or buying from the government
   d. All of the above

14. Pest inspection reports are divided into how many different portions?
   a. 1
   b. 2
   c. 4
   d. 5

15. Which of the following would not exempt a property from the requirements of the special studies zone?
   a. Alterations worth over 50% of the total value of the structure
   b. Structures in existence prior to May 4, 1975
   c. Single-family, wood-frame or steel structures not over two stories high, provided the dwelling is not part of a development consisting of four or more dwellings.
   d. Single-family, wood-frame or steel-frame structures for which geologic reports have been approved, to be built in subdivisions authorized by the Subdivision Map Act.

16. The environment hazard disclosure requires sellers of property to disclose which of the following?
   a. Formaldehyde
   b. Lead-based paint
   c. Termites
   d. Underground storage tanks

17. Flood zones are defined as areas with the potential to flood once every
   a. 500 years.
   b. 100-500 years.
   c. 100 years.
   d. 50 years.

18. Before the transfer of title to a condominium, the seller must provide the buyer with
    a. a copy of the subdivision restrictions.
    b. a financial statement of the homeowner's association.
    c. a written statement from the homeowner's association regarding any unpaid assessments if any.
    d. all of the above.

19. Within how many hours of the receipt of his or her loan application must a borrower receive a written statement detailing the expected maximum costs he or she must pay in order to secure the loan?
    a. 48
    b. 60
    c. 72
    d. 96

20. Lenders generally charge a placement fee of what percentage of the original loan amount?
    a. 1–3%
    b. 2–4%
    c. 3–5%
    d. 4–6%

CLOSING
THE
LOAN

What you will learn in this Chapter

- Risk Analysis

- Underwriting Guidelines

- Disclosures and Notice of Rights

- Closing

Test Your Knowledge

1. An underwriter analyzes
   a. a borrower's ability to repay a debt.
   b. whether the collateral is sufficient to cover the debt.
   c. the loan, to make sure it qualifies to be sold on the secondary mortgage market.
   d. all of the above.

2. Lenders wishing to sell their loans in the secondary mortgage market must follow the guidelines set by
   a. Ginnie Mae.
   b. Freddie Mac.
   c. Fannie Mae.
   d. both B and C.

3. Verification of Deposit not only determines the existence of funds to be used for a down payment, but also
   a. the account the funds will come from.
   b. a credit history.
   c. the amount of time the funds have been in the account.
   d. both A and B.

4. Which of the following is not a reason for an underwriter to do a verification of employment?
   a. Verify at least 4 years of employment with the current employer
   b. Salary is consistent with the application
   c. Overtime and bonus income is likely to occur
   d. Probability of continued employment with the same employer

5. Total housing expenses typically should not exceed what percent of the gross monthly income?
   a. 25%
   b. 28%
   c. 31%
   d. 36%

6. Occasionally a lender will make a loan to a borrower with a debt to income ratio over 36% if
   a. the borrower makes a larger down payment than normal.
   b. the borrower has a large net worth.
   c. the borrower has a lot of cash savings.
   d. all of the above.

7. Within how many days from closing must the lender give the borrower the escrow statement?
   a. 7
   b. 14
   c. 30
   d. 45

INTRODUCTION

All the paperwork has been collected by the loan processor and the loan package is complete. It is now the job of the underwriter to use the information in the loan package to determine, according to conforming guidelines, whether the loan will be funded. The purpose of sending a completed loan package to an underwriter is to accomplish the desired result: funding a loan that conforms to the standards of the secondary mortgage market and is an acceptable risk for the investor. Completing this analysis of the information relating to risk and making a decision about funding the loan is the only step left for the loan process to be concluded.

RISK ANALYSIS

The practice of analyzing the degree of risk involved in a mortgage loan is known as **underwriting**. Basically, the underwriter determines whether the borrower has the ability and willingness to repay the debt and whether the property being pledged as collateral is adequate security for the debt. The process also involves the evaluation of both the property and the borrower, to determine whether or not the loan package conforms to the guidelines for selling on the secondary mortgage market or directly to some other permanent investor.

In any case, the loan must be attractive to an investor with regard to the risk of default, as well as being profitable. If any part of the loan process is lacking, such as poor processing or underwriting, the mortgage lender might find it difficult to sell the loan. Also, if the borrower defaults on a carelessly underwritten loan, the loss to the mortgage lender could be considerable. For example, if the appraisal was too high and the borrower defaulted, the lender could end up with a loss when the property does not sell at the foreclosure sale for the amount needed to repay the loan and other costs of the default.

UNDERWRITING GUIDELINES

If lenders expect to sell their loans on the secondary market, they must follow the standards set by Fannie Mae and Freddie Mac to analyze the important information necessary to approve a borrower while protecting the assets of the lender or some future owner of the loan.

Upon receiving the loan package, the underwriter begins the process of evaluating the risk factor of certain elements at the heart of the application. There are several different categories of risk analysis. These categories include **appraisal, credit history, down payment, employment, income ratios, loan amount and loan-to-value ratios.**

Appraisal

After reviewing the loan-to-value ratios, loan amount, down payment, income ratios, employment, and credit history in the loan package, the underwriter must determine the adequacy of the security for the loan. Since the mortgage loan will be secured by the property, the value of the property must be determined to validate the loan-to- value ratio. The valuation is determined by the appraisal.

The underwriter wants to make sure that the lender is protected from loss through default and foreclosure by establishing the value of the property upon which the loan-to-value ratio is applied. For example, if the lender's loan-to-value ratio for making the loan is 80%, the loan cannot exceed 80% of the value of the property.

Example
$550,000 Property Value
x 0.80 Loan-to-Value Ratio
= $440,000 Loan Amount

If the property goes into foreclosure, the lender can feel reasonably safe as far as risk of loss goes, because of the 20% percent cushion between the loan amount and the value of the property. Lenders do make loans with higher ratios, with more risk involved for them. In that case, the comfort zone is smaller than a 20% cushion, with a greater risk of loss. The cost for 80, 90 or even 100% percent loans goes up according to the perceived risk to the lender. Interest rates and points are all increased to protect the lender in case of default, and the buyer is normally required to purchase mortgage insurance.

Credit History

A mortgage lender is concerned not only about whether a borrower can repay the loan, but whether he or she will repay the loan. An underwriter will review the **Residential**

Mortgage Credit Report to see whether the borrower has a credit history of meeting payments according to contract terms, in a timely manner. If the credit report shows a positive borrowing history, the underwriter will use that as an encouraging sign of a worthy borrower.

Down Payment

Most lenders require some kind of down payment to show that a borrower does have a monetary, or equitable, interest in the property. The thinking is that the borrower will protect his or her interest to a greater degree if there is some personal money invested in the purchase. The down payment has been verified during loan processing by checking the bank account of the borrower to make sure the money is there. The **VOD (Verification of Deposit)** will establish the existence and history of funds to be used for a down payment as well as determining how long the funds have been in the account. The reason for that is to make sure the applicant has not borrowed the money recently from a friend or relative, and therefore does not actually have any personal money invested in the purchase.

Employment

An underwriter will seek out the **VOE (Verification of Employment)** in the processed file to determine how the loan will be repaid by the borrower. The following factors are of concern to the underwriter

- Salary / wages are consistent with the application
- Probability of continued employment with the same employer
- Overtime / bonus income is likely to continue
- Dates of employment are consistent with the application
- Employer has signed the VOE

At least 2 years employment with current employer (If not, a VOE from the former employer is requested.)

Income Ratios

A lender is concerned about whether or not the borrower can repay the loan. The underwriter will use income ratios to determine the risk of default due to lack of ability to make the payments in a timely manner. Using the long history of mortgage lending as a guideline for making mortgage loans with a low risk of default, the **mortgage debt ratio** (or **front-end ratio**) is determined by calculating the percentage of monthly income necessary to meet the monthly housing expense.

The percentage of income that can be used for housing debt varies depending on what kind of loan is being made, i.e., whether it is conventional, FHA or VA. Assuming the loan is conventional (not government-sponsored or private-party), the following monthly housing expenses (or monthly share of annual expenses) are added together.

The total of the monthly housing expense should not be more than 28% of the gross monthly income of the borrower. In some cases the lender will allow a higher ratio if the borrower has strong credit and no long-term debts.

Most borrowers have monthly payments other than housing payments to make. Other expenses might include credit cards, alimony or child support, student loan repayment, car payment, or any number of installment-type expenses. These expenses, when added to the housing debt, become known as **back-end debt** or **total debt service**. Ratios for back-end debt are calculated separately from the front-end ratio of housing expense to gross monthly income.

Commonly, lenders will use the guideline that the total of all debt service should not be more than 36% of the borrower's gross monthly income. Certain other factors might be used to allow a higher debt-to-income ratio if the borrower can show

- A larger down payment than normal

- A large amount of cash in savings

- An extra-solid credit rating

- A large net worth

- A great potential for high future earnings

Loan Amount

Evaluating the **loan-to-value ratio (LTV)** is probably the most important aspect of the underwriting process. The greater the down payment from the borrower, which would lower the LTV ratio, the less risk there is for the lender. The risk involved for the mortgage lender would be the risk of the borrower defaulting, the property going into foreclosure and then selling for less than the loan amount. The lender would find itself either getting the property back at the foreclosure sale or getting a deficient amount at the sale, neither of which makes for a desirable investment. So the underwriter makes certain the LTV falls within the guidelines for that particular loan.

Loan-to-Value Ratios

The loan-to-value ratio (LTV) is the relationship between the amount borrowed and the value of the property. For example, if the property in question is valued at $100,000 and the loan amount requested is $80,000, the loan-to-value ratio would be 80%. The difference between the amount borrowed and the value is made up by the down payment from the borrower. The down payment is the equity the borrower has in the property.

DISCLOSURES AND NOTICE OF RIGHTS

Lenders who make mortgage loans and brokers who arrange mortgage loans must comply with various federal and state disclosure laws and regulations. Underwriters must be aware of these laws and act in accordance with them.

Settlement, or **closing** as it is called in some states, is the formal process by which ownership of real property passes from seller to buyer. It is the end of the home-buying process, the time when title to the property is transferred from the seller to the buyer.

Certain disclosures that protect consumers from unfair lending practices are required at different times during a loan transaction.

In the previous chapter, we discussed disclosures required when the borrower applies for the loan: the **Special Information Booklet** (not necessary for refinances); the **Good Faith Estimate**; the **Mortgage Servicing Disclosure Statement**; and **Truth-in-Lending Disclosure Statement**.

Disclosures at Settlement/Closing

The **HUD–1 Settlement Statement** is a standard form that clearly shows all charges imposed on borrowers and sellers in connection with the settlement. RESPA allows the borrower to request to see the HUD-1 Settlement Statement one day before the actual settlement. The settlement agent must then provide the borrowers with a completed HUD-1 Settlement Statement based on information known to the agent at that time.

The HUD-1 Settlement Statement shows the actual settlement costs of the loan transaction. Separate forms may be prepared for the borrower and the seller. Where it is not the practice that the borrower and the seller both attend the settlement, the HUD-1 should be mailed or delivered as soon as practicable after settlement.

The **Initial Escrow Statement** itemizes the estimated taxes, insurance premiums and other charges anticipated to be paid from the Escrow Account during the first 12 months of the loan. It lists the Escrow payment amount and any required cushion. Although the statement is usually given at settlement, the lender has 45 days from settlement to deliver it.

Disclosures after Settlement

Loan servicers must deliver to borrowers an **Annual Escrow Statement** once a year. This annual escrow account statement summarizes all escrow account deposits and payments during the servicer's 12-month computation year. It also notifies the borrower of any shortages or surpluses in the account, and advises the borrower about the course of action being taken.

A **Servicing Transfer Statement** is required if the loan servicer sells or assigns the servicing rights to a borrower's loan to another loan servicer. Generally, the loan servicer must notify the borrower 15 days before the effective date of the loan transfer. As long as the borrower makes a timely payment to the old servicer within 60 days of the loan transfer, the borrower cannot be penalized. The notice must include the name and address of the new servicer, toll-free telephone numbers, and the date the new servicer will begin accepting payments.

A. Settlement Statement

U.S. Department of Housing and Urban Development

OMB Approval No. 2502-0265

B. Type of Loan

1. ☐ FHA	2. ☐ FmHA	3. ☐ Conv. Unins.
4. ☐ VA	5. ☐ Conv. Ins.	

6. File Number: 7. Loan Number: 8. Mortgage Insurance Case Number:

C. Note: This form is furnished to give you a statement of actual settlement costs. Amounts paid to and by the settlement agent are shown. Items marked "(p.o.c.)" were paid outside the closing; they are shown here for informational purposes and are not included in the totals.

D. Name & Address of Borrower:

E. Name & Address of Seller:

F. Name & Address of Lender:

G. Property Location:

H. Settlement Agent:

Place of Settlement:

I. Settlement Date:

J. Summary of Borrower's Transaction		K. Summary of Seller's Transaction	
100. Gross Amount Due From Borrower		**400. Gross Amount Due To Seller**	
101. Contract sales price		401. Contract sales price	
102. Personal property		402. Personal property	
103. Settlement charges to borrower (line 1400)		403.	
104.		404.	
105.		405.	
Adjustments for items paid by seller in advance		**Adjustments for items paid by seller in advance**	
106. City/town taxes to		406. City/town taxes to	
107. County taxes to		407. County taxes to	
108. Assessments to		408. Assessments to	
109.		409.	
110.		410.	
111.		411.	
112.		412.	
120. Gross Amount Due From Borrower		**420. Gross Amount Due To Seller**	
200. Amounts Paid By Or In Behalf Of Borrower		**500. Reductions In Amount Due To Seller**	
201. Deposit or earnest money		501. Excess deposit (see instructions)	
202. Principal amount of new loan(s)		502. Settlement charges to seller (line 1400)	
203. Existing loan(s) taken subject to		503. Existing loan(s) taken subject to	
204.		504. Payoff of first mortgage loan	
205.		505. Payoff of second mortgage loan	
206.		506.	
207.		507.	
208.		508.	
209.		509.	
Adjustments for items unpaid by seller		**Adjustments for items unpaid by seller**	
210. City/town taxes to		510. City/town taxes to	
211. County taxes to		511. County taxes to	
212. Assessments to		512. Assessments to	
213.		513.	
214.		514.	
215.		515.	
216.		516.	
217.		517.	
218.		518.	
219.		519.	
220. Total Paid By/For Borrower		**520. Total Reduction Amount Due Seller**	
300. Cash At Settlement From/To Borrower		**600. Cash At Settlement To/From Seller**	
301. Gross Amount due from borrower (line 120)		601. Gross amount due to seller (line 420)	
302. Less amounts paid by/for borrower (line 220)	( )	602. Less reductions in amt. due seller (line 520)	( )
303. Cash ☐ From ☐ To Borrower		603. Cash ☐ To ☐ From Seller	

Section 5 of the Real Estate Settlement Procedures Act (RESPA) requires the following: • HUD must develop a Special Information Booklet to help persons borrowing money to finance the purchase of residential real estate to better understand the nature and costs of real estate settlement services; • Each lender must provide the booklet to all applicants from whom it receives or for whom it prepares a written application to borrow money to finance the purchase of residential real estate; • Lenders must prepare and distribute with the Booklet a Good Faith Estimate of the settlement costs that the borrower is likely to incur in connection with the settlement. These disclosures are mandatory.

Section 4(a) of RESPA mandates that HUD develop and prescribe this standard form to be used at the time of loan settlement to provide full disclosure of all charges imposed upon the borrower and seller. These are third party disclosures that are designed to provide the borrower with pertinent information during the settlement process in order to be a better shopper.

The Public Reporting Burden for this collection of information is estimated to average one hour per response, including the time for reviewing instructions, searching existing data sources, gathering and maintaining the data needed, and completing and reviewing the collection of information.

This agency may not collect this information, and you are not required to complete this form, unless it displays a currently valid OMB control number.

The information requested does not lend itself to confidentiality.

(continued on next page)

(continued)

L. Settlement Charges

			Paid From Borrowers Funds at Settlement	Paid From Seller's Funds at Settlement
700. Total Sales/Broker's Commission based on price $		@ % =		
Division of Commission (line 700) as follows:				
701. $	to			
702. $	to			
703. Commission paid at Settlement				
704.				
800. Items Payable In Connection With Loan				
801. Loan Origination Fee	%			
802. Loan Discount	%			
803. Appraisal Fee	to			
804. Credit Report	to			
805. Lender's Inspection Fee				
806. Mortgage Insurance Application Fee to				
807. Assumption Fee				
808.				
809.				
810.				
811.				
900. Items Required By Lender To Be Paid In Advance				
901. Interest from to	@$	/day		
902. Mortgage Insurance Premium for		months to		
903. Hazard Insurance Premium for		years to		
904.		years to		
905.				
1000. Reserves Deposited With Lender				
1001. Hazard insurance	months@$	per month		
1002. Mortgage insurance	months@$	per month		
1003. City property taxes	months@$	per month		
1004. County property taxes	months@$	per month		
1005. Annual assessments	months@$	per month		
1006.	months@$	per month		
1007.	months@$	per month		
1008.	months@$	per month		
1100. Title Charges				
1101. Settlement or closing fee	to			
1102. Abstract or title search	to			
1103. Title examination	to			
1104. Title insurance binder	to			
1105. Document preparation	to			
1106. Notary fees	to			
1107. Attorney's fees	to			
(includes above items numbers:		)		
1108. Title insurance	to			
(includes above items numbers:		)		
1109. Lender's coverage	$			
1110. Owner's coverage	$			
1111.				
1112.				
1113.				
1200. Government Recording and Transfer Charges				
1201. Recording fees: Deed $	; Mortgage $	; Releases $		
1202. City/county tax/stamps: Deed $	; Mortgage $			
1203. State tax/stamps: Deed $	; Mortgage $			
1204.				
1205.				
1300. Additional Settlement Charges				
1301. Survey to				
1302. Pest Inspection to				
1303.				
1304.				
1305.				
1400. Total Settlement Charges (enter on lines 103, Section J and 502, Section K)				

HUD created the following table illustrating the disclosures that may be relevant to the simplification and consolidation process.

Timing of Disclosures	Truth-in-Lending Act (TILA)	Real Estate Summary Procedures Act (RESPA)
At or before referral	None	Affiliated Business Arrangement Disclosure
At or before application	1. Home Equity Line of Credit (HELOC) booklet and disclosures 2. Adjustable rate booklet and disclosures	None
Within 3 days of application	TILA disclosure statement including APR and finance charges	1. Special Information Booklet 2. Good Faith Estimate 3. Required Provider Information 4. Initial Transfer of Servicing Disclosure
3 Days prior to closing	1. Section 32 disclosures (an annual adjustment of the dollar amount that triggers additional disclosures under the Truth in Lending Act for mortgage loans that bear rates or fees above a certain amount) 2. Reverse Mortgage Disclosure	None
1 Day prior to closing	None	Right to inspect HUD–1 or HUD–1A
At closing	1. TILA Disclosure 2. Rescission notice	1. HUD–1 or HUD–1A 2. Initial Escrow Account Statement (within 45 days after closing.)

C L O S I N G

After all information needed to make a decision about approving the loan has been received, processed and analyzed, and the security for the loan has been verified as sufficient, the decision must be made to accept or reject the loan application. That could be done by a loan officer whose job it is to decide which loans to fund, or by a loan committee. In any case, once approved, the loan goes to the final stage of the mortgage loan process, the loan closing, where necessary documents are prepared and executed.

The borrower receives the package of closing documents, some of which must be signed before a notary. The note and trust deed must also be signed, as well as various disclosures. When all documents have been executed by the borrower, the trust deed will be recorded and the loan funded.

S U M M A R Y

We can see from all the steps an underwriter takes that each application is checked thoroughly and carefully. From the seven risk categories analyzed, to all the necessary disclosures, the final step in the funding process is not only lengthy, but also necessary, to make sure the loan conforms to the guidelines of the secondary mortgage market in the event the mortgage is sold, and also so that the lender does not take an unnecessary or foolish risk by funding an unqualified borrower. This is the last step in the loan process before closing can occur, and the loan be funded.

T E R M S   A N D   P H R A S E S

Loan-to-Value Ratio (LTV)   relationship between the amount borrowed and the value of the property

Underwriting   practice of analyzing the degree of risk involved in a mortgage loan

Verification of Deposit (VOD)   establishes the existence and history of funds to be used for a down payment, as well as determining how long the funds have been in the account

1. Analyzing the risk associated with a mortgage is called
   a. loan-to-value
   b. underwriting.
   c. income ratio.
   d. risk analysis.

2. What factors make a loan attractive to an investor?
   a. Low risk of default, and profitable
   b. Profitable, and easy to sell in the secondary mortgage market
   c. Easy to sell in the secondary mortgage market, and low risk of default
   d. All of the above

3. An underwriter analyzes
   a. a borrower's ability to repay a debt.
   b. a property being pledged as collateral to see if it is sufficient to cover the debt.
   c. the loan, to be certain it qualifies to be sold on the secondary mortgage market.
   d. all of the above.

4. Lenders wishing to sell their loans in the secondary mortgage market must follow the guidelines set by
   a. Ginnie Mae.
   b. Freddie Mac.
   c. Fannie Mae.
   d. both B and C.

5. Which of the following is not a risk category analyzed when underwriting a loan?
   a. Credit history
   b. Employment
   c. Number of dependents
   d. Loan-to-value ratio

6. From an underwriter's point of view, an appraisal of property is most useful for
   a. determining property taxes for the property.
   b. determining the loan-to-value ratio of the property.
   c. determining the value of the property in an open market.
   d. determining the tax base for the neighborhood.

7. A large loan-to-value ratio poses a
   a. smaller risk for the lender.
   b. larger risk for the lender.
   c. smaller risk for the borrower.
   d. larger risk for the borrower.

8. A down payment is generally used to
    a. lower the monthly payments on the mortgage.
    b. establish equity or interest in the property being purchased.
    c. secure a loan.
    d. none of the above.

9. Verification of Deposit not only determines the existence of funds to be used for a down payment, but also
    a. the account the funds will come from.
    b. a credit history.
    c. the amount of time the funds have been in the account.
    d. both A and B.

10. Which of the following is not a reason for an underwriter to do a verification of employment?
    a. Verify at least 4 years of employment with the current employer.
    b. Salary is consistent with the application.
    c. Overtime and bonus income is likely to occur.
    d. Probability of continued employment with the same employer.

11. A credit history will help determine
    a. a borrower's ability to repay the note.
    b. a borrower's willingness to repay the note, based on making past payments on time.
    c. both A and B.
    d. neither A nor B.

12. A lender will generally not make a loan when the debt-to-income ratio is greater than
    a. 28%.
    b. 32%.
    c. 36%.
    d. 39%.

13. Which of the following is considered back-end debt?
    a. Car payment
    b. Mortgage insurance premiums
    c. Hazard insurance
    d. Principal

14. Total housing expenses typically should not exceed what percent of the gross monthly income?
    a. 25%
    b. 28%
    c. 31%
    d. 36%

15. Occasionally a lender will make a loan to a borrower with a debt to income ratio over 36% if
    a. the borrower makes a larger down payment than normal.
    b. the borrower has a large net worth.
    c. the borrower has a lot of cash savings.
    d. all of the above.

16. Which of the following expenses are used to determine debt-to-income ratio?
    a. Alimony
    b. Car loan
    c. Credit cards
    d. Property taxes

17. Loan-to-value ratios are typically expressed as
    a. a percentage.
    b. a fraction.
    c. a dollar figure.
    d. none of the above.

18. The lender must give the borrower the escrow statement within how many days from closing?
    a. 7
    b. 14
    c. 30
    d. 45

19. The borrower receives the annual escrow statement
    a. twice a year.
    b. once a year.
    c. only at closing.
    d. every other year.

20. The Truth-In-Lending Act disclosure must be given to the borrower
    a. within 3 days of the application.
    b. 3 days before closing.
    c. 1 day before closing.
    d. at closing.

14

REAL ESTATE INVESTMENT

What you will learn in this Chapter

- Why Invest in Real Estate?

- Types of Return on Investment (ROI)

- Investment Process

- Real Estate Investment Analysis Tools

- Real Estate Investment Tactics

Test Your Knowledge

1. Which of the following is a type of return on investment?
   a. Return on taxes
   b. Appreciation
   c. Cash flow
   d. All of the above

2. Which of the following documents should you prepare when planning to invest in property?
   a. Complete tax returns for the last 3 years
   b. Landlord contact information to verify rent history and copies of cancelled rent checks for the past 24 months
   c. Most recent two statements for all bank and asset accounts
   d. Both A and C

3. Which of the following persons would not be helpful in aiding a real estate investor in his or her transaction?
   a. A general contractor
   b. An accountant
   c. An Insurance agent
   d. A loan officer

4. Your credit score is
   a. not affected by a creditor running your score.
   b. hurt every time your credit is run.
   c. improved every time your credit is run.
   d. none of the above.

5. Which of the following is not considered a step in making a profitable investment?
   a. An attorney review
   b. Making a smart offer
   c. Preparing a business plan
   d. Updating loan approval

6. All of the following factors affect return on investment except
   a. liquidity.
   b. risk.
   c. cost.
   d. management.

7. Real estate investors can exploit tax advantages in which of the following areas?
   a. Operating losses
   b. Depreciation
   c. Capital gains
   d. All of the above

INTRODUCTION

Investing is putting money into some entity, such as property, with the hope or expectation that there will be a profit in the end. Individuals, businesses and institutions can all invest some discretionary portion of the money they earn. In order for an investor to take the risk and invest money, the benefits must exceed any other opportunities available at the time. Investing in real estate is a convenient and reliable choice when other sources for investment are not profitable or productive.

Real estate investment presents both distinctive problems and special opportunities. Real estate is a restricted, non-liquid investment opportunity; stationary, sometimes scarce, durable and physically real. It is not always easy to own buildings requiring maintenance, tenants, retrofitting and security, and that are subject to fire, earthquakes and the advantages and disadvantages of a particular locality.

Since real estate is extremely dependent on local conditions, consumers should invest in real property only if they are knowledgeable about local real estate values—including the local economy, market conditions, political environment and building controls. All of these factors can be critical to the success or failure of an investment.

WHY INVEST IN REAL ESTATE?

There are many reasons for people to invest in property. Generally speaking, these reasons can be summarized as three main reasons: to meet their personal goals and objectives, to have the capacity to meet their financial commitments, and because of the economic soundness of real property when viewed in light of the investor's objectives and capacity.

> **Remember**
>
> There are three primary reasons for people to invest in real property
>
> - To meet their personal goals and objectives
> - To have the capacity to meet their financial commitments
> - Economic soundness

Objectives

We know the reasons for investing, but what about objectives? What does an investor hope to accomplish from his or her investment? Different investors will certainly have different objectives for their investments. Investors may be seeking additional income through well-chosen properties, or a tax shelter to help reduce the bite on otherwise taxable income. Other considerations may be prestige, personal enjoyment of the properties or activities, and the creation of an estate. The investor needs to decide which of these goals, or which combination of them, is important, in order to select the property most likely to accomplish those objectives.

Capacity

Financially, investors need to be able to bear the burdens of investing. Some burdens include debt service and taxes, and the need to retain a cash reserve for emergencies. It may even be argued that the investor must be psychologically able to live with the fact that the large sums required for investment result in price increases. Prices continue to escalate with the continued rise in inflation and appreciation, so the costs of investing continue to go up.

Soundness

After deciding on objectives and analyzing financial capacity to carry a given amount of debt, the economic health of the property itself must be considered, along with the economic trends of the immediately surrounding area. Growth trends in the community, zoning (both current and planned), projections for the type of services or products to be generated, costs and competition for investment funds, and certainly the general economic picture must all be taken into account. This will create an accurate picture of the viability of the investment.

The investment should be sound from an economic point of view; that is, investors ought to look carefully at projected figures. Projected figures should ultimately reflect reality, by including market and economic analysis. For instance, one might trade off risk with growth, cash flow, and initial investment, as will be explained later. The market for the property should be properly and objectively analyzed; there should be a real need for the services the property is expected to produce. All too often, only income tax consequences are considered, irrespective of the basic soundness of the venture.

Investment Facts

- An introduction to creative real estate investment must begin with an understanding of the process. For the average consumer, real estate investing is the most common and effective method of building wealth aside from ordinary income derived from a regular paying job.

- Many programs and methods are available for consumers to build a real estate investment portfolio, regardless of income, credit, assets, gender, race or education.

- Many beginning real estate investors lose money. Those investors who do succeed sometimes have a little luck on their side; but they all tend to have a common trait: knowledge .

The three types of return on investment (ROI) found in a real estate investment are **cash flow, return on taxes** and **appreciation**.

Cash Flow

Cash flow is the amount of money returned to an investor on an ongoing basis after expenses, including debt service (mortgage payment). It represents the most direct type of return, since it is money an investor can see almost immediately. Some good investments do not have a positive cash flow at first, but the investment may be justified by the return from the other two types of ROI.

Return on Taxes

Some investors, especially those in higher tax brackets, are less concerned with cash return than they are with the tax advantages of real estate investment. Income property provides tax shelter by allowing the investor to deduct, on an annual basis, the interest on the loan, property taxes, insurance, management, maintenance, and utilities. Loss on the sale of income property may also be deducted. Another benefit of investing in income producing property is allowed **depreciation**. Depreciation may not be taken on a personal residence, but investment property may be depreciated according to a formula determined by the Internal Revenue Service (IRS).

The tax laws reward an investor for the financial risk taken, and add to the benefit from the investment by allowing the taxpayer to reduce tax liability in numerous ways. As long as an investment is income-producing, such as apartment buildings or commercial property, certain reductions in tax liability are allowed. One of the most important tax benefits of income property ownership is the **depreciation allowance**. While a homeowner can exclude a certain amount of profit from being taxed, the owner of income property may not. However, the investor can claim depreciation and other deductions, which will reduce the tax bill in ways that are not allowed for a homeowner.

Depreciation for tax purposes is not based on actual deterioration, but on the calculated useful life of the property. The theory is that improvements, but not land, deteriorate and lose their value. A building is thought to have a certain number of years during which it can generate an income, and after that it is no longer a practical investment. The investor is compensated for the loss by being allowed to deduct a certain dollar amount each year based on the useful life of the property, until, on paper at least, the property no longer has any value as an investment.

However, tax laws regarding depreciation change so often that it is advisable for the reader to check current IRS rules for calculating depreciation.

The common method used to determine the dollar amount per year that will be deducted is **straight line depreciation**, where the same amount is deducted every year over the depreciable life of a property. In calculating depreciation, the value of the improvements is divided by the depreciable life of the property, to arrive at the annual dollar amount that can be claimed as depreciation and thus deducted as such. Here is how it works.

Calculating Depreciation

- Determine what the IRS allowance for the depreciable life of a residential income property is by checking current tax law. For our purposes let's assume it is 27.5 years.

- Subtract the value of the land from the value of the property to determine the value of the building. The value of the land can be calculated from the tax assessor's bill or by using the value of similar parcels.

Value of property – Value of the land = Value of the building
$400,000 - $160,000 = $240, 000

- $240,000 divided by 27.5 years = $ 8,727 annual depreciation allowance

When the owner of income-producing property sells the property, the amount depreciated over the years will be subtracted from the cost basis to determine the tax liability or capital gain. Also, when the property is sold, the new owner is allowed to begin depreciating the building as if it were new, based on the new sales price.

The gain on an income-producing property is calculated much like that for a personal residence, except that any depreciation that has been claimed over the years must be subtracted from the cost basis. This means the dollar amount that has been deducted for depreciation over the time of property ownership, after the cost of any improvements has been added to the purchase price, must be subtracted from the cost basis to arrive at the **adjusted cost basis**. The amount of taxable gain is then calculated by subtracting the adjusted cost basis from the selling price, less the expense of the sales commission.

Unlike the sale of a primary residence, where a certain amount of gain may be excluded from being taxed, taxes are owed on any profit made whenever income-producing property is sold. However, there are ways an investor may legally defer the gain to a later time.

Installment Sale
An installment sale is one where payments are made by the buyer to the seller over a period of more than one year. This is one way capital gains and the tax payments owed can be spread out over a period of time. Part of the tax liability can be deferred by the seller taking back a note and trust deed, or an all-inclusive trust deed or contract of sale,

with monthly payments. Only the amount of the gain that is collected in the tax year is taxable income, and the tax due on the rest can be deferred until collected. Once again, the reader should check current tax laws about installment sales.

> **Computing Capital Gain on an Income Property (3 steps)**
>
> - Purchase Price (or cost basis) + Improvements – Depreciation claimed = Adjusted cost basis
>
> - Selling Price – Expenses of sale = Adjusted selling price
>
> - Adjusted selling price – Adjusted cost basis = Capital gain or Profit

Tax-Deferred Exchange (1031 Exchange)

The provisions for non-recognition of gains or losses are set out in the Internal Revenue Code, Section 1031(2), which states: "No gain or loss shall be recognized if property held for productive use in trade or business or for investment is exchanged solely for property of a like kind to be held either for productive use in trade or in business or for investment."

Property can be classified under five categories: principal residence, dealer, trade or business, rental, and investment. Only the last three classifications qualify for the tax deferral under Section 1031. Put another way, any property is like-kind property so long as it is neither personal use property (principal dwelling) nor property held for sale to customers (dealer property, such as lots in a subdivision).

> **Remember**
>
> Property can be classified into five categories
>
> - Principle residence
> - Dealer
> - Trade or Business
> - Rental
> - Investment

Whether a property falls under the qualifying categories is determined from the standpoint of the party to the transaction who is claiming the benefits. That is, so long as the taxpayer held the property being given up for income or investment, and as long as the property to be acquired will also be used for income or as an investment, the rules of Section 1031 apply. It is irrelevant that the other parties to the exchange transaction did not hold their property for income or investment. For example, a condominium unit that is used as a rental may be exchanged for another dwelling that is used by the owner as his or her principal residence, so long as the acquiring party uses it as a rental or for investment purposes. The fact that the other party used the condo as his or her dwelling does not nullify the deferral of taxes under Section 1031.

It is important to note, too, that income-producing properties may be exchanged for investment properties, or that investment properties may be traded for properties used in one's trade or business, or in any other combination of the three categories that fall under the rules of Section 1031.

Thus, for example, an apartment building can be exchanged for an office building; unimproved land can b exchanged for improved land, vacant land for a shopping center, or city investment property for ranch or farm land. The combinations are endless. "Like kind" does not consider the grade or quality or quantity of the property, but rather the nature or class of the property. Accordingly, real property cannot be exchanged for personal property, since each is of a different class. However, qualifying personal property could be exchanged for other qualifying personal property of a similar nature or class, such as furnishings in an apartment building being exchanged for, say, machinery used for business.

Remember

"Like kind" property does not mean the property needs to be used exactly the same way. A trade property can be exchanged for a trade property even if one is a retail shop and one is a repair shop.

It is not required to have an exchange agreement form to consummate an exchange, though it is a good idea to utilize standard exchange forms. Agreements can be written on deposit receipts, as long as either the agreement or the escrow instructions properly call for an exchange. The parties may decide to convert a sale to an exchange even after going to a sale escrow, so long as the exchange is properly done before closing the escrow.

Example

Equity = Property value – incumbrances

Investor A: *Property is valued at $500,000*
Less $40,000 in incumbrances
Equity = $460,000

Investor B: *Property is valued at $600,000*
Less $100,000 in incumbrances
Equity = $500,000

The difference between the two properties is $40,000

Appreciation

Appreciation is the increase in value over the original investment amount. In other words, it is the increase in the property value from the original purchase price. This gain results from many factors, but mainly from the pressures of a changing society where increasing needs and expanding use create higher demands. The greatest return on investment is typically from appreciation, which is the continuing increase in the value of a property due to higher market value each year.

Properties can have significant increases in value over time due to various forces such as high demand, low interest rates, inflation, or change in the economy. The relatively high ROI due to appreciation represents one of the primary reasons for investing in real estate. However, this return is realized only on the sale of the property, and may be dependent on an investor being able to tie up his or her money for an extended period of time. Real estate investing is not for those who need a regular, predictable return on their investment. But it can be very rewarding for those who can invest relatively large amounts and wait for favorable selling conditions.

INVESTMENT PROCESS

An introduction to real estate investment must begin with an understanding of the process. The process for acquiring investment property is similar to buying a home, but a different type of due diligence is involved, as well as an increased awareness and acceptance of the risk involved. The typical home buyer does not necessarily see the purchase of a primary residence in terms of risk, and rightly so. All a consumer has to think about in the purchase of a home, aside from qualifying for the loan and making the payments, are the intangible benefits of home ownership, which allow a consumer to purchase a home without having to think about cash flow, depreciation, tenant issues or capitalization rates.

Factors in Investing

- Appraised Value–independent appraisal value

- Availability of investors–prepare a feasibility analysis to show them

- Competition–what new properties are coming onto the market, will they help or hurt the value of yours?

- Condition–look for visual problems, not structural.

- Context–find the worst buildings in the best districts.

- Cost to rehabilitate the structure

- Demand–how much competition is there among buyers?

- Economic cycle–is the economy up or down?

- Existing leases

- Existing operating expenses

- Financial and political stability of controlling authority

- Higher and better use–will the market allow for better cash flow?

- Historic tax credits

- Location

- Price

- Redevelopment, potential general city plan, zoning or restriction changes

- Rent control

- Replacement cost–compared to new construction

- Seller's motives–why is the seller selling the property?

- Terms of financing–seller names the price while the buyer will name the terms

- Zoning–how restrictive are the zoning laws?

The successful investor must understand the nature of real estate investment, that it is vastly different from buying his or her personal residence. He or she must be knowledgeable and thorough in each stage of the process of acquiring investment property.

Stages of the Investment Process

- Preparation and planning

- Gathering resources

- Targeting the right property

- Negotiating terms

- Closing the purchase and taking over the property

Preparation and Planning

Everyone is familiar with the saying "people don't plan to fail, they fail to plan." That is especially true with real estate investing. Real estate investing is entrepreneurship; it is running a business. A consumer's chances for business success will always be greater if he or she makes adequate preparations and plans before launching a new venture.

The first preparatory steps should be to clarify the investment objectives. Personal goals and plans will influence what the investor decides to pursue. If the goal is strong positive cash flow, then the target property and the process selected would be different than if the chosen goal is resale value.

Investment Goals

- Clarify goals

- Prepare for the investment

- Prepare finances

- Develop a written plan

- Create the business

- Determine preferences and priorities

Clarify Goals

The very first step for any aspiring real estate investor is to clarify goals and objectives. The goals will determine what tactics an investor will use and what properties he or she will choose or reject. These reflections should not be left to daydreams and mental notes. They should be written down along with answers and considerations.

Can an investor acquire ten units or 50 units in a year's time? It's very do-able, although the challenges will differ according to the investor's financial and credit situation and the type of property selected by the investor. Will it be easy? No, probably not. A consumer must be willing to invest 20 to 40 hours a week searching for just the right property to fit his or her goals. With relatively stable personal finances the route will be much easier, but the investor still needs to clarify goals or complete an investment analysis questionnaire to make sure the goals are realistic. The right answers are the truly honest ones, regardless of how difficult the truth might be; the wrong answers are the ones that stray from the truth.

Here are a few questions the investor should consider about goals before making an investment in real estate.

1. Where would I like to be financially and personally next year? How about five years from now?

2. Do I want real estate investing to become my full-time or primary employment? Or do I want to make it a side hobby to my full-time job ?

3. Do I want my real estate investments to build my wealth? Or do I want them simply to add a little more to my other income sources?

4. How can investing in real estate help me with meeting those goals?

5. Are there other investments or projects that I want to pursue in the near future?

6. What are my current liabilities? Are there more coming in the future?

7. Where on my priority scale will I place my real estate investments?

8. How much time do I have available to spend on real estate investments?

9. What do I want from my short-term real estate investments? Cash flow to improve my income situation? Resale profits to put into other investments? Collateral with self liquidating liabilities that will improve my asset situation after retirement?

This last question is perhaps the most important one that a new investor must answer before moving on to other preparatory steps. For example, if the investor is seeking to increase cash flow, the properties selected probably will be very different than if the goal were to make investments that can be cashed in for profits upon retirement.

Prepare for the Investment
Sometimes real estate investing is easier for those who have had entrepreneurial experience, i.e., starting or running their own business. Investors with entrepreneurial experience are more aware of the emotional and mental needs of running a business.

The truth is, however, that anyone armed with the proper resources and knowledge can build wealth in real estate. To obtain some of the experiences of seasoned entrepreneurs, beginning real estate investors must take the time to prepare themselves for this new venture.

Avoid Bad Habits

Perhaps the biggest had habit consumers need to conquer is procrastination. Receipts should go directly into the receipt box, not dropped on the dresser with the idea of filing them later. Successful investors should get in the habit of doing tasks or as soon as possible. A "to-do" list may help.

Business Space

Even while working from home, which is common for beginning investors, the individual should try to set aside a room or desk at which business is conducted. The investor should try to avoid having business papers spill over into other areas of the home, and vice versa. If an office can be set up in a separate room, that would be great. However an investor can do just as well with a desk in the corner of a bedroom. Regardless of where the office is situated, though, it should be kept away from television or traffic that could distract and interfere with efficiency.

It's Business

It's inevitable that entrepreneurs invest their emotions, as well as their capital and energies, into their business. However, successful entrepreneurs all have the ability to separate business decisions from personal ones. This doesn't mean that an investor should abandon his or her ethics, morality, conscience, values or principles. It is rather an acknowledgment that investing is essentially like playing a game: it's only a game. At the end of the game, win or lose, the investor goes home and, if he or she is lucky, will play another game the next day or week. And if the investor is very good, this game will eventually support a desired lifestyle. Of course, it's very hard to separate business from personal life if personal well-being is entirely dependent on business. That's the challenge facing all beginning real estate investors.

Organized Systems

Real estate investing will involve a great deal of paperwork and records, especially at the beginning as the investor shops for and buys properties. If investors are actively managing their own properties, the demands on a filing system are even greater. There will be leases and tenant records, as well as property records and contracts, and files for service providers. Perhaps the most important items to save are receipts; it may he surprising to see the amount of deductions and tax savings available to real estate investors. A decent computer and software system, with an office suite of administrative programs, such as Microsoft Office, is also a must. Tasks may be automated and communications sent electronically, saving time and possibly money. The computer is also important to send and receive faxes, as well as send and receive important business email.

Patience

Business requires patience. If an investor is constantly stressed by entrepreneurship, there are a couple of probable conclusions: either the investor is doing it wrong or is not meant to be an entrepreneur. Things can and do go wrong; but that's one of the wonderful opportunities that entrepreneurship offers, the chance to learn and improve.

Perspective

When serious decisions are required, it always helps to remember objectives, goals and plans. Keep a perspective on the big picture, while concentrating on the immediate tasks.

Self-Discipline

Successful entrepreneurship requires self-discipline to do what needs to be done when it needs to be done. Self-discipline isn't necessarily genetic, and it can be learned. Moreover, self-discipline is aided by structure, such as having an office area set aside. Another structural tool to consider is to schedule specific times to take care of tasks.

Prepare Your Finances

The great thing about real estate investing is that the strengths of selected properties can overcome weaknesses in an investor's personal income, assets and credit.
At a certain point, such as if the property in question is larger than four units, a lender is only mildly curious about the buyer. Primarily, the lender wants to make sure the property supports itself, not counting the strength of the investor's financial statement. Nonetheless, each person still needs to prepare all of the important financial papers. First of all, it helps the investor to know exactly what his or her strengths and weaknesses are. Secondly, the mortgage lender will require them.

Again, the investor should only provide copies. Originals should not be released unless absolutely necessary. A mortgage loan officer can assist in clarifying what is needed, as well as reviewing the investor's credit report and arranging a mortgage pre-approval.

The following documents should be prepared

- Complete tax returns for the past 3 years

- Legible photocopy of driver's license and social security card

- Letter of explanation for credit problems

- Renters: landlord contact information (to verify rent history) and copies of canceled rent checks for the past 12 months

- Supporting documents for credit issues, such as bankruptcy papers and judgment decrees

- The most recent two statements for all bank and asset accounts

- W-2s for the past 3 years

Develop a Written Business Plan

A real estate investor has now become an entrepreneur. Nothing helps to increase the chances of success for beginning entrepreneurs better than a good business plan. This plan need not be extravagant or written in stone. At the very least, the investor should lay out goals and a basic game plan. What types of properties or investments sound good? How much can the investor afford to invest? What resources, contingencies and assistance are at his or her disposal? What are his or her personal strengths and weaknesses?

Real estate investing is about acquiring and owning a business, which also happens to be a property. The right business decision during the preparatory stage can save the investor thousands of dollars and an enormous amount of grief.

There are issues an investor must consider when venturing into a business. One of the first issues an investor should consider is whether to do this alone, or partner with key people. If time and resources are limited, a partnership definitely should be considered.

Of course, an investor needs partners that can be trusted, and a well-designed (by a professional, not the investor) partnership agreement to reinforce that trust. Partners who can complement an investor's skills and resources should be selected. For example, if a partnership is a four-person team, one partner could handle the financing responsibilities; one partner might be a real estate agent who guides the property search, acquisition and leasing; another partner might manage the fiscal and administrative operations; and the fourth partner could have intensive contractor experience to guide the work and understand properties structurally. Everyone could be involved in cleaning and repair work.

If the investor is working out of a home office, there should be an offsite post office box or local mail-store box to receive business mail, to avoid the problem of tenants and clients contacting the investor at home. Use this mailbox address on all correspondence. Also, the investor should set up a separate business phone line, and have a cell phone as well.

Determine Preferences and Priorities

As per the business plan, it is now time for the investor to focus on tactics. Specifically, what will be the initial target properties and areas? The investor must be prepared to answer why those targets were selected. Are they three units close to home or a condominium conversion project downtown? Both can be good investments—for the right person at the right time. However, the real question is what the investor is ready and able to pursue.

It goes without saying that adequate preparation will save time, aggravation and money, and this is especially true of buying real estate. After the investor has completed preparations, it is now time to begin shopping.

To further highlight the importance of adequate preparations, consider that the most successful real estate investors all make detailed analyses and plans before embarking on any venture. Detailed feasibility studies are the minimum preparations taken by experienced investors. In many cases, only a fraction of the considered projects (after feasibility studies and preparations are completed) are actually launched.

Successful real estate investing is very demanding. An investor may have to look at 25 properties before finding one that will meet investment parameters and allow the investor to make an offer. Furthermore, out of every four offers, the investor may only complete one purchase. That's actually not too bad for beginning investors. As the investor gets more experienced or works with more experienced agents, it may mean only having to look at 10 properties before finding a good one on which to make an offer.

Gathering Resources

A real estate investor should not go on the journey alone. The real estate industry has agents and resources at an investor's disposal during the entire investment process. Before starting, however, an investor should identify the key individuals as resources who will be there for much of the process. It is best to establish the relationship before starting, when possible, so that their assistance will be available when the time comes.

Because of the large amount of money involved with mortgages and real estate transactions, many agents, representatives, service providers and individuals become involved to protect the interests of the investor as well as other parties to a transaction.

Resource List
• Accountant
• Appraiser
• Attorney
• Closing or escrow agent
• Insurance agent
• Loan officer
• Property inspector
• Real estate agent

Appraiser

The appraiser determines an approximate fair market value for the subject property, based on a review and analysis of recorded data about that property and its locale. The lender will normally order the appraisal. Although the lender must approve the appraiser, the buyer sometimes has an option regarding selection of an independent appraiser.

The appraiser is separate and distinct from the real estate inspector, because the appraiser's focus is on the market value. In most cases, the appraiser assumes that the property is in normal working condition and only visits the subject property briefly.

When visiting the property, the appraiser will take floor and lot measurements, as well as photograph the property and neighborhood. The appraiser will also use the visit to confirm the property's condition. The appraiser usually will not calculate any major adjustment based on the property's condition unless the property shows visible deterioration or contains major value-inflating improvements. Still, improvements can only increase the property value so much—the neighborhood has the anchoring influence on the appraised value.

Attorney

Real estate investors need experienced attorneys with a background in commercial and investment real estate. It also helps if they or someone in their firm also can provide the investor with business planning assistance.

Investors should not assume that attorneys who help purchase homes are qualified to be investment attorneys. Real estate closings on the purchase of homes are heavily regulated and highly standardized—so much so that practically any attorney can handle the typical home closing without any problems. If there are any questions, the attorney can always turn to the closing agent, usually a representative of the title company, who is well-trained in residential closings. Investment properties have a different focus altogether.

Another point to remember is that good attorneys cost more. Experienced investment property attorneys will cost much more than regular residential property attorneys. But they are worth it.

If an investor wants to lower closing costs to the absolute minimum, the attorney's fee is not the area to look for bargains. Yes, the investor may save $200 by going with a cheaper attorney, but an experienced attorney's knowledge and experience can save thousands of dollars. The investor should find an experienced real estate attorney with a forte in investment property, and consider it a smart investment.

It may surprise some people to learn that they do not need an attorney to handle closings. Legally, anyone can do it without professional assistance. But both the buyer and seller will typically have attorney representation in some states. In other states, buyer and seller will be represented by an escrow holder who will be a dual agent dealing with both parties. In most cases, however, communication between the two parties is usually only done between the attorneys, escrow holders or real estate agents. In locales where an attorney acts as closing agent, it is the attorney's responsibility to protect his or her client's legal and financial interests. The buyer's attorney will review all documents involved with the purchase transaction, from the purchase agreement and loan good faith estimate disclosure to the closing's final settlement statement.

At the closing, the buyer's attorney will review the dozens of legal documents and disclosures that must be signed by the buyer. The buyer's attorney will explain each document to the buyer before it is signed. Also, both attorneys will calculate and verify the final transaction figures prior to concluding the closing.

In the case where an escrow holder acts as the closing agent, the same events occur as when an attorney closes the transaction, with the escrow holder explaining any disclosures that have not been explained by the real estate agent, overseeing signing of loan documents, calculating closing costs and preparing closing statements.

Closing Agent

A closing agent, who may be a representative of the title company or an escrow holder, will conduct the closing. In some locales or situations, however, the seller's attorney will act as the closing agent. The closing agent will prepare many of the closing documents, although the lender's document preparation department or provider usually packages the mortgage loan documents and disclosures.

The buyer should expect to sign numerous legal documents and disclosures. The seller will only need to sign a few documents and often skips the closing, as the seller's attorney is the only person necessary to represent the seller in some states. The closing agent will gather final transaction calculations from both attorneys and collect any necessary funds from the buyer, seller and lender. Once all documents are signed, the closing agent will notarize them and prepare them for recording with the county. After a final review and check with the lender, the closing agent will then disburse funds to the seller, attorneys, real estate agents, service providers, lien holders (to be paid off) and buyers, as required by the transaction.

Insurance Agent

At the typical closing, the buyer must provide proof of paid hazard insurance coverage for one full year. This is a common mortgage loan requirement and it is advisable for the buyer to use a respectable insurance company in the area of the property, as the buyer will want the insurance agent nearby if there is a problem. The agent will have to review the property briefly to confirm that it is in acceptable condition, though properties with serious defects may have a more difficult time obtaining affordable insurance coverage.

Loan Officer

The lender's representative is typically the loan officer, although the applicant may also have to communicate with the loan processor or underwriter. It is the loan officer's responsibility to initially pre-qualify and pre-approve the buyer's mortgage loan application, as well as eventually obtain final approval and coordinate the loan closing for the purchase mortgage loan. Because of the money and myriad government regulations involved, loan officers must provide the borrower with a good deal of information. By the same token, the loan officer must gather numerous borrower documents to support and process the application. But the loan officer also often acts as an informal advisor for the borrower, as the lender has a vested interest in the borrower's success.

Not all loan officers and lenders are alike, although most lenders tend to eventually sell their loans to investors that have nothing to do with the initial transaction. Banks may lend their own money, but usually sell the loan (through Fannie Mae and Freddie Mac) to the secondary mortgage market so that they can replenish their cash supply and make a profit on initiating the loan. Mortgage companies usually broker to dozens of banks from across the country. This allows mortgage brokers to work with more challenged borrowers, who may have a difficult time with the conservative parameters of most banks.

A consumer seeking a standard home loan or even a standard investment loan (on one-to-four units), with the usual down payment requirements and restrictions, can go to practically any bank or mortgage company for the financing. If an investor is looking for creative financing, such as a no money down, 100% mortgage for investment (rental) properties, however, he or she will probably work with a mortgage broker with ties to specialized lenders. There are considerably more lenders willing to make loans on one-to-four units than there are for larger properties with increased investment risks. Those risks include the fact that there is no seller obligation for transfer disclosures about the condition of the property, as well as no protection under RESPA (Real Estate Settlement Procedures Act) rules for properties with more than four units.

Property Inspector

The property inspector is different from the appraiser. Hiring the inspector is typically an option available to the buyers; they don't have to conduct an actual inspection of the property if they do not want to pay for one. But an investor would be unwise not to take advantage of this option. Actually, it would be a huge mistake not to have an investment property fully inspected before purchasing the property.

The property inspector will conduct a thorough examination of the property for defects, operating efficiency and overall condition. Among other things, the inspector will check heating, cooling, plumbing and electrical systems, as well as the building's structure. It is also a good idea for the investor to accompany the inspector if the investor is a first-time buyer, as it may be the first and only opportunity to learn such practicalities as restarting a furnace, locating the fuse box and checking the primary water valves.

Real Estate Agent

Real estate agents are generally free for the buyer/investor, so why not use them? Fortunately, there are real estate agents who are well equipped to help an investor find suitable investment properties. They have had training in locating profitable investment properties and experience in the successful acquisition of such properties.

An investor should look for an experienced and well-informed real estate agent when he or she starts interviewing agents. A salesperson or broker possessing certain investment designations such as **CCIM (Certified Commercial Investment Member of the Commercial Investment Institute)** would be a particularly valuable asset to an investor. The CCIM designation is awarded by the Commercial Investment Real Estate Council, an affiliate of the National Association of REALTORS®, representing the real estate industry's highest professional and ethical standards. For a real estate investment broker to earn the CCIM designation, the member must have completed a rigorous series of professional courses and passed a comprehensive final examination, along with having submitted a resume of transactions showing a certain depth of experience. The CCIM designation is rapidly growing in recognition as the hallmark of a truly experienced professional in the field of commercial investment real estate brokerage.

Agent vs. Broker Real estate agents cannot operate independently; they must work for a broker. Only a real estate broker can own and operate a real estate office. Real estate agents who take further training and pass the state broker exam can become real estate brokers. Until then, they can only list real estate or assist buyers if they work through a broker. From the point of view of an investor, the only difference is that a real estate broker may possess more knowledge or experience than a salesperson, and thus be more helpful in a transaction. There are many salespersons, however, who are extremely knowledgeable—even specialists in investment properties—who would be the perfect candidates to help an investor find properties that match his or her objectives.

Buyer's Broker Some buyers may select a more specialized agent, called a **buyer's broker**. The certified buyer's broker has only recently become a more specific type of professional, and should not be confused with other real estate agents or brokers. The buyer's broker represents only the buyer and has no allegiance to the seller. The buyer will pay the buyer's broker for his or her service. Because the buyer's broker does not depend on a seller-paid commission, the buyer's broker will look at properties that might no be listed on the **Multiple Listing Service (MLS)**. Buyer's brokers are increasingly common in commercial real estate transactions.

Listing Agent The listing agent is the real estate agent or broker responsible for selling the property. The agent works for and represents the seller. The name derives from the agent's primary task of listing the property for sale, usually through the local Multiple Listing Service (MLS). When a buyer finds a worthy property, the buyer's broker or real estate agent will approach the listing agent to make an offer, arrange preliminary inspections and negotiate a final price. The listing agent shares the property's sales commission with the buyer's real estate agent. An investor needs to keep in mind that the listing agent has a fiduciary duty to carry out the best interests of the seller, and the buyer's interest might not be first priority, beyond being honest and truthful as required by real estate law. It might be more profitable for an investor to make an offer through his or her own agent rather than depending on a listing agent to represent both buyer and seller as a dual agent.

Targeting the Right Property

The investor is now ready to begin shopping. Normally, the investor would not be committed to any obligation during a shopping process, so keeping an open mind is important to acquiring a property that is consistent with one's goals. It is not uncommon for the successful investor to change decisions a few times, each time getting closer to the property that is exactly right.

There are five steps in locating the right property. These steps are

- Review the business plan
- Obtain loan pre-approval
- Obtain available property listings
- Visit and inspect prospective properties
- Prioritize preferences

Review the Business Plan

A business plan is useless unless the investor actually applies it. Whenever a person starts to feel off-course, the first move should be to review the business plan. As the investor begins shopping, it is particularly important to recall special goals, priorities, preferences, and minimum requirements.

As mentioned earlier, an investor's goals and plans will determine which properties are right. Instead of having to look at thousands of prospective investments, the business plan should provide the focus for the search. The investor should also share the business plan with the key people assisting in the acquisition, especially the real estate agent, loan officer and accountant. As the investor starts shopping for property, this is the time to make sure the real estate agent understands the selected investment strategy and objectives.

Obtain Loan Pre-Approval

The fact is that a consumer is not really considered a serious buyer—let alone investor—unless he or she has funds backing up inquiries and offers. A loan pre-approval certificate is a powerful tool. It means that a buyer can close sooner and more assuredly than someone without a loan commitment, without delays meaning additional headaches and expenses for the seller. There are two landmarks in obtaining preliminary mortgage financing that all prospective investors should understand.

- **Pre-Qualification**   The minimum certification that most sellers will want is a pre-qualification. However, the pre-qualification carries no obligation from the lender; the pre-qualification usually entails a quick credit and income analysis conducted by the loan officer. In most cases, the borrower has yet to complete the loan application. Still, the pre-qualification certificate will often suffice for most listing agents.

- **Pre-Approval**   The pre-approval involves the processing of a full loan application, with most of the required borrower documents attached. The pre-approval is a preliminary approval and does carry significantly more weight than the pre-qualification. The preliminary approval is usually conditioned on the borrower finding an acceptable (to the lender) property, maintaining credit qualifications and providing any other items required by the lender.

Depending on the property desired, it may be easy to obtain a pre-qualification and/or pre-approval. A buyer must complete a pre-approval questionnaire and either email, fax or mail the completed form to a loan representative. Normally the lender can give a pre-qualification in a few minutes after checking the buyer's credit and analyzing the buyer's income, and can then prepare an application package for the pre-approval.

If the property in question is a large investment property, pre-approval may not be available to the buyer, since the lender is going to look at the property more than at the buyer in evaluating the risk involved in making the loan.

If an investor wants to shop around with different lenders, he or she needs to realize that there is a right way and a wrong way to do it. Following the wrong way can severely damage the investor's credit, because every time any creditor requests a credit report— for a pre-qualification or pre-approval—the investor's credit record will indicate an inquiry, and each inquiry has the potential to lower the investor's FICO or credit score by 10 to 20 points. Shopping around for the best deal is smart, but after the sixth inquiry, an investor may discover a personal credit grade that has dropped from an A to a B, thereby jeopardizing the mortgage financing.

The right way to shop around is for the investor to obtain a credit report from all three credit reporting bureaus—**TransUnion**, **Experian** and **CBI/Equifax**. This can be done online. Also, the credit reports should indicate the investor's FICO credit score.

As an investor shops around for a pre-qualification, he or she should tell the loan officers not to request a credit report, and give them a copy instead. That is more than sufficient for a pre-qualification and such credit reports are good for up to 60 to 90 days. Once the investor applies for a pre-approval or a full approval, the lender will then have to request its own credit report.

Obtain Available Property Listings
Armed with a business plan and loan approval, the investor is ready to begin some serious shopping. The next stop should be with a professional real estate agent, who

can identify the properties that meet the investor's required criteria and who has access to the Multiple Listing Service (MLS). A real estate agent can generate a computer print-out of properties that provides a wealth of information about each property, including rental income and operating expenses. The investor should review the data offered and prioritize all of the listings using the business plan as guide.

Not all properties for sale are listed through brokers. Many sellers try to market their properties themselves in order to avoid paying the 5% to 6% commission they would otherwise have to pay to list with an agent. Unfortunately, considering those properties as purchase prospects will require more legwork from investors—unless they use a buyer's broker.

Still, for-sale-by-owner (FSBO) properties are too important to ignore. An investor's best bet is to spend a couple of hours scouring the real estate classified ads for such properties. The investor should telephone the sellers of interesting properties and conduct a preliminary analysis over the phone, getting more information about the property, its expenses and its income potential, as well as discovering the seller's motivation. In some cases, an investor may be able to negotiate creative transactions with the seller.

Visit and Inspect Prospective Properties

The investor should drive by each of the preferred properties at least once before seriously previewing them. Prior to actually visiting any properties, the organized investor will have analyzed each one for its potential, and then prioritized each property according to its compatibility with the investor's goals. After the investor has done all the homework on the properties, it is time to visit those that meet the investment requirements. Only then should the real estate agent make the appointment to preview those properties.

An investor should visit each property with a totally professional attitude, asking questions about the property's history, neighborhood, repair needs and seller motivation. Most importantly, the investor should make note of every aspect of the property. If more than one property is previewed, the investor will quickly find that details get confused. To assist in the initial visits, the following property inspection checklist will help. A camera would also be beneficial in taking photos of the property and its neighborhood.

Prioritize Preferences

As an investor compares inspected properties, it is necessary to continually prioritize preferences. If necessary, the real estate agent can arrange second and third visits to a property. Investors should drive by the top preferences at various times—evenings, mornings and weekends—to become aware of the property's characteristics at different times.

Buyer's remorse is common with many new investors who make large purchases, and real estate is obviously one of the largest purchases in a lifetime. However, buyer's remorse will not be as much of an issue if the investor takes due care during the shopping stage. The investor needs to remember that as the buyer, he or she is in control. If an investor can't make a decision about whether to buy or not, it just means that the investor doesn't have enough data or information on a property, and this particular transaction requires more research before the investor can come to a decision. Even in the event that an investor passes up a good investment, experience shows that other opportunities will arise.

Negotiating Terms

When the investor finds a property that would potentially be a good investment, it is time to negotiate with the seller. The objective at this stage is to arrive at a fair contract that meets the goals of all parties. Unworthy actions on the part of an investor, such as trying to beat the seller down below a fair price at all costs, maybe even below the investor's own stated business objectives, usually are unsuccessful. These actions result in the investor failing to achieve long-term goals, not to mention the ill will generated by the conflict, and the seller's eventual perception of not wanting to do business with an investor who is unwilling to compromise. This "shoot-myself-in-the-foot" behavior should be avoided by the investor.

One tactic to remember, however, as an investor negotiates, is that an individual should never be afraid to say "no." An investor should never be afraid to lose a deal, thinking there will never be another one as profitable or desirable. Again, every transaction opportunity should be measured against the investor's business plan to validate the purchase. There will always be other opportunities for more investments.
But it may be impossible to get out of a bad deal.

An investor's decisions and actions during this stage do become more important, while moving closer toward an obligation. But the investor is also moving toward what should be a profitable investment.

Attorney Review

Before signing the contract, an investor may want to make sure that it has an **attorney review clause**. This provision normally gives a buyer a certain number of days to have an attorney review the contract. If a buyer's attorney finds something wrong or disagreeable, the attorney review clause allows the buyer to request changes or cancel the contract.

Buyer and Seller Negotiate Price and Terms

If the seller believes that the investor is making a serious offer, a series of counteroffers will often follow. With luck, both buyer and seller will eventually arrive at a fair agreement. It is important to remember during this period, however, that price is not the only determinant of value. The terms of the purchase agreement can be just as important as the price. For example, an investor may be willing to give a little on price if the seller is willing to include some valuable concessions, such as paying the closing costs or making improvements.

PROPERTY INSPECTION CHECKLIST

Property Address	Date & Time of Visit

NEIGHBORHOOD

Area Type:	Prominent Use:	General Condition:	Traffic:
☐ Urban ☐ Suburban ☐ Rural	☐ Residential ☐ Commercial ☐ Industrial ☐ Other:	☐ Excellent ☐ Stable ☐ Fair ☐ Distressed ☐ Awful	☐ Heavy ☐ Medium ☐ Light

Noise:	Lighting:	Nearby Homes:	Neighbors:
☐ Loud ☐ Medium ☐ Quiet	☐ Well Lit ☐ Fair ☐ Poorly Lit ☐ None	☐ Excellent ☐ Good ☐ Fair ☐ Distressed	☐ Seniors ☐ Families ☐ Young Singles ☐ Other

Schools:	Shopping:	Public Transportation:	Church:	Parks:
☐ < ½-mile ☐ ½-1 mile ☐ > 1 mile	☐ < ½-mile ☐ ½-1 mile ☐ > 1 mile	☐ < ½-mile ☐ ½-1 mile ☐ > 1 mile	☐ < ½-mile ☐ ½-1 mile ☐ > 1 mile	☐ < ½-mile ☐ ½-1 mile ☐ > 1 mile
Gym, Recreation Ctr:	**Hospital/Medical:**	**Employment:**	**Highways & Major Streets:**	**Entertainment:**
☐ < ½-mile ☐ ½-1 mile ☐ > 1 mile	☐ < ½-mile ☐ ½-1 mile ☐ > 1 mile	☐ < ½-mile ☐ ½-1 mile ☐ > 1 mile	☐ < ½-mile ☐ ½-1 mile ☐ > 1 mile	☐ < ½-mile ☐ ½-1 mile ☐ > 1 mile

Comments:

PROPERTY SITE & LOT

Lot Size	Topography:	Location on Block:	Driveway:	Sidewalk:
	☐ Flat ☐ Sloping ☐ Hilly ☐ Other	☐ Corner ☐ Middle ☐ Other:	☐ None ☐ Good ☐ Fair ☐ Damaged	☐ Excellent ☐ Good ☐ Fair ☐ Awful
Alley:	**Patio:**	**Visible Encumbrances:**	**Visible Easements:**	**Pool:**
☐ None ☐ Good ☐ Fair ☐ Damaged	☐ None ☐ Good ☐ Fair ☐ Damaged	☐ None ☐ Yes:	☐ None ☐ Yes:	☐ None ☐ Good ☐ Fair ☐ Damaged

Fence:	Landscaping:	Description of Landscaping & Exterior Site Elements
☐ None ☐ Good ☐ Fair ☐ Damaged	☐ None ☐ Good ☐ Fair ☐ Damaged	
Parking Type:	**Parking Condition:**	**Description of Exterior Parking Elements (paving, striping, carports, etc.)**
☐ None ☐ Garage ☐ Paved ☐ Unpaved	☐ NA ☐ Excellent ☐ Good ☐ Poor	

Comments:

BUILDING EXTERIOR

Building Style:	Levels/Stories:	Finish Type:	Finish Condition:	Curb Appeal:
		☐ Brick ☐ Vinyl ☐ Wood ☐ Other:	☐ Excellent ☐ Good ☐ Fair ☐ Damaged	☐ Excellent ☐ Good ☐ Fair ☐ Poor

Front Wall Condition:	Side Wall 1 Condition:	Side Wall 2 Condition:	Rear Wall Condition:
☐ Excellent ☐ Good ☐ Damaged:	☐ Excellent ☐ Good ☐ Damaged:	☐ Excellent ☐ Good ☐ Damaged:	☐ Excellent ☐ Good ☐ Damaged:
Front Windows Condition:	**Side 1 Windows Condition:**	**Side 2 Windows Condition:**	**Rear Windows Condition:**
☐ Excellent ☐ Good ☐ Poor/Damaged:	☐ Excellent ☐ Good ☐ Poor/Damaged:	☐ Excellent ☐ Good ☐ Poor/Damaged:	☐ Excellent ☐ Good ☐ Poor/Damaged:
Front Storm Windows:	**Side 1 Storm Windows:**	**Side 2 Storm Windows:**	**Rear Storm Windows:**
☐ None ☐ Good ☐ Fair ☐ Damaged:	☐ None ☐ Good ☐ Fair ☐ Damaged:	☐ None ☐ Good ☐ Fair ☐ Damaged:	☐ None ☐ Good ☐ Fair ☐ Damaged:
Front Window Screens:	**Side 1 Window Screens:**	**Side 2 Window Screens:**	**Rear Storm Window Screens:**
☐ None ☐ Good ☐ Fair ☐ Damaged:	☐ None ☐ Good ☐ Fair ☐ Damaged:	☐ None ☐ Good ☐ Fair ☐ Damaged:	☐ None ☐ Good ☐ Fair ☐ Damaged:

Front Door Type:	Front Door Condition:	Front Intercom:	Front Security Camera:	Front Door Lighting:
☐ Glass ☐ Metal ☐ Wood ☐ Other:	☐ Excellent ☐ Good ☐ Damaged:	☐ None ☐ Good ☐ Fair ☐ Damaged:	☐ None ☐ Good ☐ Damaged:	☐ Excellent ☐ Good ☐ Fair ☐ None
Front Door Lock:	**Inner Front Door Type:**	**Inner Front Door Condition:**	**Inner Front Door Lock:**	**Foyer/Inner-Door Light:**
☐ Excellent ☐ Good ☐ Fair ☐ Damaged	☐ None ☐ Glass ☐ Metal ☐ Wood ☐ Other:	☐ Excellent ☐ Good ☐ Damaged:	☐ Excellent ☐ Good ☐ Fair ☐ Damaged	☐ Excellent ☐ Good ☐ Fair ☐ None

Front Lighting:	Gutters:	Downspout:	Chimney:
☐ Excellent ☐ Good ☐ Poor/None:	☐ None ☐ Excellent ☐ Good ☐ Damaged:	☐ None ☐ Excellent ☐ Good ☐ Damaged:	☐ None ☐ Excellent ☐ Good ☐ Damaged:

Rear Door Type:	Rear Door Condition:	Rear Door Lock:	Rear Door Access:	Rear Door Lighting:
☐ Glass ☐ Metal ☐ Wood ☐ Other:	☐ Excellent ☐ Good ☐ Damaged:	☐ Excellent ☐ Good ☐ Fair ☐ Damaged	☐ NA ☐ Restricted ☐ Open	☐ Excellent ☐ Good ☐ Fair ☐ None

Eaves:	Roof Style:	Roofing Type:	Roof Condition:
☐ Excellent ☐ Good ☐ Poor/Damaged:	☐ Flat ☐ Pitched ☐ Other:	☐ Sheet ☐ Shingle ☐ Tar ☐ Other:	☐ Excellent ☐ Good ☐ Fair ☐ Poor/Damaged:

(continued on next page)

Additional Comments About Roof:				

Sprinklers:	Garage:	Garage Door:	Exterior Lights:	Ext. Electrical Outlets:
☐ NA ☐ Good	☐ NA ☐ Good	☐ None ☐ Good	☐ Excellent ☐ Good	☐ None ☐ Good
☐ Damaged:	☐ Damaged:	☐ Damaged:	☐ Fair ☐ None	☐ Damaged:
Comments:				

INTERIOR (General)

Interior Square Footage	Total # of Rental Units:	# of Studios/Efficiency:	# of 1-Bedrooms:	# of 2-Bedrooms:	# of 3+ Bedrooms:

Foyer:	Foyer Condition:	Lobby:	Lobby Condition:	Mgmt Office:	Office Condition:
☐ None	☐ NA ☐ Good	☐ None	☐ NA ☐ Good	☐ None	☐ NA ☐ Good
☐ Yes, Size:	☐ Fair ☐ Poor	☐ Yes, Size:	☐ Fair ☐ Poor	☐ Yes, Size:	☐ Fair ☐ Poor
1st Hall Floor Type:	1st Hall Floor Condition:	1st Hall Wall/Ceiling Type:	1st Hall Wall/Ceiling Cond.:	1st Hall Lighting:	
☐ Wood ☐ Carpet	☐ Good ☐ Fair	☐ Paint ☐ Wallpaper	☐ Good ☐ Fair	☐ Good ☐ Fair	
☐ Tile ☐ Other:	☐ Damaged:	☐ Stucco ☐ Other:	☐ Damaged:	☐ Poor	
2nd Hall Floor Type:	2nd Hall Floor Condition:	2nd Hall Wall/Ceiling Type:	2nd Hall Wall/Ceiling Cond.:	2nd Hall Lighting:	
☐ Wood ☐ Carpet	☐ Good ☐ Fair	☐ Paint ☐ Wallpaper	☐ Good ☐ Fair	☐ Good ☐ Fair	
☐ Tile ☐ Other:	☐ Damaged:	☐ Stucco ☐ Other:	☐ Damaged:	☐ Poor	
3rd Hall Floor Type:	3rd Hall Floor Condition:	3rd Hall Wall/Ceiling Type:	3rd Hall Wall/Ceiling Cond.:	3rd Hall Lighting:	
☐ Wood ☐ Carpet	☐ Good ☐ Fair	☐ Paint ☐ Wallpaper	☐ Good ☐ Fair	☐ Good ☐ Fair	
☐ Tile ☐ Other:	☐ Damaged:	☐ Stucco ☐ Other:	☐ Damaged:	☐ Poor	
# of Staircases:	Staircase Condition:	Staircase Lighting:	Secured access:	Fire Doors:	
	☐ Good ☐ Fair	☐ Good ☐ Fair	☐ Yes	☐ Yes	
	☐ Damaged:	☐ Poor	☐ No	☐ No	
# of Mgmt. Closets:	Closet Condition:	Closet Lighting:	Attic:	Attic Condition:	
	☐ Good ☐ Fair	☐ Good ☐ Fair	☐ None	☐ Good ☐ Fair	
	☐ Damaged:	☐ Poor/None	☐ Yes, Size:	☐ Damaged:	
Basement:	Basement Condition:	Basement Lighting:	Attic Walls:	Basement Floor:	
☐ None	☐ Finished ☐ Unfinished	☐ Good ☐ Fair	☐ Good ☐ Fair	☐ Good ☐ Fair	
☐ Yes, Size:	☐ Damaged:	☐ Poor/None	☐ Damaged:	☐ Damaged:	
Mechanical Room:	Mech Room Condition:	Mech Room Lighting:	Laundry Room:	Laundry Rm. Condition:	
☐ None	☐ Good ☐ Fair	☐ Good ☐ Fair	☐ None	☐ Good ☐ Fair	
☐ Yes, Size:	☐ Poor:	☐ Poor/None	☐ Yes, Size:	☐ Damaged:	
Fire Sprinklers:	Fire Extinguishers:	Fire Alarm System:	Smoke Detectors:	Emergency Lighting:	
☐ None ☐ Good	☐ None ☐ Good	☐ None ☐ Good	☐ None ☐ Good	☐ None ☐ Good	
☐ Damaged:	☐ Insufficient:	☐ Damaged:	☐ Insufficient	☐ Insufficient	
Comments:					

MECHANICALS

Furnace Type:			Furnace Condition:			Hot Water Heater:			Hot Water Tank:		
☐ None	☐ Boiler	☐ Hot Water	☐ New	☐ Good	☐ Fair	☐ None	☐ Good	☐ Fair	☐ None	☐ Good	☐ Fair
☐ Steam	☐ Electric	☐ Gas	☐ Damaged:			☐ Damaged:			☐ Damaged:		

Radiators:			Heating Ducts:			Space Heaters:			A/C Unit:		
☐ None ☐ Good	☐ Fair		☐ None ☐ Good	☐ Fair		☐ None ☐ Good	☐ Fair		☐ None ☐ Good	☐ Fair	
☐ Damaged:			☐ Damaged:			☐ Damaged:			☐ Damaged:		

A/C Ducts:	Electric Service Control:	Electric Wiring:	Elevators:	Elevator Lighting:
☐ None ☐ Good	☐ Fuse Box	☐ Good ☐ Fair	☐ None ☐ Good	☐ Good ☐ Fair
☐ Fair ☐ Damaged:	☐ Circuit-Breaker Panel	☐ Needs Upgrade	☐ Damaged:	☐ Poor
Comments:				

INTERIOR (Individual Units)

Unit 1 Type:	Unit 1 Size	Unit 1 Kitchen:	Unit 1 Kitchen Equipment:	Unit 1 Bathroom:
☐ Studio ☐ 1BR ☐ 2BR		☐ Excellent ☐ Good	☐ Refrigerator ☐ Stove ☐ Oven	☐ Excellent ☐ Good
☐ Other:		☐ Poor/Damaged:	☐ Microwave ☐ Other:	☐ Poor/Damaged:
Unit 1 Floor Types:	Unit 1 Floor Condition:	Unit 1 Wall/Ceiling Type:	Unit 1 Wall/Ceiling Cond.:	Unit 1 Lighting:
☐ Wood ☐ Carpet	☐ Good ☐ Fair	☐ Paint ☐ Wallpaper	☐ Good ☐ Fair	☐ Excellent ☐ Good
☐ Tile ☐ Other:	☐ Damaged:	☐ Stucco ☐ Other:	☐ Damaged:	☐ Fair ☐ Poor
Unit 1 Living Room:	Unit 1 Bedrooms:	Unit 1 Overall Condition:	Unit 1 Comments	
☐ Excellent ☐ Good	☐ Excellent ☐ Good	☐ Excellent ☐ Good		
☐ Poor/Damaged:	☐ Poor/Damaged:	☐ Fair ☐ Poor		

(continued on next page)

Unit 2 Type: ☐ Studio ☐ 1BR ☐ 2BR ☐ Other:	Unit 2 Size	Unit 2 Kitchen: ☐ Excellent ☐ Good ☐ Poor/Damaged:		Unit 2 Kitchen Equipment: ☐ Refrigerator ☐ Stove ☐ Oven ☐ Microwave ☐ Other:	Unit 2 Bathroom: ☐ Excellent ☐ Good ☐ Poor/Damaged:
Unit 2 Floor Types: ☐ Wood ☐ Carpet ☐ Tile ☐ Other:	Unit 2 Floor Condition: ☐ Good ☐ Fair ☐ Damaged:	Unit 2 Wall/Ceiling Type: ☐ Paint ☐ Wallpaper ☐ Stucco ☐ Other:		Unit 2 Wall/Ceiling Cond.: ☐ Good ☐ Fair ☐ Damaged:	Unit 2 Lighting: ☐ Excellent ☐ Good ☐ Fair ☐ Poor
Unit 2 Living Room: ☐ Excellent ☐ Good ☐ Poor/Damaged:	Unit 2 Bedrooms: ☐ Excellent ☐ Good ☐ Poor/Damaged:		Unit 2 Overall Condition: ☐ Excellent ☐ Good ☐ Fair ☐ Poor	Unit 2 Comments	
Unit 3 Type: ☐ Studio ☐ 1BR ☐ 2BR ☐ Other:	Unit 3 Size	Unit 3 Kitchen: ☐ Excellent ☐ Good ☐ Poor/Damaged:		Unit 3 Kitchen Equipment: ☐ Refrigerator ☐ Stove ☐ Oven ☐ Microwave ☐ Other:	Unit 3 Bathroom: ☐ Excellent ☐ Good ☐ Poor/Damaged:
Unit 3 Floor Types: ☐ Wood ☐ Carpet ☐ Tile ☐ Other:	Unit 3 Floor Condition: ☐ Good ☐ Fair ☐ Damaged:	Unit 3 Wall/Ceiling Type: ☐ Paint ☐ Wallpaper ☐ Stucco ☐ Other:		Unit 3 Wall/Ceiling Cond.: ☐ Good ☐ Fair ☐ Damaged:	Unit 3 Lighting: ☐ Excellent ☐ Good ☐ Fair ☐ Poor
Unit 3 Living Room: ☐ Excellent ☐ Good ☐ Poor/Damaged:	Unit 3 Bedrooms: ☐ Excellent ☐ Good ☐ Poor/Damaged:		Unit 3 Overall Condition: ☐ Excellent ☐ Good ☐ Fair ☐ Poor	Unit 3 Comments	
Unit 4 Type: ☐ Studio ☐ 1BR ☐ 2BR ☐ Other:	Unit 4 Size	Unit 4 Kitchen: ☐ Excellent ☐ Good ☐ Poor/Damaged:		Unit 4 Kitchen Equipment: ☐ Refrigerator ☐ Stove ☐ Oven ☐ Microwave ☐ Other:	Unit 4 Bathroom: ☐ Excellent ☐ Good ☐ Poor/Damaged:
Unit 4 Floor Types: ☐ Wood ☐ Carpet ☐ Tile ☐ Other:	Unit 4 Floor Condition: ☐ Good ☐ Fair ☐ Damaged:	Unit 4 Wall/Ceiling Type: ☐ Paint ☐ Wallpaper ☐ Stucco ☐ Other:		Unit 4 Wall/Ceiling Cond.: ☐ Good ☐ Fair ☐ Damaged:	Unit 4 Lighting: ☐ Excellent ☐ Good ☐ Fair ☐ Poor
Unit 4 Living Room: ☐ Excellent ☐ Good ☐ Poor/Damaged:	Unit 4 Bedrooms: ☐ Excellent ☐ Good ☐ Poor/Damaged:		Unit 4 Overall Condition: ☐ Excellent ☐ Good ☐ Fair ☐ Poor	Unit 4 Comments	
Unit 5 Type: ☐ Studio ☐ 1BR ☐ 2BR ☐ Other:	Unit 5 Size	Unit 5 Kitchen: ☐ Excellent ☐ Good ☐ Poor/Damaged:		Unit 5 Kitchen Equipment: ☐ Refrigerator ☐ Stove ☐ Oven ☐ Microwave ☐ Other:	Unit 5 Bathroom: ☐ Excellent ☐ Good ☐ Poor/Damaged:
Unit 5 Floor Types: ☐ Wood ☐ Carpet ☐ Tile ☐ Other:	Unit 5 Floor Condition: ☐ Good ☐ Fair ☐ Damaged:	Unit 5 Wall/Ceiling Type: ☐ Paint ☐ Wallpaper ☐ Stucco ☐ Other:		Unit 5 Wall/Ceiling Cond.: ☐ Good ☐ Fair ☐ Damaged:	Unit 5 Lighting: ☐ Excellent ☐ Good ☐ Fair ☐ Poor
Unit 5 Living Room: ☐ Excellent ☐ Good ☐ Poor/Damaged:	Unit 5 Bedrooms: ☐ Excellent ☐ Good ☐ Poor/Damaged:		Unit 5 Overall Condition: ☐ Excellent ☐ Good ☐ Fair ☐ Poor	Unit 5 Comments	
Unit 6 Type: ☐ Studio ☐ 1BR ☐ 2BR ☐ Other:	Unit 6 Size	Unit 6 Kitchen: ☐ Excellent ☐ Good ☐ Poor/Damaged:		Unit 6 Kitchen Equipment: ☐ Refrigerator ☐ Stove ☐ Oven ☐ Microwave ☐ Other:	Unit 6 Bathroom: ☐ Excellent ☐ Good ☐ Poor/Damaged:
Unit 6 Floor Types: ☐ Wood ☐ Carpet ☐ Tile ☐ Other:	Unit 6 Floor Condition: ☐ Good ☐ Fair ☐ Damaged:	Unit 6 Wall/Ceiling Type: ☐ Paint ☐ Wallpaper ☐ Stucco ☐ Other:		Unit 6 Wall/Ceiling Cond.: ☐ Good ☐ Fair ☐ Damaged:	Unit 6 Lighting: ☐ Excellent ☐ Good ☐ Fair ☐ Poor
Unit 6 Living Room: ☐ Excellent ☐ Good ☐ Poor/Damaged:	Unit 6 Bedrooms: ☐ Excellent ☐ Good ☐ Poor/Damaged:		Unit 6 Overall Condition: ☐ Excellent ☐ Good ☐ Fair ☐ Poor	Unit 6 Comments	

MISCELLANEOUS CRITERIA

COMMENTS

Comments:

Due Diligence

With residential properties, a buyer may only have a few days to conduct due diligence. Commercial properties allow the buyer a little more time and information.

Regardless of the situation, it is important that an investor gather as much information as possible about the property. Due diligence investigations normally carry three goals

- Calculating the value of the property

- Verifying the property's condition, income and expenses

- Confirming that it meets the investor's minimum requirements

A real estate agent can assist the investor at this stage by gathering information available both from city or county records as well as from the seller. Once an investor has all of the necessary facts, he or she will want to use those facts to conduct a feasibility study. The feasibility study analyzes the potential for profit and success. An accountant and a knowledgeable real estate agent are helpful assistants in the task of analyzing the property's finances to determine its projected income, expenses, capital requirements and profits.

Before making an offer and entering into negotiations with a seller, an investor should try to obtain information about the seller and the property that may be helpful during the negotiation. An important objective here should be to try to discover the seller's motivation. The simplest way is just to ask.

Making a Smart Offer

If due diligence gives the investor a green light, it is time to make an offer. What should the opening bid be? If the price matches the investor's objectives, the investor can accept it or start 5% to 10% lower—but not too much lower, unless there is a compelling reason for doing so. Due diligence may have shown the investor that the property is overpriced and that the opening bid should reflect the selling price of similar properties in the area. Before negotiations begin, the investor should already know what is needed to ensure profitability and success.

These are not clear-cut rules. Negotiating the price is more an art than a science. An investor must be aware of local economic conditions, especially whether the market is a buyer's market, which would allow the investor to bargain more aggressively, or a seller's market, in which the seller can be more demanding and there might be other offers to consider. A guiding principle should be to respect the seller. Again, the goal is to arrive at a fair and workable price.

The best negotiator is always the one who is willing to walk away from a bad deal. This assumes, of course, that the investor understands the difference between a good deal and a bad one. That is where a business plan, research and preparations are important.

Obtaining Property Insurance

Many mortgage lenders require a one-year prepaid insurance policy prior to the closing. Even if the transaction is all cash it is smart business to have insurance protection. The insurance agent should be able to provide coverage in less than an hour. Commercial properties, however, may require more time.

Preparing a Budget and Operations Plan

Before closing, the investor should prepare a budget and operations plan. The budget should rely on the due diligence and appraisal report for facts and assumptions as well as the investor's personal goals for the property. The operations plan is meant to give the investor the benefit of being prepared to be a new landlord or property owner. For example, the investor should have lease forms, notices and dedicated bank accounts ready.

Professional Inspection of the Property

As soon as the contract has been signed by all parties, the investor should immediately arrange for a professional inspection of the property. For larger properties, the certified inspector should have an engineering background. The inspector will check the property's functional, structural and economic condition. If the inspector finds major problems, the investor can negotiate with the seller for concessions or—if the property no longer makes sense—a cancellation. Generally, the contract contains a clause allowing the buyer to have a certain number of days to approve the property inspection.

Updated Loan Approval

An investor should also inform the loan officer that he or she has signed a purchase contract, and should take steps to start a formal loan application. The lender will need to order an appraisal of the property and finalize the investor's mortgage loan commitment. A lender probably will ask for additional documents and the most current information from the investor prior to the closing. An investor should be ready to satisfy these conditions immediately, as the loan cannot close and disburse without them.

Closing the Purchase and Taking over the Property

The final stage of the real estate purchase is the closing, or settlement. Depending on the state, this may be conducted at the offices of a title company, an attorney or an escrow holder. The closing is scheduled soon after the loan is fully approved and all documents and verifications have been collected by the closing agent.

In an ideal world, detailed plans can be made and expected to be carried out like clockwork. That doesn't always happen. Many real estate transactions have fallen through at the last minute, or even during the closing itself. A common problem for many beginning investors is that they make firm commitments to events that must happen immediately after the scheduled closing.

For example, say the closing is scheduled for Friday morning. The investor has already contracted for the laborers and remodeling supplies to arrive at the subject property on Friday afternoon—intending to save some money by saving a little time. Instead, the closing runs late and eventually fails to consummate. Because of those prior commitments, the investor is under even greater stress during the failed closing. As the lawyers or real estate agents try to reschedule the closing or salvage the deal, the investor must scramble to rearrange those delivery commitments.

REAL ESTATE INVESTMENT ANALYSIS TOOLS

The specific measure of a property's profitability usually depends on who is doing the analysis. How does a buyer get beyond the marketing hype of the sellers or their agents? For lenders, the bottom line often focuses on the debt service ratio. With larger investors, the focus is normally on the anticipated return on investment (ROI) and the capitalization rate. A serious investor must understand the key financial and analysis terms involved with real estate investments to be successful in the long run.

Fortunately, the technical details and analysis terms are not difficult to understand for most people. These terms are not accidental concepts. They were developed as a way to measure a subject property's chances for success. Many beginning and novice real estate investors feel overwhelmed when these terms and figures are used, but in many ways the concepts are actually common sense.

Carrying Costs

Speculators and real estate investors who purchase property with the primary goal of reselling for profit must be especially concerned with the project's carrying costs. **Carrying costs** refer to the net amount of expenditures that investors must outlay before the property is resold and profits are realized. The carrying costs usually exclude the purchase price, and deduct operating income.

Unfortunately, uninformed real estate investors often look at just the purchase and resale prices. On the surface, buying a property for $100,000 and reselling it for $150,000 would seem like a good investment. This transaction, however, would be a disastrous decision if the carrying costs came to $60,000.

Steps for a Successful Purchase

Prepare
- There are a great many tasks that the investor can do before the closing, which can ease the post-closing take-over. For example, if the investor plans to redecorate, rehab or improve the property in other ways, the property inspection results can be used to start planning the work.

Relax
- The stress of pre-closing requirements and the closing itself can be aggravating. Investors learn that they must accept this as a normal part of many closings, especially closings that involve creative financing. Successful investors learn to stay calm, as purchases occasionally fail to close on time or to close at all. This is part of the investment process, but an investor can learn from the mistakes and problems involved and avoid them on the next transaction.

Obtain Closing Instructions
- The closing agent will provide instructions on how to get to the closing and what to bring. If additional down payment and closing cost funds are required, the investor probably will be instructed to bring a cashier's check made out for the amount needed.

Close the Transaction
- The closing will last about one hour for a smooth transaction and much longer for more complicated ones. The investor should he prepared to sign numerous documents, including the trust deed or mortgage and the promissory note.

Take-Over
- The closing session ends with the investor receiving the keys to the new property, either from the closing agent, real estate agent or attorney. This is where earlier preparations, especially the operations plan, will pay off. The investor will have much to do to ensure a smooth and profitable operation, and must not delay implementing the necessary changes. A take-over check-list is provided on the following pages.

Take-Over Checklist

Current Tenancy:

☐ Tenants informed of new ownership and rent payment information? .... ☐ Yes ☐ No

☐ Seller indicated _____ of _____ units were occupied. Verified? .... ☐ Yes ☐ No

☐ Current leases executed and in place? .... ☐ Yes ☐ No

☐ Are all rents current? .... ☐ Yes ☐ No

☐ List of all residents? .... ☐ Yes ☐ No

☐ Tenant home & work phone numbers? .... ☐ Yes ☐ No

☐ Security deposit amounts verified with lease? .... ☐ Yes ☐ No

☐ Security deposit amounts verified with tenants? .... ☐ Yes ☐ No

☐ Any pending legal actions involving tenants? .... ☐ Yes ☐ No

☐ All vacant units verified as really vacant? .... ☐ Yes ☐ No

☐ Are delinquent renters in possession of their units? .... ☐ Yes ☐ No

☐ Have all delinquent renters been served Termination Notices? .... ☐ Yes ☐ No

Services Requiring Continuation:

☐ Has electric company been notified of changes? .... ☐ Yes ☐ No

☐ Has electric company made final readings? .... ☐ Yes ☐ No

☐ Has gas company been notified of changes? .... ☐ Yes ☐ No

☐ Has gas company made final readings? .... ☐ Yes ☐ No

☐ Has water company been notified of changes? .... ☐ Yes ☐ No

☐ Has water company made final readings? .... ☐ Yes ☐ No

☐ Has scavenger company been notified of changes? .... ☐ Yes ☐ No

☐ Have you provided for ongoing janitorial services? .... ☐ Yes ☐ No

☐ Have you provided for ongoing maintenance services? .... ☐ Yes ☐ No

☐ Have you provided for ongoing landscape services? .... ☐ Yes ☐ No

Building Code Issues:

☐ Have the sellers provided any existing Notices of Violations? .... ☐ Yes ☐ No

☐ Are there any existing Notices of Violations? .... ☐ Yes ☐ No

☐ Does each unit have an operating smoke detector? .... ☐ Yes ☐ No

☐ Are carbon monoxide detectors in place? .... ☐ Yes ☐ No

☐ Are there proper locks on windows and doors? .... ☐ Yes ☐ No

☐ Are all windows and screens in good repair? .... ☐ Yes ☐ No

☐ Have you provided for ongoing janitorial services? .... ☐ Yes ☐ No

Emergency Procedures:

☐ Have you contracted with an answering service for after hours? .... ☐ Yes ☐ No

☐ Have current tenants been informed of any changes they must make? .... ☐ Yes ☐ No

(continued on next page)

(continued)

Take Over Checklist

❑ Have emergency point people been identified?... ❑ Yes ❑ No

❑ Do you have an emergency procedures plan? .... ❑ Yes ❑ No

❑ Have emergency service providers been identified/contracted? .... ❑ Yes ❑ No

Reports Provide by Seller/Agent:

Regulatory Agreements .... ❑ Received ❑ Missing ❑ N/A

Financial Reports .... ❑ Received ❑ Missing ❑ N/A

Inventory .... ❑ Received ❑ Missing ❑ N/A

Security Deposit Listing .... ❑ Received ❑ Missing ❑ N/A

Waiting Lists .... ❑ Received ❑ Missing ❑ N/A

Legal Actions .... ❑ Received ❑ Missing ❑ N/A

Current Billing .... ❑ Received ❑ Missing ❑ N/A

Personnel Records .... ❑ Received ❑ Missing ❑ N/A

Service Contracts in Place .... ❑ Received ❑ Missing ❑ N/A

Immediate Actions Needed:

❑ _____
❑ _____
❑ _____
❑ _____
❑ _____
❑ _____
❑ _____
❑ _____
❑ _____
❑ _____

Comments:

Smart investors know that the purchase price is only part of the total expenses required by a real estate investment. Carrying costs include the operating expenses, as well as the acquisition costs, mortgage payments, capital improvements and selling costs.

The situation in which an investor would want a quick resale on a property rather than wait for time to build a profit is if the property is priced remarkably below market value and is in good enough condition to allow for the fast turnaround with an attractive profit.

Purchase price		$350,000
Purchase closing costs	$10,500	
Clean-up and decoration	$14,000	
Mortgage interest payments (at 8%)	$4,600	
Real estate taxes	$2,300	
Hazard insurance	$300	
Utilities	$1,000	
Supplies	$1,300	
Resale broker commission	$21,000	
Resale closing costs	$8,500	
Total 6-month carrying costs		$63,500
Total Investment		$413,500
Resale price		$425,000
Net gain/loss		$11,500

In most cases, however, an investor must resell a property for at least 11% more than the original purchase price just to break even. When the investor bought it, probably the typical total closing costs were about 3% of the purchase price. When the investor resells it, expected closing costs usually are about 1.5% to 2%. On top of that, the usual selling commission to real estate brokers will be 6%. This doesn't include the cost of the investor's time or the lost interest income from the money used to make the down payment for the purchase. This rule of thumb also assumes that the investor sells the property right away. Every day that the investor waits to resell the property means additional costs.

Understanding carrying costs is often the difference between success and failure as a real estate investor, particularly for speculators. Actually, a smart investor may still be able to make the above project work by successfully eliminating some of the expenses and/or increasing income. For example, the investor may decide to rent out the garage for storage and the house to seasonal renters for additional income of $5,000 over six months, making the property more desirable to a prospective buyer and thus encourage a faster sale.

Debt Service Ratio
The **debt service ratio (DSR)** is a lender's preferred measurement of a property's ability to pay its mortgage debts, not the borrower's ability to make the payments. Many investment property loans give the lender the right to step in and begin collecting the rent and other revenues if the borrower defaults on the loan. In some cases this right is available after default and a complete foreclosure is not required. So the DSR lets the lender gauge whether the property can support itself with decent management.

Two elements are required to calculate the property's DSR: its net operating income (NOI) and the projected loan payments. The DSR is the net operating income (NOI) divided by the projected loan payments (debt servicing).

Most lenders seek a minimum DSR of 1.2, which means that the net operating income should be large enough to cover the mortgage payments, and provide an additional 20% buffer. If the DSR is too low, the lender will lower the loan amount that it would be willing to lend. This would mean that the borrower will have to make up the difference, with a bigger down payment.

Most real estate investors do not really use the DSR themselves, but they are all familiar with it, since many banks and commercial lenders depend on it. Note that lowering the loan amount is only one way to increase the DSR ratio. The other way is to increase the net operating income by either lowering the expenses or increasing the revenue.

For example, the current owner/seller may have set rents too low, which may explain why the DSR is also low. Fortunately, the appraisal report will provide a market survey of average rents in the area for similar units. Most lenders will allow the buyer to use these market rents to calculate the property's projected NOI, thus allowing the DSR to increase.

Calculating DSR
(The following figures will all be calculated on the following pages so you can see where the numbers are coming from.)

Gross operating income	$39,920
Operating expenses	$18,050
Net operating income (NOI)	$21,870
Projected loan payments	$16,000
Projected DSR (NOI divided by the payments)	1.37

The Development Market's Cycle

Successful real estate investment and development requires good timing. Decades of modem study have uncovered a clear pattern or cycle that seems to govern most real estate markets, assuming they are exposed to normal market conditions.

Understanding this cycle will help an investor make better investment decisions. The duration, shape and severity of the different stages of the cycle will vary for each area and market, but industry professionals tend to recognize a four-part cycle that controls the supply of real estate.

- **Absorption**   Coming out of the down cycle, when construction has slowed or ceased, the market is able to absorb the existing supply of real estate. As occupancy rates increase, prices may begin to follow.

- **New Construction**   Many developers may not be able to predict areas or periods of future high demand, but they usually know it when it finally arrives. The new construction cycle generates construction to meet rising or perceived demand.

- **Saturation**   This stage begins as soon as supply has clearly over-shot demand. As such, vacancy rates begin to increase and prices may begin to plateau or actually decrease, as the market becomes a buyer's market. This is obviously not a good time to start a project that will only add unneeded supply in the face of lackluster demand.

- **Down**   The line between the saturation and down cycle stages is a blurred one, but investors know when they are in a down cycle stage. There is already too much supply to meet existing demand. High or increasing vacancy rates will force developers to slow or stop new developments.

Real estate investors, especially developers, must understand where their target area falls within this development cycle before they invest in existing or new supply. Even if demand is high, values can stagnate or still decline if the incoming supply is too great in relation to that demand.

Investors must understand this cycle when seeking to buy investment property. The investor's objectives and tactics must be grounded in such understanding. If the investor is seeking an investment with strong rental income, the best deals are often found during the new construction and early market saturation stage.

Investors seeking appreciation profit can find potential investments in all four stages, but the thinking must adapt to each stage. Nevertheless, many speculative investors focus only on areas that are in the absorption stage or late down markets—when there is strong potential for new development and construction. Smart investors may also enter during the new construction stage, if they can time their entry just right. Few investors will enter the late saturation stage, unless they spot an underperforming property.

Net Operating Income

A common method to determine the value of income producing property is to use the **projected net operating income** as the basis to calculate the value. This approach estimates the present worth of future benefits from ownership of a property by looking at the property's capacity to continue producing an income

.

The process of calculating a property's present worth on the basis of its capacity to continue producing an income stream is called **capitalization**. This process converts the future income stream into an indication of the property's present worth. The expected future income and expenses of a property are evaluated to determine its present value.

The investor, however, must determine how large and how reliable the income is, and how long the income stream will last. There are five basic steps to determine a property's present worth using the capitalization approach.

1. Calculate the annual gross income

The gross income is the total annual income from the property, minus any vacancy or rental losses. That includes rental income, plus any other income generated by the property, such as laundry room income or parking fees. Loss of income because of a vacant unit is known as the vacancy factor. Current market rents are used to determine the loss from the vacancy factor. Market rent is the rent the property should bring in the open market, while contract rent is the actual, or contracted, rent being paid by the tenants.

2. Determine operating expenses

Expenses are generally classified as being either fixed or variable. Fixed expenses are expenses such as property taxes and insurance, while variable expenses include management, maintenance and utilities.

3. Calculate net operating income

The key to this method is in correctly determining the net operating income. Starting with the annual gross income, which includes all revenues generated by the property, including rent, laundry income, late fees and parking charges (less an annual vacancy factor or any rental losses) we would subtract the operating expenses to calculate the net operating income (NOI).

The NOI is the annual gross income minus the operating expenses, as we have seen. Again, the NOI does not include mortgage and other debt servicing payments in its calculation, nor does the NOI take into account capital improvements and acquisition costs. The operative term is "operating." The net operating income consists of the annual gross income less the operating expenses.

Rental income	$32,000	
Laundry income	$3,500	
Penalties and late fees	$1,000	
Storage and parking	$3,300	
Interest income	$120	
Gross Operating Income		$39,920
Maintenance and repairs	$4,000	
Supplies and janitorial	$2,200	
Scavenger	$900	
Utilities	$3,400	
Advertising / promotion	$250	
Administrative costs	$6,300	
Tax and license cost	$300	
Insurance	$700	
Operating Expenses		$18,050
Net Operating Income (NOI)		$21,870

4. Select a capitalization rate (cap rate)

The **cap rate** provides a handy tool for comparing different types of real estate investments. It allows the investor to make a sound choice between putting money in the purchase of a shopping mall or an office building, between a farm or a car wash. The cap rate is a simple calculation involving two elements: the purchase price (or value) and the net operating income (NOI). The cap rate is calculated by dividing the NOI by the property's price.

The capitalization rate is the rate of interest which is considered a reasonable return on an investment, and it is used in the process of determining value based on net income. It may also be described as the yield rate that is necessary to attract the money of the average investor to a particular kind of investment. In the case of property with improvements (as opposed to raw land), depreciation is a factor taken into consideration in the recapture of the initial investment. The capitalization rate provides for the return of invested capital plus a return on the investment. A capitalization rate is designed to reflect the recapture of the original investment over the economic life of the improvement (building), to give the investor an acceptable rate of return on the original investment and to provide for the return of the invested equity.

The rate is dependent upon the return a buyer will demand before investing money in the property, and it measures the risk involved. For example, the greater the risk of not making a profit, the higher the cap rate and the lower the price will be. The lower the risk, the lower the cap rate and the higher the price of the property will be.

Example

Deb wants to buy a piece of land in Santa Barbara. The land currently is being leased to a luxury car dealership on a 25 year lease, generating $250,000 annually for the owner. Currently the only expense the landowner has is property taxes, which amount to roughly $25,000 per year. The property has a Net Operating Income of $225,000 yearly. The current owner wants to sell the property for $4.5 million. This would mean a cap rate of 5%

Projected NOI $225,000

Purchase Price $4.5 million

$4,500,000 divided by $225,000 = $20,000 or 5%

For many investors, a 5% cap rate is too low. But the cap rate is primarily used for income-producing properties. So a low cap rate may be acceptable for investors who are speculating on future values. For example, this same $4.5 million property may he worth more than $10 million in 10 years. In that case, the low cap rate would be acceptable if the investor can handle the carrying costs.

For most investors, their due diligence (inspection and investigation of the property) will involve a lot of time confirming the true cap rate. The following is a step-by-step guide to verifying a property's true capitalization rate

- Confirm rental rates
- Confirm vacancy rate
- Confirm all other income sources
- Check cap rates in new listings and real estate advertising
- Calculate gross operating income (make sure to deduct vacancy rate)
- Confirm past operating expenses
- Investigate deferred maintenance expenses to be absorbed
- Calculate net operating income (NOI)
- Calculate capitalization rate

5. Divide the net income by the chosen capitalization rate to determine market value

After calculating the annual gross income, determining operating expenses, calculating net operating income and selecting a capitalization rate, the investor divides the net income by the chosen cap rate to determine the present market value of the property in question.

Operating Expenses

As the name suggests, operating expenses include all regular expenses associated with the running of a property. They include trash collection, janitorial, maintenance and management services, as well as utilities, fees, service contracts, supplies, taxes, insurance and advertising. The underlying theme to operating expenses is that they are costs involved with the day-to-day operations of the investment.

It is also necessary for the beginning investor to understand the difference between operating expenses and those expenditures for the property that are not operating expenses. Just because money is spent on a property does not make that expenditure an operating expense. Understanding this difference could mean thousands of dollars in additional cash refunds from an investor's tax withholdings.

One misconception that new investors have is thinking that operating expenses include mortgage payments and other debt servicing. Not all properties have a mortgage lien against them, and mortgages are actually part of the acquisition cost, not the operating cost. The table on page 431 is a breakdown of typical costs which are considered operating expenses and others that are not.

As you can see, capital improvements are separated from operating expenses. Unlike repairs, which serve to maintain the property's current value, capital improvements are additional investments made to the property that will increase its value. For example, building additions, major renovations and installation of a security system are considered capital improvements, because they add to the value of the property. This distinction between repairs and capital improvements becomes very important when income taxes and capital gains come into play.

Accurate identification of operating expenses is important for real estate investors, primarily because the operating expenses are necessary to determine the net operating income. Investors who are investing in real estate for its cash flow and income profits need to examine operating expenses carefully.

Operating expenses are those costs that the investor can reasonably expect during the ownership of the property. A property's income stream and operating profits are improved in one of two ways: increasing revenue or lowering operating expenses. Experienced investors will often focus on the operating expenses—looking for potential reductions and savings—when analyzing a potential cash flow investment.

Another advantage with understanding the difference involves actual dollars and cents the investor can get through depreciation. The building fixtures and equipment, though not the land, can be depreciated. The process of calculating depreciation is discussed at the beginning of this chapter.

OPERATING EXPENSES	NON—OPERATING EXPENSES
Maintenance and janitorial	Acquisition (closing) costs
Repair and decoration	Mortgages and debt servicing
Service contract	Capital improvements
Supplies	Equipment and fixtures
Trash pickup	
Management fees	
Accounting and administrative services	
Advertising and leasing services	
Insurance premiums	
Real estate and corporate taxes	
Government fees and licenses	
Utilities (paid by owner)	

Return on Investment

The return on investment (ROI) is a calculation of the property's true earnings, with the emphasis on the meaning of "true." The ROI compares what the investor has put into the property and what that same investor has gotten out of it. The ROI tries to provide a big picture analysis of the property's profitability. For investors, the ROI describes how well or poorly they are investing their money.

The ROI can be used on both rental properties and speculative investments. Moreover, it can be used to compare all types of potential investments, not just real estate. The smart investor can use it to compare a stock purchase against a real estate investment.

Would the investor be better off putting a $20,000 bonus in the company's stock plan or in the purchase of a ranch? For income-producing properties, the ROI is basically the net earnings divided by the capital investments made by the investor.

To calculate the return on the investment, you must divide the projected returns into the capital investment, or the down payment or other cash input into the property, simply referred to as the capital investment.

ROI = Projected returns / Capital investment

The projected return is figured by adding net operating income with the property's appreciation in value, less any debt service (loan service).

A 25% ROI is a very good prospect, particularly for a one-year investment. Compare that to a CD that at best would garner you 4.5% (2002), or an S&P-based mutual fund generating less than 10% return.

Unfortunately, not all real estate investments are so rosy. A decrepit property may require lots of additional capital improvements and outlays from the investor. The unprepared investor may be lucky to get out of the investment with a small loss. In such a case, that very safe 4.50% CD begins to look very attractive indeed.

Again, the return on investment describes the property's true earnings. But there are also different ways to measure ROI and subsets of ROI measurements, such as the internal rate of return or the equity dividend rate.

Another way to look at and use the ROI calculation is to consider how quickly an investor can get his or her money back. Here's a concept that all beginning real estate investors must quickly realize: there are risks in all investments, but the quicker you get your investment back, the lower your risk of losing any of it.

When considering a potential investment's ROI, an investor should never consider that ROI calculation in a vacuum. It must be compared with other, possibly safer, ROI investments, such as CDs and savings accounts. The ROI must also be adjusted for other factors, both tangible and intangible, that are often overlooked.

- **Liquidity**   How long will it take and how much will it cost an investor to liquidate the investment? Real estate is a non-liquid hard asset that often takes weeks, if not months, to sell, while it can take less than 10 minutes to liquidate a CD. The ROI must be adjusted to account for the cost of selling, as well as the time involved.

- **Management**   How much is an investor's time worth? Certain investments require more time from the investor than other investments. Unfortunately, many investors fail to understand the value of their time. A CD may only be earning 5%, but the investor doesn't have to do any work. Real estate holdings may be generating 10%, but if an investor has to spend 20 hours a week on the property, it may mean losing money. Putting it another way, if an investor spent that 20 hours a week at a second job, earning a steady income, how much would the individual earn? If the absence of that hypothetical second job was considered an operating expense, how much would that drag down the overall ROI?

- **Risk**   What are the odds that the investor will lose money? Risk is an intangible element, but it is all too real for accountants, actuaries and investors. An investor has almost no risk at all with CDs, which accounts for their low rate of interest. In comparison, junk bonds are very risky and so must promise higher returns. To investors who understand and can carry the risk, the pursuit of higher returns may be worthwhile. For others, it could be unacceptable.

There may be other factors, such as tax deductions and special grants, which also affect the overall ROI. Experienced investors must look at properties over their entire investment period—from the purchase to the final resale, with everything in between.

What separates the one successful real estate investor from the nine or so other investors who lost money in real estate? Luck is often a factor. But for the serious, long-term investor, the main factor is knowledge of the different ways to make (and lose) money in any particular real estate project.

There are many ways to make money through real estate investing, and there are probably many more that have not yet been designed or uncovered. As mentioned at the start of this chapter, successful real estate investing depends on knowing how you plan to generate profits and avoid expenses.

This section introduces the most common, as well as some less common, profit-generating tactics available to real estate investors.

- Collateral
- Development
- Income stream
- Master lease
- Options
- Subdivision
- Tax free exchanges
- Tax shelters
- Value appreciation

Not all tactics are applicable to all properties. Some properties use several strategies at once to generate profits for the investor. The choice of tactics always depends on the subject property. The successful investor will be the one who can look at a piece of property and understand what its profit potential is and which tactics will unlock that potential.

There is one recommendation that fits all real estate investments: never fall in love with a property. Such properties will usually result in losses or severely depressed profits. Real estate investment requires objective decisions. Unfortunately, many novice investors become so infatuated with a specific piece of property that they completely lose objectivity. The best way to approach real estate investing is to start with a plan that works for you as an individual, then find a property that fits into that plan. An investor should avoid starting with the property, then trying to fit the plan to that property.

Collateral

A very common, but often overlooked, reason for investing in real estate is to build **collateral** for future investments. The value of real estate is widely recognized and accepted by the market. Lenders are more lenient and generous to borrowers with real estate holdings, because real estate is considered highly useful collateral.

For many consumers, the chief purpose of their only real estate holding is to provide a home for their families. Our homes actually offer much more. Americans who own real estate have a multitude of opportunities available to them that are not available to typical renters. The reason is that real estate provides the owner with a collateral instrument. Even if the property is highly mortgaged, it can still be used as collateral for more debt.

Many commercial and small business banks are often more willing to lend money to borderline enterprises, if the business owners agree to use their real estate properties as collateral for the loan.

> *Collateral Example*
> *Jennifer runs a surf retail/repair store. Business is booming, and she needs to expand. Unfortunately, the bank has reservations about lending to Jennifer, because her credit shows a few late payments, she has owned the surf shop for only two years, and the retail industry in general is always somewhat risky. The bank offers to provide the loan if Jennifer agrees to allow the bank to place a lien against her home. Jennifer is able to get her needed financing, by using her real estate as collateral.*
>
> *Of course, if her business fails, the business loan will remain as a lien against her home until it is paid off. But if Jennifer didn't own property, she would have a more difficult time obtaining a business loan. A possible alternative: if Jennifer owned other property, she could elect to have the lien placed against that property.*

Real estate can still be used as collateral for a loan, even if it has no equity available. The value of real estate goes beyond its resale or appraised value. Consider that the property's income stream is also a valuable asset that is often included in the use of real estate as collateral. For example, Fred takes out a mortgage loan on a piece of farmland that he rents out to a local farmer; if he ever defaults, his mortgage allows the bank to start collecting the rental income to offset the unpaid loan payments.

Some **Real Estate Investment Trusts (REITs)** function in a similar manner. The trust is a security instrument sold to investors; the trust itself can be collateralized by the income generated by the properties underpinning the REIT.

Another use of this collateral tactic is to create a chain-reaction acquisition scheme. When property is being used for or considered as collateral, the investor's primary responsibility will be maintaining that collateral's value. This task obviously begins with basic maintenance. The property's value, however, is affected more by its locale and location. The investor must therefore stay attuned to developments in the neighborhood and market area. Crime prevention, street improvements, zoning, new developments and tax issues will all affect the property's value, and property investors must remain aware, if not involved, to make sure that their property values are not damaged.

Development   The big money in real estate investment is most often generated through development. It is also lost there. Development entails creating or evolving an existing piece of property to a real estate project with greater market value. This may involve subdividing, or keeping the property in one piece and building on it.

Development may entail immediately selling the property upon completion, or keeping it long-term for its income stream. There are many types of developers in the real estate market today.

- **Converters**   Some developers avoid massive from-the-ground-up construction projects and focus on changing the property's use or type. For example, converters may change a factory building into stylish offices or an apartment building into condominiums.

- **Fee Developers**   Many developers do not develop their own land; instead they are hired by the property owner to develop, market, and/or manage the owner's real estate. For such developers, the risk exposure is much lower than if they were tackling their own project.

- **Land Developers**   Some developers prefer to focus on just the land preparation portion of a development project. Land developers will typically develop the land's infrastructure—such as sewers, streets and utilities— usually after subdividing the property. The prepared parcels are then sold to buyers, who will be responsible for developing their separate parcels. For example, industrial land developers may subdivide 500 acres of land into 25-acre parcels, with wide streets for semi-trucks and adequate sewers and utilities to meet the needs of manufacturers and industrial tenants.

- **Merchant Builders**   To minimize their risk exposure, many developers do not start or complete projects until they have a commitment from a buyer to purchase the completed development. Merchant builders typically develop properties for immediate resale after completion, usually with a firm commitment from the eventual buyer. For example, XYZ Home Builders are developing several parcels they own in a subdivision. Before they begin custom construction, however, the buyer must obtain a purchase loan commitment.

- **Renovators**   Similar to converters, renovators or rehabbers seek to upgrade, improve or modify a property's condition, with the goal of establishing higher value. The most widely recognized form of this approach is the rehabbers who buy cheap properties, fix them up and resell them for profit.

- **Speculative Developers**   Major developers willing to accept greater risk exposure will sometimes develop properties without any commitments from potential tenants or buyers. They are speculating that the market will have a demand for their real estate.

As you can surmise from the review of the different types of developers, there are different types of development projects. In a sense, practically all real estate investors wear the hat of developer. But beginning real estate investors should avoid major development projects without strong outside support, as the risks are as tremendous as any potential rewards.

Income Stream
Many people buy investment real estate to generate additional income for themselves. Success for such investors means positive cash flow, or profits, from the property's operation. That's easier said than done, for most consumers.

If an investor is interested in finding properties that can generate a solid income stream, the following four issues are critical to a successful venture.

- Understanding cash flow

- Improving cash flow

- Recognizing profit-generating properties

- Finding underperforming properties

Understanding Cash Flow
On a practical level, a property's rental income and other revenue must exceed its operating costs and debt servicing. Unfortunately, many novice investors fail to understand that there are two types of cash flow figures.

- **Pre-Tax Cash Flow**   The cash flow calculation before taxes due for the investment project are calculated

- **After-Tax Profits**   The net profits from an investment after taxes have been deducted

Many investors find it easy to ignore the tax implications of their investments, often because income taxes do not provide a billing statement like operating expenses do. But the bill will finally come, unless the investor takes steps to reduce the impact of income taxes.

Investors should focus more on the after-tax cash flow as the measure of the property's real profits. Depending on the precautions the investor takes, the after-tax profits can be close to, or even improve upon, pre-tax cash flow.

When analyzing the cash flow of a prospective or current purchase, real estate investors must examine the project's operating expenses, net operating income, rate of return, and capitalization rate. Experienced investors have learned never to accept the seller's estimates at face value. Sellers always try to put the best spin on their properties' numbers in order to make the sale more attractive. Investors should always insist on sufficient documentation, before making any final decisions.

- **Profit and Loss (P&L) Statement**   It is a common practice for sellers of apartment buildings and other commercial properties that are currently generating rental income to provide an annual profit and loss (P&L) statement for the property. Unfortunately, this usually does not apply to smaller two- to four-unit properties. Investors should request a previous year P&L, as well as a year-to-date P&L statement.

- **Rent Roll and Leases**   The income figures on the P&L statement should be supported by rent rolls and, preferably, lease agreements and deposit receipts. When no leases are available, some investors have their attorneys request all of the seller's tenants to sign estoppel statements, confirming their current rent status. Whenever possible, the buyer should try to ascertain the vacancy rates and history of the rental units.

- **Service Contracts**   Service contracts are standard elements for most building operation, especially for trash pick-up, elevators and some leasing services.

- **Utility Bills**   The seller should provide copies of utility bills for at least a 12-month period on those utilities that the property owner (landlord) must cover. These utilities have to be factored into the operating expenses.

- **Appraisal Reports**   The investor's lender will order an appraisal report for the property, which will survey market averages for the property's area. The investor should ask the lender for a copy, so the investor can understand what the prevailing rates for the area are.

- **Professional Inspections**   The investor has the right, in most cases, to conduct a professional inspection of the property. An experienced inspector, with an engineering background, can point out deferred maintenance and potential expenses that the investor may eventually face.

Improving Cash Flow

A thorough verification of the property's income and expenses is important, because it points to the two ways that any investor can maintain or improve cash flow.

- **Lower Expenses**   Slashing costs, without affecting quality, is the quickest way to improving a property's cash flow. Economies of scale (i.e., bulk purchases) and negotiating with service providers are effective methods for immediate results.

- **Increase Income**   Somewhat more difficult, but just as important, for successful cash flow management is increasing the property's revenue. For most properties, increasing income will primarily revolve around increasing rent rates and lowering vacancies. Experienced investors, however, must also consider alternative income sources, such as laundry income, garage rental and storage spaces.

Improving cash flow generates another benefit that is often overlooked when the investor's primary focus is the income stream: appreciation. Increasing profits will typically increase value, because the value of most income-generating investments is based on their profits, or net operating income (NOI).

Increased equity cannot be counted in the property's cash flow statement. Nevertheless, it is still there. When investors are primarily or only concentrating on the property's income stream, they often fail to consider the property's potential for value appreciation. A property may have a poor income stream and not seem worthy of purchase, but when appreciation rates in the area are considered, that same property may look like a gold mine.

The bottom line when considering income stream as a tactic is the bottom line. Investors who seek an income stream will need to be property managers, or hire and supervise a manager. Either way, that investor must keep an eye on the bottom line. Cash flow management will require the investor to always run all prospective expenses and investments through a cost-benefit analysis first, unless those repairs or improvements are absolutely necessary: what will this expense cost, and what benefit will it generate?

Investing for income stream is difficult, but still feasible, for small investors. Larger investors may be more successful, because they can save money through economies of scale. The more rental units an investor owns and manages, the less each unit will (or should) cost on a per-unit basis.

This should not discourage novice investors, however, because even large investors start small. Disciplined management and thorough preparation can ensure better odds for success, regardless of the investor's resources and experience. Before undertaking this tactic, investors should first ask themselves, "Do I have the discipline needed to be successful entrepreneur?"

Recognizing Profit-Generating Properties
Here's a somewhat discouraging piece of news: few two-to-four-unit residential properties listed for sale in America's urban centers generate enough rental income to cover their operating expenses and debt servicing. Worse still, most of those properties are in deteriorating and often undesirable areas. The situation is somewhat better with larger properties.

It seems that rental rates have not kept pace with increases in real estate prices. Still, there are opportunities to be found for those willing to search for them. The trick is to find those few properties that actually have a positive cash flow, after paying the mortgage. It comes down to the investor who must ultimately find the profitable investment, but only after becoming knowledgeable about the entire process from start to finish.

Learning how to recognize these properties is the bottom line of investing, after all is said and done. Also, after locating a property, the investor must be willing to trust his or her instincts, and research and make the offer. The following are some due diligence tips to help the investor separate the good from the bad investment.

- **The 1% Rule** A rule of thumb that some investors use is the 1% rule—to break even, the property's monthly income should be at least one percent of the sales price. This is useful when skimming through several potential properties. Be warned, however, that this is a rule of thumb that assumes average expenses, properties and markets.

- **Focus on the NOI** As you become more serious about a specific property, you must begin to focus on its annual net operating income (NOI). You must concentrate your due diligence on verifying the property's true NOI—never take the seller's word for it.

- **Cap Rate** The NOI should lead you to the capitalization rate—NOI divided by the price. If your goal is positive cash flow, you want a minimum cap rate of 10%. Single-digit cap rates should be avoided, unless you are primarily looking at the value appreciation.

Finding Underperforming Properties
Assuming that the investor understands how to distinguish properties with profitable income streams, the next logical step is finding those properties. Technology and a dynamic real estate market make this easier than one would think.

The following are several suggestions for uncovering underperforming properties.

- **Low Rents** Ignore metropolitan rent averages. Real estate investment is about location, location and location. For example, average rent for a two-bedroom in the city of Chicago may be $750; but some areas can easily demand $1,500, while some areas can't find tenants at $350. Search by areas—after researching average rent rates—and look for listings that have low rent rates and the potential for quick increases.

- **Below Median Price** Interested in something that you can buy and sell right away? First, target an area that has an active market, in which average marketing time is under 60 days. Then calculate the median price level in that target area for common property types (two-flats, single-family homes, etc.). Then concentrate on those properties whose asking price is below the median. If you find a good property in the bunch, there is a good chance that you can resell it at a price near or above the median, perhaps with a little cosmetic work.

- **Poor Management**   Some properties are underperforming because of poor management. A more dedicated, informed and organized investor can do wonders with such properties. Look for properties in promising areas that appear unkempt or ill-managed, and use that condition to your advantage.

- **Distress**   One way to increase the capitalization rate is to lower the sales price. Sellers in distress, foreclosure, bankruptcy or financial pressures are often willing to cut their asking price to drastic levels for a quick sale. However, an investor might need to be able to close right away.

- **Aggressive Advertising**   Usually, it is only the property sellers who advertise. This puts creative real estate investors in an advantageous position, as they don't have too many competitors. Use classified ads and flyers to get the word out that you are looking to buy property. Possible message: "Investor looking to buy; can close right away." The people replying to such a message probably will be in distress and would be willing to cooperate if the investor can close immediately. The investor, in turn, must be able to close immediately, and will need a firm mortgage pre-approval.

- **Spreadsheet Listings**   The Web and many Multiple Listing Services (MLS) now allow real estate agents to download all rental properties that meet your search criteria. These files can then be arranged in a spreadsheet to automatically calculate the NOI, mortgage payment and cap rate for each property. They can then be sorted based on the cap rate and neighborhood.

Master Lease

Smart real estate investors do not have to own a property in order to profit from it. The **master lease** is a tactic anyone can use to obtain possession of a property and use it to their profit for a limited period.

The master lease can and should be legally recorded, so that public notice is given to any prospective buyer of the property. Of course, the basic lease will not give a tenant the right to sell or otherwise encumber the property. Some leases do contain an option to purchase, which would be an extra bonus for the buyer/lessee.

Purchase Options

The **option instrument** is a little known tool with powerful choices for real estate investors. Usually called an **option to purchase**, the option instrument gives the real estate investor the right to purchase a piece of property, usually for a set price, to take advantage of increases in appraised market value.

This ability to set the price for a long period of time is perhaps the primary benefit that purchase options offer to the beginning investor. Successful real estate investors can exploit the equity difference between the option's set price and the property's actual market value. Investors can exploit the equity difference between the option's set price and the property's actual market value.

Subdivision

Sometimes the whole is greater than the sum of its parts. Real estate occasionally offers opportunities for the parts to be worth much more than the unified whole. That is the theory behind the tactic of subdivision. The real estate investor acquires property, cuts it up and sells the pieces for much more than the original purchase price.

The most common examples of subdivision have occurred through much of modern history whenever raw land was subdivided into smaller plots to meet the needs of a growing town or city. It continues today. Investors purchase farmland or open land and legally subdivide it into smaller parcels that are then sold to potential home builders. In such cases, subdividing normally entails the following steps.

- **Survey**   A property survey is conducted that provides for a graphic subdivision of the parcels. This survey will create a plat that establishes the boundary of each parcel, as the greater property is subdivided.

- **Easements**   The plat must be designed to provide adequate easements for all of the parcels. Easements must be provided for streets, utilities, sidewalks and other necessary access. Remember that basic property laws provide that no parcel of land be landlocked, so that the property owner must always have access to and egress from his or her parcel.

- **Legal Subdivision**   Establishing legally separated parcels involves having the subdivision plan approved and recorded by the local governing body. Subdivision and land development is now strictly controlled, as many areas have discovered too late the true cost of uncontrolled growth. Through their plat approval powers and impact fees, cities ensure minimum sewer, curb and other regulatory requirements.

In most cases, the developer undertaking a residential subdivision will build the streets, sewers, main utility lines, curbs and other elements throughout the entire project. The individual parcel buyers/owners will be responsible for building and improving their parcels. Sometimes, such as in large rural subdivisions, the developer may only establish a dirt road to the parcel entrances.

A recently more prevalent example of subdivision in urban areas has been the condominium conversion, whereby an apartment complex is subdivided into individually owned units. Condominiums demonstrate the evolution of property laws not by subdividing the land—which essentially remains intact—but by subdividing the project's air spaces.

Subdivision development can be highly profitable; the past few paragraphs have only provided a brief introduction.

Tax-Deferred Exchanges

Investors face capital gains taxes on their profits from the sale of real estate, and these capital gain taxes can be significant. However, investors have a way to defer paying any capital gains by selling their property through a trade. IRS tax codes only assess taxes on capital gains realized from a sale of property.

Through a 1031 exchange, investors can defer capital gains taxes if they trade their property—instead of selling it—for a like-kind property. The courts have taken a very lenient approach to the term "like-kind," so any type of real estate can be exchanged for any other type of real estate, as long as it is investment real estate. Cars can be traded for cars, and jewelry can be traded for jewelry.

With 1031 "Starker" exchanges, the seller/exchanger must identify the target property within 45 days of the sale of the current property. The exchanger can target up to three potential properties of any (unlimited) market value, subject to final decision. Moreover, the exchanger must receive title to that target property within 180 days of the sale of the original property. Note that sellers who are in the midst of the 180-day period should not file their tax returns—but instead ask for an extension.

Tax Shelters

Real estate no longer offers the tax shelters to institutional investors that it formerly did. Prior to the 1980s, institutional investors actively sought real estate that could provide a paper loss, which the investor could then use to offset income from other sources. Changes to the tax code have minimized or eliminated many such tax shelters, but tax advantages still remain with real estate investments.

Real estate investors can exploit tax advantages in three general areas

1. Operating losses
2. Capital gain
3. Depreciation

Operating Losses

Actively managing and operating a real estate investment is, for all practical and legal purposes, operating a business. As such, real estate investments that declare profit are taxed on that income; on the other hand, real estate investments that declare losses avoid taxes, and can sometimes use those losses to offset income in other investments. Current tax codes distinguish between passive and active income, as well as between passive and active losses. Losses from passive investments, such as most stocks, bonds and some real estate investments, can only be deducted against income from similar passive investments. They cannot be used to offset income from active endeavors, such as primary employment and personally owned and operated businesses.

This is not an issue for most beginning real estate investors, because their real estate investments are usually active income and losses. Such investors can use declared losses from their real estate investments to offset their taxable income.

Capital Gains

When investors sell their investment—whether stocks, bonds, a business or real estate—they must pay capital gains tax on the resale profit. However, there are methods for deferring these capital gains taxes.

All serious real estate investors should be aware of how capital gains may affect them. An old saying about investing is that building wealth is often not so much about how much you make, but how much you keep.

In most cases consumers only pay capital gains tax on investment properties. If a consumer is selling a property that qualifies as a primary residence (having lived in it for at least two years out of the past five years), he or she can qualify for a capital gains tax exemption. For sole owners, a capital gains exemption of up to $250,000 is allowed, with joint owners allowed exemptions of up to $500,000 on their primary residence. Recent tax changes have made this available to all homeowners once every two years.

Depreciation

For real estate investors, depreciation is perhaps one of the most important deductions to understand. Through the concept of depreciation, properties that earn a marginal profit can be made to look as if they were just breaking even or losing money. Moreover, even though a property may be appreciating in value, the investor can still deduct for the property's depreciation.

Beginners can best understand the concept of depreciation by considering a small business that has bought a new drilling machine for $10,000. This machine, according to the IRS, may have a useful life of five years. As each year passes, the drilling machine will lose some of its value. For example, by the second year, it may only be worth $8,000. If the business is allowed to depreciate the cost of this machine over five years, that business can write off $2,000 per year on its tax returns. Depreciation is not allowed on land. However, depreciation is allowed on improvements to the land, such as buildings and other developments. The amount of depreciation is governed by IRS-issued tables. Residential real estate properties are currently depreciated over 27.5 years, while commercial real estate is depreciated over 39 years, depending on when the real estate was purchased and placed into service.

Note that depreciation does not restrict appreciation. The strange thing about real estate is that the property's value will often continue to appreciate, even while the investor is deducting depreciation. There is one minor drawback with taking depreciation. When an investor sells the property, he or she has to add the total dollar amount of depreciation taken to the cost basis of the property, making the amount of the capital gain larger by the amount of the depreciation. But this is negligible for three reasons.

1. **Time Value of Money**   The money that an investor gets today from depreciation deductions is worth much more than the "paper" money that he or she has to add back to the cost basis later.

2. **Depreciation Tax Rate vs. Capital Gain Rate**   Remember that long-term capital gains are taxed at about 20%, currently. Meanwhile, depreciation deductions recapture funds in the investor's tax bracket. If you're in the 28% bracket, you're still coming out ahead by 8%.

3. **Capital Gains Deferral**   Through a trade or exchange transaction, an investor can defer capital gains indefinitely into the future.

One way an investor can conservatively take advantage of the depreciation deduction is to take the profits from those deductions and put them into high-yield CDs or market funds. When the investor finally sells the property, the investor will discover that the capital gains hit on the added-back depreciation is more than offset by the income from the depreciation deduction funds.

Value Appreciation

Many real estate investors are speculators, betting that they will be able to resell their property for much more than their purchase (and carrying) cost. The great thing about this approach is that most speculators do almost nothing with the property.
At best, they are land speculators trying to anticipate a potential development trend. At worst, they are poor investors, trying to squeeze every dime from a piece of property.

Other speculators are more proactive in increasing the value of their property. Some land speculators may survey and subdivide the larger parcel, while others may go further and begin initial development with sewer access, water lines and roads. Such speculators are actually partaking in development.

All of these real estate investors share a common tactic of pursuing potential appreciation. In truth, history is very supportive of such speculators. Although some areas have experienced reduction of property value, these periods are usually the result of a preceding boom that went too far, and the reduction periods tend to be short. In the long run, the value of real estate has continued on a steady march upwards—for practically all properties. The value of all real estate has continued to increase over the centuries, especially in areas of increasing population density.

Note that there is a relatively finite supply of real estate, at least until we begin colonizing other planets on a major scale. As such, the price of real estate—and thus its value—is really controlled by demand.

S U M M A R Y

We examined real estate investments in depth, looking at the opportunities and issues with investing. People invest in real estate primarily to meet personal goals, for the economic soundness of the investment and to meet their financial commitments.

Investors are generally looking for a good return on their investment, realized in cash flow, return on taxes and appreciation of the property. Investors are looking for high returns on their investment to make this type of investing feasible over other types.

The stages of the investment process take people through planning, gathering resources, targeting the most desirable property, negotiating terms and closing the purchase by taking over the property. It is important for investors to utilize all resources at their disposal, including contacts for advice when making a large investment.

A good investor will use all tools at his or her disposal in the form of analysis to find the properties profitability. Not doing the appropriate analysis may get the investor into a less-than-desirable property, and not achieve a very high rate of return on the investment.

Finally we looked at tactics that investors typically use when considering an investment property. These tactics include collateral, development, income stream, master lease, options, subdivision, tax free exchanges, and tax shelters.

T E R M S   A N D   P H R A S E S

Appreciation   the increase in value over the original investment

Cash Flow   net income generated by a property before depreciation and other non-cash expenses

Leverage   ratio of debt to current value

Liquidity   ability to generate cash from an investment in a hurry

Syndication   association of people, formed for the purpose of conducting and carrying out some particular business transaction where each member has mutual interest

Tax Shelter   tax laws allow special consideration for the real estate investor who desires to take advantage of allowable depreciation schedules, capital gain privileges, tax-deferred ex-changes, and other benefits

Yield   amount the investor makes on the capital invested during the time the investment is held

1. Which of the following is not a reason for investing in real estate
   a. objectives.
   b. capacity.
   c. availability.
   d. soundness.

2. Which of the following is a type of return on investment?
   a. Return on taxes
   b. Appreciation
   c. Cash flow
   d. All of the above

3. Depreciation is based on
   a. deterioration of the structure.
   b. useful life of the property.
   c. age of structure.
   d. all of the above.

4. 1031 Exchanges involves
   a. like-kind property.
   b. no gain's or losses recognized.
   c. boot.
   d. all of the above.

5. Which of the following is not a factor in investing?
   a. Cost to rehabilitate the structure
   b. Rent control
   c. Size of structure
   d. Historic tax credits

6. Which one of the following is not one of the stages in investing?
   a. Gathering resources
   b. Computing capital gain
   c. Negotiating terms
   d. Preparation and planning

7. Which of the following documents should you prepare when planning to invest in property?
   a. Complete tax returns for the last 3 years
   b. Landlord contact information to verify rent history and copies of cancelled rent checks for the past 24 months
   c. Most recent two statements for all bank and asset accounts
   d. Both A and C

8. Real estate investments involve a large amount of money, agents, representatives, service providers and others to complete the transaction. Which of the following persons would not be helpful in aiding an investor in his or her transaction?
   a. General contractor
   b. Accountant
   c. Insurance agent
   d. Loan officer

9. Which of the following is not a step in locating the right property?
   a. Review the business plan
   b. Prioritize preferences
   c. Obtain title search on each property
   d. Obtain loan pre-approval

10. A pre-qualification involves
    a. the processing of a full loan application.
    b. is weighted with more importance than a pre-approval.
    c. is the minimum certification an agent will require.
    d. conditional on the borrower finding an acceptable property.

11. Your credit score is
    a. not affected by a creditor running your score.
    b. hurt every time your credit is run.
    c. improved every time your credit is run.
    d. none of the above.

12. Which of the following is not considered a step in making a profitable investment?
    a. Attorney review
    b. Make a smart offer
    c. Prepare a business plan
    d. Updated loan approval

13. Which of the following is a goal of the due diligence investigation?
    a. Calculating the value of the property
    b. Verifying the property's condition, income and expenses
    c. Confirming that it meets the investor's minimum requirements
    d. All of the above

14. A professional inspection of a property will reveal
    a. functional condition.
    b. structural condition.
    c. economical condition.
    d. all of the above.

15. Which of the following steps is not considered a step in a successful purchase?
    a. Relax
    b. Take over
    c. Study
    d. Obtain closing instructions

16. Carrying costs include
    a. purchase price.
    b. operating income.
    c. operating expenses.
    d. all of the above.

17. Which of the following is not one of a development market's cycles?
    a. New Construction
    b. Saturation
    c. Demolition
    d. Absorption

18. Which of the following is considered an operating expense?
    a. Trash collection
    b. Purchase price
    c. Operating income
    d. All of the above

19. All of the following factors affecting return on investment except
    a. liquidity.
    b. risk
    c. cost.
    d. management.

20. Real estate investors can exploit tax advantages which of the following areas?
    a. Operating losses
    b. Depreciation
    c. Capital gain
    d. All of the above

15

REAL ESTATE
M A T H

What you will learn in this Chapter

- Interest

- Time Value of Money

- Payment Schedules

- Prorations on Closing Statements

- Measures of Profitability

- Trust Deed and Mortgage Discounting

Test Your Knowledge

1. Tom borrowed $4,000 for 1 year. He paid $480 in interest. What rate did he pay?
    a. 15%
    b. 12%
    c. 10%
    d. 9%

2. Amy signed a note for $10,000 payable in 12 months. The note had an interest rate of 9% when it was due. The note was later sold to a private investor at a 15% discount. What is the rate of return on the amount invested by the investor?
    a. 25.89%
    b. 28.24%
    c. 32.44%
    d. 35.47%

3. How much money will Julia have in her savings account at the end of year 10, assuming the initial balance is $7,000 with a rate of 4%? (Rounded up)
    a. $9,360
    b. $10,190
    c. $10,360
    d. $11,280

4. What is the present worth of $8,000 10 years from now at a discount rate of 5%? (Rounded to the nearest dollar)
    a. $4,753
    b. $4,825
    c. $4901
    d. $4911

5. A fire insurance policy was prepaid for three years. Assume it is currently September 1, 2004 and the policy will expire November 15, 2005. The policy costs $400 per year. How much of the unused portion of the policy is left?
    a. $521
    b. $501
    c. $497
    d. $483

6. An apartment complex brings in $800 per month per unit, with 9 units. June is interested in purchasing the property as an investment property, and needs a 9% rate of return or capitalization rate. How should June pay for the complex?
    a. $960,000
    b. $80,000
    c. $106,667
    d. $550,000

7. Assuming a fixed cost requirement of $115,000 annually and a variable cost ratio of 19% per rental dollar, the gross income needed to break even would be: (rounded)
    a. $141,158
    b. $141,975
    c. $142,068
    d. $142,687

INTRODUCTION

A great many calculations go into figuring out various factors in real estate finance. How principal and interest are partitioned in mortgage payments and how this varies over time; property taxes; income taxes; insurance premiums; assessments; depreciation; discounts; returns on investments; and other numbers resulting from calculations are all indicators of the risk and potential profitability of investing in real estate or lending funds to buy real estate.

Most homebuyers are initially concerned about the down payment and closing costs, especially if points are involved. Then, they examine the monthly payment as part of their total fixed costs to determine if they can afford the home. Buyers, of course, also study the asking price relative to similar homes in the area, interest on different types of loans, the term length of the loan in connection to the interest rate, property taxes, and insurance premiums to determine their total cost of ownership.

Buyers of commercial property also must consider cash flow and the breakeven point used to estimate their returns on investment. People contemplating commercial property must do a great deal of estimating revenue streams and outlays to determine whether an investment is not only feasible, but eventually profitable, as well.

This chapter reviews methods of calculating interest rates, the time value of money, alternative loan repayment schedules, closing statement prorating, profitability, and discounting mortgages and trust deeds. The rates of interest used in this chapter are for illustration only, and may not reflect current market rates.

INTEREST

Interest can be viewed as rent paid for the use of money. Lenders and investors see interest as money earned in exchange for taking on the risk of accepting responsibility for making a loan. Rent is paid by a tenant and received by a landlord in return for the use of an apartment, house, office, or store under the conditions of a lease. In a similar way, in real estate finance, interest and principal are paid by the borrower and received by the lender under the terms and conditions of a mortgage or trust deed. Money is borrowed (leased) at a certain interest rate (rent) for a specified time period, during which the amount borrowed is repaid.

The rent that a landlord can charge to a tenant depends on the market for that type of real estate—which depends on the supply of such real estate and demand for it. Similarly, the rate of interest that a lender can charge a borrower depends on the money market. A rational borrower pays a lender no more than the lowest interest rate available on a specific loan at the time.

When we borrow money, there is a charge for the use of this money, called interest. The rate charged for the interest is called the **interest rate**, which is a dynamic (i.e., constantly changing) figure. Most payments toward a loan include a monthly interest payment, and a monthly principal amount, combined as one sum. The variables used when solving interest and loan problems are

- Dollar amount of interest (I)
- Principal or the loan amount (P)
- Interest rate (R)
- Number of years the loan will last (length of the loan) (T)

Equations used to solve these problems look like this

- Principal = Dollar amount of interest/(Annual interest rate × Length of the loan) $P = I/(R \times T)$

- Annual Interest Rate = Dollar amount of interest/(Principal × Length of the loan) $R = I/(P \times T)$

- Dollar amount of interest = Principal × Interest Rate × Length of the Loan
  $I = P \times R \times T$

Example 1
Andrew and Tammy borrowed $10,000 for one year, paying $900 in interest. What was the interest rate they paid?

P = $10,000
I = $900
T = 1 year
R = ?
R = $900 / ($10,000 × 1)
R = 9%

Example 2
One month's interest on a five-year, straight interest-only loan is $65. If the interest rate on the note is 10% per year, what is the amount of the loan?

R = 10%
I = $65 / mo, $780 / year
T = 1 year
P = ?
P = I / (R × T)
P = $780 / (10% × 1)
P = $78,000

Add-on Interest

Usually **simple** interest is calculated for real estate loans, but in certain circumstances, a lender may use **add-on** interest. You first determine the total amount of interest on the loan for the entire term of the loan. This interest is then added to the principal owed before the monthly payments are figured out. Usually, this interest calculation appears in home improvement loans and junior liens offered by private mortgage companies. Bottom line, when add-on interest is used, the simple interest rate is just about doubled.

The formula for computing the add-on interest rate (AIR) is

$$2 \, IC \, / \, P(n+1)$$

I = Number of installment payments per year

C = Total loan charge

P = Principal

n = Number of installments in the contract

Note: Parentheses ( ) around terms indicates multiplication of that term with the term just outside the parenthesis; for example, 3(30) = 90

Nominal (Contractual) and Effective (Actual) Rates of Interest

If simple interest is used, the **nominal rate** of interest or the **contracted rate**, is the same as the **effective rate**—the actual rate paid by the borrower. However, if add-on interest is used, then an add-on interest rate of 8% has a nominal rate of 8%, but an actual, or effective, rate, of about 15%—nearly double the nominal rate, as mentioned earlier.

Even if simple interest is used, the nominal rate can be different from the actual rate. For example, let's say a new mortgage loan is made for $100,000, and to get the interest rate, a three point discount fee is charged along with other fees. As a result, the borrower receives only somewhere between $96,000 and $97,000. However, that borrower has to pay interest on the full $100,000 loan, which makes the actual (effective) interest rate higher than the nominal rate.

The secondary mortgage market and bond and government securities markets all operate based on effective interest rates, usually called yields. When the nominal interest rate on the security is less than market interest rates, the security is usually sold at a discount, or for less than its face value, in order to maintain the required yield. In the same way, when nominal rates for securities are higher than market rates, the security commands a premium—or a price above its face value.

Compound Interest

Compound interest essentially is interest paid on interest earned. This is most dramatically demonstrated by looking a compound interest tables and realizing that $1 deposited in a savings account at the beginning of a year at 3% interest results in $1.03

balance in the account at the end of the year ($1.00 × 0.03 = $.03 + $1.00 = $1.03). If this new $1.03 balance is allowed to remain on deposit and the interest rate remains at 3%, the balance at the end of the second year is $1.0609 ($1.03 × .03 = $.0309 + $1.03 = $1.0609). Of course, most people deposit far more in a savings account than just $1, plus they usually make deposits periodically throughout the years. So, this example is very simplistic. But the concept is the same, and is the major reason young people are encouraged to start saving for retirement by making contributions to their employers' 401K plans as soon as they can.

The **compound interest** formula is

$$CS = BD(1 + i)^n$$

CS = compound sum
BD = beginning deposit
i = interest rate per period
n = number of periods

Compound Value of an Annuity

As noted earlier, most people do not make a single deposit into a savings account or other investment. So, you are interested in how compounding affects a series of deposits or earnings. An **annuity** is the term used to describe a series of set payments or receipts, for example, mortgage payments and annual payments you receive if you win a state lottery, respectively.

To determine the future value of a series of regular deposits, or an annuity, each made at the beginning of a period, use the following formula that incorporates compound interest

$$CS = RD [(1 + i)^{n-1} + (1 + i)^{n-2} + (1 + i)^{n-n} \text{ or } 1]$$

CS = compound sum
RD = regular deposit
i = interest rate per period
n = number of periods

Based on this formula, a regular deposit of $1 made at the beginning of each year for three years at 3% compound interest is worth $3.09 at the beginning of the third year, as shown below

$$CS = \$1 [(1 + 0.03)^{3-1} + (1 + 0.03)^{3-2} + 1]$$
$$CS = \$1 [(1.03)^2 + (1.03)^1 + 1]$$
$$CS = \$1 [(1.0609) + (1.03) + 1]$$
$$CS = \$1 [3.0909]$$
$$CS = \$3.0909 \text{ or } \$3.09 \text{ rounded}$$

Many calculators have built-in compound interest functions, so figuring out the value of a much larger annuity held for a much longer time is much less cumbersome than this formula would indicate.

TIME VALUE OF MONEY

Time is obviously a major component of the compound interest formula. The longer the time the money is put aside and invested, the more its value rises. This growth is also dependent on the interest rate, or yield, of the investment. Therefore, money you will receive in the future is worth less today. How much less it is worth also depends on the yield rate and time, i.e., how long you have to wait to receive the funds.

For example, if the yield rate is 3%, $1 that you do not receive until a year from today has a real worth of only $0.97 today. If that $1 could be deposited today at 3% interest earned annually, the account would have $1.03 in it at the end of this year. But, if you have to wait a year before you get your hands on that $1, you have lost the opportunity to earn $.03. The $.03 that has not been earned is called the opportunity cost or the discount rate that reduces the present value of the $1 that you won't receive until the end of the year to $0.97 right now.

Present Value of $1
The net present value of $1 is mathematically the reciprocal of the compound value of $1. The formula is

$$PV = A \times 1/(1+i)^n$$
PV = present value
A = amount of deposit
i = interest rate per period
n = number of periods

For example, the present value of $1,000 that will not be received until 10 years from today at a discount rate of 3% is

$$PV = \$1,000 \times 1/(1 + 0.03)^{10}$$
$$PV = \$1,000 \times (1/1.344)$$
$$PV = \$1,000 [0.744]$$
$$PV = \$744.00$$

So, $1,000 that you expect to receive in 10 years is only worth $744 today at a discount rate of 3%. If the return on your investment is higher, then the value of your $1,000 is even lower because you are losing the opportunity to invest those dollars at that higher rate of return for the 10 years.

Present Value of an Annuity

We have just seen how the present value of $1 is the reciprocal of its compound rate. The same function is true for the present value of an annuity: its calculation is made by determining the reciprocal of its compound formula, as follows

Present value of annuities (PVA)= RA $[1/(1+i)^n + 1/(1+i)^{n-1} + 1/(1+i)^{n-2} +...]$

RA = regular amount deposited or received

i = interest rate per period

n = number of periods

For example, the present value of $1 received at the end of each year for three years at 3% interest would be $2.83, as shown below.

PVA = $1 $[1/(1+.03)^3 + 1/(1+.03)^2 + 1/(1+.06)^1]$

PVA = $1[1/1.0927 + 1/1.0609 + 1/1.03]$

PWA = $1 [0.9152 + 0.9426 + 0.9708]$

PWA = $1 [2.8286]$

PWA = $2.83 when rounded to the nearest cent

Present value tables online or in financial textbooks and functions built into calculators reduce the amount of arithmetic that must be done to make these calculations.

PAYMENT SCHEDULES

A good part of a real estate loan agreement involves arrangements for its repayment. Depending to some degree on the needs of the borrower, payments can be made annually, semiannually, quarterly, or monthly. Some payments can be interest-only, and not include any paydown of the principal. While most conventional residential loans of the past almost always involved a specific monthly payment that included principal and interest amounts that varied in proportion but totaled the same, today some repayment schedules can involve higher or lower payments at different times. Furthermore, with term agreements, only interest is paid regularly; the principal is due in a lump sum—or "balloon payment"—at a specific time.

Amortization

The regular, equal payment made monthly for a certain number of years—usually 15 or 30—is still the most common arrangement. When these payments include both principal and interest, the process is called **amortization**.

Annual Payments

In some circumstances, real estate loans are repaid in equal annual installments and are considered annuities. These payment amounts can be calculated using the present worth of an annuity formula we have already discussed. The formula can be adjusted to determine the schedule of equal payments of principal and interest necessary to repay the loan at the nominal interest rate.

In the case of loan repayment, the formula for the present value of an annuity (PVA) is

PVA = RA (IF)

RA = regular amount

IF = interest factor, found in financial textbooks and online, based on the present value of $1 at a specified interest rate.

So, for example, to calculate the annual payment on a loan of $100,000 at 6% interest to be paid back over 15 years

RA = PVA/IF

RA = $100,000/9.712249

RA = $10,296.28

Monthly Payments

The most common amortization schedules involve equal monthly payments. However, the annual payment calculated using the annuity formula above cannot simply be divided by 12. Monthly compounding does not precisely have the same results as annual compounding. So, to calculate the equal monthly payment accurately, the formula must include a monthly interest factor (IF), and not the annual interest factor. The formula for monthly payments is

RA = PVA/IF

The interest factor (IF) for monthly payments is also found in compound interest tables or amortization tables available in financial textbooks and online.

So, for example, a $100,000 loan to be repaid over 15 years at 6% percent interest has the following level monthly payment:

RA= PVA/IF

RA = $100,000/118.503514 (IF = PVA of $1 at 6% for 180 months) (15 years × 12 months per year)

RA = $843.86 as the regular monthly principal and interest payment

So, with monthly payments, the annual amount paid is $10,126.32 ($843.85 × 12), slightly less than the calculated annual payment above, because of monthly compounding.

Loan Constants

Many real estate investors use a loan constant to measure the annual principal and interest amounts required to amortize their debt known as the **annual loan constant**. A loan constant represents the relationship between the regular equal payments and the total loan amount in terms of an annual percentage rate. In the previous example, where the $100,000, 6%, 15-year loan requires $843.86 in monthly principal and interest payment, the loan constant is 10.13% ($843.86 × 12= $10,126.32 ÷ $100,000 = 0.1013). In other words, the loan is being repaid at an annual rate of 10.13% of the face amount. This repayment includes both principal and interest.

Distribution of Principal and Interest

The term, amortization, refers to how the total equal monthly payment is split between interest and principal repayment. Amortization schedules are computed based on the interest rate and the term of the loan. The $100,000 loan example we have used earlier has an interest rate of 6% and a term of 15 years, or 180 months. At the beginning of the term, a larger proportion of the monthly payment is used to pay interest, with less going toward principal. As time goes on, this distribution equalizes and eventually, more goes toward principal repayment and less toward interest. In other words, the interest is paid upfront.

The amortization table below shows the monthly payment made in December of every year for a $100,000, 6% interest, 15-year loan initiated in August 2005. The payments made monthly between Decembers are distributed somewhere in between the December figures. A full amortization table would show the precise amounts paid against principal and interest for each and every month. As you can see, the total loan balance is reduced by the monthly payments to principal. So, as time goes on, the interest is charged against a shrinking amount—which is why, over time, the interest proportion goes down and the amount paid against principal increases.

Date	Amt. to Principal	Amt. to Interest	Loan Balance
Dec 2005	$352.54	$491.32	$97910.90
Dec 2006	$374.28	$469.57	$93540.38
Dec 2007	$397.37	$446.49	$88900.30
Dec 2008	$421.88	$421.98	$83974.02
Dec 2009	$447.9	$395.96	$78743.91
Dec 2010	$475.52	$368.33	$73191.21
Dec 2011	$504.85	$339.00	$67296.04
Dec 2012	$535.99	$307.87	$61037.26
Dec 2013	$569.05	$274.81	$54392.46
Dec 2014	$604.15	$239.71	$47337.82
Dec 2015	$641.41	$202.45	$39848.06
Dec 2016	$680.97	$162.89	$31896.35
Dec 2017	$722.97	$120.89	$23454.20
Dec 2018	$767.56	$76.29	$14491.36
Dec 2019	$814.9	$28.95	$4975.70

The basic formula for the remaining principal balance of a real estate loan is

B = (Present value of $1 per period of term remaining/Present value of $1 for full period) × Original Principal

Term Loans

A **term loan** is a nonamortized repayment arrangement. It is also called a **straight loan** and **bullet loan**. With this loan, only interest is paid regularly. The entire principal is due at a pre-determined time in the future called the **stop date**. At that point, the loan is fully paid by a balloon payment of the principal and any interest still owed.

For example, a loan for $100,000 repaid at not less than interest only at 6% annually, with the full amount due in 15 years requires monthly payments of at least $500 interest for 180 months, The "not less than interest" only stipulation in this loan allows the borrower to pay more than interest only if he or she desires. As a result, this loan can be paid down or paid in full at any time without penalties, i.e., there is no pre-payment penalty. At the end of the 15 years, the principal amount of $100,000, or the outstanding balance if any payments have been made toward principal, is due.

Impound Funds (Escrow Accounts)

As discussed earlier, most real estate loans are made for single-family, owner-occupied homes. Often, lenders require that borrowers include in their monthly payments an amount that is impounded—or held in escrow—for annual or semi-annual payment of property taxes, insurance premiums, and property improvement assessments. The resulting monthly payment is abbreviated PITI, referring to its components of principal, interest, taxes, and insurance.

Property Taxes

Property taxes are charged to property owners usually by counties, but they can be sources of funds for the public services provided by states, cities, school districts, and other local governments. Governments can place liens on property whose owners are delinquent in paying property taxes, and these liens have a priority over any others. So, when the property is sold, the property taxes are first to paid before any profits from the sale are distributed to the seller. To avoid any problems of this nature, lenders often demand that monthly payments toward taxes be made along with principal and interest to ensure that property taxes are paid on time and the mortgage's position as primary lien is protected. The property tax amount owed by each property owner depends on the funds needed by the government entities to provide necessary services in the area where the property is located and the valuation of all taxable properties in that area.

The property tax rate is calculated by dividing the total budgetary requirements of the taxing district by the total value of taxable property in the jurisdiction. Property tax rates are usually expressed in terms of mills (1/10 of a cent) per $1,000 of the property's assessed value.

Proposition 13, voted on in 1978, set California's property tax policy. It limits the maximum annual tax on real property to 1% of the property's full cash value plus a

DISTRICT COURT   main trial court in the federal court system and the lowest federal court that has jurisdiction in civil cases where the plaintiffs and defendants are from different states (diversity of citizenship) and the amount in controversy is over $10,000, and in cases involving a federal question

DIVESTMENT   elimination or removal of a right or title, usually applied to the cancellation of an estate in land

DOMICILE   person's permanent residence

DOMINANT TENEMENT   tenement obtaining the benefit of an easement appurtenant (servient tenement)

DONEE   person to whom a gift is made

DONOR   person who makes a gift

DOUBLE ESCROW   second escrow that is contingent upon and tied to the first escrow; while not illegal, unless there is full and fair disclosure of the second escrow, there may be a possibility of fraud or other actionable conduct by the parties

DOWER   right (abolished in California) that a wife has in her husband's estate at his death

DUE PROCESS OF LAW   constitutional guarantee that the government will not interfere with a person's private property rights without following procedural safeguards prescribed by law

DUE-ON-ENCUMBRANCE CLAUSE   clause in a deed of trust or mortgage that provides that upon the execration of additional deeds of trust or other encumbrances against a secured parcel of property, the lender may declare the entire unpaid balance of principal and interest due and owing

DUE-ON-SALE CLAUSE   also called an alienation clause, is a clause in a deed of trust or mortgage that provides that if the secured property is sold or transferred, the lender may declare the entire unpaid balance immediately due and payable; its use has been severely limited by recent court decisions

DURESS   unlawful constraint by force or fear

E

E.I.R.   abbreviation for Environmental Impact Report

EARNEST MONEY DEPOSIT   deposit of money paid by a buyer for real property as evidence of good faith, and cannot be given back to the buyer unless he obtains written permission from the seller

EASEMENT APPURTENANT   easement created for the benefit of a particular parcel of property

EASEMENT IN GROSS   easement that benefits a particular individual, not a parcel of property, and involves only a servient estate

EASEMENT   right, privilege, or interest that one party has to use the land of another

EASY QUALIFIER MORTGAGE   may be referred to as "low doc" or "no doc" loan.

EAVES   lower projecting edge of a roof over the wall

ECONOMIC LIFE   remaining useful life of an improvement or structure; that period during which an improvement will yield a return on the investment

ECONOMIC OBSOLESCENCE   or social obsolescence, is a loss in value to property due to external causes such as zoning or a deteriorating neighborhood

EFFECTIVE GROSS INCOME   amount of net income that remains after the deduction from gross income of vacancy and credit losses

EGRESS   exit; the act or avenue or leaving property

EMBLEMENTS   things that grow on the land require annual planting and cultivation

EMINENT DOMAIN   constitutional or inherent right of a government and certain others, such as public utilities, to take private property for public good upon the payment of just compensation

ENCROACHMENT   structure or natural object that unlawfully extends into another's property

ENCUMBRANCE   any claim, interest, or right improperly possessed by another that may diminish the true owner's rights or value in the estate. Examples include mortgages, easements, or restrictions of any kind. A claim, lien, or charge on property

ENDORSEMENT   see Indorsement.

ENVIRONMENTAL IMPACT REPORT- A report that must be prepared whenever any agency or individual considers a project that may have a significant impact on the environment, as directed by the California Environmental Quality Act

EQUAL CREDIT OPPORTUNITY ACT   prohibits discrimination amongst lenders

EQUAL HOUSING OPPORTUNITY   prohibits discrimination in the listing, sale, lease, rental or financing of real property due to race, creed, religion, sex, marital status or handicap

EQUAL PROTECTION   the Fourteenth Amendment to the U.S. Constitution and similar provisions in the California Constitution require each citizen to receive equal protection of the laws. There are no minimum standards of protection; all equally situated individuals must simply be treated equally. (The due process clause of the Constitution imposes certain minimum standards of protection)

EQUITY BUILD-UP   increase of the owner's equity due to mortgage principal reduction and value appreciation

EQUITY OF REDEMPTION   right to redeem property during the foreclosure period; in California the mortgagor has the right to redeem within 12 months after the foreclosure sale

EQUITY   (1) ownership in property, determined by calculating the fair market value less the amount of liens and encumbrances, or (2) part of our justice system by which courts seek to supplement the strict terms of the law to fairness under the circumstances, rather than on fixed legal principles or statutes

EROSION   wearing away of the surface of the land by the action of wind, water, and glaciers

ESCALATOR CLAUSE   clause in a promissory note, lease, or other document that provides that upon the passage of a specified time or the happening of a stated event, the interest rate shall increase

ESCHEAT   reversion of property to the state when there are no devisees or heirs capable of inheritance

ESCROW   deposit of instruments with a neutral third party (stakeholder) with instructions to carry out the provisions of an agreement or contract

ESTATE AT WILL   occupation of real property by a tenant for an indefinite period which one or both parties may terminate it at will. Thirty days' notice is now required to terminate this type of estate in California

ESTATE FOR LIFE   freehold estate whose duration is measured by and limited to the life or lives of one or more persons

ESTATE FOR PERIOD TO PERIOD   often called a month-to-month tenancy.is a leasehold tenancy that continues indefinitely for successive periods of time, until terminated by proper notice

ESTATE FOR YEARS   leasehold tenancy of a fixed duration, being a definite and ascertainable period of a year or any fraction of multiple thereof

ESTATE OF INHERITANCE   estate that may go to the heirs of the deceased

ESTATE   degree, quantity, nature, and extent of the interest that a person has in real property

ESTOP   to ban, stop, or impede

ESTOPPEL   doctrine whereby one is forbidden to contradict or deny his or her own previous statement, act, or position

ET AL   abbreviation meaning and others

ET UX   abbreviation meaning "and wife"

ETHICS   standard of conduct that is based on what each individual feels is good or bad and cannot be legislated and that all members of a given profession owe to the public, clients or patrons, and to other members of that profession

ETHNIC   racial background of a person which the seller of a property is not permitted, by law, to question a buyer about

EVICTION   dispossession by legal process, as in the termination of a tenant's right to possession through re-entry or other legal proceedings

EVIDENCE   all relevant information, facts, and exhibits admissible in a trial

EX PARTE by only one party or side without the other side being present

EXCEPTION see Reservation

EXCHANGE reciprocal transfer of properties between two or more parties

EXCLUSIVE AGENCY LISTING written agreement giving one agent the exclusive right to sell property for a specified period of time, but reserving the right of the owner to sell the property by his or herself without liability for the payment of a commission

EXCLUSIVE AGENCY contract hiring the broker as the exclusive agent for the seller

EXCLUSIVE RIGHT TO SELL AGENCY contract hiring the broker as the only person authorized to sell property; should anyone, including the seller, find a buyer, the broker still earns the commission

EXCLUSIVE-RIGHT-TO-SELL LISTING an agent has the exclusive right to sell property for a specified period of time and may collect a commission if the property is sold by anyone, including the owner, during the term of the listing agreement

EXCULPATORY CLAUSE provision in leases and other instruments seeking to relieve one party of liability for his negligence and other acts. In residential leases such clauses are invalid, and in other leases the courts have limited the landlord's ability to escape liability for intentional acts, and for acts of affirmative negligence

EXECUTE to complete, make, perform, do or to follow out. To sign a document, intending to make it a binding instrument; also used to indicate the performance of a contract

EXECUTION LIEN lien arising because of an execution on property; a judgment is not self-executing; however, when a writ of execution has been obtained, the sheriff will levy (seize) property, which creates a lien on the property

EXECUTOR personal representative appointed by the testator a will to administer a decedent's estate

EXPANSIBLE HOUSE home designed for expansion and additions in the future

EXPANSION JOINT fiber strip used to separate units of concrete to prevent cracking due to expansion as a result of temperature changes

F

FACADE face of a building, especially the front face

FAIR MARKET VALUE amount of money that would be paid for a property offered on the open market for a reasonable length of time with both the buyer and the seller knowing all uses to which the property could be put and with neither party being under pressure to buy or sell; see market value

FALSE PROMISE statement used to influence or persuade

FANNIE MAE the Federal National Mortgage Association (FNMA)

FARM specific geographical location in which an agent walks every month in order to obtain listings

FEDERAL DEPOSIT INSURANCE (FDIC)   federal corporation that insures deposits in commercial banks

FEDERAL FAIR HOUSING ACT   established under Title VIII of the United States Civil Rights Act of 1969, and amended in 1988, it was created to provide fair housing through out the United States

FEDERAL HOME LOAN BANK (FHLB)   district bank of the Federal Home Loan Bank System that lends only to savings and loan associations who are members

FEDERAL HOME LOAN MORTGAGE CORPORATION (FHLMC)   also known as Freddie Mac, it is a federal corporation that provides savings and loan associations with a secondary mortgage money market for loans

FEDERAL HOUSING ADMINISTRATION (FHA)   agency of the federal government that insures mortgage loans

FEDERAL NATIONAL MORTGAGE ASSOCIATION (FNMA)   federal corporation that provides lenders with a secondary mortgage money market

FEDERAL RESERVE SYSTEM   federal banking system of the United States under the control of a central board of governors (Federal Reserve Board) which consists of a central bank in 12 geographical districts, with broad powers in controlling credit and the amount of money in circulation

FEDERAL SAVINGS AND LOAN INSURANCE CORPORATION (FSLIC)   federal corporation that insures deposits in savings and loan associations

FEE SIMPLE ABSOLUTE   highest estate known at law that is a freehold estate of indefinite duration, incapable of being defeated by conditions or limitations

FEE SIMPLE DEFEASIBLE   fee simple estate to which certain conditions or limitations attach, such that the estate may be defeated or terminated upon the happening of an act or event; also called a fee simple subject to condition subsequent estates

FEE SIMPLE SUBJECT TO A CONDITION SUBSEQUENT   fee simple defeasible estate that requires the holder of the future interest to act promptly to terminate the present interest, in order for that interest to be terminated

FEE SIMPLE   estate in real property by which the owner has the greatest possible power over the title; he or she may dispose of it by sale, trade, or will, as he or she chooses

FEE   estate of inheritance in real property for life

FIDUCIARY   person in a position of trust and confidence, as between principal and broker who may not make a profit from his or her position without first disclosing it to the beneficiary

FINANCIAL FREEDOM   freedom to make purchases with no restraint

FINANCING STATEMENT   instrument filed to perfect the security agreement and give constructive notice of the security interest, thereby protecting the interest of the secured parties. (See Security Agreement; Security Interest; and Secured Party.) It is analogous to a mortgage on real property, except that it secures personal property, and, under the U.C.C., it may be filed in Sacramento with the secretary of state

FINDER'S FEE   money paid to a person for finding someone interested in selling or buying property; to conduct any negotiations of sale terms, the finder must be a licensed broker or he violates the law

FINISH FLOOR   final covering on the floor, such as wood, linoleum, cork, or carpet

FIRE STOP   solid, tight closure of a concealed space placed to prevent the spread of fire and smoke through a space

FIRST AMENDMENT   constitutional amendment guaranteeing freedom of speech, press, assembly, and religion

FIXTURES   items that were originally personal property but that have become part of the real property, usually because they are attached to the real property more or less permanently

FLASHING   sheet metal or similar material used to protect a building from water seepage

FLIPPER PROPERTY   any property bought for immediate resale and profit

FOOTING   base or bottom of a foundation wall, pier or column

FORCIBLE DETAINER   wrongful retention of property by actual or constructive force

FORCIBLE ENTRY   entry into property without the consent of the owner, by acts that constitute more than mere trespass

FORECLOSURE   legal proceeding by which a secured property is seized and sold to enforce a lien on such as a mortgage or deed of trust; a sale under a deed of trust may be either by court action or through a private trustee's sale

FOREFEITURE   loss of a legal right, interest, or title by default

FORMAL WILL   will signed by the testator in the presence of two or more witnesses, who must themselves sign the will

FOUNDATION   the part of a structure or wall wholly or partly below the surface of the ground that is the base or support, including the footings

FOURTEENTH AMENDMENT   constitutional amendment that directs that no state can deprive a person of life, liberty, or property without due process or equal protection of the law

FRAUD   false representation or concealment of material facts that induces another person to justifiably to rely on it to his detriment or a deception that deprives another person of his her rights or causes injury

FREEHOLD   estate in real property that is either a life estate or an estate in fee

FRONT FOOT   property measurement along the street line for sale or valuation purposes; each front foot extends to the depth of the lot, and is usually used in connection with commercial property

FROSTLINE   depth of frost penetration in the soil

FRUCTUS   fruits, crops, and other plants. If the vegetation is produced by human labor, such as crops, it is called fructus industrials; vegetation growing naturally is called fructus naturales

FURRING   strips of wood or metal fastened to wall to even it, form air space, or to give the wall greater thickness

FUTURE ADVANCES   future (additional) loans made by a lender and secured under the original deed of trust; they may be either optional or obligatory, but the deed of trust or mortgage must provide in the security instrument that it will cover any such future advances

FUTURE INTEREST   estate that does not or may entitle one to possession or enjoyment until a future time

G

GABLE ROOF   pitched roof with sloping sides

GAMBREL ROOF   curb roof, having a steep lower slope with a flatter upper slope above

GARNISHMENT   legal process to seize a debtor's property or money in the possession of a third party

GAURANTEED NOTE   permit must be received from the real estate commissioner before being allowed to sell a guaranteed note

GENERAL PLAN RESTRICTIONS   covenants, conditions, and restrictions placed on a subdivision or other large tract of land, designed to benefit and burden each lot in the tract

GIFT DEED   deed for which there is no material consideration

GIFT   voluntary transfer of property without consideration

GIRDER   beam used to support other beams, joists, and partitions

GOVERNMENT NATIONAL MORTGAGE ASSOCIATION (GNMA)   also known as Ginnie Mae, is the federal corporation that assists in financing special assistance programs for federally aided housing

GRADE   ground level at the foundation

GRADUATED LEASE   usually a long-term lease that provides for adjustments in the rental rate on the basis of some future determination. For example, the rent may be based upon the result of appraisals to be made at predetermined times in the future.

GRANT DEED   in California, a deed in which the word grant is used as a work of conveyance and therefore by law implies certain warranties deed used to transfer property in California, and by statute it contains only two limited warranties

GRANT   to transfer; a deed

GRANTEE   buyer; a person to whom a grant is made

GRANTOR seller; one who signs a deed

GRID chart used in rating the borrower, property, and neighborhood

GROSS INCOME total income before expenses are deducted

GROSS RENT MUTIPLIER number that reflects the ratio between the sales price of a property and its gross monthly rent and is used in the income approach of appraising property

GROUND LEASE agreement leasing land only, without improvements, ordinarily with the understanding that improvements will be placed on the land by the tenant

GROUND RENT perpetual rent that a grantor in some states may reserve to himself or herself and his or her heirs when he or she conveys real property, or earnings from the ground only

GROWTH EQUITY MORTGAGE type of mortgage will be paid back faster than the typical 30 year fully amortized mortgage

H

HANDICAP includes, but is not limited to, a physical or mental impairment that substantially limits one or more of a person's major life activities

HAZARD INSURANCE insurance that protects the owner and lender against physical hazards to property such as fire and windstorm damage

HEADER beam placed perpendicularly to joists and to which joists are nailed in the framing of openings such as windows, doors, and stairways

HEIRS persons who succeed to the estate of someone who dies intestate (without a will); it may sometimes indicate anyone who is entitled to inherit a decedent's property

HEREDITAMENT term usually referring to real estate and all that goes with it as being incidental

HIGHEST AND BEST USE appraisal phrase that means that use of real property that is most likely to produce the greatest net return on land or buildings, or both, over a given period of time

HIP ROOF pitched roof with sloping sides and ends

HOLDEN ACT specifically states that "redlining" is illegal in California

HOLDER IN DUE COURSE person who has taken a negotiable note, check, or bill of exchange in due course (1) before it was past due, (2) in good faith, (3) without knowledge that it has been previously dishonored and without notice of any defect at the time it was negotiated to him or her, or (4) for value; someone who acquires a negotiable instrument in good faith and without any actual or constructive notice of defect. The acquisition must occur before the note's maturity. Such a holder takes the note free from any personal defenses (such as failure of consideration, fraud in the inducement) that may be available against the maker

HOLOGRAPHIC WILL will that is entirely written, dated, and signed by the testator in the testator's handwriting; no witnesses are needed

California Real Estate Finance

HOMEOWNER'S EXEMPTION   exemption or reduction in real property taxes available to those who reside on their property as of March 1; the current amount is $70 off the normal tax bill otherwise due

HOMESTEAD   (1) home upon which the owner or owners have recorded a Declaration of Homestead, as provided by California statutes, that protects the home against judgments up to a specified amount, or **(2)** a probate homestead is a similarly protected home property set aside by a California probate court for a widow or minor children. A special, limited exemption against certain judgments available to qualified homeowners

HUNDRED PERCENT LOCATION   retail business location considered the best available for attracting business

I

ILLUSORY CONTRACT   agreement that gives the appearance of a contract, but in fact is not a contract because it lacks one of the essential elements

IMPLIED   not expressed by words, but presumed from facts, acts, or circumstances

IMPOUND ACCOUNT   trust account established by the lender to pay property taxes and hazard insurance

INCOME APPROACH   also known as the capitalization approach, is an appraisal technique used on income producing properties

INCOME TAX   cost to remodel vacant property may be deducted from the income tax

INCOMPETENT   someone incapable of managing his or her own affairs by reason of age, disease, weakness of mind, or any other cause

INCREMENT - any increase, or (1) the increased value of land because of population growth and increased wealth in the community, and (2) "unearned increment" is used in this connection since the values increased without effort on the part of the owner

INDEBTEDNESS   debt or obligation

INDEMNIFICATION   compensation to a person who has already sustained a loss

INDIRECT LIGHTING   method of illumination in which the light is reflected from the ceiling or other object outside the fixture

INDORSEMENT   (1) act of signing one's name on the back of a check or a note, with or without further qualification, or **(2)** the signature itself

INFLATION   occurs when prices rise faster than wages

INFLATIONARY HEDGE   security against the financial hazards of inflation; real estate is considered to be the best bet against inflation

INGRESS   act of or avenue for entering property

INHERIT   to receive property through a deceased's estate

INJUNCTION   court order prohibiting certain acts or ordering specific acts

INSTALLMENT NOTE   note that provides that payments of a certain sum or amount be paid in more than one payment on the dates specified in the instrument

INSTALLMENT SALES CONTRACT   also known as an agreement of sale or a land contract, it is a contract providing for a buyer to purchase a property by making installment payments to a seller; the title remains vested in the seller until the specified purchase price is paid in full

INSTALLMENT   partial payment of a debt due in a series of payments

INSTALLMENT-SALE METHOD   method of reporting capital gains by installments for successive tax years to minimize the impact of capital gains tax in the year of the sale

INSTITUTIONAL LENDER   lenders who make a substantial number of real estate loans, such as banks, savings and loan associations, and insurance companies

INSTRUMENT   written legal document created to affect the rights of the parties

INTEREST DEDUCTION   amount of a home equity loan that qualifies for an interest deduction cannot exceed $100,000.00

INTEREST RATE CAP   maximum increase in interest rate permitted in an ARM.

INTEREST RATE   percentage of a sum of money charged for its use

INTEREST   charge or cost for the use of money

INTERPLEADER   court proceeding initiated by a stakeholder, such as a broker or escrow agent; this decides the ownership or disposition of trust funds

INTESTATE   to die without a will

INVESTOR   person who holds property primarily for future appreciation in value for federal and state income tax purposes

INVITEE   person who enters another's land because of an express or implied social invitation, such as a social guest; it also covers certain government workers who enter someone's land, such as police officers and firefighters. Classification of such status was revoked by a recent court case

INVOLUNTARY CONVERSION   loss of real property due to destruction, seizure, condemnation, foreclosure sale, or tax sale

INVOLUNTARY LIEN   any lien imposed on property without the consent of the owner

IRREVOCABLE   incapable of being recalled or revoked; unchangeable

IRRIGATION DISTRICTS   quasi-political districts created under special laws to provide for water services to property-owners in the district

J

JALOUSIE   screen or shutter consisting of overlapping horizontal slats that is used on the exterior to keep out sun and rain while admitting light and air

JAMB   side post or lining of a doorway, window, or other opening

JOINT NOTE   note signed by two or more persons who have equal liability for payment.

JOINT TENANCY   joint ownership by two or more persons with right of survivorship; four unities must be present: time, title, interest, and possession. Property held by two or more people with right of survivorship

JOINT VENTURE   partnership for a limited, specific business project

JOINT   space between the adjacent surfaces of two components joined and held together by nails, glue, or cement

JOISTS   one of a series of parallel beams to which the boards of floor and ceiling laths or plaster boards are nailed and supported in turn by larger beams, girders, or bearing walls

JUDGMENT AFFIRMED   decision by an appellate court reaffirming, approving, and agreeing with an inferior court's decision

JUDGMENT DEBTOR   person who has an unsatisfied money judgment levied against him or her

JUDGMENT LIEN   money judgment that, because it has been recorded, has become a lien against the judgment debtor's real property

JUDGMENT REVERSED   decision by an appellate court disagreeing with an inferior

JUDGMENT   court of competent jurisdiction's final determination of a matter presented to it; the final decision by a court in a lawsuit, motion, or other matter

JUNIOR LIEN   lien lower in priority or rank than another or other liens

JUNIOR MORTGAGE   mortgage second in lien to a previous mortgage

JURISDICTION   authority of a court to hear and decide a particular type of case

L

LACHES   unreasonable delay in asserting one's legal rights

LAND CONTRACT   or installment sales contract or an agreement of sale, is a contract used in the sale of real property when the seller wishes to retain legal title until all or a certain part of the purchase price is paid by the buyer. It is also referred to as an

LAND SALES CONTRACT   contract for the sale of property, by which possession is delivered to the buyer, but title remains with the seller until full payment or the satisfaction of other stated conditions

LANDLOCKED   property totally surrounded by other property with no means of ingress or egress

LANDLORD   person who leases property; the owner of the property

LANDS, TENEMENTS, AND HEREDITAMENT   inheritable lands or interest

LATE CHARGE   charge made by a lender against a borrower who fails to make loan installments when due

LATE SUPPORT   support that the soil of an adjoining owner gives to his or her neighbor's land

LATH   building material of wood, metal gypsum, or insulating board fastened to the frame of a building to act as a plaster base

LEASE   contract between owner and tenant, setting forth conditions upon which the tenant may occupy and use the property and the term of the occupancy

LEASEHOLD ESTATE   estate of a tenant under a lease; see Estate for Years

LEGACY   gift of money by will

LEGAL DESCRIPTION   description recognized by law; a description by which property can be definitely located by reference to government surveys or approved recorded maps

LENDER GUIDELINES   most lenders use Fannie Mae and Freddie Mac underwriting guidelines

LESSEE   tenant; the person who is entitled to possession of property under a lease

LESSOR   landlord; the property owner who executes a lease

LETTER OF INTENT   expression of intent to invest, develop, or purchase without creating any firm legal obligation to do so

LEVY   to execute upon; to seize and sell property to obtain money to satisfy a judgment

LIABILITIES   debts or claims that creditors have against assets

LICENSE   personal, non-assignable authorization to enter and perform certain acts on another's land

LICENSEE   under the law before 1968, which classified persons who entered upon others' land, a licensee was someone who entered upon land with the owner's express or implied permission for a business purpose

LIEN   charge or claim against property as security for payment of a debt or obligation

LIFE ESTATE   estate in real property that continues for the life of a particular person; the "life" involved may be that of the owner or that of some other person

LIGHT COLORS   light colors make a room look larger

LIMITED PARTNERSHIP   partnership composed of some partners whose contribution and liability are limited; there must always be one or more general partners with unlimited liability and one or more limited partners with limited liability

LINTEL   horizontal board that supports the load over an opening such as a door or window

LIQUIDATED DAMAGES CLAUSE   agreement between the parties that in the event of a breach, the amount of damages shall be set or fixed; the amount is set before the breach, usually at the time of making the contract, on the assumption that the exact amount of damages is difficult to determine because of the nature of the contract

LIS PENDENS   notice that a lawsuit is pending, the outcome of which may affect title to property

LISTING AGREEMENT   employment contract authorizing a broker to sell, lease, or exchange an owner's property

LISTING   employment contract between a broker and his principal (client); a listing is automatically canceled upon the death of the agent (real estate broker) or the principal (owner)

LITIGATION   civil lawsuit; a judicial controversy

LOAN COMMITTEE   committee in a lending institution that reviews and approves or disapproves the loan applications recommended by a loan officer

LOAN CORRESPONDENT   loan agent usually used by distant lenders to help the lender make real estate loans

LOAN PACKAGE   group of documents prepared along with a loan application to give the prospective lender complete details about the proposed loan

LOAN TRUST FUND ACOUNT   see impound account

LOAN VALUE   lender's appraised value of the property

LOUVER   opening with a series of horizontal slats set at an angle to permit ventilation without admitting rain, sunlight, or vision

LTV   these initials mean "loan to valuation"

M

MAI   term that designates a person who is a member of the American Institute of Appraisers of the National Association of Realtors

MANDAMUS   court decree ordering a lower court judge, public official, or corporate officer to perform an act acquired of that office

MARGIN OF SECURITY   difference between the amount of secured loan(s) on a property and its appraised value

MARGINAL LAND   land which barely pays the cost of working or using it

MARKET DATA APPROACH   see Comparative Market Analysis

MARKET PRICE   price paid regardless of pressures, motives, or intelligence

MARKET VALUE   (1) price at which a willing seller would sell and a willing buyer would buy, neither being under abnormal pressure, or (2) as defined by the courts, it is the highest price estimated in terms of money that a property would bring if exposed for sale in the open market, allowing a reasonable time to find a purchaser with knowledge of the property's use and capabilities for use

MARKETABLE TITLE   or merchantable title, is a title free and clear of reasonable objections and doubts

MATERIAL FACT   fact that would be likely to affect a person's decision in determining whether to enter into a particular transaction

MECHANIC'S LIEN   lien granted when a contractor, laborer, or materialman provides labor or materials to improve real property and is not paid, that person is entitled to a lien against the property as a means of securing payment

MENACE   threat to use duress

MERCHANTABLE TITLE   see Marketable Title

MERGER OF TITLE   combination of two estates; also refers to the joining of one estate burdened by an encumbrance and another estate benefited by the encumbrance

MERIDIANS   imaginary north-south lines that intersect base lines to form a starting point for the measurement of land

METES AND BOUNDS   terms used to describe the boundary lines of land, setting forth all the boundary lines together with their terminal points and angles

MILLIONAIRE   person having cash or material assets amounting to one million dollars or more; 90% of all millionaires become that way from owning property

MINOR   person under the age of majority; in California it is any person under the age of 18

MINUS CASH FLOW   event that takes place when there is not enough cash to cover expenses and service the mortgage debt

MISREPRESENTATION   intentional or negligent suggestion or statement of a material fact in a false manner with the intent of deceiving someone into taking a course of action he would not otherwise normally pursue; in real estate, a licensee may be disciplined for misrepresentation even though the misrepresentation did not result in a loss to the principal

MITIGATION   facts or circumstances that tend to justify or excuse an act or course of conduct

MOBILE HOME   stationary, non-motorized vehicle designed and equipped for human habitation

MOLDING   usually patterned strips used to provide ornamental variation of outline or contour, such as cornices, bases, window and doorjambs

MONEY TO MAKE MONEY   in real estate is the general belief that it takes money to make money

MONTH-TO-MONTH TENANCY   lease of property for a month at a time, under a periodic tenancy that continues for successive months until terminated by proper notice; usually 30 days

MONUMENT   fixed object and point established by surveyors or others to establish land locations

MORATORIUM   temporary suspension, usually by stature, of the enforcement of liability for debt

MORTGAGE CONVERTIBLE ADJUSTABLE RATE   allows the borrower to adjust to a fixed interest rate

MORTGAGE CONVEYANCE   instrument that transfers an interest in real property from one person to another

MORTGAGE GUARANTY INSURANCE   insurance against financial loss available to mortgage lenders from the Mortgage Guaranty Insurance Corporation, a private company organized in 1956

MORTGAGE LOAN BROKER   loan broker who is also required to have a real estate license

MORTGAGE   instrument by which property is hypothecated to secure the payment of a debt or obligation

MORTGAGEE   person to whom a mortgagor gives a mortgage to secure a loan or performance of an obligation: the lender under a mortgage; see Secured Party

MORTGAGOR   person who gives a mortgage on his or her property to secure a loan or assure performance of an obligation; the borrower under a mortgage; see Debtor

MULTIPLE LISTING   generally exclusive right to sell listings taken by a broker and shared with other brokers through a specialized distribution service, usually provided by the local real estate board

MUNICIPAL COURT   inferior trial court having jurisdiction in cases involving up to $15,000 in money damages and in unlawful detainer actions in which the rental value is under $1,000 per month

MUTUAL ASSENT   agreement between the parties in a contract; the offer and acceptance of a contract

MUTUAL WATER COMPANY   water company organized by or for water-users to whom stock is issued, in a given district, with the object of securing an ample water supply at a reasonable rate

N

NAR   National Association of Realtors

NAREB   National Association of Real Estate Boards; currently known as the National Association of Realtors

NEGATIVE AMORTIZATION   occurs when normal payments on a loan are insufficient to cover all interest then due, so that unpaid interest is added to principal; though payments are timely made, the principal grows with each payment; This type of note should only be used in area that is appreciating in value

NEGLIGENCE   either the failure to act as a reasonable, prudent person, or the performance of an act that would not be done by a reasonable, prudent person

NEGOTIABLE INSTRUMENT   check or promissory note that meets specified statutory requirements and is therefore easily transferable in somewhat the same manner as money. The negotiable instrument can be passed by endorsement and delivery (or in some cases by mere delivery), and the transferee takes title free of certain real defenses (such as failure of consideration, fraud in the inducement) that might exist against the original maker of the negotiable instrument

NEPA   abbreviation for the National Environmental Protection Act, a federal statute requiring all federal agencies to prepare an Environmental Impact Statement and meet other requirements whenever a major federal action is anticipated that could significantly affect the environment

NET LISTING   provides that the agent may retain as compensation for his or her services all sums received over and above a stated net price to the owner

NONFREEHOLD ESTATE   lease tenancy; see under Estates for the four types of leasehold estates

NONJUDICIAL FORECLOSURE   foreclosure and sale of property without resort to court action, by private sale; for deeds of trust the foreclosure provisions are outlined by the statutes and the requirements in the security instrument, which include a notice of default, right to reinstate, publication of sale, and trustee's sale

NOTARY PUBLIC   individual licensed by the state to charge a fee for acknowledging signatures on instruments

NOTE   signed written instrument promising payment of a stated sum of money

NOTICE OF COMPLETION   notice recorded after termination of work on improvements, limiting the time in which mechanic's liens can be filed against the property

NOTICE OF DEFAULT   notice that is recorded in the county recorder's office stating that a trust deed is in default and that the holder has chosen to have the property sold; the property owner has three months after the date of recording to reinstate the loan

NOTICE OF NONRESPONSIBILITY   notice provided by law designed to relieve a property owner from responsibility for the cost of work done on the property or materials furnished for it when the work or materials were ordered by a person in possession

NOTICE TO QUIT   also called a three-day notice, that is given to a tenant in default of his lease terms or on his rent, which directs the tenant to either to cure the default or to vacate the premises

NOVATION   acceptance of a new contract in substitution for the old contract, with the intent that the new contract will extinguish the original contract; this is sometimes encountered in transfers of deeds of trust, where the new owner assumes the debt and the lender, through novation, releases the former owner from any liability under the original promissory note and deed of trust

NUISANCE   anything that is injurious to health or indecent or offensive to the senses, or any obstruction to the free use of property so as to interfere with the comfortable enjoyment of life or property or unlawfully obstructs the free passage or use, in the customary manner, of any navigable lake or river, bay, stream, canal, or basin, or any public park, square, street, or highway

O

OBLIGEE   promisor; a person to whom another is bound by a promise or another obligation

OBSOLESCENCE   loss in value due to reduced desirability and usefulness of a structure because its design and construction become obsolete; loss because of becoming old-fashioned and not in keeping with modern needs

OFFER   proposal to create a contract, which signifies the present intent of the offeror to be legally bound by his proposal

OFFEREE   person to whom an offer is made

OFFEROR   person who makes an offer

OFFSET STATEMENT   also called a beneficiary statement, is a statement by the owner of a deed of trust or mortgage against the property, setting forth the present status of the debt and lien

OPEN HOUSE   although not the most efficient method to advertise a piece of rental property, it is an opportunity for a licensee to meet potential buyers and sellers, and therefore is considered to be in the best interest of the licensee and not the seller

OPEN LISTING   authorization given by a property-owner to a real estate agent in which the agent is given the nonexclusive right to secure a purchaser; these listings may be given to any number of agents without liability to compensate any except the one who first secures a buyer ready, willing, and able to meet the terms of the listing or who secures the acceptance by the seller of a satisfactory offer

OPEN-END MORTGAGE OR DEED OF TRUST   mortgage containing a clause that permits the mortgagor or trustor to borrow additional money without rewriting the mortgage or deed of trust

OPTION LISTING   listing that also includes an option, permitting the broker to buy the property at the stated price at any time during the listing period

OPTION   right to have an act performed in the future; a right given for a consideration to purchase or lease a property upon specified terms within a specified time; a contract to keep an offer open for a particular period of time. The right of a person to buy or lease property at a set price at any time during the life of a contract

ORAL CONTRACT   verbal agreement, one not reduced to writing

ORDINANCE   law passed by a political subdivision of the state, such as a town, city, or county

ORIENTATION   placement of a house on its lot with regard to its exposure to the rays of the sun, prevailing winds, privacy from the street, and protection from outside noises

OR-MORE CLAUSE   simple prepayment clause that permits the borrower to make a normal payment or any larger amount, up to and including the entire outstanding balance, without a prepayment penalty

OSTENSIBLE AGENCY   agency implied by law because the principal intentionally or inadvertently caused a third person to believe someone to be his agent, and that third person acted as if that other person was in fact the principal's agent

OVER IMPROVEMENT   improvement that is not the highest and best use for the site on which it is placed, by reason of excessive size or cost

OVERAGES IN TRUST ACCOUNT   any unexplained overages in the trust account must be held in trust by the licensee and must be maintained in a separate record

OVERHANG   part of the roof that extends beyond the walls and that shades buildings and covers walks

OWNERSHIP   right of a person to use and possess property to the exclusion of others

P

PARITY WALL   wall erected on the line between two adjoining properties that are under different ownership for the use of both owners

PAROL EVIDENCE RULE   rule of courtroom evidence that once the parties make a written contract, they may not then introduce oral agreements or statements to modify the terms of that written agreement.; an exception exists for fraud or mistake, which will permit the parties to offer evidence to vary the terms of the writing

PAROL   oral or verbal

PARQUET FLOOR   hardwood flooring laid in squares or patterns

PARTIAL RECONVEYANCE   in a deed of trust or mortgage, a clause that permits release of a parcel or part of a parcel from the effects and lien of that security instrument, and usually occurs upon the payment of a specified sum of money

PARTITION ACTION   action by which co-owners seek to sever their joint ownership of a property; usually through court action

PARTNERSHIP   association of two or more persons to unite their property, labor or skill, or any one or combination thereof, in prosecution of some joint business, and to share the profits in certain proportions; if it is a general partnership, all partners have unlimited liability and, absent other agreements, share equally in the management and profits of the business

PART-TIME STATUS - many real estate agents have other full-time jobs, therefore a part time agent cannot devote a full time effort to represent a client, thus the failure to disclose a part time status is considered unethical real estate practice

PATENT   conveyance of title to government land

PAYMENT CLAUSE   provision in a promissory note, deed of trust, or mortgage, permitting the debtor to pay off the obligation before maturity

PENNY   term, as applied to nails, which serves as a measure of nail length and is abbreviated by the letter "d"

PERCENTAGE LEASE   lease on property, the rental for which is determined by the amount of business done by the tenant, usually a percentage of gross receipts from the business, with provision for a minimum rental

PERIMETER HEATING   baseboard heating or any system in which the heat registers are located along the outside walls of a room, especially under the windows

PERIODIC TENANCY   leasehold estate that continues indefinitely for successive periods of time, until terminated by proper notice; when the periods are one month in duration, it is often called a month-to-month lease

PERSONAL INJURY   term commonly used in tort (e.g. negligence cases) indicating an injury to one's being or body such as cuts or broken bones, as opposed to injury to his property

PERSONAL PROPERTY   any property that is not real property, usually property that is movable, as opposed to real property, which is immovable; also includes intangible property and leasehold estates

PETITIONER   person who petitions the court on a special proceeding or a motion

PIER   column of masonry used to support other structural members

PITCH   incline or rise of a roof

PLAINTIFF   party who initiates a lawsuit

PLATE   horizontal board placed on a wall or supported on posts or studs to carry the trusses of a roof or rafters directly; a shoe or base member, as of a partition or other frame; a small flat board placed on or in a wall to support girders and rafters

PLEDGE   deposition of personal property by a debtor with a creditor as security for a debt or engagement

PLEDGEE   person who is given a pledge as security; see Security Party

PLEDGOR   person who gives a pledge as security; see Debtor

PLOTTAGE INCREMENT   appreciation in unit value created by joining smaller ownerships into a single ownership

PLYWOOD   several thickness of wood glued or laminated together with grains at different angles for strength.

POCKET LISTING   when a real estate licensee convinces a seller that he can procure a buyer for the property and wants to withhold the information from the multiple listing services; this is considered unethical

POINTS   in real estate, 1 point reflects 1% of the value of the loan; points are paid over the life of the loan and are tax deductible

POLICE POWER   right of the state to enact laws and regulations and its right to enforce them for the order, safety, health, morals, and general welfare of the public; zoning and building codes are examples of exercise of the police power

POWER OF ATTORNEY   instrument authorizing a person to act as the agent of the person granting it; a special power of attorney limits the agent to a particular or specific act, as a landowner may grant an agent special power of attorney to convey a single and specific parcel of property; under a general power of attorney, the agent may do almost anything for the principal that the principal could do

POWER OF TERMINATION   future interest created whenever there is a grant of a fee simple subject to a condition subsequent estate; future interest matures into a present interest estate only if the holder timely and properly exercises his right upon a breach by the current holder of the fee estate

PREFABRICATED HOUSE   house manufactured, and sometimes partly assembled, before delivery to the building site

PREJUDGEMENT ATTACHMENT   attachment of property made before the trial, with the intent of holding that property as security, to have an asset to sell if the court judgment is favorable to the attaching party

PREPAYMENT PENALTY   penalty for the payment of a note before it actually becomes due; not all prepayment clauses provide for a penalty, and in many real estate transactions the law regulates the amount of penalty that may be charged

PRESCRIPTION   securing of an easement by open, notorious, and uninterrupted use, adverse to the owner of the land for the period required by statute, which, in California, is five years

PRESENT INTEREST   estate in land that gives the owner the right to occupy his property immediately; as opposed to a future interest, which grants only the right to occupy the premises at some future date

PRESUMPTION   that which may be assumed without proof; a conclusion or assumption that is binding in the absence of sufficient proof to the contrary

PRIMA FACIE   presumptive on its face; assumed correct until overcome by further proof; facts, evidence, or documents that are taken at face value and presumed to be as they appear unless proven otherwise

PRINCIPAL   person who hires an agent to act on his or her behalf; also refers to the amount of an outstanding loan. exclusive of interest

PRIORITY   that which comes first in point of time or right

PRIVITY   closeness or mutuality of a contractual relationship

PROBATE   court supervision of the collection and distribution of a deceased person's estate; this takes place in Superior Court within the county where the property is located

PROCEDURAL LAW   the opposite of substantative law, it is the law of how to present and proceed with legal rights

PROCURING CAUSE   a broker is the procuring cause of a sale if his or her efforts set in motion an unbroken chain of events that resulted in the sale

PROFIT A PRENDRE   easement coupled with a power to consume resources on the burdened property

PROMISSORY NOTE   written promise to pay a designated sum of money at a future date

California Real Estate Finance

PROPERTY   anything of value for which the law permits ownership

PRORATION OF TAXES   division of the taxes equally or proportionately between buyer and seller on the basis of time of ownership

PUFFING   putting things in their best perspective is not subject to disciplinary action

PUNITIVE DAMAGES   money awarded by the court for the sole purpose of punishing the wrongdoer, and not designed to compensate the injured party for his damages

PURCHASE MONEY INSTRUMENT   mortgage or deed of trust that does not permit a deficiency judgment in the event of foreclosure and sale of the secured property for less than the amount due on the promissory note; it is called purchase money since the deed of trust and mortgage was used to buy all or part of the property

PURCHASE-MONEY MORTGAGE OR PURCHASE-MONEY DEED OF TRUST   mortgage or deed of trust given as part or all of the consideration for the purchase of property or given as security for a loan to obtain money for all or part of the purchase price

Q

QUARTER ROUND   molding whose profile resembles a quarter of a circle

QUASI   almost as if it were

QUASI-CONTRACT   contract implied by law; that is, the law will imply and consider certain relationships as if they were a contract

QUIET ENJOYMENT   right of an owner to the use of property without interference with his or her possession or use

QUIET TITLE ACTION   lawsuit designed to remove any clouds on a title to property; it forces the claimant of an adverse interest in property to prove his right to title, otherwise he or she will be forever barred from asserting it.

QUITCLAIM DEED   deed to relinquish any interest in property that the grantor may have, but implying no warranties

QUIET TITLE   court action brought to establish title and to remove a cloud from the title

R

RADIANT HEATING   method of heating, usually consisting of coils or pipes placed in the floor, wall, or ceiling

RAFTER   one of a series of boards of a roof designed to support roof loads

RANGE   strip of land six miles wide, determined by a government survey, running in a north-south direction

RATIFICATION   approval and confirmation of a prior act performed on person's behalf by another person without previous authority

READY, WILLING, AND ABLE BUYER   purchaser of property, who is willing to buy on terms acceptable to the seller, and who further possesses the financial ability to consummate the sale

REAL ESTATE BOARD   organization whose members consist primarily of real estate brokers and salespersons

REAL ESTATE INVESTMENT TRUST (REIT)   specialized form of holding title to property that enables investors to pool their resources and purchase property, while still receiving considerable tax advantages, without being taxed as a corporation

REAL ESTATE LICENSEE   person who holds a license to sell real estate

REAL ESTATE TRUST   special arrangement under federal and state law whereby investors may pool funds for investments in real estate and mortgages and yet escape corporation taxes

REAL ESTSATE SETTLEMENT PROCEURE (RESPA) - federal statute enacted by the U.S. Department of Housing and Urban Development (HUD) and passed in 1974, it governs the real estate settlement process by mandating all parties fully disclose to borrowers all closing costs, lender servicing and escrow account practices, business relationships between closing service providers and other parties to the transaction

REAL PROPERTY   land and anything affixed, incidental, or appurtenant to it, and anything considered immovable under the law such as land, buildings, and other attached permanently immovable property

REALTOR   real estate broker holding active membership in a real estate board affiliated with the National Association of Realtors

REBUTTABLE PRESUMPTION   presumption that applies unless proven inapplicable by the introduction of contradictory evidence

RECAPTURE   rate of interest necessary to provide for the return of an investment or a provision in tax laws that reduces certain benefits from claiming depreciation

RECEIVER   neutral third party, appointed by the court to collect the rents and profits from property, and distribute them as ordered by the court; often used as a remedy when mere damages are inadequate

RECONVEYANCE   transfer of property back from a lender who holds an interest as security for the payment of a debt; in a deed of trust, the beneficiary reconveys property upon satisfaction of the promissory note

RECORDATION   filing of instruments for record in the office of the county recorder, which, once recorded, gives constructive notice to the world

REDEMPTION   buying back one's property after a judicial sale

REFORMATION   legal action to correct a mistake in a deed or other document

REINSTATEMENT   right available to anyone under an accelerated promissory note secured by a deed of trust or mortgage on property stating that a debtor may have up to three months from the recording of the notice of default to pay the amount in arrears plus interest and costs, thereby completely curing the default (reinstating) without penalty

REJECTION   refusal to accept an offer; repudiation of an offer automatically terminates the offer

RELEASE CLAUSE   stipulation in a deed of trust or mortgage that upon the payment of a specific sum of money to the holder of the deed of trust or mortgage, a particular lot or area shall be removed from the blanket lien on the whole area involved

RELEASE   to give up or abandon a right; the release of rights may be voluntary, as when one voluntarily discharges an obligation under a contract, or involuntary, by operation of the law; for example, one's wrongful conduct may bar him from asserting his rights. In deeds of trust a partial release clause frees certain property from the security of the deed of trust upon the payment of specified sums of money

RELICTION   gradual lowering of water from the usual watermark

REMAINDER   estate that vests after the termination of the prior estate, such as after a life estate, for example, a life estate may be granted to Adams, with the remainder granted to Baker; most commonly, an estate (future interest) that arises in favor of a third person after a life estate

REMAND   to send back to a lower court for further action

REMEDY   means by which a right is enforced, preserved, or compensated; some of the more common remedies are damages, injunctions, rescission, and specific performance

RENT   consideration paid by a tenant for possession of property under a lease

RENTAL PROPERTY   real property, such as houses or apartment complexes, rented primarily for use as dwelling unit for income or investment purposes

RENUNCIATION   cancellation of an agency relationship by the real estate agent requires written notice to the principal

RESCISSION OF CONTRACT   cancellation of a contract by either mutual consent of the parties or legal action

RESCISSION   unmaking of a contract, and the restoring of each party to the same position each held before the contract arose

RESERVATION   right or interest retained by a grantor when conveying property; also called an exception

RESIDUE   portion of a person's estate that has not been specifically devised

RESPONDEAT SUPERIOR   Latin phrase meaning, "let the master answer, holds an employer liable for the tortuous acts of an employee, and a principal is liable for the acts of an agent; to be liable, the acts must be within the "course and scope" of the agency or employment

RESPONDENT   person against whom an appeal is taken

RESTRICTION   encumbrance on property that limits the use of it; usually a covenant or condition

RETALIATORY EVICTION   landlord's attempt to evict a tenant from a lease because the tenant has used the remedies available under the warranty of habitability

REVERSION   right a grantor keeps when he or she grants someone an estate that will or may end in the future

REVOCATION   withdrawal of an offer or other right, thereby voiding and destroying that offer or right; it is a recall with intent to rescind

RIDGE BOARD   board placed on edge at the ridge of the roof to support the upper ends of the rafters; also called rooftree, ridge piece, ridge plate, or ridgepole

RIDGE   horizontal line at the junction of the top edges of two sloping roof surfaces

RIGHT OF OWNERSHIP   evidence of a person's ownership or interest in property

RIGHT OF SURVIVORSHIP   right to acquire the interest of a deceased joint-owner, it is the distinguishing feature of a joint tenancy

RIGHT OF WAY   easement granting a person the right to pass across another's property

RIPARIAN RIGHTS   right of a landowner with regard to a stream crossing or adjoining his or her property

RISER   upright board at the back of each step of a stairway; in heating, a riser is a duct slanted upward to carry hot air from the furnace to the room above

RULE AGAINST PERPETUITIES   complex set of laws designed to prevent excessive restrictions on the transferability of property

RUMFORD ACT   prohibits discrimination in employment and housing, and is enforced by the Department of Fair Employment and Housing

S

SAFETY CLAUSE   provision in a listing agreement specifying that if anyone found by the broker during his listing period purchases the property within a specified time after the expiration of the listing, the broker receives his full commission

SALE-LEASEBACK   situation in which the owner of a piece of property sells it and retains occupancy by leasing it from the buyer

SALES CONTRACT   contract between buyer and seller setting out the terms of sale

SALESPERSON   individual licensed to sell property, but who must at all times be under the supervision and direction of a broker

SANDWICH LEASE   leasehold interest that lies between the primary lease and the operating lease, for example: A leases to B; B subleases to C; C subleases to D. C's lease is a sandwich lease

SASH   wood or metal frame containing one or more windowpanes

SATISFACTION   discharge of a mortgage or deed of trust lien from the records upon payment of the secured debt

SAVINGS ACCOUNT   balancing account to a person's checking account into which transfers from checking occur and which earns interest; funds saved for future use for special purposes as desired by the depositor

SEAL   impression mark or stamp made to attest to the execution of an instrument

SECONDARY FINANCING   loan secured by a second mortgage or a second deed of trust

SECONDARY MONEY MARKET   where loans are bought and sold

SECTION   square mile of land, as established by government survey, containing 640 acres

SECURED DEBT   obligation that includes property held as security for the payment of that debt; upon default, the property may be sold to satisfy the debt

SECURED PARTY   party having the security interest in personal property; the mortgagee, conditional seller, or pledgee is referred to as the secured party

SECURITY AGREEMENT   agreement between the secured party and the debtor that creates a security interest in personal property, it replaced such terms as chattel mortgage, pledge, trust receipt, chattel trust, equipment trust, conditional sale, and inventory lien

SECURITY DEPOSIT   deposit made to assure performance of an obligation, usually by a tenant

SECURITY INTEREST   term designating the interest of a secured creditor in the personal property of the debtor

SEIZIN   the possession of land under a claim of freehold

SENIOR LIEN   lien that is superior to or has priority over another lien; the first deed of trust or lien on a property

SEPARATE PROPERTY   property that is owned by a husband or wife and that is not community property, usually it is property acquired by either spouse prior to marriage or by gift or inheritance after marriage; also, in California, it is the income from separate property after marriage

SEPTIC TANK   underground tank in which sewage from the house is reduced to liquid by bacterial action and drained off

SERVIENT ESTATE   parcel of property, which is burdened by and encumbered with an easement

SERVIENT TENEMENT   estate burdened by an easement

SET-BACK ORDINANCE   ordinance prohibiting the erection of a building or structure between the curb and the set-back line; see Building Line

SEVERALTY   ownership of property by one person

SEVERALTY OWNERSHIP   ownership by only one person; sole ownership

SHAKE   hand-split shingle, usually edge-grained

SHEATHING   structural covering, such as boards, plywood, or wallboard, placed over the exterior studding or rafters of a house

SHERIFF'S DEED   deed given by court order in connection with the sale of property to satisfy a judgment

SILL   board or piece of metal forming the lower side of an opening, such as a doorsill or windowsill

SINKING FUND   fund set aside from the income from property that, with accrued interest, will eventually pay for replacement of the improvements, a similar fund is set aside to pay a debt

SMALL CLAIMS COURT   branch of the Municipal Court. The rules of this court forbid parties to be assisted by attorneys and dispenses with most formal rules of evidence. All trials are heard by judges. The monetary limit of cases before the court is $1,500

SOIL PIPE   pipe carrying waste from the house to the main sewer line

SOLD TO THE STATE   bookkeeping entry on the county tax rolls indicating that the property taxes are delinquent; the entry begins the five-year redemption period, after which the property may be physically sold to the public for back taxes

SOLE OR SOLE PLATE   structural member, usually two-by-four, on which wall and partition studs rest

SPAN   distance between structural supports, such as walls, columns, piers, beams, and girders

SPECIAL ASSESSMENT   legal charge against real estate by a public authority to pay the cost of public improvement, as distinguished from taxes levied for the general support of government

SPECIFIC PERFORMANCE   legal action to compel performance of a contract; for example a contract for the sale of land

SPOUSE   a person's husband or wife

SQUARE FOOTAGE OF BUILDING   exterior dimensions of a building used by an appraiser to calculate the square footage of a building

SRA   Society of Real Estate Appraisers

STARE DECISIS   fundamental principle of law, which holds that courts should follow prior decisions on a point of law; a proper decision is a binding precedent on equal or lower courts having the same facts in controversy

STATUTE   written law

STATUTE OF FRAUDS   state law that requires certain contracts, including most real estate contracts, to be in writing to be enforceable

STATUTE OF LIMITATIONS   statute that requires lawsuits to be brought within a certain time to be enforceable; the basic periods are one year for personal injury, two years for oral contracts, three years for damages to real or personal property, four years for written contracts, and three years from date of discovery for fraud

STEERING   illegal procedure where individual buyers, who are usually minorities, are only shown properties in specific neighborhoods

STEPPED-UP BASIS   higher, increased tax value of property given as the result of most sales or taxable transfers; the tax basis is used in computing capital gains and losses on the transfer of property

STOP NOTICE   notice served on the owner of property or custodian of funds; it requests, with certain penalties for noncompliance, that any funds due to a general contractor be paid to the claimant, laborer, or materialman

STRAIGHT MORTGAGE OR DEED OF TRUST   mortgage or deed of trust in which there is no reduction of the principal during the term of the instrument; payments to interest are usually made on an annual, semiannual, or quarterly basis

STRAIGHT NOTE   promissory note that is unamortized. The principal is paid at the end of the term of the note

STRAIGHT-LINE DEPRECIATION   accounting procedure that sets the rate of depreciation as a fixed percentage of the amount to be depreciated; the percentage stays the same each year

STRING, STRINGER   timber or other support for cross-members; stairs, it is the support on which the stair treads rest

STUDS OR STUDDING   vertical supporting timbers in walls and partitions

SUBCHAPTER-S CORPORATION   corporation that, for federal tax purposes only, is taxed similarly to a partnership; this corporate entity is disregarded for most federal tax purposes, and the shareholders are generally taxed as individual partners

SUBJACENT SUPPORT   support given by the soil beneath the surface, to the soil on top

SUBJECT TO   burdened by and liable for an obligation, or a method of taking over a loan without becoming personally liable for its payment

"SUBJECT TO" MORTGAGE OR DEED OF TRUST   when a grantee takes a title to real property subject to a mortgage or deed of trust, he or she is not responsible to the holder of the promissory note for the payment of any portion of the amount due. The most that he or she can lose in the event of a foreclosure is his or her equity in the property. In neither case is the original maker of the note released from his or her responsibility; see also Assumption of Mortgage or Deed of Trust

SUBLEASE   lease given by a tenant to another person

SUBORDINATE   to make subject or junior to

SUBORDINATION AGREEMENT   in a mortgage or deed of trust, a provision that a later lien shall have a priority interest over the existing lien. It makes the existing lien inferior to a later lien, in effect exchanging priorities with that later lien

SUBORDINATION CLAUSE   senior lien that makes it inferior to what would otherwise be a junior lien

SUBROGATE   to substitute one person for another's legal rights to a claim or debt

SUBROGATION   substitution of another person in place of the creditor with regard to an obligation

SUBSTANTIVE LAW   laws describing rights and duties

SUCCESSION   inheritance of property

SUCCESSOR IN INTEREST   next succeeding owner of an interest in property

SUPERIOR COURT   principal trial court of the state; a court of unlimited monetary and subject matter jurisdiction, and an appeal court for decisions of municipal courts and small claims courts

SUPREME COURT   highest court in the California and the federal court structure, this court is almost exclusively an appeals court, accepting (by certiorari) only those cases that, in the court's discretion, involve issues of significant magnitude and social importance

SURETY   person who guarantees the performance by another, a guarantor

SURVEY   process by which a parcel of land is located on the ground and measured

SWING LOAN   short-term equity loan

SYNDICATION   group of individuals pooling their resources to purchase property through the holding vehicle of a partnership, corporation, or other association; in this arrangement, each individual owns shares in the legal entity formed to acquire and hold title to the property. This is an alternative method to finance and purchase real estate and allows an investment in real estate with out having to do any of the work

T

TAX   compulsory charge on property or individuals, the payment of which supports a government

TAX BASIS   tax value of property to the taxpayer; it is a figure used to compute capital gains and losses

TAX DEED   deed issued to the purchaser at a tax sale

TAX SALE   sale of property after a period of nonpayment of taxes

TENANCY   leasehold estate; for specific types of leases see Estates

TENANCY-IN-COMMON   ownership by two or more persons who hold an undivided interest in real property, without right of survivorship; the interests need not be equal

TENANT   person who leases real property from the owner

TENEMENTS   all rights in real property that pass with a conveyance of it

TENTATIVE MAP   Subdivision Map Act requires subdividers to submit a tentative map of their tract to the local planning commission for study; the approval or disapproval of the planning commission is noted on the map, and thereafter, the planning commission requests a final map of the tract embodying any changes

TENURE IN LAND   manner in which land is held

TERMITE SHIELD .   shield, usually of non-corrodible metal, placed on top of the foundation wall or around pipes to prevent passage of termites

TERMITES   ant-like insects that feed on wood

TESTAMENT   written declaration of one's last will

TESTAMENTARY DISPOSITION   gift passing by will to an inheritor

TESTATE   person who dies leaving a will

TESTATOR   person who makes a will; technically, a testator is a male and a testatrix is a female, although in common use testator refers to anyone who makes a will

THIRTY-DAY NOTICE   notice terminating a periodic tenancy without cause, by ending a tenancy thirty days from date of service

THREE-DAY NOTICE   notice giving a tenant three days in which to cure a default or quit the premises; it is the first step in an unlawful detainer action, as the means of terminating a lease for cause; when rent is delinquent, it is sometimes called a notice to quit or pay rent.

THRESHOLD   strip of wood or metal beveled on each edge and used above the finished floor under outside doors

"TIME IS OF THE ESSENCE"   these words, when placed in an agreement, make it necessary that all time limitations and requirements be strictly observed

TITLE   evidence of the owner's right or interest in property

TITLE INSURANCE   insurance written by a title company to protect a property-owner against loss if title is defective or not marketable; the policy may be either a CLTA policy, issued to the property owner and to non-institutional lenders, or an ALTA policy, issued to institutional lenders

TOPOGRAPHY   nature of the surface of the land; it may be level, rolling, or mountainous

TORRENS TITLE   title included in a state-insured title system no longer used in California

TORT   a civil wrong, not arising from a breach of contract; most torts arise via negligence, although they could also be intentional torts such as assault and battery, trespass, or strict liability torts

TORTFEASOR   person who commits a tort

TORTIOUS   conduct which amounts to a tort

TOWNSHIP territorial subdivision that is six miles long and six miles wide and that contains 36 sections, each one mile square

TRADE FIXTURES articles of personal property that are annexed to real property but that are necessary to the carrying on of a trade and are removable by the owner; they are an exception to the general rule that fixtures are part of a building, and may be removed by the tenant before the expiration of the tenancy

TRADE-IN method of guaranteeing an owner a minimum amount of cash on the sale of his or her present property in order to permit him or her to purchase another; if the property is not sold within a specified time at the listed price, the broker agrees to arrange financing to purchase the property at an agreed-upon discount

TRANSFER conveyance; passage of title

TRANSFER DISCLOSURE STATEMENT good faith disclosure by the seller to the buyer of all known conditions of the property including easements, water damage any defects in construction, environmental hazards or noise nuisances

TRANSFEREE person to whom a transfer is made

TRANSFEROR person who makes a transfer

TREADS horizontal boards of a stairway

TRESPASS invasion of an owner's rights in his or her property or unauthorized entry onto another's lands

TRESPASSER who trespasses; the importance of this classification of individuals on

property is created by the methods for removal and the liability of the property owner if the trespasser is injured on his property

TRIM finish materials in a building, such as moldings applied around openings; window trim, door trim, or at the floor and ceiling; baseboard, cornice, picture molding

TRUST right of property, real or personal, held by one party called the trustee for the benefit of another party called the beneficiary

TRUST DEED deed of trust given by a borrower to a trustee to be held pending fulfillment of an obligation, which is usually repayment of a loan to a beneficiary; trust deed investments should be on improved property rather than on unimproved property

TRUST FUNDS consist of money or property received by a real estate licensee on behalf of others, and cannot be given to the seller without the permission of the buyer; it is against the law for these funds to be commingled; these records are subject to audit and examination by the D.R.E. and all records and corresponding instruments must be kept for a period of (3) three years

TRUSTEE person who holds property in trust for another; in a deed of trust, the person who holds bare legal title in trust

TRUSTEE'S DEED deed issued by the beneficiary after the foreclosure and sale under a deed of trust

TRUSTEE'S SALE   private sale of property held by a trustee under a deed of trust as part of the foreclosure proceedings

TRUSTEE'S SALE   public sale of a property that has been foreclosed on

TRUSTOR   person who conveys his or her property to a trustee, or the borrower or debtor under a deed of trust

TRUSTOR'S REINSTATEMENT RIGHTS   rights which continue for five business days prior to the date of the trustee's sale

TRUTH IN LENDING LAW   complex set of federal statutes designed to provide a borrower with a means of discovering and comparing the true costs of credit. Under Regulation Z of the act, certain borrowers of property have three days after accepting a loan to rescind without cost or liability

U

UNDUE INFLUENCE   compulsory charge on property or individuals, the payment of

UNEARNED INCREMENT   increase in value of real estate due to no effort on the part of the owner, often due to an increase in population

UNENFORCEABLE   incapable of being enforced at law; an example of an unenforceable contract is an oral listing agreement to pay a broker a commission

UNIFORM COMMERCIAL CODE   group of statutes establishing a unified and comprehensive scheme for regulation of security transactions in personal property and other commercial matters, superseding the existing statutes on chattel mortgages conditional sales, trust receipts, assignment of accounts receivable, and other similar matters

UNILATERAL   one-sided, ex parte

UNJUST ENRICHMENT   legal doctrine that prevents a person from inequitably benefiting from another's mistake, poor judgment, or loss; in a land sales contract the vender may no longer keep both the property and the buyer's excess payments (over his damages) in the event of breach, because to do so would unjustly enrich him at the buyer's expense

UNLAWFUL DETAINER   action to recover possession of real property; lawsuit designed to evict a defaulting tenant, or anyone unlawfully in possession of property, from premises. It is summary in nature, entitled to a priority court trial, and litigates only the right to possession of property and damages resulting there from

UNLAWFUL   against the law

UNRUH CIVIL RIGHTS ACT   deals with equal rights in business establishments, prohibits age limitations in housing, and sets age limitations necessary for senior housing; it states that all persons within California are free and equal no matter what their sex, race color, ancestry, national origin or disability, they are entitled to full and equal accommodations

UNSECURED DEBT   debt not backed by specific property to satisfy the indebtedness in case of default

URBAN PROPERT   city property; closely settled property

USURY   charging a greater rate of interest on loans than the rate allowed by law which supports a government, taking any fraudulent or unfair advantage of another's necessity or weakness of mind, or using a position of trust and confidence improperly to persuade a person to take a course of action in which, by relying on the trusted confidant, the decision maker fails to exercise his free will and independent judgment

V

VALID   legally sufficient and authorized by law; having force or binding force; fully effective at law; legally sufficient

VALLEY   internal angle formed by the junction of two sloping sides of a roof

VALOAN   loan which does not contain a "due on sale " clause

VALUATION   estimated worth or price, or the act of valuing by appraisal

VARIABLE INTEREST RATE   interest rate that fluctuates in a set proportion to changes in an economic index, such as the cost of money; extensive regulations cover use of VIRs in loans on residential property

VARIANCE   exception granted to a property owner, relieving him from obeying certain aspects of a zoning ordinance; it's granting is discretionary with the zoning authorities and is based on undue hardship suffered by the property owner because of unique circumstances affecting his property

VENDEE   purchaser or buyer or real property

VENDOR   seller of real property

VENEER   thin sheets of wood placed over another material

VENT   pipe installed to provide a flow of air to or from a drainage system or to provide a circulation of air within such system to protect trap seals from siphonage and backpressure

VENUE   location in which a cause of action occurs; it determines the court having jurisdiction to hear and decide the case; for real estate, the court having proper venue is one in the county in which the property is located

VERIFICATION   sworn statement under oath and/or penalty before a duly qualified officer as to the correctness of the contents of an instrument

VERSUS   against (abbreviated v. or vs.). Used in case names, with the plaintiff's name given first

VESTED   bestowed upon someone, such as title to property; absolute, not contingent or subject to being defeated

VETERAN'S EXEMPTION   deduction from the annual property tax allowed to a qualified veteran residing on residential property; since July 1978, it has amounted to $40 off the normal tax bill.

VOID   to have no legal force or effect; that which is unenforceable

VOIDABLE instrument that appears to be valid and enforceable on its face but is, in fact, lacking some essential requirement; it may be declared void, but is valid unless and until declared void.

VOLUNTARY AFFIRMATIVE MARKETING AGREEMENT voluntary commitment by real estate licensees to promote fair housing by using methodology that is fairer than government regulations

VOLUNTARY LIEN any lien placed on property with the consent of the owner or as a result of the voluntary act of the owner

W

WAIVE to give up a right

WAIVER giving up of certain rights or privileges; the relinquishment may be voluntary and knowing, or it may occur involuntarily through action of the parties, the action resulting in the waiver is unilateral, and requires no action or reliance by the other party

WARRANTY DEED deed that is used to convey real property and that contains warranties of title and quiet possession; the grantor agrees to defend the premises against of third persons and although used predominantly in states without title insurance, in California the grant deed has replaced it; this deed contains six full warranties of protection to the buyer, including warranties that the seller owns the property, that it is unencumbered, and that the seller will defend title against any defects

WARRANTY OF HABITABILITY landlord covenants, by implication, that the premises are suitable for human occupancy; these implied warranties are found in the statutes and implied by common law

WARRANTY absolute undertaking or promise that certain facts are as represented; occasionally used interchangeably with guarantee

WASTE destruction, injury, material alteration, or abusive use of property by a person rightfully in possession, but who does not own the fee or entire estate, for example, a lessee or life tenant

WATER TABLE distance from the surface of the ground to a depth at which natural groundwater is found

WILL document that directs the disposition of one's property after death

WITNESSED WILL formal will, signed by the testator in the presence of two or more witnesses, each of whom must also sign the will

WRAP AROUND MORTGAGE see All-Inclusive Deed of Trust

WRAP-AROUND DEED OF TRUST sophisticated financing package that permits the seller to sell his property without paying off the outstanding deed of trust; the buyer's larger loan, which is used to purchase the property, includes provisions for paying off the seller's existing loan

WRIT OF ATTACHMENT writ authorizing and directing the physical attachment (seizure) of property

WRIT OF EXECUTION   order directing the sheriff to seize property to satisfy a judgment

WRIT OF IMMEDIATE POSSESSION   order authorizing a landlord to obtain immediate possession of a tenant's premises, pending the outcome of an unlawful detainer action or other court proceeding

WRIT   process of the court under which property may be seized; an order from the court to the sheriff or other law enforcement officer directing and authorizing a specific act

Z

ZONE   area set off by the proper authorities in which the real property can be used for only specific purposes

ZONING   a government's division of a city or other geographic area into districts, and the regulation of property uses within each district

INDEX

A

Abandonment, in real estate, 71, 73
Absorption, in development market cycle, 426
Abstract of title, 74–75, 358
Abstractors, title search and, 74
Acceleration clause, in promissory notes, 99
Actual interest, 453
Add-on interest, 453
Adjustable rate mortgages (ARMs), 87, 89–95
    characteristics of, 90–93
    graduated payment, 116
    indexes for, 94–95
    loans in, 321–323
    VA-insured, 222
Adjusted cost basis, depreciation and, 396
Adjustments, in appraisals, 300
Administered price system, of Federal National
    Mortgage Association (Fannie Mae), 179
Adverse possession, easement terminated by,
    71–72
Advertisements, real estate, 35
Age
    credit and, 240–241, 248
    housing and, 267–268
    Senior Housing Opportunities program of
        Federal National Mortgage
        Association (Fannie Mae) and, 332–
        333
Age Discrimination Act of 1975, 269
Age Discrimination in Employment Act of 1967
    (ADEA), 270
Airspace, 55
Alienation clause, in promissory notes, 99
Alimony, 242, 248
All-inclusive trust deeds (AITD), 111–114, 345–
    347
Allodial system of ownership, 5
Alquist-Priolo Special Studies Zones Act, 363
American Association of Retired Persons
    (AARP), 331
American Land Title Association (ALTA), 76,
    358, 368
Americans with Disabilities Act (ADA) of 1990,
    270
Amortization
    full and partial, 87, 101
    negative, 260
    payment schedules calculation for, 456–460
Amount financed, 259. See also Truth-in-
    Lending disclosures (Regulation Z)
Angeles National Forest, 11
Annual Escrow Loan Statement, 254, 382

Annual percentage rate (APR), 257, 259, 368.
    See also Truth-in-Lending disclosures
    (Regulation Z)
Annuities, value of, 454–456
Anticipation principle, in appraisals, 288
Appraisals, 277–318
    cost approach to, 299, 302–305
    definition of, 279–280
    example of, 308–309
    in home equity lines of credit, 110
    house style in, 296–298
    income capitalization approach to, 299, 305–
        306
    license to do, 307, 310
    lot type in, 291–293
    overstated, 18
    process of, 290–292
    race discrimination and, 241–242
    in real estate investing, 407, 437
    reconciliation in, 306–307
    in risk analysis, 377–378
    roof type in, 294–295
    sales comparison approach to, 299–302
    in VA-insured loans, 224
    valuation principles in, 287–289
    value determination in, 280–287
        demand, utility, scarcity and transferability,
            282–283
        economic influences on, 283–284, 286–
            287
        environmental influences on, 284, 286–
            287
        highest and best use in, 285–286
        market, 280–281
        physical influences on, 283–284, 287
        political influences on, 284–287
        social influences on, 284, 286–287
        supply and demand in, 285
Appreciation, of real estate value, 100, 116, 399,
    426, 444
Appurtenances, 57, 69
Architectural and Transportation Barriers Board
    (ATBCB), 270
Architectural Barriers Act of 1968, 270
"Arms-length" transactions, 301
Asbestos disclosure, 364
Assemblage, in appraisals, 285
Assessment liens, 460
Assignees of promissory notes, 88
Assignment, power of, 4
Assignment of rents clause, 130
Assumption clause, in promissory notes, 99
Attachments on real estate, 68–69

P

Package loans, 111, 334, 343–344
Paired sales approach in appraisals, 300
Paper money, 28–29
Partial coverage mortgage default insurance, 217
Partially amortized promissory notes, 87–88, 101
Participation loans, 339–341
Partnerships of borrowers, 340
Partnerships of lenders, in participation loans, 339–340
Partnerships of lenders and borrowers, 340–341
Pass-through mortgage-backed securities, 183
Payment, priority of, in foreclosure, 158–160
Payment bonds, 66
Payment caps, in ARMs, 93, 323
Payment rate, in ARMs, 322
Payment schedules calculations, 456–460
Period-to-period, estate for, 9, 54
Permanence of real estate, 11
Permanent attachments to real estate, 56
Personal property, 7, 51, 55–58, 344
Physical depreciation, 304
Placement fees, for loans, 367
Plat maps, 60–61
Pledged account mortgages (PAMs), 324
Plottage, in appraisals, 285
Points, 110, 367, 466–467
Police power, 11
Political attitudes, real estate and, 17
Population, real estate and, 16
Power of assignment, 4
Power of sale clause, 129–131, 138
Pre-approval for loans, 411–412
Precedent, condition, 72
Prepayment penalties, 35, 100, 225, 256, 261, 323, 368
Pre-qualification, for loans, 412
Prescription, easements created by, 70, 72
Present value calculations, 455–456
Price of real estate, 282
Primary lenders, 173
Prime lenders, 333
Prime rate, 32–33, 90
Principal, distribution of, 458–459
Principal meridians, in land survey, 62
Principal-only (PO) tranches, of Real Estate Mortgage Investment Conduit (REMIC), 186
Principle of anticipation, in appraisals, 288
Principle of balance, in appraisals, 289
Principle of change, in appraisals, 288
Principle of competition, in appraisals, 289
Principle of conformity, in appraisals, 287
Principle of contribution, in appraisals, 288
Principle of highest and best use, in appraisals, 288
Principle of progression, in appraisals, 286, 288
Principle of regression, in appraisals, 286, 288
Principle of substitution, in appraisals, 286, 288, 300
Principle of supply and demand, in appraisals, 288
Principle of three-stage life cycle, in appraisals, 289
Priority of payment, in foreclosure, 158–160
Private mortgage insurance, 228
Private mortgage insurance (PMI), 230–233, 368, 460
Processing loans. See Loan processing
Profitability calculation, 463–466
Profit and loss (P&L) statement, in real estate investing, 437
Profit generation, 438–439
Progression, principle of, in appraisals, 286, 288
Promissory note. See Financing real estate
Property inspections, 409, 415–417, 419, 437
Property Report, in Interstate Land Sales Full Disclosure Act, 264
Property taxes, 359–360, 459–460, 462
Proposition 65 (exposure to cancer-causing agents), 364
Providential Home Income Plan, Inc., 332
Public aid programs, of Federal National Mortgage Association (Fannie Mae), 177
Public assistance, credit and, 241, 248
Public Land Survey (PLS) system, 62–65
Purchase money loans, 34, 101–102, 133, 345
Purchase standby commitments, in construction loans, 338

Q

Qualified, fee simple, 52
Qualified Thrift Lender guidelines (QTL), of Federal Home Loan Bank Board, 203
Qualifying rate, in ARMs, 322
Quantity survey method, in appraisals, 303
Quia Emptores, statute of 1290, 5
"Quiet title," 359

R

Radon gas, 364
Rancho grants, 5
Ranges, in land survey, 63
Rates. See Interest rates
Real estate, 1–23. See also Estates in real property
    California agencies related to, 42–43
    cycles in, 15–18
    definition of, 6–7
    fixtures on, 7

profitability calculations for, 463–466

tax advantages as, 395–396

in tax-deferred exchanges (1031 exchange), 397–399

Revenue Act of 1913, 198

Revenue Act of 1962, 200

Reverse annuity mortgages (RAMs), 116–117, 219, 331–332

Reversion, in life estates, 53

Right of appropriation, in water rights, 56

Right of redemption, 131

Right-of-way. *See* Easements

Right to Financial Privacy Act, 263

Right to rescind, 34–35, 255–256

Riparian water rights, 56

Risk, in real estate investing, 377, 432

Rollover mortgages, 116

Roman Civil Law, 5

Roof types, in appraisals, 294–295

Roosevelt, Franklin D., 174, 176, 199

Rule-of-thumb method, for discounts, 467–468

Rumford Act (California Fair Employment and Housing Act), 268

S

Sale-leaseback arrangements, for seniors, 333

Sales comparison approach to appraisals, 299–303

Saturation, in development market cycle, 426

Savings and loan associations, 196–202

Depository Institutions Deregulation and Monetary Control Act and, 197–198

Federal Home Loan Bank Act of 1932 and, 199

Federal Savings and Loan Insurance Corporation (FSLIC) and, 199

Financial Institutions Reform, Recovery, and Enforcement Act (FIRREA) and, 202–203

Garn-St. Germain Depository Institutions Act of 1982 and, 201

history of, 198–199

Home Owner's Loan Act of 1933 and, 199

identifying, 271–272

Internal Revenue Code of 1939 and, 199

Revenue Act of 1962 and, 200

Tax Reform Act of 1969 and, 200

Tax Reform Act of 1976 and, 200

Tax Reform Act of 1986 and, 202

U. S. Department of Housing and Urban Development (HUD) (FIRREA) and, 203–204

Savings Association Insurance Fund (SAIF), 27, 39, 202

Savings banks, 205–206, 271–272

Scarcity value of real estate, 10–11, 282–283

Secondary market for mortgages. *See* Mortgages, secondary market for

Second Bank of the United States, 30

Second mortgages, 110–111. *See also* Junior trust deeds

Section 32 Mortgages, 259–260

Sections, in land survey, 62, 63, 64

Securities, U. S. Treasury, 33, 36

Securities and Exchange Commission, 27

Securities pools, 182–183

Security instruments, 97, 129

Security interest, 97

Security of real estate, 10

Seismic Safety Commission, 363

Self-insurance, in mortgage default insurance, 217

Seller financing, 101, 112, 133, 345

Senior citizens. *See* Age

Senior Housing Opportunities program of Federal National Mortgage Association (Fannie Mae), 332–333

Service contracts, in real estate investing, 437

Serviceman's Readjustment Act of 1944, 220

Servicing Transfer Statement, 254

Servient tenement, 69, 71

Settlement. *See* Closing loans; Truth-in-Lending disclosures (Regulation Z)

Shape of lots, in appraisals, 284

Shared appreciation mortgages (SAMs), 116, 324, 341

Short form of appraisals, 307

Short pay, in financing real estate, 117–118

Silver certificates, 28

Size of property, in appraisals, 285

Social Security (FICA), 36

Spanish, in California, 3, 5

Special clauses, in promissory notes, 99–100

Special Flood Hazard Area disclosure, 365

Special Information Booklet, 381

Special studies zones, geologic, 363

Specific liens, 65–66, 68

Speculative developers, in real estate development, 436

Square foot method, in appraisals, 303

Stagnation, economic, 14

Standard title insurance policy, 75

Standby commitments, in construction loans, 337–338

"Starker" 1031 exchanges, 442

Statute of limitation, 140

Statutory reinstatement period, 153

Stock institutions, savings banks as, 206

Straight-line depreciation, 304, 395

Straight loans, 459

Straight pass-through mortgage-backed securities, 183

Regulation M of, 258
requirements of, 33–35, 256–259, 367–368
right to rescind of, 34–35, 255–256
Section 32 Mortgages and, 259–260
Two-Step Mortgage Plan of Federal National
    Mortgage Association (Fannie Mae), 333

U

U. S. Army Corps of Engineers, 369
U. S. Congress, 18, 29–30, 182
U. S. Department of Housing and Urban
    Development (HUD)
  area median income determination of, 41
  Fair Housing Amendments Act 1988 and,
    266–269
  Government National Mortgage Association
    (Ginnie Mae) and, 179, 182
  HUD-1 Settlement Statement of, 253–254,
    381, 385
  institutional mortgage lenders and, 203–204
  Office of Fair Housing and Equal Opportunity
    (FHEO) of, 269
  Real Estate Settlement Procedures Act
    (RESPA) and, 252
  reverse annuity mortgages of, 331
U. S. Department of Justice, 269
U. S. Government Section and Township
    Survey, 62–65
U. S. Savings and Loan League, 196
U. S. Supreme Court, 11
U. S. Treasury
  control of money supply by, 27
  Deposit Insurance Fund (DIF) and, 39–40
  Federal Deposit Insurance Corporation
    (FDIC) and, 38–39
  Federal Home Loan Mortgage Corporation
    (Freddie Mac) and, 181
  Federal National Mortgage Association
    (Fannie Mae) and, 176, 178
  Financial Institutions Reform, Recovery, and
    Enforcement Act of 1989 (FIRREA)
    and, 37–38
  functions of, 36–37
  gold and, 28
  indexes tied to, 90, 94, 322
  Office of Thrift Supervision (OTS) in, 41
  real estate cycles and, 17
  securities of, 33, 36
Underground water rights, 56
Underperforming properties, 439–440
Underwriting
  electronic, 184–186
  guidelines for, 377–381
Uniform Commercial Code (UCC), 334, 343
United States District Court, 4
Unit-in-place method, in appraisals, 303

Unlawful detainer, 131
Unsecured loans, 114
Utility bills, in real estate investing, 437
Utility value of real estate, 282–284

V

Valuation principles in appraisals, 287–289
Value. *See also* Appraisals
  appreciation of, 100, 116, 399, 426, 444
  Certificate of reasonable value, in VA-insured
    loans and, 222–223
  ratio of loan to, 340, 377–378, 380–381
  time, of money, 444, 455–456
Variable rate mortgages, 116. *See also*
    Adjustable rate mortgages (ARMs)
Velocity of circulation, of money, 29
Verification of Deposit (VOD), 379
Verification of Employment (VOE), 379
Veterans Administration (VA)
  benefits of loans insured by, 224–225
  eligible loan types of, 222–223
  FHA and Cal-Vet loans *versus,* 229
  Guaranteed Loan Program of, 174, 176
  loan costs of, 369
  obtaining loans insured by, 223–224
  in secondary mortgage market, 173
  Serviceman's Readjustment Act of 1944 and,
    220
  veteran's entitlement loan guarantees of, 221
Voluntary liens, 66

W

Wall Street Journal, 95
Warehousing entities, mortgage companies as,
    208
Water rights, 56
Weighted capitalization rates, 465–466
Will, estate at, 9, 54
Wilson, Woodrow, 30
Wrap-around loans, 111–114, 345–347
Writ of execution, 69

Y

Years, estate for, 9, 54

Z

Zero percent financing, 330
Zoning, 14, 72, 284, 290, 359–360

A N S W E R   K E Y

Chapter 1
Test Your Knowledge 1-C, 2-D, 3-B, 4-B, 5-A, 6-D, 7-C
Chapter Quiz 1-C, 2-A, 3-D, 4-B, 5-A, 6-C, 7-B, 8-D, 9-C, 10-A, 11-A, 12-B, 13-B, 14-A, 15-C, 16-B, 17-B, 18-D, 19-D, 20-A

Chapter 2
Test Your Knowledge 1-C, 2-B, 3-C, 4-B, 5-C, 6-C, 7-A
Chapter Quiz 1-D, 2-C, 3-B, 4-B, 5-A, 6-B, 7-C, 8-D, 9-B, 10-B, 11-A, 12-B, 13-C, 14-C, 15-C, 16-D, 17-C, 18-C, 19-A, 20-B

Chapter 3
Test Your Knowledge 1-A, 2-D, 3-A, 4-C, 5-A, 6-D, 7-C
Chapter Quiz 1-B, 2-D, 3-C, 4-A, 5-D, 6-B, 7-A, 8-C, 9-B, 10-D, 11-C, 12-D, 13-A, 14-A, 15-B, 16-B, 17-A, 18-D, 19-A, 20-D

Chapter 4
Test Your Knowledge 1-A, 2-A, 3-D, 4-C, 5-B, 6-B, 7-D
Chapter Quiz 1-D, 2-A, 3-B, 4-A, 5-B, 6-D, 7-C, 8-D, 9-A, 10-B, 11-D, 12-D, 13-A, 14-D, 15-C, 16-B, 17-A, 18-D, 19-A, 20-D

Chapter 5
Test Your Knowledge 1-A, 2-B, 3-A, 4-D, 5-C, 6-B, 7-B
Chapter Quiz 1-B, 2-C, 3-B, 4-A, 5-C, 6-C, 7-C, 8-B, 9-D, 10-A, 11-B, 12-C, 13-A, 14-B, 15-C, 16-B, 17-D, 18-A, 19-C, 20-B

Chapter 6
Test Your Knowledge 1-A, 2-B, 3-C, 4-A, 5-C, 6-D, 7-B
Chapter Quiz 1-A, 2-A, 3-C, 4-C, 5-A, 6-B, 7-C, 8-A, 9-C, 10-D, 11-B, 12-C, 13-D, 14-C, 15-A, 16-C, 17-A, 18-B, 19-C, 20-D

Chapter 7
Test Your Knowledge 1-D, 2-A, 3-D, 4-C, 5-C, 6-D, 7-A
Chapter Quiz 1-D, 2-C, 3-A, 4-A, 5-D, 6-D, 7-D, 8-D, 9-A, 10-C, 11-B, 12-A, 13-B, 14-C, 15-C, 16-B, 17-D, 18-B, 19-A, 20-C

Chapter 8
Test Your Knowledge 1-B, 2-B, 3-B, 4-C, 5-D, 6-B, 7-B
Chapter Quiz 1-B, 2-A, 3-D, 4-B, 5-C, 6-A, 7-B, 8-A, 9-C, 10-C, 11-C, 12-B, 13-D, 14-D, 15-D, 16-B, 17-C, 18-B, 19-A, 20-B

Chapter 9
Test Your Knowledge 1-D, 2-D, 3-C, 4-D, 5-B, 6-D, 7-D

Chapter Quiz 1-D, 2-D, 3-C, 4-D, 5-B, 6-D, 7-B, 8-D, 9-A, 10-D, 11-C, 12-A, 13-D, 14-B, 15-C, 16-D, 17-B, 18-C, 19-D, 20-D

Chapter 10
Test Your Knowledge 1-D, 2-A, 3-B, 4-C, 5-D, 6-D, 7-B
Chapter Quiz 1-D, 2-B, 3-C, 4-A, 5-C, 6-B, 7-D, 8-A, 9-B, 10-C, 11-A, 12-C, 13-D, 14-D, 15-A, 16-D, 17-B, 18-A, 19-C, 20-D

Chapter 11
Test Your Knowledge 1-D, 2-A, 3-A, 4-C, 5-B, 6-D, 7-C
Chapter Quiz 1-D, 2-A, 3-D, 4-B, 5-A, 6-D, 7-A, 8-B, 9-A, 10-C, 11-D, 12-B, 13-B, 14-B, 15-C, 16-D, 17-A, 18-D, 19-C, 20-C

Chapter 12
Test Your Knowledge 1-C, 2-B, 3-D, 4-B, 5-B, 6-C, 7-D
Chapter Quiz 1-C, 2-C, 3-D, 4-B, 5-A, 6-B, 7-A, 8-B, 9-D, 10-D, 11-C, 12-B, 13-B, 14-B, 15-A, 16-C, 17-C, 18-D, 19-C, 20-A

Chapter 13
Test Your Knowledge 1-D, 2-D, 3-C, 4-A, 5-B, 6-D, 7-D
Chapter Quiz 1-B, 2-A, 3-D, 4-D, 5-C, 6-B, 7-B, 8-B, 9-C, 10-A, 11-C, 12-C, 13-A, 14-B, 15-D, 16-D, 17-A, 18-D, 19-B, 20-A

Chapter 14
Test Your Knowledge 1-D, 2-D, 3-A, 4-B, 5-C, 6-C, 7-D
Chapter Quiz 1-C, 2-D, 3-B, 4-D, 5-C, 6-B, 7-D, 8-A, 9-C, 10-C, 11-B, 12-C, 13-D, 14-D, 15-C, 16-C, 17-C, 18-A, 19-C, 20-D

Chapter 15
Test Your Knowledge 1-B, 2-B, 3-C, 4-D, 5-D, 6-A, 7-B
Chapter Quiz 1-B, 2-B, 3-B, 4-C, 5-D, 6-D, 7-A, 8-A, 9-B, 10-B
522